booksonline

Read SAP PRESS online also

With booksonline we offer you online access to leading SAP experts' knowledge. Whether you use it as a beneficial supplement or as an alternative to the printed book – with booksonline you can:

• Access any book at any time
• Quickly look up and find what you need
• Compile your own SAP library

Your advantage as the reader of this book

Register your book on our website and obtain an exclusive and free test access to its online version. You're convinced you like the online book? Then you can purchase it at a preferential price!

And here's how to make use of your advantage

1. Visit www.sap-press.com
2. Click on the link for SAP PRESS booksonline
3. Enter your free trial license key
4. Test-drive your online book with full access for a limited time!

Your personal **license key** for your test access including the preferential offer

8tik-7u5m-np3w-26jd

Reporting and Analytics with SAP® BusinessObjects

 **PRESS**

SAP PRESS is a joint initiative of SAP and Galileo Press. The know-how offered by SAP specialists combined with the expertise of the Galileo Press publishing house offers the reader expert books in the field. SAP PRESS features first-hand information and expert advice, and provides useful skills for professional decision-making.

SAP PRESS offers a variety of books on technical and business related topics for the SAP user. For further information, please visit our website: *www.sap-press.com*.

Ingo Hilgefort
Integrating SAP BusinessObjects XI 3.1 Tools with SAP NetWeaver
2009, 260 pp.
978-1-59229-274-5

Larry Sackett
MDX Reporting and Analytics with SAP NetWeaver BW
2009, 380 pp.
978-1-59229-249-3

Muke Abdelnaby, Subhendu Roy, Hisham Ismail, Vu Pham, and Joseph Chica
Mastering Information Broadcasting with SAP NetWeaver BW 7.0
2009, 220 pp.
978-1-59229-276-9

Daniel Knapp
SAP NetWeaver BI 7.0 Migration Guide
2008, 180 pp.
978-1-59229-228-8

Ingo Hilgefort

Reporting and Analytics with SAP® BusinessObjects

Galileo Press

Bonn • Boston

Galileo Press is named after the Italian physicist, mathematician and philosopher Galileo Galilei (1564–1642). He is known as one of the founders of modern science and an advocate of our contemporary, heliocentric worldview. His words *Eppur se muove* (And yet it moves) have become legendary. The Galileo Press logo depicts Jupiter orbited by the four Galilean moons, which were discovered by Galileo in 1610.

Editor Erik Herman
Copyeditor Mike Beady
Cover Design Jill Winitzer
Photo Credit Image Copyright Colour Wheel. Used under license from Shutterstock.com
Layout Design Vera Brauner
Production Editor Kelly O'Callaghan
Assistant Production Editor Graham Geary
Typesetting Publishers' Design and Production Services, Inc.
Printed and bound in Canada

ISBN 978-1-59229-310-0

© 2010 by Galileo Press Inc., Boston (MA)

1st Edition 2010

Library of Congress Cataloging-in-Publication Data
Hilgefort, Ingo.
 Reporting and analytics with SAP BusinessObjects / Ingo Hilgefort. — 1st ed.
  p. cm.
 Includes bibliographical references and index.
 ISBN-13: 978-1-59229-310-0 (alk. paper)
 ISBN-10: 1-59229-310-7 (alk. paper)
 1. BusinessObjects. 2. SAP NetWeaver BW. 3. SAP ERP. 4. Management
information systems. 5. Business intelligence — Data processing. I. Title.
 HF5548.4.B875H55 2010
 005.74 — dc22   2009045231

Contents at a Glance

Contents

4 Ad Hoc Query and Analysis 131

7   Data Exploration and Searching 385

Foreword

The world in which we live has changed dramatically over the past decade. Especially in our consumer lives, the Internet has given us access to more information than we had ever dreamed possible. On the one hand, we are more empowered as individuals. Yet at work we lack the visibility of information, the accessibility to it and the ease of use that we all crave.

We need the right information to be available to us at the right time, and in a form that we can act on — quickly, intelligently, and confidently. People need to be able to make critical, fact-based business decisions, with clean, quality data at their fingertips. It's no longer acceptable to make "gut-level" decisions based on intuition or hearsay. Business executives, knowledge workers, and really, anyone who works anywhere doing anything, must have access to high-quality data that's accessible anytime, anyplace, from any device. Companies must be able to explore their business at the speed of thought. We are ushering in a new era of business. A transformation of how we work.

As one of the largest and most successful software companies in the world, SAP is well-positioned to lead this transformation. We are determined to ensure that every person within an organization has trusted, immediate access to the information they need to do their jobs — just as easily as they have access to email and the Internet. We are breaking down the walls between the stand-alone silos of the past — differentiated by technical infrastructures, separate operating processes, and isolated individuals. Our vision is to enable business intelligence (BI) for everyone within an enterprise — regardless of IT infrastructure or line-of-business role/location of the individual. We're bridging the information divide between the technically capable and the professionally informed. With the integration of SAP and Business Objects, we have a tremendous opportunity to bring together previously disparate worlds and unify processes, data, people, and actions into seamless, intuitive experiences of our customers.

Over the last couple of years, we've been working diligently on this vision, creating stronger integrations between our BI tools and SAP. Ingo Hilgefort, a senior product manager responsible for SAP integration within SAP Business Objects, has been at the forefront of this effort. Ingo has a long history with integrating SAP and Business Objects solutions, going all the way back to 2000 when he drove the integration of Crystal Reports/Crystal Enterprise into SAP BW. Over the course of his career, Ingo has helped hundreds of our customers directly and thousands indirectly by sharing his knowledge and insight via his blogs, documentation, speaking engagements and publications. I'm thrilled to support Ingo in publishing his latest book, *Reporting and Analytics with SAP BusinessObjects*. This book is an essential read for any SAP customer and/or practitioner looking to take advantage of the opportunity created by our BI solutions, and will help them derive maximum value from bringing SAP data to their end users.

Marge Breya
Executive Vice President and General Manager
Intelligence Platform and NetWeaver Group
SAP

Introduction

After I finished my first book, *Integrating BusinessObjects XI 3.1 BI Tools with SAP NetWeaver,* it became obvious that SAP users were still looking for more information regarding BusinessObjects. Questions such as "Which tool should I use?" or "How do I create my balance sheet?" seemed to come up more and more. Apparently, users had overcome the first hurdle of installing and deploying the Business Objects software, but now they were not clear on the broad range of tools offered with SAP BusinessObjects and how to move forward. That's where the idea for a second book was born.

The goal of this book is to provide an overview of the SAP BusinessObjects toolset in the Business Intelligence (BI) area and to provide guidance on the question, "When do I use which tool?" This book tries to cover as much as possible in one book and the first part provides you with a set of criteria that can be used to drive a tool selection for your own implementation.

The second part of the book focuses on the actual creation of content and provides you with step-by-step guidance for certain types of reports in each of the tools based on Business Content in SAP NetWeaver Business Warehouse (BW), so you should be able to follow along in your own system.

I hope this book provides you a great overview of the capabilities of each tool, insight into the selection of the tools based on your requirements, and a great reference on how you can use each tool to create content on top of your SAP data.

Target Group

The target audience for this book is twofold. On the one hand, I hope that BI team leads, BI project managers, and BI decision makers can use this book to understand the different tools and get a better understanding at which tool is best suited for which kind of requirements.

On the other hand, the audience for this book is anyone that will implement and create content with the SAP BusinessObjects software. For this audience, I hope the book provides guidance on tool selection, and the required information to understand which metadata and data is available and how they can be used in each tool.

The focus of this book is not to make you an expert in the installation and deployment of the SAP BusinessObjects software in an SAP landscape. If you are looking for material in this area, you might want to consider my first book. *Integrating BusinessObjects XI 3.1 BI Tools with SAP NetWeaver.*

As a reader, you should have some prior knowledge of SAP NetWeaver BW and SAP ERP. With SAP BusinessObjects, I tried to keep the need for prior knowledge to a minimum and you should be able to follow this book even without any SAP BusinessObjects experience, but you should consider further training.

Technical Prerequisites

All steps and examples are based on the BusinessObjects XI 3.1 Service Pack 02 Release in combination with an SAP NetWeaver BW 7.x and ERP 2005 system. However, you can also use previous releases from SAP NetWeaver BW and SAP ERP as long as they are a supported with the XI 3.1 Service Pack 02 Release. In specific cases, new functionality might require a new version of SAP NetWeaver BW software, which will be mentioned in the text. For example, the Xcelsius connectivity towards SAP NetWeaver BW requires SAP NetWeaver BW 7.0 Enhancement Package 01 SP05 at a minimum.

All of the SAP BusinessObjects software can be downloaded from the SAP Service Marketplace and you can receive temporary license keys from *http://service.sap. com/licensekeys*. The book is very practical, so I highly recommend you download the following components so you can follow all of the outlined steps:

- BusinessObjects Enterprise XI 3.1
- Crystal Reports 2008
- Xcelsius 2008

▶ Live Office XI 3.1

▶ BusinessObjects Integration for SAP Solutions XI 3.1

▶ SAP BusinessObjects Explorer XI 3.1

Ensure that you update the software to at least Service Pack 02.

You should also make sure you have access to an SAP NetWeaver BW and SAP ERP system so that you can follow the examples. If you can't get access to an existing system, you can download a trial version of SAP NetWeaver via the Download section in the SAP Developer Network (SDN).

Structure of the book

When I started this book and outlined all of the topics I wanted to write about, it quickly became obvious that it would become a large book, which made a proper structure very important. I tried to keep it very practical with lots of examples and step-by-step guidance.

Here is a short overview of the content of the chapters:

Chapter 1 — BusinessObjects Product Overview

This chapter introduces you to the BusinessObjects Enterprise platform and the BusinessObjects BI Clients that you will use in the following chapters. You will get a short overview of the different BI tools.

Chapter 2 — Customer Requirements and Usage Scenarios

In the second chapter we look at a list of typical requirements for your BI landscape and use this list to evaluate which tool is best used for which type of requirement.

Chapters 3 through 8 — BusinessObjects Tools Area

In each of these chapters we'll take a look at some requirements and how each of the areas in the SAP BusinessObjects portfolio is able to fulfill those requirements and how you can use the tool to create content for these areas. Each chapter will provide an overview on the usage of the tools, the connectivity, and provide concrete examples with step-by-step instructions.

Chapter 9 — Dashboard Manager

In this chapter, we'll look at how you can leverage the Dashboard Manager as part of your BusinessObjects Enterprise deployment and combine content from different sources and tools into compelling dashboards.

Chapter 10 — InfoView

In this chapter we look at how you can use InfoView to view, schedule, or edit content. In addition, we will take a look at some features that are specific to using BusinessObjects Enterprise in combination with SAP NetWeaver.

Chapter 11 — Best Practices

This chapter provides tips, recommendations, and Best Practices for the design of BW queries and Universes and steps you can take to improve the overall performance and stability of your system.

Chapter 12 — Outlook

Chapter 12 offers a short list of topics that might be of interest to you and your deployment. These topics are part of the integration roadmap given out by SAP and BusinessObjects, but were technically not final at the point of writing this book

Acknowledgments

First, I would like to thank the team from SAP PRESS, and especially Erik Herman, for providing the opportunity to write this book and for providing such a smooth process.

In addition, special thanks are going to the following people for reviewing early drafts of the book and providing their input and feedback:

Matt Stultz, Newell Rubbermaid

Yatkwai Kee, Newell Rubbermaid

Rajeev Kapur, Newell Rubbermaid

Alexander Schuchman, Colgate-Palmolive

Jay Thoden van Velzen, SAP BusinessObjects

Ty Miller, SAP BusinessObjects

And most of all, my thanks go out to Jacob Klein for continuously being my mentor and for providing me the opportunity to take this journey.

Learn about the SAP BusinessObjects reporting and analytics portfolio and how it relates to your SAP landscape.

1   Introduction to the SAP BusinessObjects Reporting and Analysis Tools

In this chapter, we'll look at the SAP BusinessObjects portfolio for Business Intelligence (BI) tools and provide a quick introduction to, and the main usage of, each. A more detailed analysis of the portfolio, including which tool should be used for each type of usage, is discussed in the Chapter 2, "Reporting and Analysis — A Customer Case Study.

1.1   Overview of the SAP BusinessObjects Tools

Before we get into the overview of the SAP BusinessObjects BI portfolio, please note that even though not all of the products from the SAP BusinessObjects portfolio are mentioned in this book, it is not a statement about the importance of those products. The focus here is on the reporting and analysis capabilities of the SAP BusinessObjects products in the XI 3.1 release.

During the integration of the SAP and SAP BusinessObjects (formerly BusinessObjects) reporting and analysis product portfolios, the overall portfolio was grouped into usage scenarios, which we'll use to understand the product portfolio and some typical customer requirements (see Figure 1.1).

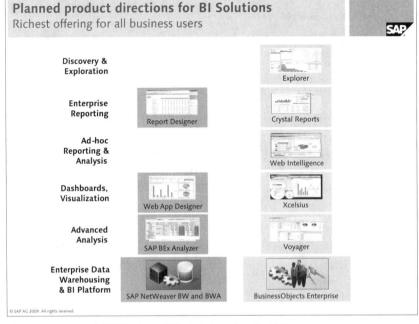

Figure 1.1 SAP and SAP BusinessObjects Integration Portfolio

As you can see in Figure 1.1, with the exception of the Ad-hoc Reporting and Analysis area, SAP and SAP BusinessObjects offer products in each area that serve similar customer requirements. Now, as a single company, SAP will merge these tools over time (we'll spend more time on these products in Chapter 12, Product Integration Outlook), but for users that want to start leveraging the solutions today, Figure 1.2 shows the decisions that have been made during the process of combining the products from SAP and SAP BusinessObjects.

The most important information that Figure 1.2 provides is which product offerings are taking the lead in the BI tools categories. All of the products listed are either already available to you, such as Crystal Reports, Xcelsius, and Web Intelligence, or will be in the very near future, such as Pioneer.

In the next couple of sections, we'll use these BI tool categories to look at which SAP BusinessObjects products are being offered to you today and what the main usage scenarios for these tools are.

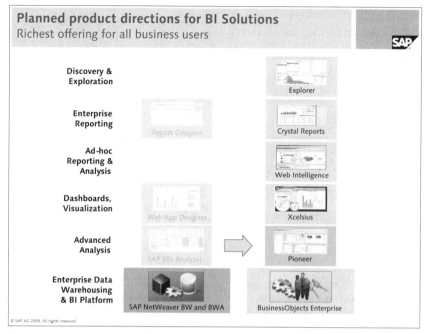

Figure 1.2   SAP and SAP BusinessObjects- Combined Portfolio

1.1.1   Enterprise Reporting

Crystal Reports is the de facto standard reporting tool in Enterprise Reporting. In this category, Crystal Reports replaces the Business Explorer (BEx) Report Designer and provides the following reporting capabilities to the end user:

▶ Highly formatted and print-optimized reporting

▶ Layout-focused reporting

▶ Static reporting

▶ Parameterized reporting

Based on the preceding capabilities, you might think Crystal Reports is only capable of creating well-formatted, pixel-perfect invoices (i.e., purchase orders, account balance statements, etc.) (see Figure 1.3), but Crystal Reports has evolved into a reporting tool that is capable of creating reports that include very sophisticated user interactivity up to an integration of Xcelsius data visualizations as part of your report (see Figure 1.4).

G/L Accounts: Balances

Fiscal Year: 2008   Period: 1 - [OFIS]   Ledger: [OAC_]   Page 1 of 3

Last Data Update: 7/7/2009   Printed by: on 7/7/2009

Selection Criteria

Company Code: [0COMP_CODE].[1000]
Profit Center:
Currency Type: 10

Company Code: 1000   SAP A.G.

Currency Type: 10   Currency: EUR

Account Number	G/L Account	Balance Carryforward	Balance Previous	Cum. Balance Previous	Debit Total	Credit Total	Cumulated Debit Balance	Cumulated Credit Balance	Cumulated Balance
IHT/1000	Real estate and similar rights	-26,273.54	0.00	-26,273.54	225,216.24	939,007.93	0.00	-740,065.23	-740,065.23
IHT/100000	Petty cash	-7,000.00	0.00	-7,000.00	0.00	0.00	0.00	-7,000.00	-7,000.00
IHT/1010	Accumltd. Deprctn - Real Estate and Similar Rights	-644,077.00	0.00	-644,077.00	0.00	268,565.00	0.00	-912,642.00	-912,642.00
IHT/11000	Machinery and equipment	2,000.00	0.00	2,000.00	2,000.00	0.00	4,000.00	0.00	4,000.00
IHT/11010	Accumulated depreciation-plant and machinery	-493,188.00	0.00	-493,188.00	0.00	204,074.00	0.00	-697,262.00	-697,262.00
IHT/113100	G.L Account	-3,322.00	0.00	-3,322.00	1,300.00	1,000.00	0.00	-3,022.00	-3,022.00
IHT/113105	Bank 1 (other interim postings)	0.00	0.00	0.00	1,000.00	1,000.00	0.00	0.00	0.00
IHT/140000	Customers - Domestic Receivables 1	0.00	0.00	0.00	2,100.00	1,100.00	1,000.00	0.00	1,000.00
IHT/154000	Input tax	43.90	0.00	43.90	689.65	0.00	733.55	0.00	733.55
IHT/160000	Accounts payable-domestic	-318.25	0.00	-318.25	0.00	7,300.00	0.00	-7,618.25	-7,618.25
IHT/175000	Output tax	0.00	0.00	0.00	13.79	0.00	13.79	0.00	13.79
IHT/191000	GR/IR clearing - own production	0.00	0.00	0.00	0.00	0.00	0.00	0.00	0.00

Figure 1.3   Crystal Reports — Account Balances

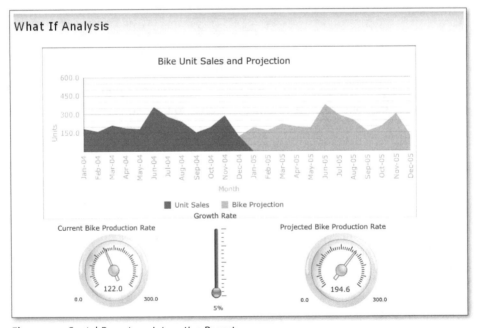

Figure 1.4   Crystal Reports — Interactive Report

Crystal Reports is a tool that is very easy to learn and use, as you will see your-self in the following chapters. It allows you to access any kind of data source and create a wide variety of reports and navigations inside them. Nevertheless, the primary purpose of Crystal Reports as a reporting tool is to provide you with the functionality to create content while you have complete control over the layout, font, positioning of objects, and the rendering and printing on all different types of clients.

1.1.2 Ad Hoc Query and Reporting

In ad hoc query and reporting, Web Intelligence takes the lead and provides you with the functionality to establish a self-service environment for your end users to easily create, edit, and share reports based on any data source. Web Intelligence is a very simple and intuitive reporting tool that allows you to create and edit reports in a web-based environment.

You can leverage Web Intelligence to consume and analyze information in a self-service-oriented environment so that there is no need for you to rely on your Information Technology (IT) department to specify and create a new report for you. You can easily specify which data you would like to leverage in your report using the Web Intelligence query panel (see Figure 1.5).

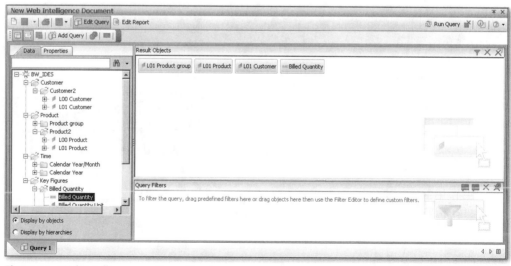

Figure 1.5 Web Intelligence — Query Panel

You can also leverage Web Intelligence to either create a new report or use an existing report, as shown in Figure 1.6, and change the report based on your needs. With some very simple steps, covered in depth in the following chapters, you can change the report to not only provide a different layout, but to also show different information, as shown in Figure 1.7.

L01 Product group	L01 Product	L01 Customer	Billed Quantity	Net Sales
Office	Lamy Pencil	9999 Hotel Ltd	502	2,535
Office	Lamy Pencil	Abbey Coffee & Tea Group Inc	1,760	8,873
Office	Lamy Pencil	Abbey Co Inc	1,446	7,288
Office	Lamy Pencil	Abbey Enterprises Group Inc	502	2,535
Office	Lamy Pencil	Abbey Fine Foods Inc	502	2,535
Office	Lamy Pencil	Abbey Foods Ltd	660	3,327
Office	Lamy Pencil	Abbey Group Inc	1,917	9,665
Office	Lamy Pencil	Abbey Ltd	4,651	23,449
Office	Lamy Pencil	Abbey Lumber Co Inc	1,288	6,496
Office	Lamy Pencil	Abbey Motor Group Inc	1,131	5,704
Office	Lamy Pencil	Abbey Services Co Inc	502	2,535
Office	Lamy Pencil	Abbey Solutions Group Inc	345	1,743

Figure 1.6 Web Intelligence — Simple Report

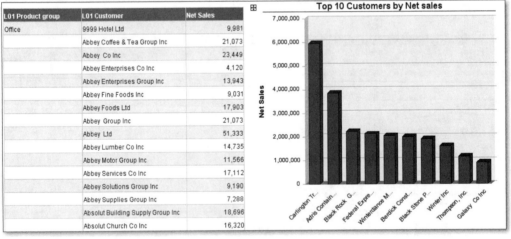

Figure 1.7 Web Intelligence — Modified Report

In addition, Web Intelligence offers you the choice of a fully web-based solution or a rich client solution for your ad hoc reporting needs.

1.1.3 Advanced Analysis

A key area in the BI tools portfolio is the functionality of an in-depth, online analytical processing (OLAP) analysis client that provides you with the capability to create predefined workbooks that include guided navigation and the option to leverage the tool for an ad hoc OLAP analysis.

As you saw in Figure 1.1 and Figure 1.2, this area was occupied by the BusinessExplorer Analyzer on the SAP side and by Voyager on the SAP BusinessObjects side. Voyager was created to compete with the BusinessExplorer Analyzer before the acquisition of BusinessObjects by SAP. In this BI tools category, a new product is being created with the project name Pioneer, which will combine the best of both offerings and offer a Microsoft Office version (see Figure 1.8) and a web-based version (see Figure 1.9).

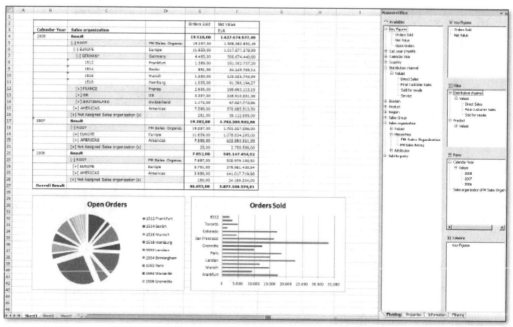

Figure 1.8 Pioneer and Microsoft Office

In addition to the great analysis feature, Pioneer will provide functionality that allows you to interact with other client tools such as Web Intelligence and Crystal Reports. Most importantly, Pioneer will provide you with a migration from either your existing BusinessExplorer Analyzer workbooks or your Voyager workspaces.

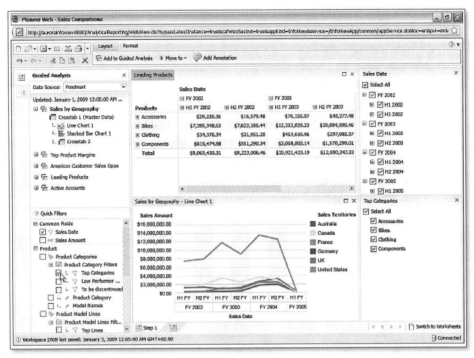

Figure 1.9 Pioneer Web Client

1.1.4   Dashboarding and Data Visualization

Xcelsius is becoming the leading tool for dashboarding and data visualization and is being positioned as the environment to create dashboard-style reports and analytics. Xcelsius is a very simple and intuitive tool that allows you to create a broad range of data visualizations; starting from a very simple chart (see Figure 1.10) up to very complex interactive dashboards (see Figure 1.11).

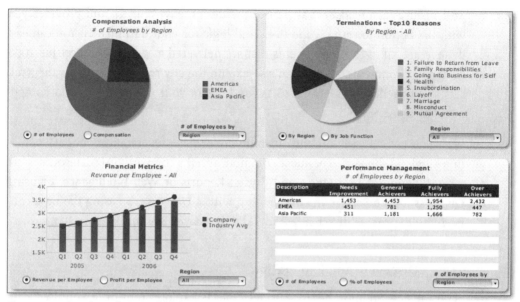

Figure 1.10 Simple Xcelsius Dashboard

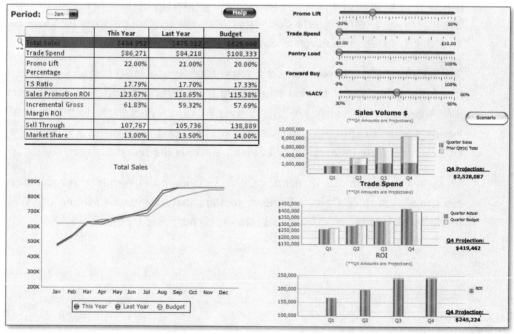

Figure 1.11 Complex Xcelsius Dashboard

Xcelsius uses a spreadsheet as part of the design environment and provides you with the option to set up conditions and logic for your dashboards. You can easily leverage all of the components that are delivered as part of the Xcelsius 2008 design environment, but you can also extend the environment by using the Xcelsius software development kit (SDK) and create your own visualization components using Adobe Flex.

Xcelsius provides you with the capability to leverage several different datasources in a single dashboard. The most common options for your SAP datasources are a combination of Live Office and Crystal Reports or Web Intelligence, or using Query as a Web Service in combination with a Universe, or using the new connectivity to provide direct access to SAP NetWeaver BW InfoProvider.

1.1.5 Discovery and Exploration

With the new addition of SAP BusinessObjects Explorer (not to be confused with SAP Business Explorer) you now have available a very different but intuitive tool as part of your BI portfolio. SAP BusinessObjects Explorer provides you with the functionality to use a search interface on top of your data set. You can then use SAP BusinessObjects Explorer to navigate and explore the data further (see Figure 1.12).

SAP BusinessObjects Explorer, accelerated version, is a tool that provides you access to a large volume of data, and when used in conjunction with SAP NetWeaver BW Accelerator (formerly SAP NetWeaver BIA), offers high performance. SAP BusinessObjects Explorer is able to leverage the semantic layer of SAP BusinessObjects and create indexes of the available data via the semantic layer.

With the integration of SAP BusinessObjects Explorer and Web Intelligence, users can use SAP BusinessObjects Explorer to start analyzing data and then use Web Intelligence for further sharing and formatting purposes (see Figure 1.13).

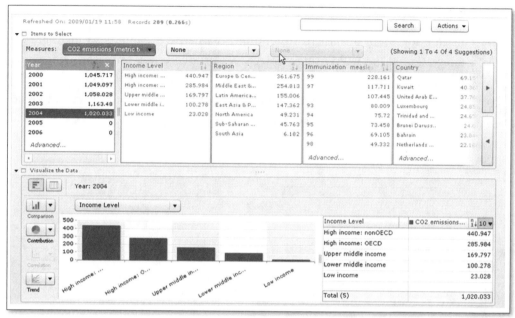

Figure 1.12 SAP BusinessObjects Explorer

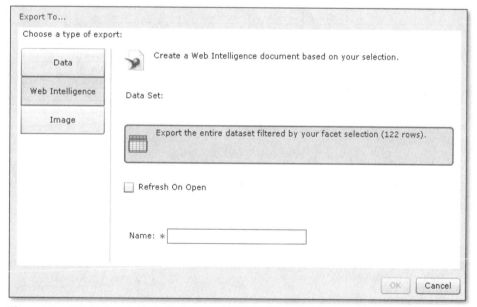

Figure 1.13 SAP BusinessObjects Explorer and Web Intelligence

1.1.6 SAP BusinessObjects BI and Microsoft Office

In addition to all of the areas mentioned earlier, we should also highlight the integration of the SAP BusinessObjects BI portfolio into a Microsoft Office environment, which allows you to leverage your BI content as part of your day-to-day Microsoft Office environment, and at the same time keep the BI data and visualizations intact and refreshable (see Figure 1.14).

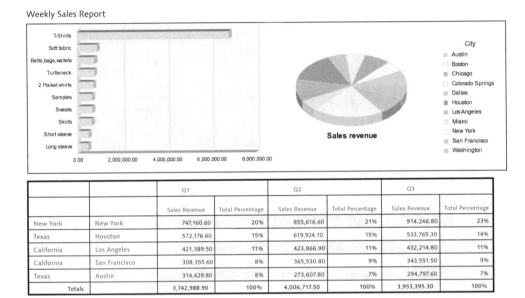

Figure 1.14 Live Office and Microsoft PowerPoint

With Live Office you can provide accurate and trusted data via the SAP BusinessObjects BI toolset to Microsoft Excel, Microsoft Word, Microsoft PowerPoint, and Microsoft Outlook (see Figure 1.15).

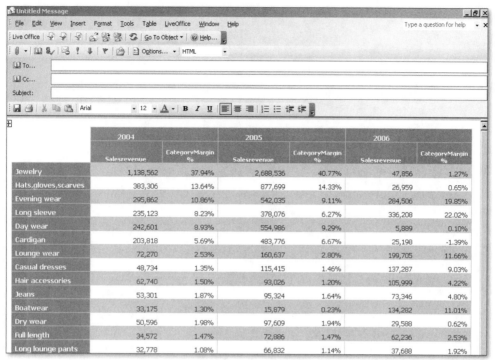

Figure 1.15 Live Office Used in Microsoft Outlook

1.2 Summary

In this chapter, we looked at the existing and upcoming offerings in the BI port-folio from SAP and SAP BusinessObjects as a newly combined company. In the next chapter, we'll go into more detail and look at typical customer requirements from different areas and show how those can be mapped to the offerings in the BI portfolio.

By first understanding the typical customer requirements for a reporting and analysis solution, we can then map those requirements to the SAP BusinessObjects portfolio and to typical user profiles in the Business Intelligence (BI) area.

2 Reporting and Analysis — Customer Case Study

In the following sections, we'll map the SAP BusinessObjects BI client tools to typical customer requirements and user profiles. Based on the scope of this book, coverage will be limited to the most common scenarios, but this should provide a good overview of the main criteria for the SAP BusinessObjects portfolio and how to select the right tool for the right job.

2.1 Motivation

When SAP acquired BusinessObjects, many customers began looking for some simple guidance on "Why" and "When" they should use the new options offered in the BusinessObjects portfolio. In the past, SAP NetWeaver Business Warehouse (BW) customers bought their BI solution from companies such as Cognos, Microstrategy, or BusinessObjects. However, in the postacquisition landscape, the standard choices offered by SAP BusinessObjects are much broader and offer a greater number of tools. Not only are customers looking for some general guidance on the capabilities of the SAP BusinessObjects portfolio, they are also looking for guidance on the migration of their existing environments to the new software.

This is the starting point for this chapter. We'll provide a list of criteria based on different conditions so that you can use your reporting and analysis requirements to find the right tools. It should be noted, a single chapter can't replace the experience and guidance of a BI consultant, and that is not the intent here. We'll provide you with the tools and information you need to ensure you understand the main criteria to make your own decisions. You will be able to understand the major differences between the tools, so that you can ask the questions you need to ask during the gathering of your reporting and analysis requirements.

2.2 Customer Requirements and Usage Scenarios

We'll now outline some common customer requirements from different areas that we'll then match to the SAP BusinessObjects toolset. The requirements are broken into separate areas because we'll use those areas in the following chapters to provide more detail on creating the actual reports and analytics. The requirements are based on common usage scenarios or use cases. We'll focus on the following areas: Financials, Sales and Distribution (SD), Human Resources (HR), Management/Executive Information Systems. We won't explain each of these areas in full, but rather focus on typical requirements and scenarios so that you can differentiate the tools and see which scenarios lend themselves to which tools. Please keep in mind, the goal of this book is to explain the usage of the reporting and analytics tools from SAP BusinessObjects and not to describe all SAP NetWeaver BW– or SAP ERP–related topics for each area.

2.2.1 Financial Reporting and Analysis Requirements

The following is a brief description of the typical requirements for financial reporting. These requirements represent a typical usage scenario and focus on reporting and analytics for customers in the financial area. Please note that references to "content" refer to the objects created with the SAP BusinessObjects BI tools.

▶ The content must be available in a web-based environment and in a Microsoft Office environment (especially Microsoft Excel).

▶ For specific content (such as an income statement or a balance sheet), the design needs to be layout focused with the actual print of the report being a high priority.

▶ The reporting and analysis tools need to let the user create new calculations and formulas and share those with other consumers of the content.

- The reporting and analysis tools need to allow for the usage of hierarchies and navigation along those hierarchies in the actual content.

- The reporting and analysis tools need to leverage custom structures that have been defined on a BW query layer.

- The content needs to resolve the time dependency defined for the financial cost and profit center hierarchies.

- Some of the content can leverage precalculated data, but the user needs to refresh all of the content on-demand, when needed.

- The consumer of the reports should be able to call the content in real-time with historical data.

- The user needs to navigate from aggregated data to more granular items, for example, navigating from a cost center aggregated value to the actual line items per cost element.

- In some content, it's required to navigate into the actual SAP transaction to retrieve further detail.

Example content from the financial area:

- Income Statement
- Balance Sheet
- Cost Center — Actual and Plan Comparison
- Profit Center — Actual/Plan/Variance Comparison

As you can see, based on the preceding descriptions, there is a wide range of requirements in the financial area alone. Without going into detail, it should be clear that those requirements will need more than one tool from the BusinessObjects BI portfolio to fulfill them.

2.2.2   Sales Reporting and Analysis Requirements

The following is a brief description of the typical requirements for the sales area. We'll use these requirements in combination with the other reporting and analytics deliverables to determine which tools will be used to fulfill these requirements.

- Content must be available online and offline (for sales representatives on the road).

▸ Distribution of content via email may be required.

▸ Users need the capability to change the view of the actual content. For example, changing a weekly sales statistics broken down by country into a weekly sales statistics broken down by sales region and quarter.

▸ Content has to leverage real-time data in most of the reports. Historical data may be required for comparisons.

▸ The content is often compared to data from different time series.

▸ Ideally, users should be able to modify existing reports or create new reports ad hoc.

▸ Users should be able to drill down or navigate to more detail-oriented data.

▸ Users should be able to perform scenario-based analysis, where the user is able to see the data but can also influence certain factors and see the impact on the overall numbers. For example, a what-if analysis in a sales planning workflow.

Example content from the sales area:

▸ Opportunity Pipeline Analysis

▸ Sales Opportunity Planning

▸ Opportunity Monitoring

▸ Incoming Orders from Customers

▸ Product Profitability Analysis

2.2.3 HR Reporting and Analysis Requirements

Similar to the previous sections, the following is a list of requirements for reporting and analytics in the HR area.

▸ The content needs to leverage data from several different sources (SAP and non-SAP) and present it in a single report.

▸ The content needs to present highly textual information in a layout-focused format.

▸ Some of the content (such as employee appraisals or performance reviews) will be used as official documentation and therefore needs to follow strict layout rules.

- All of the tools need to leverage the security of the underlying system.

- The leveraged tools for the content need to leverage specific features, such as date-specific aggregation to show the correct numbers for items like a head-count statistic or a salary at a given date for an employee. Resolving these time-dependent key figures is very important for the content.

Example content from the HR area:

- Personal Development — Appraisals and Qualifications

- Employee Master Sheet

- Employee Termination Statistics

- Termination Trend Analysis

- Employee Recruitment Planning

- Salary and Bonus Comparisons per Year

2.2.4 Executive Leadership and Management Reporting and Analysis Requirements

In this section, we'll highlight the executive and management reporting requirements, which are valid for all of the previous areas as well but should be discussed separately. These requirements come up in all of the areas that require a BI solution, because all of those areas need to deliver numbers to their management team. The following are the typical requirements for the executive and management areas:

- The content needs to present highly aggregated information with alerts for important key performance indicators (KPIs).

- The data needs to be shown in a highly visualized manner and the main KPIs need to be presented in a single dashboard.

- The reports and analytics need to allow for further navigation to more detailed-oriented reports and further analysis of the summarized data.

- The consumption of the reports and analytics needs to be simple and easy to use and critical information needs to be identifiable right away.

- The response time for this audience is critical and the information needs to be presented in a dashboard within 5 - 10 seconds (otherwise people might navigate away from the page).

Example content for the executive and management area:

- Sales Management Overview
- Sales Pipeline Overview and Forecast
- Operational KPI Dashboard
- Employee Turnover

2.3 Mapping SAP BusinessObjects Tools to Customer Requirements

In this section, we'll look at all of the requirements from the previous sections and map them to the different tools. Based on the requirements we previously identified, it should be obvious that no solution using the BI portfolio involves only a single tool. The requirements go from simple printable reports in the financial area to highly visualized dashboards for the executive team. To simplify the mapping of SAP BusinessObjects BI tools to the actual requirements, we have grouped the requirements into areas and ranked the BusinessObjects tools based on how well they fulfill the criteria (see Figure 2.1). Please keep in mind, the focus of this book is on the BusinessObjects XI 3.x release of products. As such, Pioneer, which will be released with the next major release of the SAP BusinessObjects platform, will be referenced alongside the Business Explorer (BEx) Suite (BEx Analyzer, BEx Web reporting). Pioneer and the BEx Suite are mentioned in parallel and, depending on when you consider using the tools, you can either choose to keep using the BEx Suite of tools or move to Pioneer.

In Figure 2.1, you can see a ranking of the SAP BusinessObjects BI tools mapped to several key requirement areas. Now let's take a look at the details of these requirements and provide more background and insight into the ranking.

- **Highly Formatted Layout**
  In this category, it's important that the tool provides full control over the layout and that you are able to create a report that is going to look identical in all web clients or when exported to an external format, such as portable document format (PDF). The extreme example for this is creating reports that are identical to legal forms. However, formatted layouts can be very important in other areas

as well where it is important to have a well-structured and formatted report, such as a delivery notice, customer invoice, or a balance sheet.

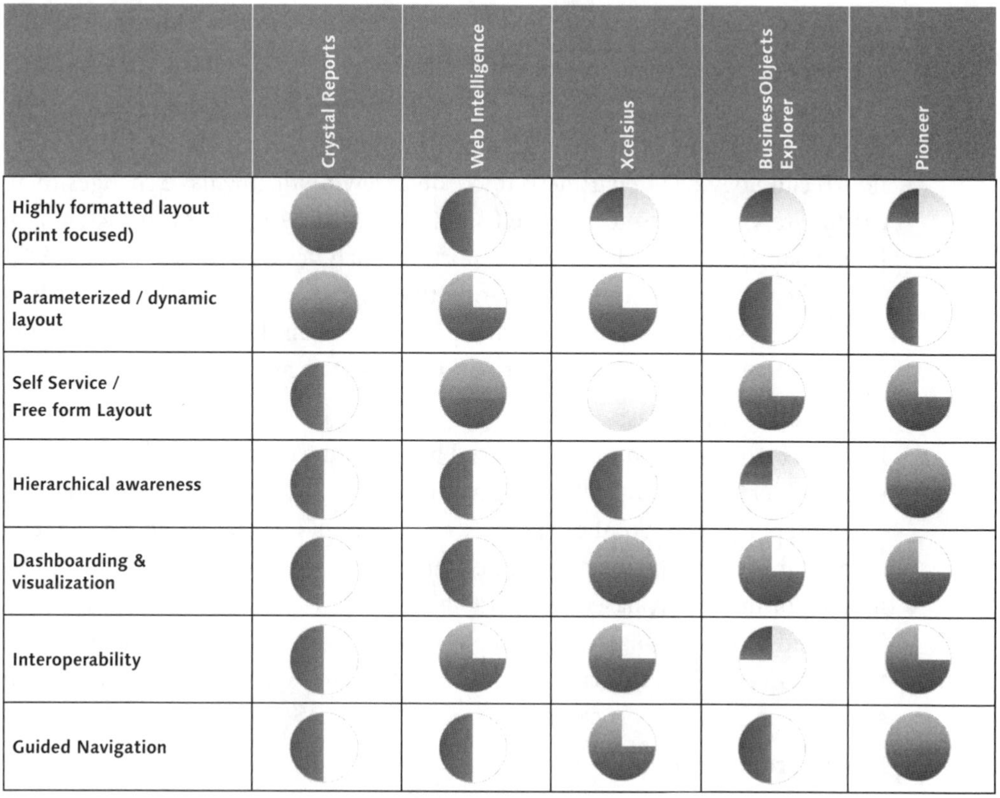

	Crystal Reports	Web Intelligence	Xcelsius	BusinessObjects Explorer	Pioneer
Highly formatted layout (print focused)					
Parameterized / dynamic layout					
Self Service / Free form Layout					
Hierarchical awareness					
Dashboarding & visualization					
Interoperability					
Guided Navigation					

Figure 2.1 SAP BusinessObjects BI Tools Mapped to Requirements

▶ **Parameterized Layout**

With parameterized layouts, we're referring to the concept that the layout can be influenced by the consumer of the report simply by changing some parameters. A good example is a report that allows you to see the data grouped, or as a simple list, or as a chart. The user is able to influence the layout of the report by simply setting a value for a parameter that selects one of those options. The other example of a parameterized layout is one that has the capability to show different types of data visualization based on user input. For example, showing a weekly, quarterly, or monthly comparison after the user has selected one of the three options. In addition, part of a parameterized layout is its capability to influence the layout based on defined conditions and the data being retrieved. The simplest example of this functionality is the ability to highlight a key figure based on a value and thresholds. A more complete example is to completely suppress a Top 5 chart in cases where only three values exist and thus would all be shown.

▶ **Self-Service/Free Form Layout**
Self-service reporting (sometimes referred to as free form layout-driven reporting) allows the user to create or change content without involving the Information Technology (IT) department to create a new report or make changes to an existing report. The concept of self-service reporting is more of the actual tool functionality than it is the type of reports or analytics that can be created. Self-service reporting is focused on offering the consumer a tool that provides him with an easy-to-use environment that puts the user in the "driver's seat" of the report —enabling him to create or edit the report as needed.

▶ **Hierarchical Awareness**
In this category, the tools are compared based on the capability of leveraging an existing hierarchy from SAP NetWeaver BW and being able to present the hierarchy properly as part of the report. The tool should not only be able to actually identify the hierarchy, but also create a hierarchical organized report; allow formatting of the report based on hierarchical information, such as the hierarchy level; and also recognize things like a hierarchy variable and hierarchy node variable. In addition, this category also includes the actual hierarchy navigation a consumer of the report can perform.

▶ **Dashboarding and Visualization**
This category focuses on the set of capabilities needed to visualize actual data and to provide a dashboard of capabilities. It is important to recognize that this is not a comparison of all of the different charting options of the tools. Charting is one element of the data visualization capabilities. Other elements include interactive navigation and the ease-of-use of the visualization.

▶ **Interoperability**
Interoperability is the term used to describe the capability of the BusinessObjects BI client tools to work together. A typical workflow for this category could be that the sales manager starts in SAP BusinessObjects Explorer and searches for the revenue numbers for a specific product. After he finds the numbers and navigates in SAP BusinessObjects Explorer to see further details, he can then

use the data and navigate to Web Intelligence so that he can conduct further analysis in Web Intelligence.

As you can see in the ranking in Figure 2.1, not all of the SAP BusinessObjects tools have the same ranking. These rankings are based on how easy or how difficult it is to set up the navigation from one tool to any other tool.

▶ **Guided Navigation**
The term "guided navigation" is used to describe the capability to provide ad hoc analysis and to limit the scope of change for the user, so that the user is only able to change specific parts of the analysis workflow. In addition, guided navigation refers to the functionality that the designer of the analysis workflow can create a pre-determined workflow for the actual consumer of the information. Think about a sales management analysis, where the user is able to see his Top 10 customers and the Top 10 opportunities in his pipeline on the initial view of the analysis. In addition, he can see the Top 10 opportunities with the highest risk factor of not getting closed in the current quarter. Instead of having to navigate through the data, the sales manager can click on a button and be "guided" to the second page of his analysis, where he sees more details regarding the 10 opportunities that are at risk. You can see that guided navigation helps create a predefined workflow for the consumer that is geared towards anticipating and providing answers to the most commonly asked questions.

Based on the preceding reporting and analysis categories and the brief descriptions of the compared functionality in each of them, you should now have a much better understanding of the strengths and weaknesses of each tool — even though this chapter did not show and compare every detail of every tool. The material up to this point is meant to provide you with an overview. We'll use these categories and the use cases to help you to determine which SAP BusinessObjects tool to use for your requirements. You will see how the tools differentiate from each other in the following chapters, where you are going to use the products and create the reports, analytics, and dashboards yourself.

In the following section, we'll look at the different user types of the BI solutions and how the tools align with those user types. We'll also look at some of the skills that define each user type. It's important to understand both, the requirements and the audience, when making a decision on actual product usage. For example, you might need a report that provides information along several characteristics, which can be created with Crystal Reports, Web Intelligence, and Pioneer. However, because your audience is a group of not-very-IT-oriented information consumers, you may decide to use prepared reports with a small set of parameters (category: parameterized layout) to offer such functionality. Based on your understanding of report requirements and user type, you decide to go with Crystal Reports.

2.4   Mapping SAP BusinessObjects Tools to User Types

It's very important to understand the different user types for the SAP BusinessObjects BI tools and how those user types map to the different products. Before we begin, it should be stated that not every product from the SAP BusinessObjects BI portfolio has been created for each user type. Each tool delivers a specific reporting and analysis user experience to a defined group of user types and has not been created with each user type in mind.

Before we start mapping the BI toolset to the user types, we need to clarify what those user types are, and more importantly, the needs and skills associated with the user types. We must look at this issue from two sides: what the user wants and what he actually needs to do his day-to-day job. Beyond these two points, you must also consider the skill level of the user. Sometimes the choice of tool can be based solely on product features and functionality, but other times you also have to consider the skills of the person using the tool.

To keep it relatively simple we will break down our user types into three categories:

▸ Information Consumer

▸ Business Analyst

▸ Executive/Leadership/Management

You may notice that these user types do not include a role called "Report Designer" or "IT Administrator." The reason is that we want to focus on the consumption of information and how a user can leverage the BI tools to make informed decisions based on the provided information. The person creating the reports and analytics may have a different skill set compared to these user types. We'll focus on the actual creation of the content in this book, but it is important to understand the consumer types of the reporting and analysis content. By doing so, you'll be better equipped to provide them with the right information in the right tool. Let's define the typical characteristics and skills of our user types. We'll characterize each user type based on the following:

▶ What are some typical goals of users working in a BI environment?

▶ What are some typical tasks for the user type?

▶ What other software does the user work with on a regular basis?

These tasks and goals are not meant to be specific to an area such as sales or finance, but should rather be seen as generic descriptions of a certain type of task or goal.

User Type: Information Consumer

Goals

▶ Review regular sales reports and monitor individual accounts and sales status.

▶ Review regular account statements to control customer invoices and vendor accounts.

▶ Review actual operational measures against goals.

▶ Fulfill management requests for information as simply as possible.

Tasks

▶ Find a prepared report, view the information, and print or export the information.

▶ Receive and review alerts from prepared reports and analytics.

▶ Schedule prebuilt reports and review the resulting information.

▶ Use predefined navigation steps and alerts to receive needed information.

▶ If required, provide information to the IT department for additional reports and analytics based on the needed information.

Regularly Used Software

▶ Microsoft Excel

▶ Microsoft PowerPoint

- Microsoft Word
- Microsoft Outlook
- Internet Browser

User Type: Business Analyst

Goals

- Analyze KPIs to find areas for improvement.
- Create deeper analysis to find details on anomalies.
- Leverage actual data and historical data to create detailed planning scenarios to enable more realistic forecasting and planning of future company key goals.
- Leverage the data and tools to provide answers ad hoc to the management and leadership team so that decisions are based on solid information.

Tasks

- Review prepared reports for KPIs and analyze the prepared data for anomalies.
- Edit existing reports and, if required, create new reports and analytics on the fly to answer related business questions.
- Share analysis and results with a larger audience and the management/leadership team.
- Act as the go-to person for the management/leadership team by providing required analysis for informed decisions.

Regularly Used Software

- Microsoft Excel
- Microsoft PowerPoint
- Microsoft Word
- Microsoft Outlook
- Microsoft Access
- Internet Browser

User Type: Executive and Management Team

Goals

- Analyze overall companywide operational metrics and ensure agreed targets are met.
- Analyze department/line-of-business performance and evaluate different scenarios for planning and forecasting purposes.
- Leverage the information for analyzing, monitoring, and planning purposes to continuously improve company performance.
- Combine the analytics with company strategies and goals and integrate these strategies and goals into each employee's workflow and goals.

Tasks

- Review companywide metrics (including past, actual, and forecasted values) and make informed decisions and take necessary actions.
- Set goals and targets for middle management and link them back to companywide goals and metrics. Continuously monitor and review those goals and targets.
- Regularly review operational KPIs and look for opportunities to improve operations and profit.

Regularly Used Software

- Microsoft Excel
- Microsoft Outlook
- Internet Browser

Now that we've defined our user types, we need to map these user types (based on their needs and skills) to the SAP BusinessObjects BI tools.

Figure 2.2 shows the three user types and the optional tools to address their needs. This does not mean, for example, that you cannot use SAP BusinessObjects Explorer for a typical business analyst audience, but it is possible that business analysts will not be 100% satisfied with the tool and they may prefer a tool like Pioneer to perform their work.

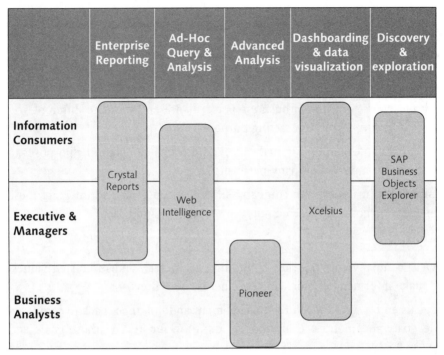

Figure 2.2 Mapping BusinessObjects BI Tools to User Types

Figure 2.2 is not an exclusive statement, meaning that the user types can only use the tools shown. It is a guide for tool selection. As you become more familiar with the tools in SAP BusinessObjects you will be able to use your own judgment and add your own criteria to the decision-making process. In cases where a tool only covers part of a user type (for example, Web Intelligence and Business Analyst), you can assume that you will be able to address some of the requirements and needs of that particular user type with the tool, but that there still will be some areas that might be better addressed by a different tool. In addition, keep in mind when selecting the tool, there is no single tool that provides all of the functionality that you might need. However, each tool does have a main purpose (see Figure 2.1).

In Figure 2.3, you can see the tools in a slightly different way. The tools are ordered based on the skill set required from the consumer's point of view (not the report designer's point of view). This figure also shows the recommended user type matched to the products as well.

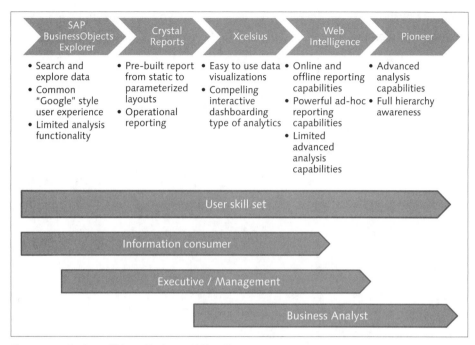

Figure 2.3 BusinessObjects Toolset and User Types

All three previous figures (Figure 2.1, Figure 2.2, and Figure 2.3) should provide you with a good overview on how to differentiate the tools and make an informed decision on which tool to use for the different user types. In the next section, we will create a simple decision based on some key questions to determine the best tool for your requirements.

2.5   Decision Path for SAP BusinessObjects Tools

Based on all of the information provided in the previous section, we'll now try to combine all of this information and criteria to provide a simplified decision tree that can be used to select a tool based on your requirements. Please keep in mind, such a simplified approach can never be perfect and it's recommended you use this decision tree in combination with all of the other information presented in the previous sections (and the upcoming chapters) to make a fully informed decision. The purpose of this decision tree is to provide you with a simplistic view of a complex topic.

In Figure 2.4 you can see the first part of the overall decision tree.

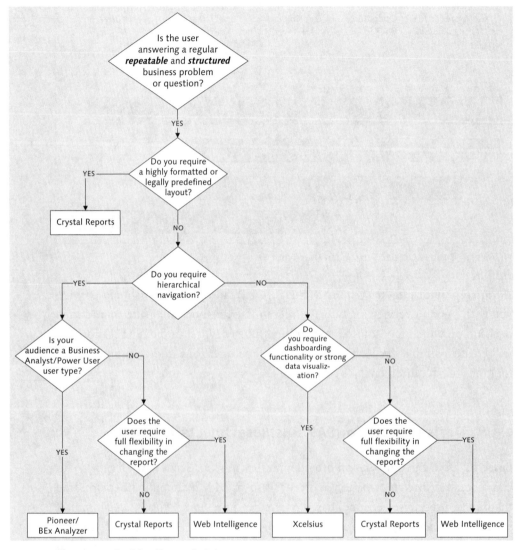

Figure 2.4 Decision Tree — Part 1

In Figure 2.5, you can see the second part of the decision tree.

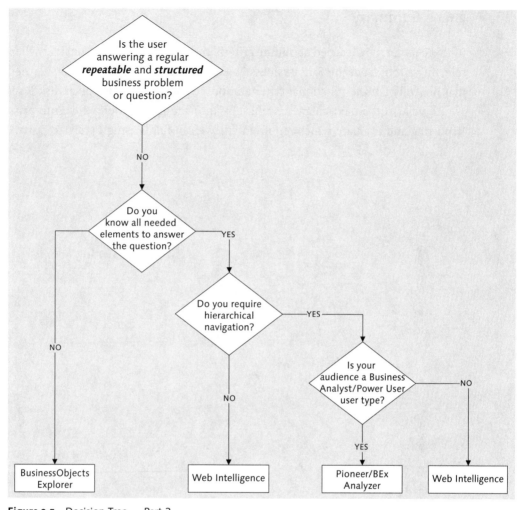

Figure 2.5 Decision Tree — Part 2

As previously mentioned, the decision tree is not intended to provide you a perfect answer just by answering a set of four to five questions. The intention is to provide you with guidance on the toolset and to provide you some criteria that you can use to make the right decision.

2.6   Summary

In this chapter, you learned about the criteria that are important to consider when selecting a tool from the SAP BusinessObjects portfolio. In addition, you learned that not only are the functional criteria important, but the user type and skill set are as well. In the next chapter, we'll look into the requirements for Enterprise Reporting and evaluate which requirements we can fulfill using Crystal Reports.

In the first half of this chapter, we'll look at the requirements that can be fulfilled by Crystal Reports. In the second part, we'll use Crystal Reports to create reports based on those requirements.

3 Enterprise Reporting with Crystal Reports

Let's look at Enterprise Reporting and how Crystal Reports can be leveraged to fulfill your requirements. We will cover the installation of the software and then focus on the requirements from our case study and see how Crystal Reports creates reports based on such requirements.

3.1 Installation and Deployment Overview

In this section, we'll focus on the installation of the tools required to create reports with Crystal Reports. This section does not cover the installation and deployment of BusinessObjects Enterprise in combination with your SAP landscape. We will only focus on the client-side components.

Integrating BusinessObjects XI 3.1 BI Tools with SAP NetWeaver

With regard to the installation and deployment of the BusinessObjects XI 3.1 release in combination with your SAP landscape, please see the author's first book, *Integrating BusinessObjects XI 3.1 BI Tools with SAP NetWeaver*.

Assuming you downloaded the software for Crystal Reports from the SAP Service Marketplace, you should be able to unpack the downloaded file and start the installation of Crystal Reports. The necessary steps are covered in the following sections.

3.1.1 Crystal Reports Installation

1. Navigate to the folder for the unpackaged download and start the installation by double-clicking on setup.exe.

2. The first screen of the installation will ask you which language you want to use for the actual setup routine (see Figure 3.1). This setting is only valid for the setup routine.

Figure 3.1 Crystal Reports 2008 — Setup Language

3. In the next steps, you need to accept the license agreement and enter the license key code for the product. After that is completed, you can select the language packs that you want to install for Crystal Reports (see Figure 3.2). In our installation we will select ENGLISH. These language packs influence which languages you can work with in Crystal Reports. If you select — as an example — English and French, then you can switch between English and French menus in Crystal Reports Designer.

Figure 3.2 Crystal Reports 2008 — Language Packs

In the next screen you can select the INSTALLATION TYPE (see Figure 3.3). The TYPI-CAL option will install Crystal Reports with the most common elements and the CUSTOM option will allow you to select the components you would like to install. If you are not sure which option to select, the TYPICAL option is recommended.

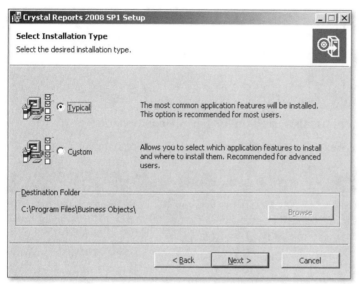

Figure 3.3 Crystal Reports 2008 — Installation Type

4. In the CUSTOM installation type, you can select the components that you would like to install on your client. In our example we will select all components.

5. In the next step you can configure the option to update your Crystal Reports installation automatically. This option depends on your personal preference and if you want Crystal Reports to download updates automatically or if you want to update the software manually.

6. In the final step, you can start the actual installation routine for Crystal Reports.

7. The installation of Crystal Reports will start and you should be able to use Crystal Reports when it's completed.

This completes the installation of Crystal Reports Designer. In the next section, we will continue with the installation of the SAP BusinessObjects Integration for SAP solutions.

3.1.2 SAP BusinessObjects Integration for SAP Solutions

After successfully installing Crystal Reports, you need to install the SAP frontend components and the client components from the SAP BusinessObjects Integration for SAP Solutions.

SAP Frontend Components

You need to ensure that the following components of the SAP frontend are available on the client:

- SAP Graphic User Interface (GUI)
- SAP Business Warehouse (BW) add-on for BW 3.5 components
- SAP Business Explorer (BEx) for SAP NetWeaver BW 7.x systems

BEx 3.5 Components

Even if you are leveraging SAP NetWeaver BW 7.x, you still need to install the BW 3.5 add-on components from the SAP frontend because Crystal Reports is leveraging user interface (UI) components from the BW 3.5 add-on.

This is a prerequisite for BusinessObjects XI Release 3.1 products and may change in future releases.

BusinessObjects Integration for SAP Solutions – Client Components

1. After installing the SAP frontend with the BW add-on (BW 3.x) and BI add-on (SAP NetWeaver BW 7.x) components, you can start the installation of the SAP BusinessObjects Integration for SAP Solutions. In the first screen of the installation routine you will be asked which language you prefer for the UI of the installation.

2. In the next two screens you will be asked to accept the license agreement and you will have to enter the license key code for the product. After these two steps you will be presented with a list of language packs. This time the language refers to the language of the BusinessObjects software that you are installing. For our installation we will select ENGLISH.

3. Now you will be asked if you want to install the CLIENT component, the SERVER component (see Figure 3.4), or if you would like to make a custom selection of the components.

4. You can select the CUSTOM option so that you can see all of the available options (see Figure 3.5).

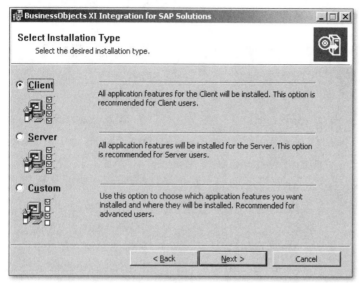

Figure 3.4 BusinessObjects XI Integration for SAP Solutions — Installation Type

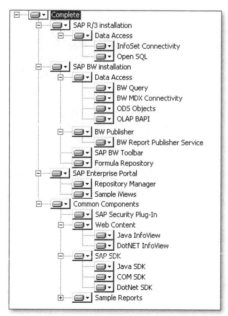

Figure 3.5 SAP BusinessObjects XI Integration for SAP Solutions — Components

5. Now you can select all of the necessary components for the client-side installation as shown in Figure 3.5. The components listed in Table 3.1 are those components needed to leverage the BusinessObjects client tools with the SAP BusinessObjects Integration for SAP Solutions.

Installation area	Installation component	Detailed selection
SAP R/3 INSTALLATION	DATA ACCESS	INFOSET CONNECTIVITY
	DATA ACCESS	OPEN SQL
SAP BW INSTALLATION	DATA ACCESS	BW MDX CONNECTIVITY
	DATA ACCESS	ODS OBJECTS
	SAP BW TOOLBAR	
COMMON COMPONENTS	SAP SECURITY PLUG-IN	
	SAMPLE REPORTS	BW QUERY SAMPLE REPORTS
	SAMPLE REPORTS	INFOSET SAMPLE REPORTS
	SAMPLE REPORTS	OPENSQL SAMPLE REPORTS

Table 3.1 BusinessObjects XI Integration for SAP Solutions — Client components for Crystal Reports

BW Query vs. BW MDX Connectivity

You will notice that the SAP BusinessObjects Integration for SAP Solutions includes BW Query connectivity and BW Multi-Dimensional eXpression (MDX) connectivity. It is highly recommended to leverage the BW MDX connectivity. The BW MDX connectivity is more enhanced for your SAP NetWeaver BW system and, when compared to the BW Query connectivity, it provides support for BW queries with multiple structures and display attributes.

After you have installed Crystal Reports Designer, the SAP frontend with the BW add-on and BI add-on components, and the client components from the SAP BusinessObjects Integration for SAP Solutions, you should be able to start the Crystal Reports Designer tool and see the newly added SAP menu and toolbar (see Figure 3.6).

In the next section, we will look at the connectivity options for Crystal Reports as part of your overall SAP landscape.

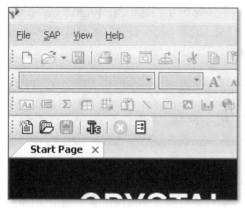

Figure 3.6 Crystal Reports with SAP Menu and Toolbar

3.2 SAP Data Connectivity for Crystal Reports

In this section, we will provide you with a short overview of the options for data retrieval when using Crystal Reports.

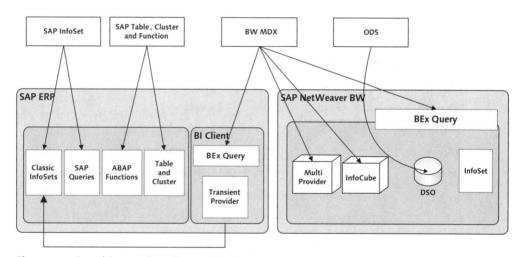

Figure 3.7 Crystal Reports Data Connectivity Options

In Figure 3.7, you can see that Crystal Reports is able to connect to the SAP ERP system and the SAP NetWeaver BW system. For the SAP ERP system, Crystal Reports gives you direct connectivity to the Advanced Business Application Programming (ABAP) dictionary — providing access to the tables and ABAP functions in your SAP system. In addition, Crystal Reports can connect to the classic InfoSets and InfoSet/ABAP queries in your SAP ERP system.

On the SAP NetWeaver BW side, Crystal Reports can connect to the BW query layer and therefore connect to all of the different InfoProviders in your data warehouse. Crystal Reports can also connect directly to the InfoCube and MultiProvider level, but such connectivity is not recommended (see Table 3.2). Table 3.2 shows the different levels of metadata support between a connectivity with the BW query and a direct connectivity with the InfoProvider. You can see that a direct connectivity with the InfoProvider is losing metadata from your SAP system and therefore is not recommended. Keep in mind that Crystal Reports is using the public Online Analytical Processing (OLAP) Business Application Programming Interface (BAPI) when connecting to SAP NetWeaver BW and that this approach might change in a future release.

SAP NetWeaver BW Metadata Element	SAP OLAP BAPI Support Level
Characteristics (incl. Time and Unit)	InfoCube and BI Query
Hierarchies	InfoCube and BI Query
Basic Key Figures	InfoCube and BI Query
Navigational Attributes	BI Query only
Display Attributes	InfoCube and BI Query
Calculated Key Figures / Formulas	BI Query only
Restricted Key Figures	BI Query only
Custom Structures	BI Query only
Variables	BI Query only

Table 3.2 SAP NetWeaver BW Metadata Support

InfoCube Access

In addition to the differences shown in Table 3.2, you should also consider that when accessing the InfoCube directly you do not have the functionality to create Authorization variables to filter the data based on user authorizations.

With regard to the mapping of the SAP NetWeaver BW metadata, Table 3.3 lists further details.

BW Query Element	Crystal Reports Designer Element
Characteristic	For each characteristic you will receive a field representing a key value and a field for the description.
Hierarchy	A hierarchy is represented by a parent-child relationship.
Key Figure	Each key figure can have up to three elements: numeric value, unit, and formatted value. The formatted value is based on user preferences configured in the SAP system.
Calculated and Restricted Key Figures	Each calculated/restricted key figure is treated like a key figure. The user does not have access to the underlying definition in Crystal Reports Designer.
Filter	Filters will be applied to the underlying query but are not visible in Crystal Reports Designer.
Navigational Attribute	Navigational attributes are treated exactly like a characteristic.
Display Attribute	Display attributes are standard fields in the Field Explorer and will be grouped as subordinates to the linked characteristic.
SAP Variables	Each variable with the property "Ready for Input" will result in a parameter field in Crystal Reports.

Table 3.3 SAP NetWeaver BW Metadata Mapping for Crystal Reports

---

SAP PRESS: Integrating SAP BusinessObjects XI 3.1 Tools with SAP NetWeaver

You can find more detail on the data connectivity options, metadata mapping, and the installation and configuration of the BusinessObjects Integration for SAP solutions in the author's book, *Integrating SAP BusinessObjects XI 3.1 Tools with SAP NetWeaver.*

In addition to the BW query connectivity we just discussed, we will highlight the option to leverage a BW query on top of the newly available Transient Info-Provider. The Transient InfoProvider allows you to connect to an ERP data source — specifically an ERP InfoSet — without any data modeling required by SAP NetWeaver BW. By using the Transient InfoProvider your SAP NetWeaver BW system becomes your single point of entry for data retrieval against your SAP ERP and SAP NetWeaver BW data sources.

In the next section, we will evaluate the requirements for Enterprise Reporting.

3.3 Customer Case Study — Enterprise Reporting Requirements

Now that you have installed the required software to leverage Crystal Reports in conjunction with your SAP landscape, and learned about the possible data connectivity options, we are now going to look at the enterprise reporting requirements and evaluate which of those requirements best fit Crystal Reports.

We'll start with the financial area requirements previously mentioned in Chapter 2, Section 2.2.1, "Financial Reporting and Analysis Requirements." We will filter the list to those requirements that cannot be fulfilled with Crystal Reports or where we think Crystal Reports is not a good match. It is important to realize that some requirements can be fulfilled with more than one tool, which does not mean that Crystal Reports wouldn't be able to fulfill these requirements that we are listing here, but we are trying to find the best combination of requirements for Crystal Reports and we need to understand that not all requirements will be satisfied using a single BI tool.

Financial Area Requirements — NOT Fulfilled by Crystal Reports

Based on the list of requirements, there is only one item that we think Crystal Reports will not be able to fulfill.

> **Unfulfilled Financial Area Requirements**
>
> ► The reporting and analysis tools need to allow the user create new calculations and formulas and share those with other consumers of the content.

Crystal Reports is not a tool that provides the end user/consumer the capability to add new calculations and formulas. Crystal Reports is a tool that provides highly formatted reports for the consumer to view and leverage information, but not to customize or change the actual content of the report.

This requirement is better suited for Web Intelligence or Pioneer, which allow the user to add calculations and formulas on demand.

Sales Area Requirements — NOT Fulfilled by Crystal Reports

There are several requirements in the sales area that cannot be fulfilled with Crystal Reports.

Unfulfilled Sales Area Requirements
▶ Users need the ability to change the view of the actual content. For example, changing a weekly sales statistic broken down by country into a weekly sales statistic broken down by sales region and quarter.
▶ Users need to modify existing reports or create new reports ad hoc.
▶ Users should be able to perform scenario-based analysis, where the user can see the data and influence certain factors to see the impact on the overall numbers. For example, a what-if analysis in a sales planning workflow.

Three out of the six sales area requirements we identified cannot be fulfilled with Crystal Reports. This could mean that most of the reports in the sales area will be delivered by another tool.

Let's now look at the three unfulfilled requirements and determine which tool is best suited to fulfill them:

▶ For users to modify existing reports or create new reports would mean that those users have access to the Crystal Reports designer tool. Providing those users a tool like Web Intelligence could offer such functionality in a web-based environment.

▶ For users to change the view of the report as previously described, Crystal Reports can be used to a certain degree, but if this is a very frequent requirement another tool, such as Pioneer or Web Intelligence, might be better suited.

▶ Scenario-based analysis is not possible with Crystal Reports. You can integrate Xcelsius into Crystal Reports objects providing such capabilities, but it is not something that Crystal Reports can fulfill on its own.

Human Resources (HR) Area Requirements — NOT Fulfilled by Crystal Reports

Based on the list of requirements there are no requirements, that Crystal Reports cannot fulfill, which is not surprising because Crystal Reports is a tool that allows you to create content with highly textual information.

Executive and Management Requirements — Not Fulfilled by Crystal Reports

There are a couple of requirements in the executive and management area that Crystal Reports does not fulfill.

> **Unfulfilled Executive Management Requirements**
>
> ▸ The data needs to be shown in a highly visual manner and the main Key Performance Indicators (KPIs) need to be presented on a single dashboard.
>
> ▸ The consumption of the reports and analytics need to be simple and easy to use and critical information needs to be identifiable right away.

Crystal Reports lacks the functionality for data visualization and the ease of consumption those visualizations offer. This does not mean that Crystal Reports is not an easy-to-use tool. Crystal Reports is, in fact, very easy to use, but the strength of the tool is not suited for data visualization (see Figure 2.1).

Data visualization requirements are better fulfilled by other tools, such as Xcelsius, Web Intelligence, and Pioneer.

Based on the evaluation of Crystal Reports against our requirements, we will use Crystal Reports as the tool to fulfill most of our financial and HR area requirements. Requirements from the sales and executive/management area are better suited for another tool.

In the next section, we will learn the first basic steps for using Crystal Reports as a design tool for reports.

3.4   Crystal Reports Designer — Quick Basics

Before we begin building reports, let's take a quick look at some of the basic functionality of Crystal Reports. If you already have a basic familiarity with Crystal Reports as a reporting tool, you can move on to the next section. However, if you are new to Crystal Reports, you should spend time reading this section to become familiar with the new environment.

In the following sections, we will look at some basic elements of Crystal Reports and how to use them to build a compelling report. You certainly won't become an expert after reading these sections, but they will provide you with an overview of the most important elements in Crystal Reports. Throughout these sections we will explain the topics as simply as possible and reference examples so that you can see how each functionality works.

3.4.1 Crystal Reports Designer Environment

When you start Crystal Reports for the first time you will be presented with a start page. This page gives you the option of opening an existing report or using wizards to create a new report. In this exercise, we'll create an empty report without any data connectivity. This will allow us to concentrate on the tool itself.

1. Follow the FILE • NEW • BLANK REPORT menu path.

2. In the next screen that comes up, click CANCEL.

3. You should now have an empty report in front of you (see Figure 3.8).

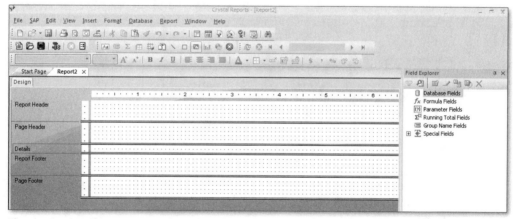

Figure 3.8 Crystal Reports Designer with an Empty Report

Before we look at the menu items, let's look at the empty report. Crystal Reports created a report with five areas called sections. These five sections are: REPORT HEADER, PAGE HEADER, DETAILS, REPORT FOOTER, and PAGE FOOTER. These sections provide the basic structure of your report. The number and type of sections can change depending on the design of your report. For example, if you need your report to group the revenue by country, then your report will also receive a group header and a group footer section.

The Report Header and Report Footer sections are placed at the beginning and end of your report. These sections are often used to present summary information about the report or the data that is being shown.

The Page Header and Page Footer are shown on the top and bottom of each page and are mostly used to show information such as the page number or the date of the report.

The Details section is the area that shows each record that has been received from the underlying data source. For example, a report with 500 records of data received from the SAP ERP system would have 500 Detail sections — unless you suppress or hide them.

Based on the preceding descriptions, you should realize that Crystal Reports is a tool that is well structured and allows you to create structured, layout-driven reports.

Now let's look at the FILE • OPTIONS menu items to understand some of the available customization options (see Figure 3.9).

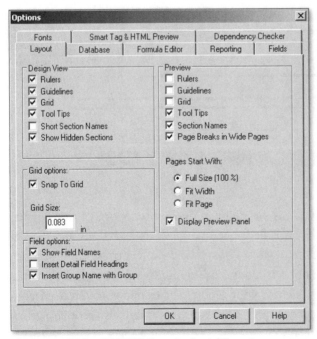

Figure 3.9 FILE • OPTIONS Menu in Crystal Reports

You can customize the look and feel of Crystal Reports Designer on your system. Let's look at some of the customization settings that are available.

In the LAYOUT tab you can specify how your design and preview of the report look. Please take note of the guidelines and the grid in Crystal Reports, you will use these when creating your first financial report and they allow you to make sure all of the elements of your report are nicely aligned and easily moveable and resizable. You want to make sure that the rules, guidelines, and the grid are checked so that you can use them on your system.

In the DATABASE tab (see Figure 3.10), you want to make sure that you check the TABLES AND FIELDS option, which basically means that you will see the technical names and the descriptions for all of the fields from your data source. In addition, you can use the TABLE NAME LIKE field to enter a technical name for a table, Info-Set, BW query, or any other data source to limit the list of available entries when connecting to your system.

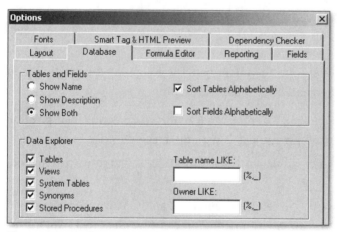

Figure 3.10 Database Options for Crystal Reports

In the FIELDS and FONTS tabs (see Figure 3.11) you can set default values for the formatting of fields and the usage of fonts based on field types for your system. This is especially useful for reports where you have to use company standards for fonts, font sizes, or number formats. You can specify those settings here once and all new reports will automatically leverage these settings; but keep in mind that these settings will not apply to all of your existing reports — only new reports will leverage them.

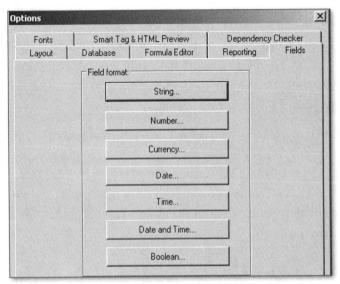

Figure 3.11 Field Options in Crystal Reports

There are several menu items on the menu bar. The following information is to help you understand when and how to use each option:

▶ The FILE menu is for creating, opening, and saving your reports, and printing and setting up your environment just as with the FILE • OPTIONS menu path.

▶ The EDIT menu has tasks similar to Microsoft Office (e.g., copy, paste, redo, undo, etc.).

▶ The VIEW menu allows you to select the elements and tools you want to see in your Crystal Reports design environment. You can turn the Field Explorer or rules and guidelines on and off, for example.

▶ The INSERT menu is one the most useful menus in Crystal Reports. Here, you can find all of the available elements you can add to your report, such as creating a group, creating a chart, or adding a textbox.

▶ The FORMAT menu allows you to not only format the selected objects, but you can also configure highlighting and align and size several objects in a single step.

▶ The DATABASE menu concerns your data connectivity. For example, you can verify the database for changes or just simply log on to or log off of the database.

▶ The REPORT menu is probably the second most useful menu after the INSERT menu. Here, you can create additional filters or conditions, such as a Top 10 setting for your report. You can also set properties for all of the sections in your report.

▶ Menu SAP allows you to create, save, and open a Crystal Reports object using SAP dialogs when communicating with your SAP NetWeaver BW system. These dialogs are not relevant when connecting to your SAP ERP system.

Over time you will start to leverage more and more of the toolbars with the respective icons for all of the menu items. When calling the menus, Crystal Reports shows the icons that are shown on the toolbars in front of each of the menu items, which will help you remember them.

3.4.2 Field Explorer

The Field Explorer (see Figure 3.12) is an element of your Crystal Reports design environment that you will use almost all of the time.

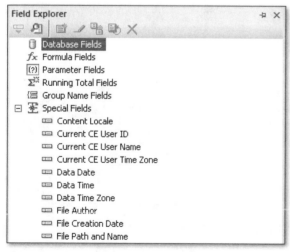

Figure 3.12 Crystal Reports — Field Explorer

The FIELD EXPLORER provides you with all of the fields that you either received from the underlying source, shown as DATABASE FIELDS, or elements that you created yourself, such as FORMULA FIELDS, PARAMETER FIELDS, RUNNING TOTAL FIELDS, and GROUP NAME FIELDS. The list of SPECIAL FIELDS is a list of common elements, such as the actual date or time, page numbers, or the report title. In the VIEW menu you can switch the display of the FIELD EXPLORER on and off.

Now let's create a simple report on top of a simple BW query.

As you can see in Figure 3.13, we created a BW query on top of the InfoProvider DalSegno Company Sales Data (technical name: 0D_DX_C01). This is a standard demo content InfoCube, which means you can create the same query in your own system. In the BW query we used the following elements:

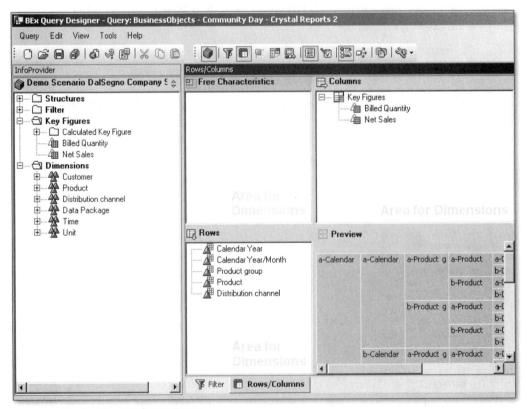

Figure 3.13 Simple BW Query

▶ In the rows:

  ▶ Calendar Year

  ▶ Calendar Year/Month

  ▶ Product Group

  ▶ Product

  ▶ Distribution Channel

▶ In the columns:

  ▶ Billed Quantity

  ▶ Net Sales

Now we can start creating a simple report and take a further look at some of the common elements of Crystal Reports.

1. Follow the SAP • SETTINGS menu path.

2. Ensure that the USE MDX DRIVER WITH SUPPORT FOR MULTIPLE STRUCTURES setting is checked, which ensures that you are using the BW MDX Driver and not the old BW Query connectivity.

3. Follow the SAP • CREATE NEW REPORT FROM A QUERY menu path.

4. The SAP logon dialog will come up and you need to select your SAP NetWeaver BW system and provide your credentials.

5. In the next step, you will be presented with the standard dialog for selecting your BW query (see Figure 3.14).

6. Select the BW query you created and Crystal Reports will create a new report with the BW query as the datasource.

7. Follow the VIEW • FIELD EXPLORER menu path to see the FIELD EXPLORER. Here, the list of DATABASE FIELDS shows the elements of your BW query (see Figure 3.15). In cases where a field is shown with a "+" symbol in front of the name, and the field is offering more than a single field, you can open the list for more detail. A good example is a characteristic from your BW query with a key value and a description.

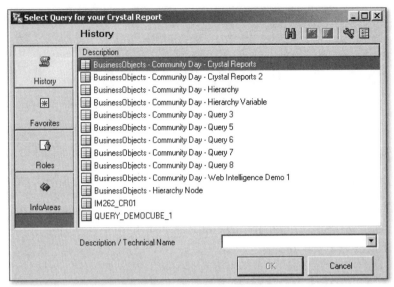

Figure 3.14   Dialog for Selecting BW Query

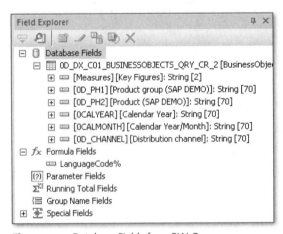

Figure 3.15   Database Fields from BW Query

8. Now use the FIELD EXPLORER and drag and drop the following fields into the Detail section of your new report:

   ▶ Distribution Channel Name

   ▶ Product Group Name

   ▶ Net Sales Value

9. Your report in the DESIGN view should look similar to Figure 3.16.

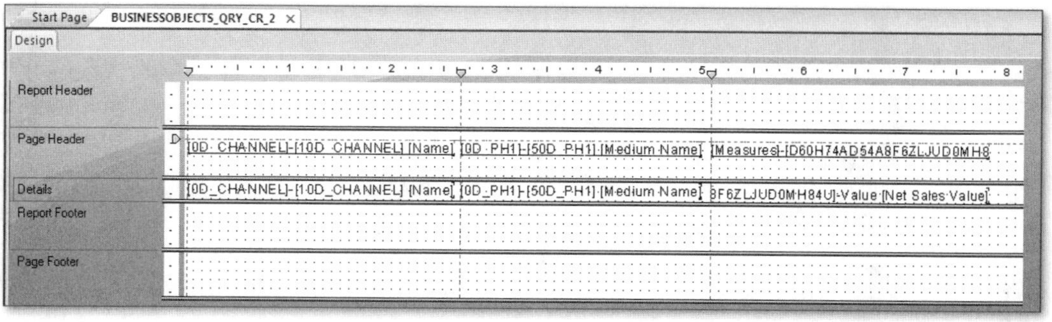

Figure 3.16 Design View of the Report

10. Now you can see the guidelines that have been created automatically during insertion of the fields onto the report. The red corners on the left side of the fields show that the field is attached to the guideline. You can create your own guidelines — as shown here in the example — by clicking on the horizontal or vertical ruler. As you can see, we created a ruler in the Page Header section and we moved all three field headings up so that they are attached to the guideline and aligned on the top.

11. In addition, Crystal Reports created field headings for each field that you placed in the Details section. The content of the field heading depends on the setting you configured in the FILE • OPTIONS menu on the DATABASE tab for the TABLES AND FIELDS area. When selecting the BOTH option, your field heading will include the technical name and the description. You can edit the field headings with a simple double-click and then you can type your own headings. If you prefer to create your own field headings, you can use the FILE • OPTIONS menu and uncheck the INSERT DETAILS FIELD HEADING setting on the LAYOUT tab in the FIELD OPTIONS area (bottom left corner).

12. Follow the VIEW • PRINT PREVIEW menu path (see Figure 3.17).

13. Crystal Reports is showing you a preview of your report, so you can decide if you want to work in the design view of the report (by clicking on the DESIGN tab) or the PREVIEW mode, where your changes are reflected with the actual data.

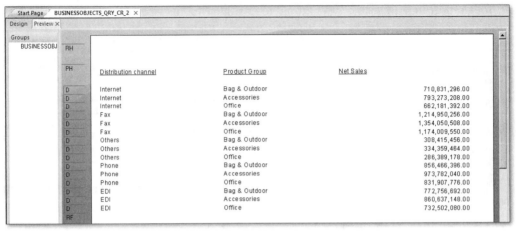

Figure 3.17   Crystal Reports Preview

3.4.3   Groupings

We will now use the basic report we just created and create our first grouping in the report.

14. Follow the INSERT • GROUP menu path (see Figure 3.18).

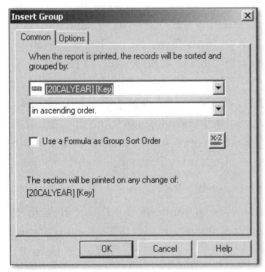

Figure 3.18   Insert Group Dialog

15. Using our example, let's select the [20CALYEAR] [KEY] field to group on. In the second list box you can choose if the grouping should happen in ascending, descending, or a customized order.

16. On the OPTIONS tab (see Figure 3.19), you can specify the behavior of your grouping. You can customize a different field to be displayed for the report instead of the field that you used for the grouping. This is a great option for reports where you summarize (for example) based on a Product key value, but would also like to show the product description. In such cases you would select the product description field here. In addition, you can use the option KEEP GROUP TOGETHER so that — if possible — the information from a single group is not split over two pages in your report. But in cases where you can't prevent such a situation, you can use the option REPEAT GROUP HEADER ON EACH PAGE to show the heading from your group on each page that contains information from this group.

Figure 3.19 Insert Group Options Dialog

17. Click OK to create the group in your REPORT.

18. Your report should look similar to Figure 3.20, and when you click on the DESIGN tab you will see that your report now also contains a Group Header and a Group Footer section.

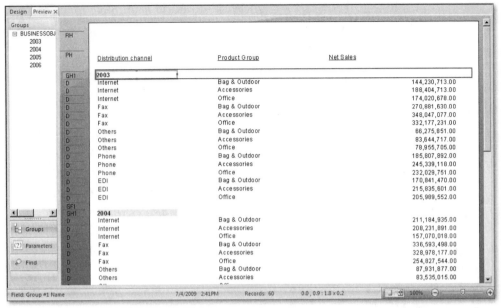

Figure 3.20   Crystal Reports Preview

Because we created the group based on the CALENDAR YEAR we can now summarize our Net Sales per year.

19. Right-click (or follow the INSERT • SUMMARY menu path) on the NET SALES field and select the INSERT • SUMMARY option (see Figure 3.21).

20. In the first list box you can select the field you want to summarize. In our example, NET SALES is pre-selected because we called the menu when we selected NET SALES. In the second list box you can set the type of summary, which depends on the type of field. For example, a summary based on customer name would not offer you the SUM option, but you could use the distinct count option to count your customers.

21. The summary location let's you specify if you want to create a GRAND TOTAL or, as in our case, a summary for your first group.

22. Click OK to create the subtotal.

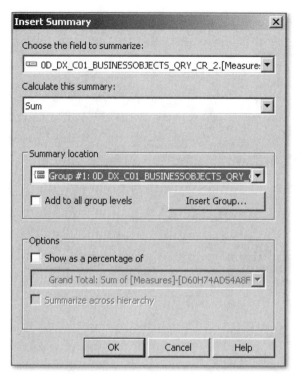

Figure 3.21   Insert Summary

3.4.4   Section Expert

Now that we created a report that shows the data grouped by Calendar Year and summarizes the Net Sales per year, let's look at what kind of formatting options you have for the sections in your report.

1. Follow the REPORT • SECTION EXPERT menu path (see Figure 3.22).

2. In SECTION EXPERT, you will be presented with a list of all of the sections your report contains at that point on the left side. On the right-hand side are the options you can configure. The most common options are also available on the context menu, when you right-click on the section you would like to configure.

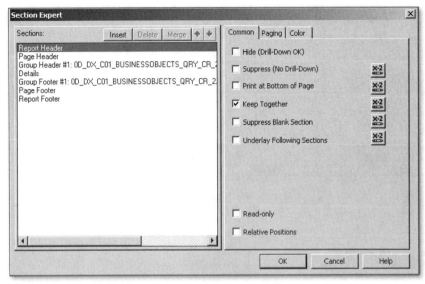

Figure 3.22 Section Expert

Now let's look at some typical options using our report as an example.

3. Select the DETAILS section on the left side.

4. You can configure the options for the details section. In our example, we will look at the HIDE (DRILL DOWN OK) and SUPPRESS (NO DRILL DOWN) options.

   ▸ HIDE (DRILL DOWN OK) lets you hide the section you select — in our example, the Details section — from the user in the initial view, but the user can double-click on a group header and drill down to the details. A drill down will be shown in a new tab.

   ▸ SUPPRESS (NO DRILL DOWN) is the opposite of the hide option. The selected section will be suppressed and the user does not have the option to drill down.

5. In our example, we will select the HIDE (DRILL DOWN OK) option for the Details section. That way, the detailed information about the products is hidden in the initial view (see Figure 3.23), but the user can drill down by double-clicking on the group header or group footer (in our case, the subtotal) information (see Figure 3.24). Each drill down will be shown as a separate tab next to the DESIGN and PREVIEW tabs.

Figure 3.23 Crystal Report Showing Summary Information Only

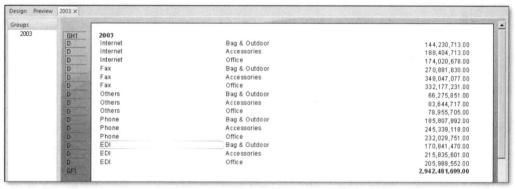

Figure 3.24 Drill Down Showing Detailed Information

Crystal Reports Designer vs. Viewing Experience

Keep in mind that all of the workflows that you are following right now are done with the Crystal Reports Designer tool, but the user consuming your report can perform most of the tasks, such as a drill down, when viewing the report as well.

6. As you can see in Figure 3.23, in our report the group header — calendar year — and the subtotal are not next to each other. Therefore, we navigate to the DESIGN tab and move the subtotal from the group footer to the group header (see Figure 3.25).

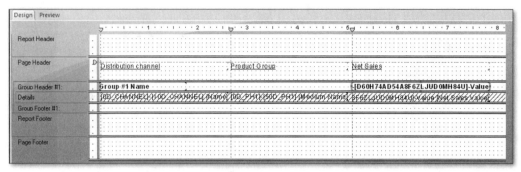

Figure 3.25 Crystal Reports Design

7. Because our group footer is now empty we can suppress it. Right-click on the GROUP FOOTER #1 section and select the menu option SUPPRESS (NO DRILL DOWN).

3.4.5 Conditional Formatting

Now let's look at one of the most powerful tools in Crystal Reports, the capability to influence formatting settings with formulas, called conditional formatting. Right now our report shows Net Sales broken down by Calendar Year and, via a drilldown, the user can see the Distribution Channel and each sold product with the Net Sales for each line item. We will now add some highlighting to the report to identify the highest Net Sales products.

1. Navigate to the DESIGN tab of your report.

2. Right-click on the NET SALES value field in the DETAILS section.

3. Select HIGHLIGHTING EXPERT.

4. In HIGHLIGHTING EXPERT, you can set boundary conditions for numeric values. Click NEW in the HIGHLIGHTING EXPERT dialog and set a boundary condition that sets the font to red and the background to yellow when the Net Sales value is larger than 1,000,000 (see Figure 3.26).

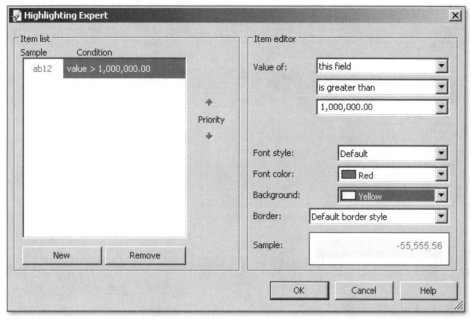

Figure 3.26 Crystal Reports Highlighting Expert

5. Click OK and navigate to the report preview.

6. Now, when performing a drilldown, values larger than 1,000,000 get highlighted in the specified manner.

7. Navigate back to the DESIGN tab of your report.

8. Right-click on the DETAILS section and select SECTION EXPERT.

9. Navigate to the COLOR tab on the right-hand side (see Figure 3.27).

10. Anywhere you see the symbol ☒ next to a property, as shown in Figure 3.27 for the COLOR property, you can use formulas to set the property.

11. Click on the symbol to go to the Formula Workshop in Crystal Reports (see Figure 3.28).

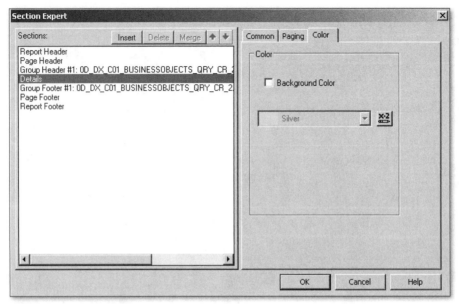

Figure 3.27 Section Expert

Figure 3.28 Crystal Reports Formula Workshop

You can create very simple to very complex formulas in the Formula Workshop to set the property.

12. We will use a very simple example. Enter the following formula:

```
if recordnumber mod 2 = 1 then crNoColor else crGreen
```

The formula is basically dividing the recordnumber by 2 and in case there is a remainder it sets the background color for the detail section to no color and in case there is no remainder it sets the color to green. In simple terms it means that the background for each second row will become green.

13. Click SAVE AND CLOSE in the Formula Workshop. You will recognize that the color of the symbol next to the color setting has changed to red to indicate that a formula has been created to influence the behavior.

14. Click OK in the Section Expert and navigate to the Preview tab of your report.

15. Now when you drill down on one of the Calendar Years you will see that each second row per Calendar Year received a green background. In addition, you will notice that the number highlighting has a higher priority than the background color (see Figure 3.29).

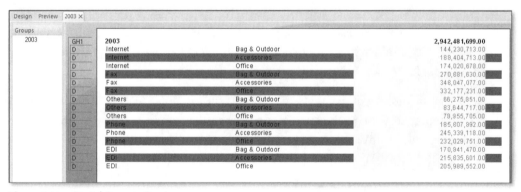

Figure 3.29 Crystal Reports Preview

3.4.6 Saving to BusinessObjects Enterprise

Now that we finished the design of our report we can save it to our BusinessObjects Enterprise system and share it with our consumers.

1. Follow the FILE • SAVE AS menu path.

2. Select ENTERPRISE in the list of possible locations (see Figure 3.30).

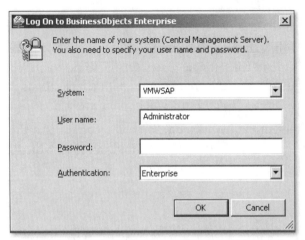

Figure 3.30 Crystal Reports Logon to BusinessObjects Enterprise

3. Enter the details to log on to your SAP BusinessObjects Enterprise system. The System entry is the name of your SAP BusinessObjects server, in our example it is VMWSAP.

4. After you authenticate against the BusinessObjects system you will be presented with a folder structure where you can select the location and name for your report.

Congratulations, you created a new report on top of a SAP BW query and saved the report to your BusinessObjects server so that other consumers can leverage the report in InfoView.

3.4.7   SAP-Specific Options

After you install the SAP BusinessObjects Integration for SAP solutions in combination with Crystal Reports on your client computer you will see that you now have a SAP-specific menu item as part of the Crystal Reports designer. In this section, we will look at some of the SAP-specific items that are relevant to Crystal Reports.

Table 3.4 explains the items listed in the SAP menu.

Button	Menu Item	Function
	Create a new report from SAP BW Query	Creates a new report based on an SAP BW query that is already defined.
	Open Report	Opens a Crystal Report file from SAP BW.
	Save Report	Saves the current report to SAP BW.
	Save Report as	Saves the report to BW with the option to define a new name or choose a different SAP BW role.
	Start SAP BW Query Designer	Starts the SAP BW Query Designer.
	Disconnect	Closes the current connection to SAP BW.
	Settings	Allows configuring settings for the connectivity to SAP BW. The settings are specific for the Crystal Reports designer installation.

Table 3.4 SAP Menu in Crystal Reports

SAP NetWeaver BW vs. SAP ER Connectivity

Keep in mind that SAP menu items are used solely for connecting to your SAP NetWeaver BW system. When connecting to your SAP ERP system you use the standard Crystal Reports menu items.

The SAP menu items provide you with some advantages over the normal Crystal Reports menu items when connecting to SAP NetWeaver BW:

► SAP variables will be generated as parameters in Crystal Reports with a list of values when using the SAP menu items. When using the standard Crystal Reports menu items the list of values will be empty.

► When using the SAP menus to create, edit, or open a report you will be presented with the standard SAP dialogs allowing you to select the report or BW query (in the case of create) based on your SAP roles. When using the standard Crystal Reports menus you will receive a list of BW queries based on the technical names without the option to distinguish based on SAP roles.

> **SAP Toolbar vs. Menu FILE • NEW**
>
> You can use the SAP Toolbar to create a report on top of your SAP NetWeaver BW system and you can use the FILE • NEW menu path to select the proper SAP connectivity. It is important that if you start to create a report with the SAP Toolbar that you also publish the report to your BusinessObjects Enterprise system (and to not use the FILE • SAVE menu path) because otherwise the report object will have incomplete information and a Single Sign-On (SSO) will not be possible.

In the next section, we will use the requirements from the financial area and use Crystal Reports to fulfill parts of them.

3.5 Customer Requirements — Financial Reporting with Crystal Reports

Now that we learned some basic functionality for Crystal Reports we will look at how we can realize the requirements from the previous section and what steps we need to take to create a report with Crystal Reports that matches these requirements. Based on the requirements and the matching tools of these requirements, we see that Crystal Reports is a great fit for the financial reporting part of the requirements, so we can start with reports from the financial area and take a look at how we can create a Crystal Report for this area.

The first report that we are going to create is a General Ledger (G/L) Accounting balance (see Figure 3.31) showing key figures such as the opening balance, debit, credit, and a total balance. The report should let us select certain items like the financial period, the currency, or the company code upfront.

To create this report we will use a SAP BW query from the Business Content. The BW query 0FIGL_M20_Q0002 is based on the G/L Accounting cube 0FIGL_M20. The BW query contains several variables that let you select the appropriate timeframe, financial periods, and currencies (see Figure 3.32).

G/L Accounts: Balances

Fiscal Year: 2008   Perbd: 1 - [PFD]   Ledger: [0AC_   Page 1 of 3

Last Data Update: 7/17/2009   Printed by: o1 7/17/2009

Selection Criteria

Company Code: [0COMP_CODE].[1000]
Profit Center:
Currency Type: 10

Company Code: 1000   SAP A.G.

Currency Type: 10   Currency: EUR

Account Number	G/L Account	Balance Carryforward	Balance Previous	Cum. Balance Previous	Debit Total	Credit Total	Cumulated Debit Balance	Cumulated Credit Balance	Cumulated Balance
INT/1000	Real estate and similar rights	-26,273.54	0.00	-26,273.54	225,216.24	939,007.93	0.00	-740,065.23	-740,065.23
INT/100000	Petty cash	-7,000.00	0.00	-7,000.00	0.00	0.00	0.00	-7,000.00	-7,000.00
INT/1010	Accumlt d. Deprctn - Real Estate and Similar Rights	-644,077.00	0.00	-644,077.00	0.00	268,565.00	0.00	-912,642.00	-912,642.00
INT/11000	Machinery and equipment	2,000.00	0.00	2,000.00	2,000.00	0.00	4,000.00	0.00	4,000.00
INT/11010	Accumulated depreciation-plant and machinery	-493,188.00	0.00	-493,188.00	0.00	204,074.00	0.00	-697,262.00	-697,262.00
INT/113100	G/L Account	-3,322.00	0.00	-3,322.00	1,300.00	1,000.00	0.00	-3,022.00	-3,022.00
INT/113105	Bank 1 (other interim postings)	0.00	0.00	0.00	1,000.00	1,000.00	0.00	0.00	0.00
INT/140000	Customers - Domestic Receivables 1	0.00	0.00	0.00	2,100.00	1,100.00	1,000.00	0.00	1,000.00
INT/154000	Input tax	43.90	0.00	43.90	689.65	0.00	733.55	0.00	733.55
INT/160000	Accounts payable-domestic	-318.25	0.00	-318.25	0.00	7,300.00	0.00	-7,618.25	-7,618.25
INT/175000	Output tax	0.00	0.00	0.00	13.79	0.00	13.79	0.00	13.79
INT/191000	GR/IR clearing - own production	0.00	0.00	0.00	0.00	0.00	0.00	0.00	0.00
INT/192100	Freight clearing (MM)	0.00	0.00	0.00	0.00	0.00	0.00	0.00	0.00
INT/199990	Clearing account fixed asset acquisition	-2,000.00	0.00	-2,000.00	0.00	160,000.00	0.00	-162,000.00	-162,000.00
INT/200010	Loss on assets scrapped	0.00	0.00	0.00	828,645.46	0.00	828,645.46	0.00	828,645.46
INT/202000	Loss from allocation of special items	0.00	0.00	0.00	72.00	0.00	72.00	0.00	72.00
INT/21010	Accumulated depreciation - fixtures and fittings	-276,235.15	0.00	-276,235.15	110,421.47	117,379.89	0.00	-283,193.57	-283,193.57

Figure 3.31 G/L Account Balances

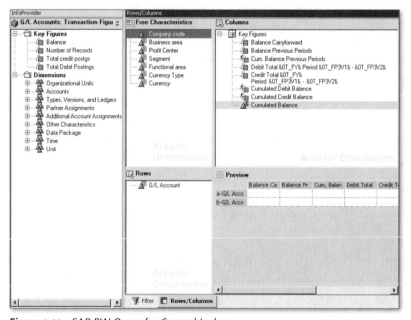

Figure 3.32 SAP BW Query for General Ledger

In the rows, the BW query contains the characteristics for the G/L account, and in the free characteristics we have the following:

- ▶ Company Code
- ▶ Business Area
- ▶ Profit Center
- ▶ Segment
- ▶ Functional Area
- ▶ Currency Type
- ▶ Currency

In the columns, we have several key figures providing us with the actual balances for the current period, carried forward balances, debit and credit balances, and the cumulated balance.

In addition to this information, you should know that the BW query contains several text variables that are used as part of the key figure descriptions; the problem is that text variables that influence the description of a key figure or a characteristic are not properly supported with Crystal Reports, and therefore the field description in the Crystal Reports Field Explorer contains the name of the variables and not the actual values. The second important item about the query is that the G/L Account characteristic is compounded with the chart of accounts characteristic. A compounded characteristic will show the combined key in Crystal Reports, which might not always be what you were looking for. We will address this in our report:

1. Start Crystal Reports Designer.
2. Follow the SAP • CREATE NEW REPORT FROM A QUERY menu path.
3. Authenticate towards your SAP system.
4. Select the BW query for the G/L report.
5. Crystal Reports will generate an empty report with the BW query as the data source.

Before we continue creating the report, let's review the goal for the report. We want to create a detailed report showing all of the accounts with key figures and descriptions and the key figures for the balances. In addition, we want to show the information that was used as selection criteria on the report. We will group the information per company code in our example; if other groupings make more sense for your company you should still be able to follow along. Based on these items, you might initially think that a cross tab is the perfect choice for such a report, but here are some thoughts:

▸ When you use a cross tab you can only have one field (similar to grouping) that distinguishes the groups. You can have several groups encapsulated, but each group is configured by one field. In our case we want to show the key and description for the account, so that would mean we have to combine the number and the description, but that gives us one field where the number will not be right-aligned with a left-aligned description — you can only align the combination of the text.

▸ The field that is being used to distinguish the rows in the cross tab — in our example, the G/L account — is losing the CAN GROW property for the field formatting. The CAN GROW option is relevant for our report because we might have G/L account descriptions that are relatively long and we want to ensure the complete description is shown. In a cross tab we would have to size all elements from the cross tab accordingly, which would lead to a lot of wasted space on our report because we would have to resize all of the rows — not just those where the description of the G/L account field needs more than a single line.

Based on the preceding items we will not use a cross tab but instead use the details sections of our report and build the structure.

6. First, we need to resolve the compounded characteristic situation for the G/L account and the chart of accounts. The key value of the G/L account characteristic is combined with the key value of the chart of accounts because these two are configured as a compounded characteristic; for example, INT/1000 for the chart of accounts INT and the G/L account 1000.

7. Follow the VIEW • FIELD EXPLORER menu path.

8. Right-click on FORMULA FIELDS in the Field Explorer and select NEW.

9. Enter `fn_GL_Account` as the Formula Field and click OK.

10. Enter the following formula:

```
ToNumber(
    (Split (
```

```
        <GL Account field>
    ,"/"
        )
  [2])
)
```

Replace the placeholder <GL Account field> with the key of the G/L account characteristic.

11. Place the newly created formula into the details section of your report.

12. Drag and drop the description field (short, medium, or long) from the G/L account characteristic next to the formula in the details section.

Guidelines

Because this report has lots of fields in the details section we recommend using guidelines to ensure the fields are left and right aligned and easily resizable and moveable. You can set your own guidelines by clicking on the horizontal or vertical rules and you can attach the fields to the guidelines by moving the fields to them.

---

13. Now place the VALUE field from each of the key figures/measures into the details section.

		Balance Carry	Balance Previ	Cum. Balance	Debit Total &0	Credit Total &	Cumulated De	Cumulated Cr	Cumulated Ba
400,000.00	Consumption, raw material	0.00	0.00	0.00	1,085.21	999.00	86.21	0.00	86.21
1,000.00	Real estate and similar righ	-26,273.54	0.00	-26,273.54	225,216.24	939,007.93	0.00	-740,065.23	-740,065.23
1,010.00	Accum ltd. Deprctn - Real E	-644,077.00	0.00	-644,077.00	0.00	268,565.00	0.00	-912,642.00	-912,642.00
11,000.00	Machinery and equipment	2,000.00	0.00	2,000.00	2,000.00	0.00	4,000.00	0.00	4,000.00
11,010.00	Accumulated depreciation-j	-493,188.00	0.00	-493,188.00	0.00	204,074.00	0.00	-697,262.00	-697,262.00
21,010.00	Accumulated depreciation -	-276,235.15	0.00	-276,235.15	110,421.47	117,379.89	0.00	-283,193.57	-283,193.57
22,010.00	Accumulated depreciation-I	4.00	0.00	4.00	0.00	0.00	4.00	0.00	4.00
72,010.00	Reserves from defined IFB-	-332.00	0.00	-332.00	0.00	110.00	0.00	-442.00	-442.00
78,000.00	Balance of special items	-159,806.00	0.00	-159,806.00	8,728.00	2.00	0.00	-151,080.00	-151,080.00
78,300.00	Investment receivables rec	332.00	0.00	332.00	110.00	0.00	442.00	0.00	442.00
100,000.00	Petty cash	-7,000.00	0.00	-7,000.00	0.00	0.00	0.00	-7,000.00	-7,000.00
113,100.00	G/L Account	-3,322.00	0.00	-3,322.00	1,300.00	1,000.00	0.00	-3,022.00	-3,022.00
113,105.00	Bank 1 (other interim postir	0.00	0.00	0.00	1,000.00	1,000.00	0.00	0.00	0.00
140,000.00	Customers - Domestic Rec	0.00	0.00	0.00	2,100.00	1,100.00	1,000.00	0.00	1,000.00
154,000.00	Input tax	43.90	0.00	43.90	689.65	0.00	733.55	0.00	733.55
160,000.00	Accounts payable-domestic	-318.25	0.00	-318.25	0.00	7,300.00	0.00	-7,618.25	-7,618.25
175,000.00	Output tax	0.00	0.00	0.00	13.79	0.00	13.79	0.00	13.79
191,000.00	GR/IR clearing - own produ	0.00	0.00	0.00	0.00	0.00	0.00	0.00	0.00
192,100.00	Freight clearing (MM)	0.00	0.00	0.00	0.00	0.00	0.00	0.00	0.00
199,990.00	Clearing account fixed asse	-2,000.00	0.00	-2,000.00	0.00	160,000.00	0.00	-162,000.00	-162,000.00
200,010.00	Loss on assets scrapped	0.00	0.00	0.00	828,645.46	0.00	828,645.46	0.00	828,645.46
202,000.00	Loss from allocation of spe	0.00	0.00	0.00	72.00	0.00	72.00	0.00	72.00
211,100.00	Scheduled depreciation of t	0.00	0.00	0.00	270,549.00	42.00	270,507.00	0.00	270,507.00
211,200.00	Unplanned depreciation-fixe	0.00	0.00	0.00	268,565.00	0.00	268,565.00	0.00	268,565.00
250,000.00	Profits on disposals ale of f	0.00	0.00	0.00	0.00	99.00	0.00	-99.00	-99.00
252,000.00	Gain from release of specia	0.00	0.00	0.00	0.00	8,798.00	0.00	-8,798.00	-8,798.00
253,000.00	Gain-asset write-up	0.00	0.00	0.00	0.00	20.00	0.00	-20.00	-20.00
261,000.00	Clearing-estimated deprei	##########	0.00	##########	18,938.00	1,444,544.00	0.00	##########	##########
261,001.00	Clearing estimated deprec	-2,333.00	0.00	-2,333.00	0.00	972.00	0.00	-3,305.00	-3,305.00
263,000.00	Clearing estimated interest	0.00	0.00	0.00	0.00	1,069,981.00	0.00	##########	##########
399,999.00	Initial entry of stock (offsetti	0.00	0.00	0.00	0.00	100.00	0.00	-100.00	-100.00
415,000.00	External procurement costs	0.00	0.00	0.00	333.00	333.00	0.00	0.00	0.00
415,100.00	External Procurement / Hou	0.00	0.00	0.00	4,469.00	4,469.00	0.00	0.00	0.00

Figure 3.33 Crystal Reports Preview

Your report should look similar to Figure 3.33. As you can see, we need to resize and align the column headers, sort our report by G/L Account, and resize the columns to fit the numbers.

14. Create a horizontal guideline by clicking on the ruler in the DESIGN view, attach the column headers, and resize them so that the complete description is visible. When you click on a field there are four squares on the outside to resize the field in all directions.

Field Size and Alignment

By selecting several fields (using the `Ctrl` button) and using the FORMAT • ALIGN and FORMAT • MAKE SAME SIZE menu paths, you can easily align and size several fields with a single click. These menus are also available by right-clicking.

---

15. Manually edit the column headers of measures with Text variables and remove the technical name of the text variable.

16. Right-click on the field for the G/L account and select Format Field.

17. Select the number format without decimals and without a thousand separator.

18. Right-click on the description field for the G/L account field and select Format Field.

19. Navigate to the COMMON tab and set the CAN GROW option (see Figure 3.34).

20. By setting this option the field can increase in size if the description of the G/L account is longer than the field size.

21. Select all of the values that we placed into the Details section of the report.

22. Right-click and select FORMAT OBJECTS.

23. Navigate to the NUMBER tab.

24. Select the number format without decimals and with a thousand separator.

25. To sort the data based on the G/L account number, follow the REPORT • RECORD SORT EXPERT menu path and add the formula for the G/L Account number to the list of sort fields and set the ascending sort option.

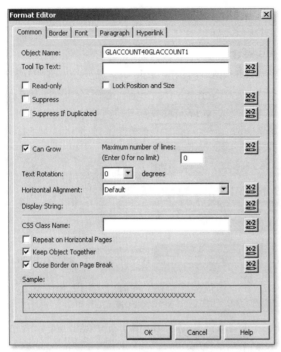

Figure 3.34 Common Options for Field Formatting

26. Because we want to show the information per company, we now need to create a new group per company. Follow the INSERT • GROUP menu path and select the company code key as the field to group in (see Figure 3.35).

27. Navigate to the tab OPTIONS and select the option CUSTOMIZE GROUP NAME FIELD and select the company description as the field to be displayed.

28. In the Design view of your report, you will see that you have the sections Group Header #1 and Group Footer #1. Because we showing the information per company, we can also move all of our column headers into the group header so that it is shown per company.

29. Navigate to the Design tab of your report.

30. Right-click on the Group Header #1 section.

31. Select the menu item INSERT SECTION BELOW to create an additional Group Header #1b area.

32. Move all column headers into the Group Header #1b section.

Figure 3.35 Insert Group

33. Now we need to add some formatting and layout to the report to make it more compelling. Navigate to the DESIGN tab of your report and right-click on the DETAILS section. Select the menu INSERT SECTION BELOW to create a Details b area.

34. Select the menu INSERT • LINE and add a line to the top of the Details b section. Add a second line into the Group header #1b area below your column headers.

35. Select the menu FILE • SUMMARY INFO and put in the title of the report to the field TITLE (see Figure 3.36).

36. Open the list of SPECIAL FIELDS in FIELD EXPLORER and drag and drop the REPORT TITLE field onto your report header.

37. Navigate to the preview of your report. Your report should look similar to Figure 3.37 by now.

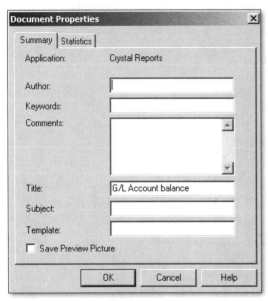

Figure 3.36 Document Properties

G/L Account balance

SAP A.G.

G/L account	Balance Carryforward	Balance Previous Periods	Cum. Balance Previous Periods	Debit Total	Credit Total	Cumulated Debit Balance	Cumulated Credit Balance	Cumulated Balance
1000 Real estate and similar rights	-26,274	0	-26,274	225,216	939,008	0	-740,065	-740,065
1010 Accumltd. Deprctn - Real Estate and Similar Rights	-644,077	0	-644,077	0	268,565	0	-912,642	-912,642
11000 Machinery and equipment	2,000	0	2,000	2,000	0	4,000	0	4,000
11010 Accumulated depreciation- plant and machinery	-493,188	0	-493,188	0	204,074	0	-697,262	-697,262
21010 Accumulated depreciation - fixtures and fittings	-276,235	0	-276,235	110,421	117,380	0	-283,194	-283,194
22010 Accumulated depreciation-LVA (fixtures/fittings)	4	0	4	0	0	4	0	4
72010 Reserves from defined IFB-reversal	-332	0	-332	0	110	0	-442	-442
78000 Balance of special items	-159,806	0	-159,806	8,728	2	0	-151,080	-151,080
78300 Investment receivables received	332	0	332	110	0	442	0	442
100000 Petty cash	-7,000	0	-7,000	0	0	0	-7,000	-7,000
113100 G/L Account	-3,322	0	-3,322	1,300	1,000	0	-3,022	-3,022
113105 Bank 1 (other interim postings)	0	0	0	1,000	1,000	0	0	0
140000 Customers - Domestic Receivables 1	0	0	0	2,100	1,100	1,000	0	1,000

Figure 3.37 Crystal Reports Preview

38. Navigate to the Design tab of your report and open the list of Special Fields in Field Explorer.

39. Add the DATA DATE field to the top left corner of the Page Footer section and add the Page N of M field to the top right corner of the section Page Footer.

Date vs. Data Date

The Data Date special field gives you the information when the data was last refreshed instead of the standard date, which would only provide you the actual date when you opened the report.

40. Based on the query we selected we received eight key figures for our report: BALANCE CARRYFORWARD, BALANCE PREVIOUS PERIODS, CUMULATED BALANCE PREVIOUS PERIODS, DEBIT TOTAL, CREDIT TOTAL, CUMULATED DEBIT BALANCE, CUMULATED CREDIT BALANCE, and CUMULATED BALANCE. To highlight the context of these key figures, we want to show the first three measures as one block, then Debit and Credit Total as one block, then the cumulated balances for credit and debit as one block, and then the overall cumulated balance. The easiest way to do so is to draw boxes around the column headers and the numbers shown in the details areas.

41. Navigate to the DESIGN tab of your report. Follow the INSERT • BOX menu path. You will see a pencil and as soon as you click on it and drag it you will draw a box starting from the top left corner and end at the bottom right corner. Draw a box around the first three key figures that start in the Group Header #1b section and end in the Group Footer #1 section. Because the box goes across the Details section, your box will cover all rows from the key figures shown in your report.

42. Repeat the steps and create three more boxes around the key figures as outlined in the previous steps. After that, your report should look similar to Figure 3.38.

43. Right-click on the first box you created (the easiest way is to click on the box frame) and select FORMAT BOX.

44. In the FILL area, activate the COLOR option and select a color for the box.

45. Repeat this step for your third box and the box around the cumulated balance.

G/L Account balance

SAP A.G.

G/L account	Balance Carryforward	Balance Previous Periods	Cum. Balance Previous Periods	Debit Total	Credit Total	Cumulated Debit Balance	Cumulated Credit Balance	Cumulated Balance
1000 Real estate and similar rights	-26,274	0	-26,274	225,216	939,008	0	-740,065	-740,065
1010 Accumltd. Deprctn - Real Estate and Similar Rights	-644,077	0	-644,077	0	268,565	0	-912,642	-912,642
11000 Machinery and equipment	2,000	0	2,000	2,000	0	4,000	0	4,000
11010 Accumulated depreciation-plant and machinery	-493,188	0	-493,188	0	204,074	0	-697,262	-697,262
21010 Accumulated depreciation - fixtures and fittings	-276,235	0	-276,235	110,421	117,380	0	-283,194	-283,194
22010 Accumulated depreciation-LVA (fixtures/fittings)	4	0	4	0	0	4	0	4
72010 Reserves from defined IFB-reversal	-332	0	-332	0	110	0	-442	-442
78000 Balance of special items	-159,806	0	-159,806	8,728	2	0	-151,080	-151,080
78300 Investment receivables received	332	0	332	110	0	442	0	442
100000 Petty cash	-7,000	0	-7,000	0	0	0	-7,000	-7,000
113100 G/L Account	-3,322	0	-3,322	1,300	1,000	0	-3,022	-3,022
113105 Bank 1 (other interim postings)	0	0	0	1,000	1,000	0	0	0
140000 Customers - Domestic Receivables 1	0	0	0	2,100	1,100	1,000	0	1,000
154000 Input tax	44	0	44	690	0	734	0	734
160000 Accounts payable-domestic	-318	0	-318	0	7,300	0	-7,618	-7,618

Figure 3.38 Crystal Reports Preview

46. Navigate to the DESIGN tab of your report and right-click on the first key figure in the DETAILS section. Select HIGHLIGHTING EXPERT.

47. Click NEW to create a new condition. Add a condition where the color switches to a red font for values less than 0 (see Figure 3.39).

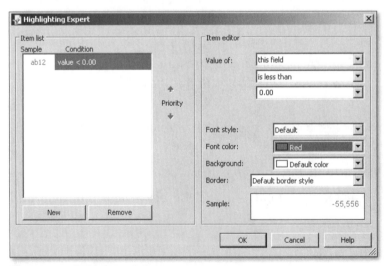

Figure 3.39 Highlighting Expert

48. Repeat this step for all of your key figures in the Details section.

> **Conditional Formatting vs. Highlighting Expert**
>
> It might seem awkward that we have to do the steps for each key figure separately and when you become more familiar with Crystal Reports you might prefer using formulas to influence the behavior of several fields in a single step, but because we are just starting with Crystal Reports we are using the Highlighting Expert to become familiar with the tool.

49. Your report should look similar to Figure 3.40 by now.

G/L Account balance

SAP A.G.

G/L account		Balance Carryforward	Balance Previous Periods	Cum. Balance Previous Periods	Debit Total	Credit Total	Cumulated Debit Balance	Cumulated Credit Balance	Cumulated Balance
1000	Real estate and similar rights	-26,274	0	-26,274	225,216	939,008	0	-740,065	-740,065
1010	Accumltd. Deprctn - Real Estate and Similar Rights	-644,077	0	-644,077	0	268,565	0	-912,642	-912,642
11000	Machinery and equipment	2,000	0	2,000	2,000	0	4,000	0	4,000
11010	Accumulated depreciation- plant and machinery	-493,188	0	-493,188	0	204,074	0	-697,262	-697,262
21010	Accumulated depreciation - fixtures and fittings	-276,235	0	-276,235	110,421	117,380	0	-283,194	-283,194
22010	Accumulated depreciation-LVA (fixtures/fittings)	4	0	4	0	0	4	0	4
72010	Reserves from defined IFB-reversal	-332	0	-332	0	110	0	-442	-442
78000	Balance of special items	-159,806	0	-159,806	8,728	2	0	-151,080	-151,080
78300	Investment receivables received	332	0	332	110	0	442	0	442
100000	Petty cash	-7,000	0	-7,000	0	0	0	-7,000	-7,000
113100	G/L Account	-3,322	0	-3,322	1,300	1,000	0	-3,022	-3,022
113105	Bank 1 (other interim postings)	0	0	0	1,000	1,000	0	0	0
140000	Customers - Domestic Receivables 1	0	0	0	2,100	1,100	1,000	0	1,000
154000	Input tax	44	0	44	690	0	734	0	734
160000	Accounts payable-domestic	-318	0	-318	0	7,300	0	-7,618	-7,618

Figure 3.40 Crystal Reports Preview

The next part is to include an area to show the values for the parameters.

50. Navigate to the Design tab of your report and right-click on the Report Header section. Select Insert Section.

51. The information we need to provide has two parts: the selection option and the selected value.

52. Follow the Insert • Text Objects menu path, and place the text object into the Report Header b section, and enter the text `Currency`.

53. Select the parameter for the Currency from the area parameter fields in the Field Explorer and place it next to the text box.

54. Repeat the previous step for all of the parameters you want to show on the report.

55. In cases where the parameter allows you to enter more than a single value you need to create a formula to retrieve the selected values. The values are basically stored in an array that you need to retrieve them from.

56. A formula for retrieving the values would look like this:

```
StringVar variable_value:="";
Local NumberVar i;
FOR i := 1 To UBOUND(<VARIABLE NAME>)
DO
if i=1 then
(
   IF MINIMUM(<VARIABLE NAME> [i]) = MAXIMUM<VARIABLE NAME> [i])
   THEN variable_value :=MINIMUM(<VARIABLE NAME> [i])
   ELSE variable_value :=MINIMUM(<VARIABLE NAME> [i]) + "-" +
MAXIMUM(<VARIABLE NAME> [i]);
)
else
(
   IF MINIMUM(<VARIABLE NAME> [i]) = MAXIMUM(<VARIABLE NAME> [i])
   THEN variable_value:= variable_value + "; " + MINIMUM(<VARIABLE
NAME> [i])
   ELSE variable_value:= variable_value + "; " + MINIMUM(<VARIABLE
NAME> [i]) + "-" + MAXIMUM(<VARIABLE NAME> [i]);
);
variable_value
```

Replace the place holder <VARIABLE NAME> with the parameter from your Crystal Reports Field Explorer. The formula is going from one to the size of the array (ubound) and verifies if the minimum and maximum are identical (then it is a single value) and, depending on the values, then creates a string that can be displayed on the report. The reason for adding an extra check for the first entry is to avoid a situation where you see a ";" added to the first value. The formula is only needed for parameters that let you select more than just a single value.

57. With such a formula per parameter you should be able to display all selections made by the consumer.

Display Parameter Values

One of the major limitations in Crystal Reports is the capability to display selected values from a parameter on the report. As of Service Pack 2 in the XI 3.1 Release (and Crystal Reports 2008), you cannot show the parameter description at all and to display the key values you might have to leverage a formula as described earlier.

58. Your report should look similar to Figure 3.41.

G/L Account balance

Selection criteria

Currency:	EUR
Currency Type	10
Company Code:	1000

SAP A.G.

G/L account	Balance Carryforward	Balance Previous Periods	Cum. Balance Previous Periods	Debit Total	Credit Total	Cumulated Debit Balance	Cumulated Credit Balance	Cumulated Balance
1000 Real estate and similar rights	-26,274	0	-26,274	225,216	939,008	0	-740,065	-740,065
1010 Accum ltd. Deprotn - Real Estate and Similar Rights	-644,077	0	-644,077	0	268,565	0	-912,642	-912,642
11000 Machinery and equipment	2,000	0	2,000	2,000	0	4,000	0	4,000
11010 Accumulated depreciation-plant and machinery	-493,188	0	-493,188	0	204,074	0	-697,262	-697,262
21010 Accumulated depreciation - fixtures and fittings	-276,235	0	-276,235	110,421	117,380	0	-283,194	-283,194
22010 Accumulated depreciation-LVA (fixtures/fittings)	4	0	4	0	0	4	0	4
72010 Reserves from defined IFB-reversal	-332	0	-332	0	110	0	-442	-442
78000 Balance of special items	-159,806	0	-159,806	8,728	2	0	-151,080	-151,080
78300 Investment receivables received	332	0	332	110	0	442	0	442
100000 Petty cash	-7,000	0	-7,000	0	0	0	-7,000	-7,000
113100 G/L Account	-3,322	0	-3,322	1,300	1,000	0	-3,022	-3,022
113105 Bank 1 (other interim postings)	0	0	0	1,000	1,000	0	0	0
140000 Customers - Domestic Receivables 1	0	0	0	2,100	1,100	1,000	0	1,000

Figure 3.41 Crystal Reports Preview

We finished the design of the report and now we can save it to our SAP Business-Objects Enterprise environment and share it with our consumers.

The second financial report we are going to create is a balance sheet based on a hierarchy that is being defined in SAP NetWeaver BW (see Figure 3.42).

Balance Sheet			Fiscal Year: 2008	Period: 0 FISCP		Ledger: 0AC LE	Currency:		Page 1 of 1
Last Data Update : 7/24/2009									Printed by: on 7/24/2009

Selection Criteria

Company Code: [0COMP_CODE].[P001]
Profit Center:

Assets	Current Year	Previous Year	Liabilities & Shareholders' Equity	Current Year	Previous Year
Fixed Assets	0.00	0.00	Capital and reserves	0.00	22,680.00
Intangible Assets	0.00	0.00	Subscribed Capital	0.00	0.00
Tangible Assets	0.00	0.00	Capital Reserves	0.00	0.00
Financial Assets	0.00	0.00	Retained Earnings	0.00	0.00
Current Assets	0.00	-11,080.00	Retained Earnings	0.00	22,680.00
Stocks	0.00	1,320.00	Provisions	0.00	0.00
Receivable and other assets	0.00	1,600.00	Payables	0.00	-11,600.00
Securities	0.00	0.00	Other Liability Items	0.00	0.00
Cash	0.00	-14,000.00	Total Liabilities	0.00	11,080.00
Other Asset Items	0.00	0.00			
Total Assets	0.00	-11,080.00			

Figure 3.42 Balance Sheet with Crystal Reports

We will use a query from Business Content so that you can follow along with the steps. The query we are using is the BW query 0FIGL_M30_Q0002 for the cube 0FIGL_M30. The BW query contains the key figures Actual, Plan, and Difference along a Financial Statement hierarchy (see Figure 3.43).

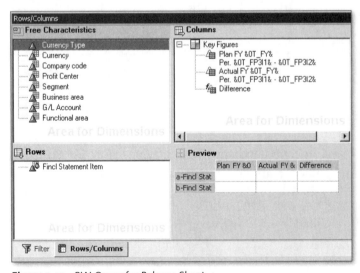

Figure 3.43 BW Query for Balance Sheet

1. Follow the SAP • CREATE NEW REPORT FROM QUERY menu path.

2. Enter your credentials to log on to the SAP system.

3. Select the BW query from the list of available queries.

4. First, we need to create the hierarchical and column structure in the report. Follow the INSERT • GROUP menu path.

5. Select FINANCIAL STATEMENT ITEM NODE ID as the field to group on.

6. Select the OPTIONS tab and activate the CUSTOMIZE GROUP NAME FIELD option.

7. Select the description field of the Financial Statement Item to group on the ID but show the description.

8. Click OK.

9. Follow the REPORT • HIERARCHICAL GROUPING OPTIONS menu path.

10. Activate the SORT DATA HIERARCHICALLY option.

11. Select the FINANCIAL STATEMENT ITEM PARENT NODE ID as the PARENT ID FIELD (see Figure 3.44).

12. Do not configure a value for the GROUP INDENT option. We will configure the indent differently later on because the GROUP INDENT option would lead to a situation where all fields (group names and key figures) are being indented and we only need to indent the group name and keep the key figures aligned.

13. Click OK.

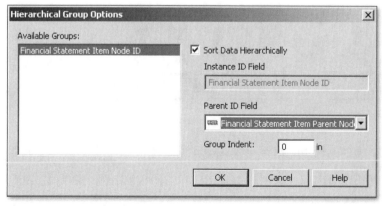

Figure 3.44 Hierarchical Group Options

14. Follow the FILE • PAGE SETUP menu path and configure your report to a landscape orientation.

15. Follow the REPORT • SECTION EXPERT menu path.

16. Select the GROUP FOOTER #1 section and check SUPPRESS (NO DRILLDOWN).

17. Select the DETAILS section and check SUPPRESS (NO DRILLDOWN).

18. Select the DETAILS section and check FORMAT WITH MULTIPLE COLUMNS.

19. Navigate to the LAYOUT tab that appears after you activate the multiple columns option.

20. Set the WIDTH of the columns to 5 inches (this value can change depending on your paper size) and activate the FORMAT GROUPS WITH MULTIPLE COLUMNS option (see Figure 3.45).

21. Select the DOWN THEN ACROSS for the PRINTING DIRECTION option.

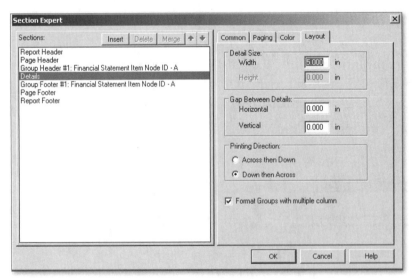

Figure 3.45 Section Expert

22. When you navigate to the preview of your report it should look similar to Figure 3.46.

```
A S S E T S                                    Investment subsidies received
Fixed assets                                   Provisions
Tangible assets                                Other provisions
Acquisition value                              Freight Clearing Account (MM)
Real estate and similar rights                 Payables
Accumulated depreciation                       Amounts owed to credit institu
Accum. depn - real estate and similar rights   Due within one year
Plant and machinery                            D B
Acquisition value                              Deutsche Bank (domestic)
Machinery and equipment                        Deutsche Bank - checks payable
Accumulated depreciation                       Deutsche Bank - other postings
Accumulated depreciation - machinery and equ   Accounts payable
Other fixtures and fitings,                    Due within one year
Accumulated depreciation                       Trade Payables - domestic
Accumulated depreciation - fixtures and fitting:
Depreciation - LVA office equipment
Current assets
Stocks
Work in process
Unfinished products
Receivables and other assets
Accounts receivable
Due within one year
Trade Receivables - domestic
Other assets
Due within one year
Taxes on sales/purchases
Input tax (See account assignment text)
Output tax
Checks, cash on hand, deposit
Other
Petty cash
L I A B I L I T I E S
Capital and reserves
Balance sheet profit or loss
Calculated Profit
Profit reserves
```

Figure 3.46 Crystal Reports preview

We managed to get the hierarchical data organized into two columns but we need to ensure that LIABILITIES is starting in the second column of our balance sheet.

23. Follow the REPORT • SECTION EXPERT menu path.

24. Select the GROUP HEADER #1 section from the report. Click INSERT in the SECTION EXPERT.

25. In the newly created second GROUP HEADER #1B section, use the blue arrows to move GROUP HEADER #1B up so that it becomes GROUP HEADER #1A.

26. Now select the GROUP HEADER#1A section in SECTION EXPERT (see Figure 3.47).

27. Activate the PRINT AT BOTTOM OF PAGE option.

28. Click on the ⊠ symbol next to the SUPPRESS (NO DRILL DOWN) option.

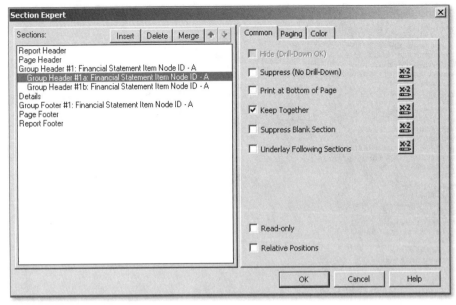

Figure 3.47 Section Expert

29. Now we need to enter a formula that ensures that GROUP HEADER #1A is suppressed unless the value is the top-level node for the liabilities part of our balance sheet.

30. Double-click on the key value of the Financial Statement item in the list of Report Fields so that the field is shown in your formula.

31. Now you need to add the comparison and the key value to the liabilities node of your hierarchy. In this case the key value for the liabilities node is INT 0LIABILITS.

> **How to Retrieve the Key Value**
>
> In this case, the easiest step is to include the key value for the required hierarchy node onto the group header of the report so that the value will be shown. The alternative would be to go to the Administrator Workbench in SAP NetWeaver BW and display the hierarchies for the InfoObjects.

32. The formula in the example looks like the following:

```
not({0FIGL_M30_0FIGL_M30_Q0002_IH.[0GLACCEXT
INT]-[20GLACCEXT]}="INT 0LIABILITS")
```

By using such logic we suppress the GROUP FOOTER #1A section except when the node for the liabilities has been shown in the report. In that case the GROUP HEADER #1A section is being printed at the bottom of the page and GROUP HEADER #1B starts in the second column.

33. Navigate back to the DESIGN tab of your report. You will see that you report is now in the design view formatted with two columns.

34. Include the key figure into the Details section by dragging and dropping it from the Field Explorer and move the field to the far right side of your first column.

35. Right-click the key figure in the Details section and follow the INSERT • SUMMARY menu path. Select SUMMARY LOCATION as your Group#1 and do *not* select the SUMMARIZE ACROSS HIERARCHY option (see Figure 3.48).

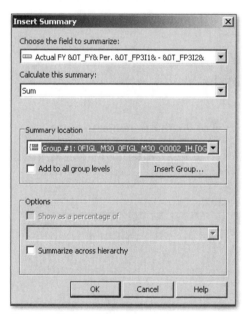

Figure 3.48   Insert Summary

36. Move the newly created summary field into the group header.

37. You report should look similar to Figure 3.49.

ASSETS		LIABILITIES	
A S S E T S	-2,633,284	L I A B I L I T I E S	2,633,284
Fixed assets	-2,628,175	Capital and reserves	2,795,895
Tangible assets	-2,628,175	Balance sheet profit or loss	2,796,337
Acquisition value	-739,065	Calculated Profit	2,796,337
Real estate and similar rights	-739,065	Profit reserves	-442
Accumulated depreciation	-912,642	Legal reserve	-442
Accum. depn - real estate and similar rights	-912,642	Reserves from defined IFB -reversal (s.acc.ass.)	-442
Plant and machinery	-693,262	Special items with reserves	-150,638
Acquisition value	4,000	Tax-related special depreciati	-151,080
Machinery and equipment	4,000	Balance of special items	-151,080
Accumulated depreciation	-697,262	Special items with reserves	442
Accumulated depreciation - machinery and equ	-697,262	Investment subsidies received	442
Other fixtures and fittings,	-283,206	Provisions	0
Accumulated depreciation	-283,206	Other provisions	0
Accumulated depreciation - fixtures and fitting:	-283,210	Freight Clearing Account (MM)	0
Depreciation - LVA office equipment	4	Payables	-11,973
Current assets	-5,109	Amounts owed to credit institu	-3,022
Stocks	114	Due within one year	-3,022
Work in process	114	DB	-3,022
Unfinished products	114	Deutsche Bank (domestic)	-3,799
Receivables and other assets	1,778	Deutsche Bank - checks payable	777
Accounts receivable	1,000	Deutsche Bank - other postings	0
Due within one year	1,000	Accounts payable	-8,951
Trade Receivables - domestic	1,000	Due within one year	-8,951
Other assets	778	Trade Payables - domestic	-8,951
Due within one year	778		
Taxes on sales/purchases	778		
Input tax (See account assignment text)	764		

Figure 3.49 Crystal Reports Preview

We have three things left to do:

► Create an indention for the hierarchy levels

► Highlight the totals for the different levels

► Provide a way to select the maximum level of depth of the hierarchy

38. Right-click on the description field in the group header and select SIZE AND POSITION.

39. Click on the ![X-2] symbol next to the X value.

40. Enter the following formula:

```
HierarchyLevel (
    GroupingLevel (
        {0FIGL_M30_0FIGL_M30_Q0002_IH.[0GLACCEXT
INT]-NodeId}
        )
)
* 150
```

The field that you are using ({OFIGL_M30_OFIGL_M30_Q0002_IH.[OGLACCEXT INT]-NodeId} in the given example) is the Node ID field from your hierarchy. By using this formula you retrieve the hierarchy level and move each field 150 pixels per level but the key figure stays aligned.

41. Follow the VIEW • FIELD EXPLORER menu path.

42. Right-click on FORMULA FIELDS in the Field Explorer and select NEW.

43. Enter fn_HierarchyLevel for the formula name.

44. Enter the following formula:

```
HierarchyLevel (
    GroupingLevel (
        {OFIGL_M30_OFIGL_M30_Q0002_IH.[OGLACCEXT
INT]-NodeId}
        )
)
```

The field that you are using ({OFIGL_M30_OFIGL_M30_Q0002_IH.[OGLACCEXT INT]-NodeId} in the given example) is the Node ID field from your hierarchy. This formula will return the actual hierarchy level and we can use the hierarchy level to format the totals in our balance sheet.

45. Follow the REPORT • SECTION EXPERT menu path.

46. Select GROUP HEADER #1B.

47. Select the COLOR tab.

48. Click on the [x-2] icon next to the color selection.

49. Enter the following formula:

```
select {@fn_HierarchyLevel}
case 2: crYellow
case 3: crGray
default: crNoColor
```

The formula evaluates the hierarchy level being returned by the formula fn_HierarchyLevel and assigns background colors for different hierarchy levels (see Figure 3.50).

Hierarchy Level Information

The information regarding the hierarchy level is very useful for conditional reporting in Crystal Reports. You can use the information to not only use different colors as background but also to influence font size, font color, number formatting, and other appearances in the report.

Top Hierarchy Level

Depending on how the actual hierarchy has been created, the asset and liabilities top-level nodes might be on hierarchy level two because there is an additional top-level node.

ASSETS		LIABILITIES	
ASSETS	-2,633,284	LIABILITIES	2,633,284
Fixed assets	-2,628,175	Capital and reserves	2,795,895
Tangible assets	-2,628,175	Balance sheet profit or loss	2,796,337
Acquisition value	-739,065	Calculated Profit	2,796,337
Real estate and similar rights	-739,065	Profit reserves	-442
Accumulated depreciation	-912,642	Legal reserve	-442
Accum. depn - real estate and similar rights	-912,642	Reserves from defined IFB-reversal (s.acc.ass.)	-442
Plant and machinery	-693,262	Special items with reserves	-150,638
Acquisition value	4,000	Tax-related special depreciati	-151,080
Machinery and equipment	4,000	Balance of special items	-151,080
Accumulated depreciation	-697,262	Special items with reserves	442
Accumulated depreciation - machinery and equ	-697,262	Investment subsidies received	442
Other fixtures and fitings,	-283,206	Provisions	0
Accumulated depreciation	-283,206	Other provisions	0
Accumulated depreciation - fixtures and fitting:	-283,210	Freight Clearing Account (MM)	0
Depreciation - LVA office equipment	4	Payables	-11,973
Current assets	-5,109	Amounts owed to credit institu	-3,022
Stocks	114	Due within one year	-3,022
Work in process	114	DB	-3,022
Unfinished products	114	Deutsche Bank (domestic)	-3,799
Receivables and other assets	1,778	Deutsche Bank - checks payable	777
Accounts receivable	1,000	Deutsche Bank - other postings	0
Due within one year	1,000	Accounts payable	-8,951
Trade Receivables - domestic	1,000	Due within one year	-8,951
Other assets	778	Trade Payables - domestic	-8,951
Due within one year	778		
Taxes on sales/purchases	778		
Input tax (See account assignment text)	764		
Output tax	14		
Checks, cash on hand, deposit	-7,000		
Other	-7,000		
Petty cash	-7,000		

Figure 3.50 Crystal Reports Preview

50. Follow the VIEW • FIELD EXPLORER menu path.

51. Right-click on PARAMETER FIELDS in the Field Explorer and select NEW.

52. Enter Number of Hierarchy Levels for the parameter name.

53. Select NUMBER as Type.

54. Follow the REPORT • SECTION EXPERT menu path.

55. Select Group Header #1B.

56. Click on the [x-2] icon next to the Suppress (No Drill-Down) option.

57. Enter the following formula:

```
{@fn_HierarchyLevel}>{?Number of Hierarchy levels}
```

That way, the user can decide how many levels of the hierarchy should be shown in the report.

Your final report should look similar to Figure 3.51

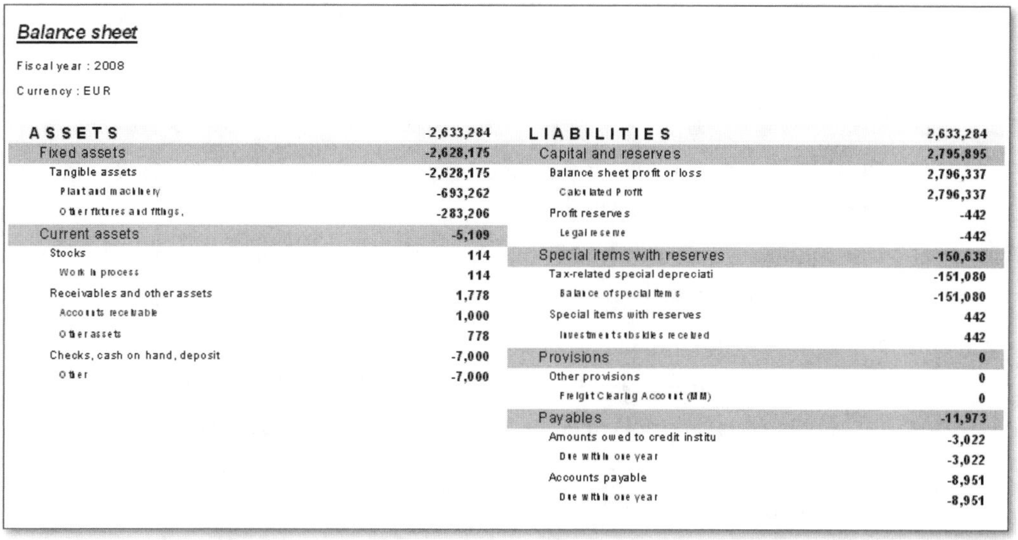

Figure 3.51 Crystal Reports Balance Sheet

Hierarchical Reports Based on Master Data

As of BusinessObjects XI 3.1 Service Pack 2, the connectivity of SAP NetWeaver BW for Crystal Reports explicitly asks for nonempty records from the BW query. This leads to situations where you will only retrieve records (including hierarchy nodes) that actually have at least one value in the InfoProvider or, to put it another way, you cannot show the complete hierarchy based on the master data definition unless each item has a record in the InfoProvider.

This behavior might change in future versions of data connectivity for Crystal Reports.

In the next section, we will look at the requirements of HR and how we can leverage Crystal Reports to fulfill them.

3.6 Customer Requirements — HR Reporting with Crystal Reports

Based on the previous sections, we identified Crystal Reports as a good fit for the reporting requirements for the HR department. This does not mean that other tools would not be able to fulfill most of the requirements as well but Crystal Reports is a very good fit for the requirements articulated here.

The requirements for the HR department are:

- The content needs to leverage data from several different sources (SAP and non-SAP) and present it in a single report.
- The content needs to present highly textual information and present it in a layout-focused format.
- Some of the content (such as employee appraisals or performance reviews) will be used as official documents and therefore need to follow strict layout rules.
- All of the leveraged tools need to leverage the security established by the underlying system.
- The leveraged tools for the content need to leverage specific features, such as date-specific aggregation, to show the correct numbers for items like headcount statistics or a salary at a given date for an employee. Resolving these time-dependent key figures is very important for the content.

Next, we'll use Crystal Reports to fulfill these requirements. We will create a report showing the employee master data information, which is highly textual information. In addition, we will combine the employee data with the qualifications and appraisals for each employee in a single report (see Figure 3.52).

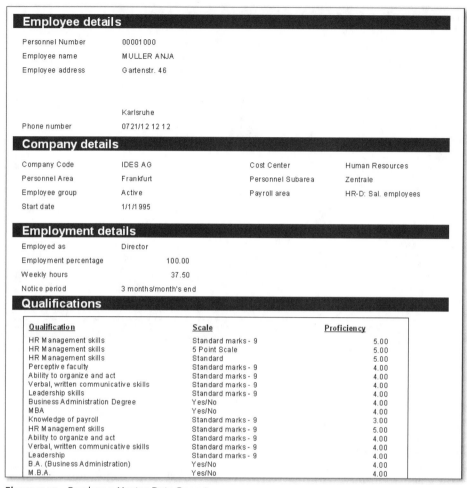

Figure 3.52 Employee Master Data Report

1. Start Crystal Reports Designer.

2. Follow the FILE • REPORT • BLANK REPORT menu path.

3. Crystal Reports generates an empty report and the DATABASE EXPERT will establish data connectivity (see Figure 3.53).

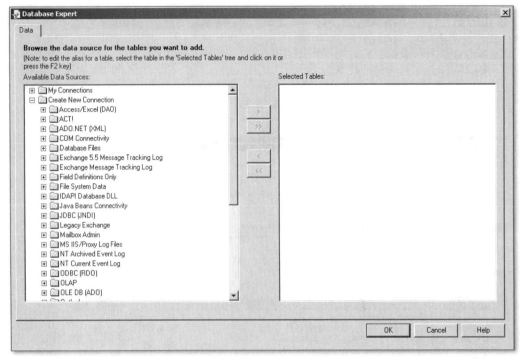

Figure 3.53   Database Expert

4. In CREATE NEW CONNECTION, scroll down to SAP INFO SETS.

5. Double-click on SAP INFO SETS.

6. Double-click on MAKE NEW CONNECTION.

7. A dialog box showing the list of available SAP systems comes up. The list of SAP systems is based on the entries in your SAP logon pad, which is part of the SAP frontend.

8. Select your SAP system and click NEXT.

9. Enter the details for client, username, and password and click NEXT.

Preferred Viewing Locale

When you authenticate against an SAP system, you are not asked for a logon language. Crystal Reports has a so-called preferred viewing locale, which is used as the logon language for the SAP system with SAP ERP. For the SAP NetWeaver BW connectivity, you can use the SAP-specific toolbar and menu, which then provides the typical SAP logon language.

Each user also has a preferred viewing locale as part of the user preferences in InfoView, which also influences the logon language for the SAP connectivity.

10. Click FINISH on the next screen.

11. The connectivity provides you with the option of selecting INFOSET or SAP QUERY (sometimes referred to as InfoSet query or ABAP query) from your SAP ERP system (see Figure 3.54).

Figure 3.54 SAP Info Sets Connectivity

12. Double-click I [CLASSIC INFOSET].

13. Next, select an InfoSet to leverage from the GLOBAL or LOCAL area.

14. In our example, double-click G [GLOBAL, CLIENT INDEPENDENT OBJECTS].

15. The list of InfoSets is shown to you. In our case, we are interested in InfoSet / SAPQUERY/HR_ADM, which is a standard delivered InfoSet.

Infoset Groups and User Assignment

If you do not see the InfoSet listed for your user, it might be because your SAP credentials are not assigned to the user group for the InfoSet (not to be confused with SAP roles). You can make this assignment with Transaction SQ03.

16. Double-click the /SAPQUERY/HR_ADM InfoSet.

17. You will be presented with a set of parameters from the InfoSet. You will see the Set to Null option for those parameters that are optional and you can leave them empty.

18. Click OK.

19. The InfoSet should now be listed under Selected Tables (see Figure 3.55).

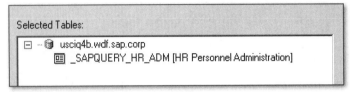

Figure 3.55 Selected Tables

20. Click OK.

21. Follow the View • Field Explorer menu path to look at the retrieved metadata.

22. Remember, we wanted to create a report showing the employee master data per employee in combination with the appraisals and qualifications. To show the actual data per employee we need to group our report based on employee ID and create several sections in our report with different sets of information.

23. Follow the View • Field Explorer menu path.

24. Right-click on Formula Fields in Field Explorer and select New.

25. Enter `fn_Personel Number` for the new formula.

26. Enter the following formula:

    `ToNumber({_SAPQUERY_HR_ADM.P0000-PERNR}).`

27. By using the formula we are converting the field for the personal number from InfoType 0000 (Actions) to a numeric field.

28. Click on the Save and Close icon.

29. Follow the Insert • Group menu path.

30. Select the newly created formula `fn_Personel Number` as the field to group on and click OK.

31. You have now added a Group Header and Group Footer to your report.

    Because we want to show several sets of information per employee (Employee details, Company details, Employment details, and Qualifications) we need to create several areas in our new group.

32. Follow the REPORT • SECTION EXPERT menu path.

33. Select GROUP HEADER #1 (see Figure 3.56).

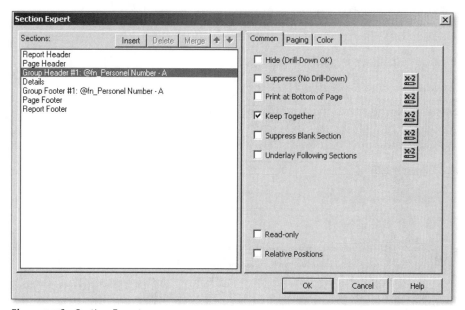

Figure 3.56 Section Expert

34. For each information area we need two sections (one for a heading and one for the information). So, in our example, we will need four areas with two sections each.

35. Select the INSERT button and create seven additional sections for GROUP HEADER #1.

36. Click OK.

37. Navigate to the DESIGN tab of your report.

38. Remove the GROUP #1 NAME field from GROUP HEADER #1A.

39. Follow the INSERT • TEXT OBJECT menu path.

40. Your mouse cursor turns into a "+" symbol which represents the top left of your text box. Click on GROUP HEADER #1A and create a new text object.

41. Enter `Employee Details` into the text box.

42. Copy and paste the text box from GROUP HEADER #1A to every second group header section (#1c, #1e, and #1g).

43. Change the text in the text objects to show the following information:

44. GROUP HEADER #1A: EMPLOYEE DETAILS

45. GROUP HEADER #1C: COMPANY DETAILS

46. GROUP HEADER #1E: EMPLOYMENT DETAILS

47. GROUP HEADER #1G: QUALIFICATIONS

48. The design of your report should look similar to Figure 3.57.

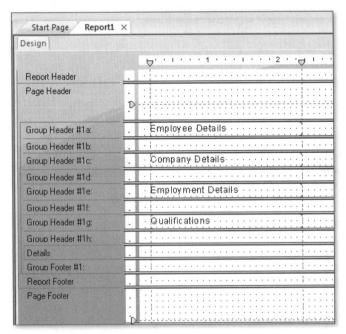

Figure 3.57 Design View

49. Follow the REPORT • SECTION EXPERT menu path.

50. Select GROUP HEADER #1A and select the COLOR tab.

51. Activate the BACKGROUND COLOR option and select a color from the list.

52. Repeat the steps for GROUP HEADER #1C, #1E, and #1G.

53. Click OK.

54. Select all of the text objects we added to the report.

55. Right-click on one of the text objects and select FORMAT OBJECTS.

56. Select the FONT tab (see Figure 3.58).

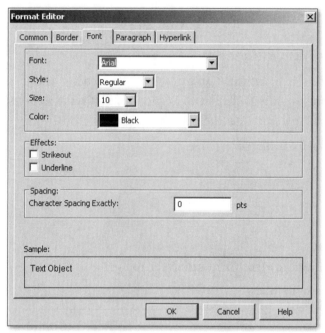

Figure 3.58 Format Editor

57. Set the SIZE to 16, the COLOR to white, and the STYLE to bold.

58. Click OK.

59. Resize the sections by selecting the dividing line between them and moving it so that the fields fit into the sections. You also need to resize the fields to align them with the change in font size.

60. For resizing the fields, you can resize one field and then select all of the text objects and use menu path FORMAT • MAKE SAME SIZE • BOTH to align all of the fields in height and width.

Make Same Size

The Make Same Size option uses the menu activated/selected field as a reference. You can identify the selected field by the frame with the small dots around the frame for resizing.

---

61. Resize GROUP HEADER #1B to allow more space for the fields that we will add to it. You can make the section very large for now because you can always use the Fit Section menu to reduce its size.

62. Next, we'll add several sets of information to each of the sections, and it is recommended that you use the guidelines in Section 3.4.1, "Crystal Reports Designer Environment," to ensure that the fields are aligned.

63. Add text objects for the following text items:
    ▸ Personnel number
    ▸ Employee name
    ▸ Employee address
    ▸ Phone number

64. Add the following fields from FIELD EXPLORER to the report:

    P0000-PERNR (Personnel number)

    P0001-SNAME (Employees name)

    P0006-STRAS (House number and street)

    P0006-ADR03 (Street 2)

    P0006-ADR04 (Street 3)

    P0006-ORT01 (Location)

    P0006-TELNR (Telephone number)

    Because we are using an InfoSet with different InfoTypes as a datasource, the list of fields is broken down by InfoType and the prefix in front of the actual field represents the InfoType.

As you can see in Figure 3.59, the guidelines are used to align the fields on the horizontal and vertical axis.

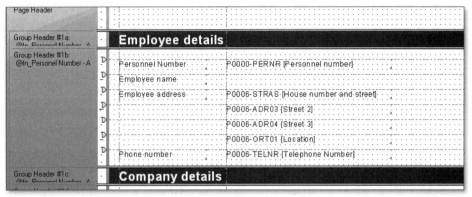

Figure 3.59 Design View

65. Insert the text objects and fields in Table 3.5 into the Company details section:

Text Object	InfoSet Field
Company code	SYHR_T_P0001_BUKRS
Personnel Areas	SYHR_T_P0001_WERKS
Personnel Subarea	SYHR_T_P0001_BTRTL
Employee group	SYHR_T_P0001_PERSG
Payroll area	SYHR_T_P0001_ABKRS
Start date	SYHR_A_P0000_AF_HIREDATE
Cost center	SYHR_T_P0001-KOSTL

Table 3.5 Company Details

InfoSet and Description Fields

The description of a field, for example, the description field for the personnel area SYHR_T_P0001_WERKS, is not organized in the groups like the other objects. In the given example, you will find the P0001_WERKS field in the P0001 group and the SYHR_T_P0001_WERKS description field is not listed in a group. All of the description fields in an InfoSet connectivity case are listed without a specific group.

Sorting fields in the Field Explorer

In the FILE • OPTIONS menu path in the DATABASE tab, you can activate an alphabetical sorting of all of the fields shown in FIELD EXPLORER.

---

66. Insert the text objects and fields in Table 3.6 into the Employment details section.

Text Object	InfoSet Field
Employed as	SYHR_T_P0001_STELL
Employment percentage	P0007-EMPCT
Weekly hours	P0007-WOSTD
Notice period	SYHR_T_P0016_KDGF2

Table 3.6 Employment Details

67. By now, the report design should look similar to Figure 3.60.

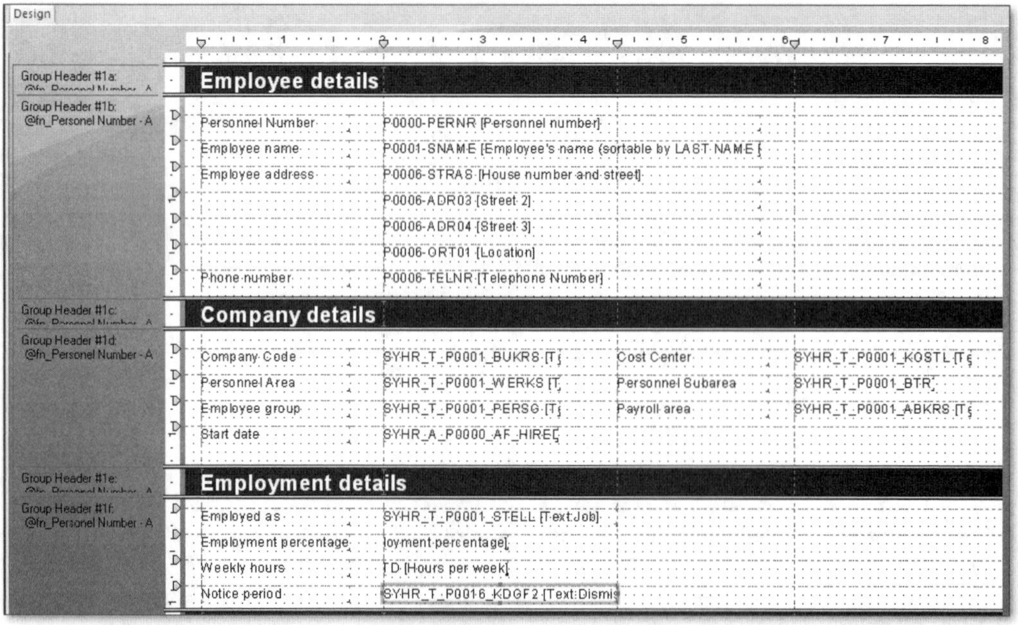

Figure 3.60 Crystal Reports Design View

For the qualifications part, let's insert a subreport linking to a BW query. We created a BW query on top of InfoProvider 0PAPD_C01 for Qualifications (see Figure 3.61).

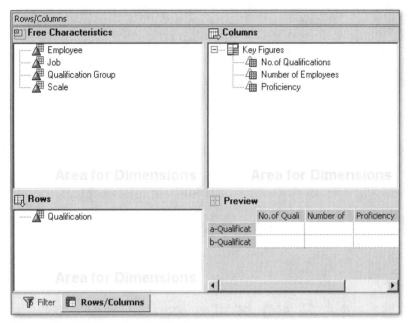

Figure 3.61 BW Query for Qualifications

The BW query contains the EMPLOYEE, QUALIFICATION, PROFICIENCY Q/R, SCALE, and QUALIFICATIONS GROUP characteristics and the NUMBER OF EMPLOYEES key figure.

Allow External Access

When using a subreport in Crystal Reports Designer you can't leverage the SAP-specific menu items. Therefore, you need to make sure the BW query is configured to allow external access. This property can be set in the BW Query designer as part of the properties on the query level.

---

68. Follow the INSERT • SUBREPORT menu path.

69. Select the CREATE A SUBREPORT WITH THE REPORT WIZARD option and enter Qualifications as the report name (see Figure 3.62).

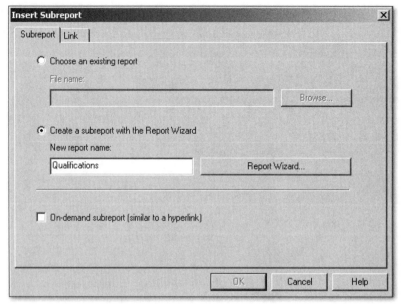

Figure 3.62 Insert Subreport

70. Click REPORT WIZARD.

71. You will be shown the DATABASE EXPERT and you can now select your data source. In our example, we will use the SAP BW MDX query connection.

72. Double-click the SAP BW MDX QUERY entry.

73. Select the SAP NetWeaver BW system from the list of available systems.

74. Click NEXT.

75. Provide the SAP credentials to authenticate against the system.

76. Click NEXT.

77. Click FINISH.

78. Double-click QC (QUERIES).

79. A list with BW queries will be shown in the syntax: [Technical name of the InfoProvider]/[Technical name of the BW query].

80. Double-click your BW query.

81. Click FINISH in the Database Expert.

82. Click OK.

83. You will now have the option to place a box onto your main report. This box represents the space that will be available for the subreport. Place the box into our GROUP HEADER #1H section.

84. Double-click on the box and you will be brought to a new tab representing the actual design of your subreport.

85. Include the following fields into the Details section of your newly created subreport:

   ► Qualification Name

   ► Scale Name

   ► Proficiency

86. Follow the REPORT • SECTION EXPERT menu path.

87. Select REPORT HEADER A and the SUPPRESS (NO DRILL-DOWN) option.

88. Select REPORT FOOTER and the SUPPRESS (NO DRILLDOWN) option.

89. Navigate to the DESIGN tab of your main report.

90. Right-click on the subreport box in your main report and select FORMAT SUB-REPORT (see Figure 3.63).

91. Ensure the option CAN GROW is activated. By using this option you allow the subreport to grow in regards to the height as part of your main report in case the amount of data of the subreport requires more space

92. We need to ensure that the Employee number is being linked from the main report to the subreport, so that the employee number is acting as a filter for the subreport, but in addition we have the issue that the InfoSet is delivering a value with leading zeros and the BW query is not delivering leading zeros in the value.

93. Therefore we will create a formula field in the main report and in the subreport which ensures that we are linking identical values.

94. In your main report select the menu VIEW • FIELD EXPLORER.

95. Right-click on FORMULA FIELDS and select NEW.

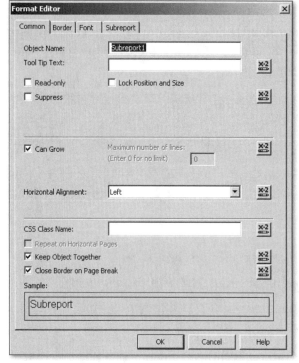

Figure 3.63 Format Editor

96. Enter `fn_EmployeeNumber` as the name of the new formula.

97. Enter the following formula:

    `ToNumber({_SAPQUERY_HR_ADM.P0000-PERNR})`

    Here, `{_SAPQUERY_HR_ADM.P0000-PERNR}` is the Personnel Number field from the InfoSet.

98. Click SAVE AND CLOSE.

99. Navigate to the design of your subreport.

100. Follow the VIEW • FIELD EXPLORER menu path.

101. Right-click on FORMULA FIELDS and select NEW.

102. Enter `fn_BW_EmployeeNumber` as the name of the new formula.

103. Enter the following formula:

    `Tonumber({0PAPD_C01_Z_PAPD_C01_Q001.[0EMPLOYEE]-[20EMPLOYEE]})`

Here, `{OPAPD_CO1_Z_PAPD_CO1_Q001.[OEMPLOYEE]-[20EMPLOYEE]}` is the Employee Key field from the BW query.

104. Click SAVE AND CLOSE.

105. Navigate to the DESIGN tab of your main report.

106. Right-click on the subreport box in your main report and select CHANGE SUB-REPORT LINKS (see Figure 3.64).

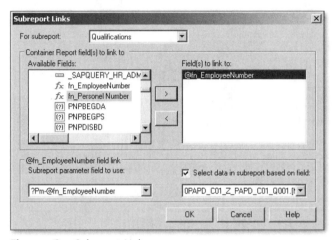

Figure 3.64 Subreport Links

107. Select the formula field `fn_EmployeeNumber` from AVAILABLE FIELDS and move it to FIELD(S) TO LINK TO (see Figure 3.64).

108. In the list of fields below the SELECT DATA IN SUBREPORT BASED ON FIELD option select the formula field `fn_BW_EmployeeNumber` (see Figure 3.65).

109. Click OK.

110. Before we refresh the report we need to suppress some sections and create a page break per employee.

111. Follow the REPORT • SECTION EXPERT menu path.

112. Select the DETAILS section and activate the SUPPRESS (NO DRILL DOWN) option.

113. Select REPORT HEADER, REPORT FOOTER, and GROUP FOOTER #1 and select the SUPPRESS (NO DRILL DOWN) option.

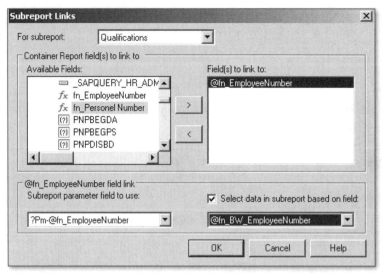

Figure 3.65 Subreport Links

114. Select GROUP FOOTER #1.

115. Navigate to the PAGING tab.

116. Activate the NEW PAGE AFTER option (see Figure 3.66).

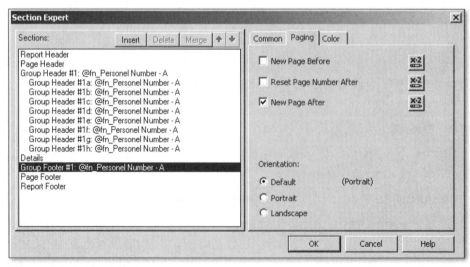

Figure 3.66 Section Expert

117. Click OK.

118. Now follow the VIEW • PRINT PREVIEW menu path to see a preview of your report (see Figure 3.67).

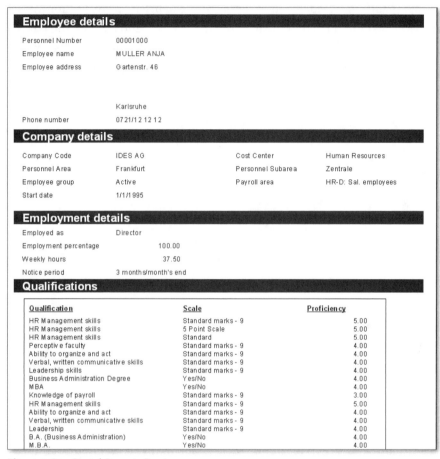

Figure 3.67 Crystal Reports Preview

The subreport will be executed for each employee in your main report and it will show the qualifications of each employee as part of the master data sheet.

SSO

When using two SAP systems you must have the SAP authentication configured for both systems on your BusinessObjects Enterprise system for your end users.

3.7   Summary

In this chapter, you not only learned about the basic functionality of Crystal Reports as a design environment for Enterprise Reporting, we also reviewed the requirements and evaluated which of these requirements are a great fit for Crystal Reports. We also used the requirements from the financial and HR area and created concrete reports to fulfill these requirements. In the next chapter we will continue our journey and try to fulfill our reporting requirements in the ad hoc query and analysis areas using Web Intelligence.

In this chapter, we'll look at how we can use Web Intelligence for customer requirements in ad hoc queries and analysis reporting.

4   Ad Hoc Query and Analysis

After covering the requirements for Enterprise Reporting, we will now focus on the ad hoc query and analysis-type reports — particularly Web Intelligence. We'll look at the technical requirements to use the tool, continue with the different connectivity options that can be leveraged, and then evaluate the requirements from the previous chapter and see how Web Intelligence can fulfill them.

4.1   Installation and Deployment Overview

The installation requirements to leverage Web Intelligence include three components:

▶ BusinessObjects Enterprise

▶ Universe designer

▶ BusinessObjects Integration for SAP Solutions

Web Intelligence is a fully web-based reporting tool and an integral part of BusinessObjects Enterprise; therefore, a BusinessObjects Enterprise deployment is required. The second component is the Universe designer, which lets you create a Universe on top of the SAP system. A Universe is a semantic layer created on top of the actual data source that enables you to provide a less technical and more business-type view of your data to your end users. The third component is the BusinessObjects Integration for SAP solutions, which enables the connectivity and SAP authentication of your BusinessObjects server landscape to your client computer.

> **Integrating BusinessObjects XI 3.1 Business Intelligence (BI) Tools with SAP NetWeaver**
>
> With regard to the installation and deployment of the BusinessObjects XI 3.1 Release in conjunction with your SAP landscape, you can find all of the details in the author's first book, *Integrating BusinessObjects XI 3.1 BI Tools with SAP NetWeaver*, published by SAP Press.

Universe Designer Installation

The Universe designer can be deployed in two ways. You can use the BusinessObjects Enterprise installation software or the BusinessObjects client deployment software, which is available as a separate download.

The following steps show how to install the Universe designer using the BusinessObjects Enterprise installation software:

1. After you start the installation routine, you'll be asked to select a language for it. This does not influence the language for the actual deployment of the software. In our example, we'll select ENGLISH as the setup language.

2. In the next two screens you'll be asked to accept the license agreement and enter the license key code. After this step, you have the choice of language packs. This time, the selection influences the software language. For our installation, we'll select ENGLISH.

3. Next, select the type of installation you want to perform. To install parts of the client tools you need to select the CUSTOM option (see Figure 4.1).

4. In the next screen, you can select the client components from BusinessObjects Enterprise (see Figure 4.2). In our case, we are interested in the Universe designer.

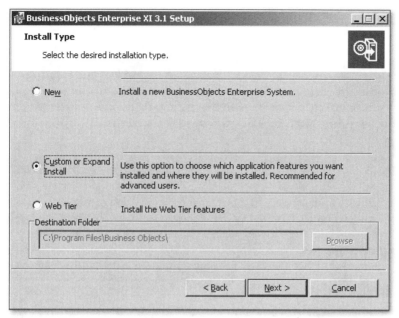

Figure 4.1   BusinessObjects Enterprise Setup

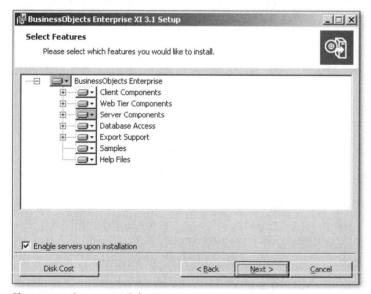

Figure 4.2   Component Selection

5. You can use the NEXT button to continue and start the actual installation process.

SAP BusinessObjects Client Setup

When you download the specific SAP BusinessObjects client installation software, you will see that the steps are very similar to the custom setup with the major difference being that you can only select client components in the client installation.

BusinessObjects Integration for SAP Solutions

The installation of the BusinessObjects Integration for SAP Solutions is shown in Chapter 3, Section 3.1, Installation and Deployment Overview, with a reference to Crystal Reports, but the installation routine itself does not change, except the list of components that need to be selected for Web Intelligence. Web Intelligence needs SAP authentication and the Online Analytical Processing (OLAP) Business Application Programming Interface (BAPI) connectivity installed on the client side so that you can create a Universe on top of SAP NetWeaver Business Warehouse (BW).

Data Federator

The installation and configuration of relational Universes on top of SAP NetWeaver BW is shown in detail in the Appendix, Section 13.1, Installation Configuration of the Data Federator Connectivity.

In the next section, we'll describe the possibilities for connecting Web Intelligence to your SAP data source.

4.2 SAP Data Connectivity for Web Intelligence and Universes

In this section, we'll look at the connectivity options for Web Intelligence using a Universe on top of your SAP landscape.

As shown in Figure 4.3, Web Intelligence does not have any direct data connectivity to your SAP ERP system. The only option available at this point is to leverage the new TRANSIENT PROVIDER, made available as part of SAP NetWeaver BW 7.02. This lets you leverage a classic InfoSet directly from your SAP ERP system via a BW query.

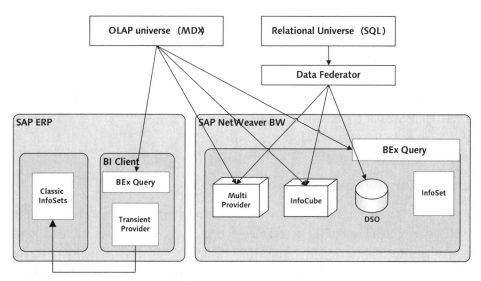

Figure 4.3 Data Connectivity for Web Intelligence

SAP NetWeaver BW Transient Provider

The TRANSIENT PROVIDER lets you leverage a BW query connecting directly to a classic InfoSet from you SAP ERP system without the requirement of modeling an InfoProvider. This functionality is — as of this writing — scheduled for release with SAP NetWeaver BW 7.02 in the first half of 2010.

When using SAP BW with Web Intelligence there are two options — a data access based on SQL providing a relational view or a data access based on Multi-Dimensional eXpressions (MDX) providing a multidimensional view. Both of these options have pros and cons, which we'll cover in detail in the next section. Please note that the OLAP Universe provides the capability to connect directly to the InfoCube level, which will limit the leverage of existing metadata as shown in Table 3.2.

In the next section, we'll go into more detail on how to leverage the already-modeled metadata in conjunction with Universes.

4.3   Metadata Management with Universes

In this section, we'll look at the role of the Universe on top of your SAP landscape and how you can leverage the Universe for ad hoc reporting and analysis. After we discuss the general role of the Universe, we'll look at the options for creating OLAP Universes and relational Universes on top of SAP NetWeaver BW and how those can add value to your reporting landscape.

4.3.1   Overview on Universes

A Universe is a layer on top of your actual data source that lets you create a more business-oriented view of the actual metadata provided by your source. This additional layer (often referred to as the semantic layer) provides the ability to create business semantics and hide the logic and terms of your SAP data source from the end user. In addition to hiding the complex logic of the underlying source system from the end user, you can now also create common definitions of your metadata and ensure that each user is leveraging the same definition of objects, such as a calculation of your margin or a hierarchy of your sales regions.

In general, a Universe differentiates between a class and an object. A class is a combination of objects in the form of a folder structure or category. An object can be of type dimension, detail, or measure and represents an actual item from the underlying source, for example, a customer number or a calculation for the variance of actual and budget.

The overall benefits of a Universe are:

- Only one person needs to design and customize a Universe on top of your SAP source — not every consumer of information.
- All consumers are sharing the same definition of metadata and the same definition of calculations.
- All consumers are sharing the same terms being used as metadata.

It is important to note that in the SAP BusinessObjects XI 3.1 portfolio not all of the client tools leverage the Universe in the same way.

- ▶ For Web Intelligence, the existence of a Universe is a must; otherwise you can't connect to your data source.

- ▶ Crystal Reports does not support OLAP Universes and instead uses the BW MDX driver to connect to the SAP NetWeaver BW system.

- ▶ Crystal Reports is connected to the SAP ERP landscape directly because there is no SAP ERP connectivity for the Universe at this point of time.

- ▶ SAP BusinessObjects Explorer can leverage the Universe for indexing data, and a Business Warehouse Accelerator (BWA) index.

- ▶ Xcelsius can leverage a Universe via the Query as a Web service tool, and also offers a direct connectivity for SAP NetWeaver BW.

The Universe plays an important role for Web Intelligence and SAP Business-Objects Explorer, and the other tools — even though they offer direct connectivity. We'll continue this topic on a more strategic level when we take a look at the roadmap going forward in Chapter 12, Product Integration Outlook.

4.3.2 OLAP Universes and SAP NetWeaver BW

In this section, we'll look at how an OLAP Universe leverages the existing meta-data from your SAP NetWeaver BW system and provides a view on top of your SAP NetWeaver BW metadata. As shown in Figure 4.3, an OLAP Universe lets you connect to the BW query layer and to the InfoCube level directly. At first, this might look like an additional layer when using the Universe on top of a BW query, where the Universe is not delivering a lot of added value, but keep in mind that as of now the only way to connect to SAP NetWeaver BW from Web Intelligence is via the Universe. With regard to the comparison between the metadata delivered from a BW query and by an InfoCube directly, you should consider Table 3.2. In addition, you should consider that you can't use authorization variables when connecting directly to the InfoCube level. This leads to a situation where, as the report designer, you have to ensure that in each report each user is setting the correct filter values. When using the BW query as your meta-data layer for the universe you can leverage the authorization variable and in that way leverage the defined BI authorizations from your SAP NetWeaver BW system.

Best Practices on Query Design

In Chapter 11, Best Practices for SAP BusinessObjects BI Tools, we'll look into more detail on how to leverage the BW queries in your system. We'll also look at Best Practices for the integration of SAP NetWeaver and SAP BusinessObjects XI 3.1.

BW Query Element	OLAP Universe Element
Cube Dimension	Each dimension of the InfoCube will result in a top level class and provides the structure for the Universe.
Characteristic	Each characteristic results in a Subclass folder with a Level 00 and a Level 01 dimension object where the Level 00 object represents the All members view for the characteristic.
Hierarchy	**BI Query as source**: A characteristic with an activated hierarchy results in a Subclass folder with the amount of dimension objects representing the number of hierarchy levels available at the point of creating the Universe. **BI InfoCube as source**: If the Universe is created directly on top of an InfoCube, each available hierarchy for each characteristic is represented by a Subclass folder and the amount of dimension object depending on the number of levels for each hierarchy available at the point of creating the Universe.
Key Figure	Each key figure can have up to three elements: numeric value, unit, and formatted value and therefore each key figure is created in a Subclass folder below the Key figures class folder with up to one measure object (numeric value) and two dimension objects (Unit and Formatted value). The formatted value is based on the user preferences configured in the SAP system.
Calculated and Restricted Key Figures	Each calculated/restricted key figure is treated like a key figure. The user does not have access to the underlying definition in the OLAP Universe.
Filter	Filters will be applied to the underlying query but are not visible in the Universe designer.

Table 4.1 SAP NetWeaver BW Metadata Mapping for OLAP Universes

BW Query Element	OLAP Universe Element
Navigational Attribute	Navigational attributes are treated just like a characteristic.
Display Attribute	Display attributes become detail objects and are subordinates of the linked characteristic.
SAP Variables	Each variable with the Ready for Input property will result in a pre-defined filter in the OLAP Universe.
Conditions	Conditions are not transferred to the Universe. This means that a created condition — like a Top 10 condition — is not leveraged and that Web Intelligence receives all of the data and not just the Top 10 records.
Exceptions	Exceptions are not transferred to the Universe or Web Intelligence report. You can easily create Alerts in the Web Intelligence report.
Custom Structure	A custom structure created in the BW query will result in a single dimension object in the OLAP Universe. When using this object in the report, each structure element will have a record in the report.

Table 4.1 SAP NetWeaver BW Metadata Mapping for OLAP Universes (Cont.)

In Table 4.2, you can see how the OLAP Universe supports the different data types that you can create in your SAP NetWeaver BW system.

Data type	Data type in OLAP Universe	Additional information
Characteristics		
CHAR	Character	
NUMC	Character	A conversion to a Numeric data type is not possible in the Universe as of Release XI 3.1 Service Pack 2. A possible workaround is to use the ToNumber function in the report.
DATS	Date	
TIMS	Character	A conversion to a data object type in the Universe is not possible as of Release XI 3.1 Service Pack 2. A possible workaround is to use the ToDate function in the report.

Table 4.2 SAP NetWeaver BW Data Type Support in OLAP Universes

Data type	Data type in OLAP Universe	Additional information
Key figures		
Amount	Number	
Quantity	Number	
Number	Number	
Integer	Number	
Date	Date	
Time	Date	A key figure of type Time is transferred to a type Date, which leads to an issue in the report. You can use the formatted value of the key figure as an alternative by changing the definition of the object in the Universe to show the Formatted Value.

Table 4.2 SAP NetWeaver BW Data Type Support in OLAP Universes (Cont.)

As you can tell by the level of support for the existing metadata from the SAP NetWeaver BW system, the OLAP Universe provides the multidimensional view of your data warehouse. We'll take a look at a more detailed comparison with the relational universe in Section 4.3.4, OLAP Universes and Relational Universes — a Comparison.

4.3.3   Relational Universes and SAP NetWeaver BW

In this section, we'll focus on how building a relational Universe on top of SAP NetWeaver BW supports the existing metadata in your data warehouse. As shown in Table 4.3, the option to connect to SAP NetWeaver BW via Data Federator provides you with the functionality to connect to MultiProvider, InfoCubes, and Data Store Objects (DSOs). The connectivity via Data Federator exposes the actual star schema to you in the Universe so you can build your own universe.

InfoCube/ MultiProivder Element	Relational Universe via Data Federator
Cube Dimension	Each dimension of the InfoCube results in a top-level class and provides the structure for the Universe.
Characteristic	Each characteristic is shown as part of the initial Universe creation process and can be integrated into the Universe. In addition, the star schema is shown and can be integrated at any time.
Hierarchy	**Not supported via Data Federator in Relese XI 3.1 Service Pack 2.**
Key Figure	Key figures are created as part of the Measures class.
Calculated and Restricted Key Figures	**Not supported via Data Federator in Release XI 3.1 Service Pack 2, but you can create calculated or filtered measures as part of the Universe.**
Filter	Filters can be created on a Universe level. Predefined filters from a BW query can't be leveraged because the Data Federator connectivity uses the InfoCube/ MultiProvider level.
Navigational Attribute	Navigational attributes are treated just like a characteristic.
Display Attribute	Display attributes are not part of the initial Universe but you can add them to the master data tables.
SAP Variables	**Not supported via Data Federator in Release XI 3.1 Service Pack 2, but you can create prompts in the Universe.**
Conditions	**Not supported via Data Federator in Release XI 3.1 Service Pack 2, but filters on a measure level can be created in the Universe.**
Exceptions	**Not supported via Data Federator in Release XI 3.1 Service Pack 2, but ranking can be created on a report level in Web Intelligence.**
Custom Structure	A custom structure is not available when connecting directly to the InfoCube, therefore, the Data Federator–based approach cannot provide support for the structure.
Currency/Unit conversion	Not available in the initial Universe, but can be enabled using target tables in the Universe.

Table 4.3 SAP NetWeaver BW Metadata Mapping for Relational Universes

As you can see, based on the metadata support show in Table 4.3, the solution to connect to SAP NetWeaver BW is to offer basic metadata-level support for the InfoCube, MultiProvider, and DSO level.

4.3.4 OLAP Universes and Relational Universes – a Comparison

In the previous sections, you learned how each of the approaches — relational Universe and OLAP Universe — supports the metadata from your SAP NetWeaver BW system. This leads to the question, when is it best to use each of the solutions?

In Table 4.4, there are some key elements that might be of importance for your decision-making process and show which approach supports those elements.

Criteria	OLAP Universe	Relational Universe Using Data Federator
BW hierarchies	X	-
Calculated and restricted key figures	X	-
Exception aggregation required	X	-
Standard aggregation (AVG, COUNT, SUM, MIN, MAX)	X	X
Data Federation (SAP, non-SAP)	-	X
Access to DSO objects required	X	X
Use of Exit variables required	X	-
Currency/Unit conversion	X	-
Use of BW query variables	X	-
Support for BW queries	X	-
BI Authorizations	X	X
Single Sign-On (SSO)	X	-

Table 4.4 OLAP Universe and Relational Universe Comparison

Table 4.4 should not be seen as the only criteria to make a decision on how to leverage metadata from SAP NetWeaver BW. For some of the criteria that are not directly available with Data Federator there are possible workarounds (for example, SAP variables can be replaced by prompts). You need to consider all of the options and requirements.

Table 4.4 indicates that SSO is not supported for relational universe created by Data Federator on top of SAP NetWeaver BW as of this book's writing. SSO is on the product roadmap for this functionality and you should check back on a regular basis for an estimated time of delivery. In addition, you can see that both approaches support BI authorizations, but because the Data Federator solution doesn't offer an SSO solution yet, honoring BI authorizations in conjunction with Data Federator involves maintenance of users on the SAP BusinessObjects Enterprise system, Data Federator, and SAP NetWeaver BW system. You can find more details on this topic in the Appendix.

The following items should provide a summary for when you should consider using OLAP Universes or Relational Universes with Data Federator:

► OLAP Universes:

  ► You invested in InfoCube design with hierarchies, and restricted and calculated key figures.

  ► You invested in BW queries at the data entry level.

  ► You need a solution using SSO.

  ► Your users need advanced analytic workflows with features such as hierarchies, variables, and currency translations.

► Relational Universes:

  ► You are not leveraging OLAP concepts as part of your data modeling.

  ► You want to combine SAP NetWeaver BW data sources with other non-SAP data sources.

  ► You want to use the DSO layer for reporting.

  ► You don't need a full SSO solution.

4.3.5 Creating Your First OLAP Universe on Top of SAP NetWeaver BW

Now that we understand how an OLAP Universe can support metadata from SAP NetWeaver BW, let's look at the workflow for creating an OLAP Universe and how to customize it and create custom objects in the Universe.

In our example, we'll leverage a BW query based on the demo content cube 0D_DX_M01 (SAP Demo Scenario DalSegno Company Reporting cube) (see Figure 4.4).

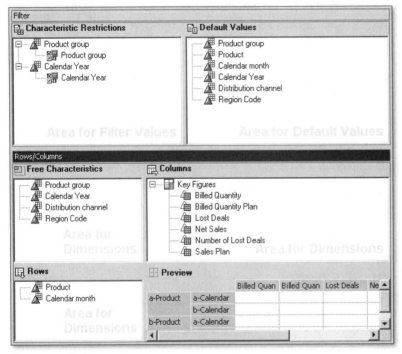

Figure 4.4 BW Demo Query

The BW query contains the following elements:

▶ Elements in Rows

   ▸ PRODUCT

   ▸ CALENDAR MONTH

- ► Elements in COLUMNS
  - ► BILLED QUANTITY
  - ► BILLED QUANTITY PLAN
  - ► LOST DEALS
  - ► NET SALES
  - ► NUMBER OF LOST DEALS
  - ► SALES PLAN
- ► Elements in FREE CHARACTERISTICS
  - ► PRODUCT GROUP
  - ► CALENDAR YEAR
  - ► DISTRIBUTION CHANNEL
  - ► REGION CODE
- ► Elements in FILTER/CHARACTERISTICS RESTRICTIONS
  - ► Optional interval variable for PRODUCT GROUP
  - ► Optional single value variable CALENDAR YEAR

To leverage the BW query with the Universe designer, we need to make sure the BW query is configured to allow external access.

1. In the BW query designer, follow the menu path: QUERY • PROPERTIES.

2. Navigate to the ADVANCED tab in the properties.

3. Activate the ALLOW EXTERNAL ACCESS TO THIS QUERY option (see Figure 4.5).

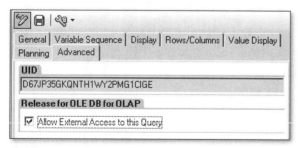

Figure 4.5 Query Properties

4. Save your changes and close the BW query designer.

Now we can start creating our first OLAP Universe.

1. Start the Universe designer via the menu path START • PROGRAMS • BUSINESS-OBJECTS XI 3.1 • BUSINESSOBJECTS ENTERPRISE • DESIGNER.

2. You will see the logon screen for the Universe designer and you need to provide the system name and your user credentials.

3. In our example, we'll use SAP authentication and our SAP credentials. For the system, we'll enter the name of the Central Management Server of our Business-Objects Enterprise system — VMWSAP20 (see Figure 4.6).

Figure 4.6 User Identification

4. Because the Universe designer doesn't offer the SAP System ID and the SAP client number as input fields as part of the logon mask, you need to enter your SAP credentials in the following format:

`[SAP System ID]~800/[SAP user name]`

For example:

`CIM~800/DEMO`

5. Click OK.

6. In the Universe designer, follow the menu path FILE • NEW.

7. The UNIVERSE PARAMETERS dialog appears (see Figure 4.7) and you can use the NEW button to create a new connection to your SAP NetWeaver BW system.

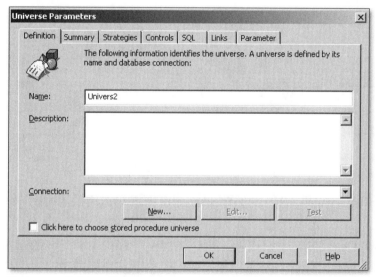

Figure 4.7 Universe Parameters

8. Click NEXT to start the Connection Wizard.

9. Enter a name for the connection into the field CONNECTION NAME and scroll down to select the SAP BUSINESS WAREHOUSE connectivity type (see Figure 4.8).

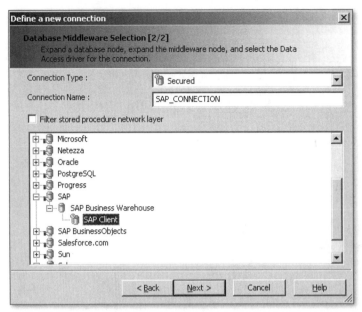

Figure 4.8 Database Middleware Selection

10. Click NEXT.

11. Enter the details to connect to your SAP system as shown in Figure 4.9.

12. The LOGIN MODE lets you switch between an Application server and a Message server.

13. If you used your SAP credentials to log on to the Universe designer you can set the AUTHENTICATION MODE to USE SINGLE SIGN ON WHEN REFRESHING REPORTS AT VIEW TIME. If the SAP authentication is not configured on your BusinessObjects Enterprise system, you can continue with the USE SPECIFIED USERNAME AND PASSWORD setting and change the setting later on.

14. Click NEXT.

15. The list of available BW queries is shown in tree form with the InfoProvider listed at the top and the BW queries below each InfoProvider. $INFOCUBE lets you connect directly to all InfoCubes without a BW query (see Figure 4.10).

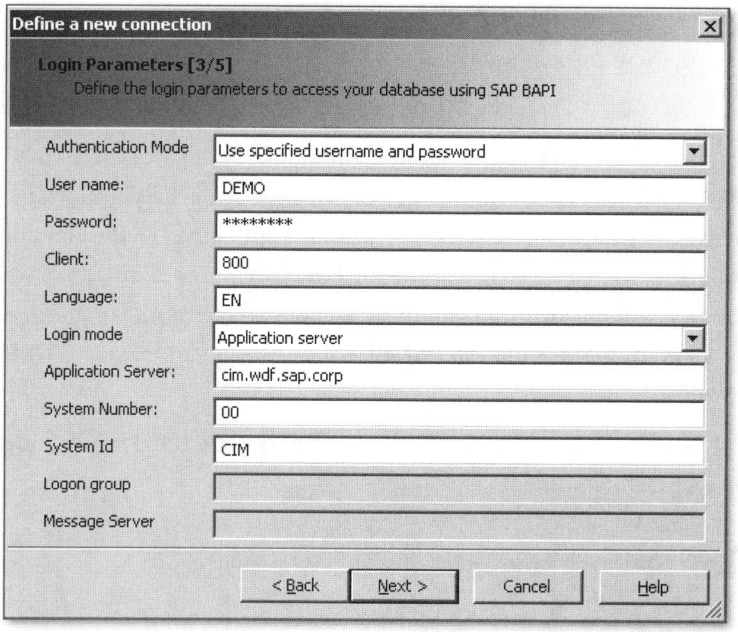

Figure 4.9 Login Parameters

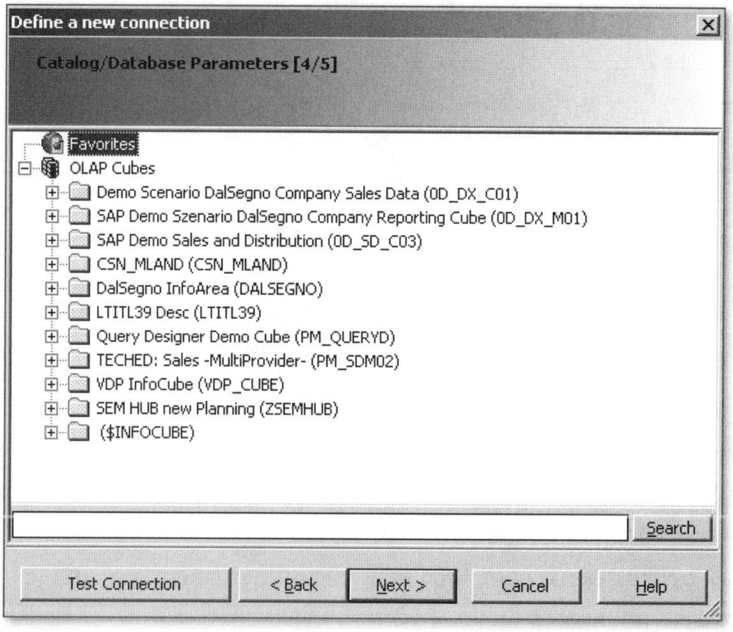

Figure 4.10 Selection of BW Query

16. In our example, let's open the list of BW queries for InfoProvider 0D_DX_ M01 and select the BW query.

17. Click NEXT.

18. In the next screen, you can define connection parameters for your SAP NetWeaver BW system. The CONNECTION POOL MODE is especially important. Here, you define how long the connection will be kept active — the default value is 10 minutes. You can also select the DISCONNECT AFTER EACH TRANSACTION option, but you want to avoid doing so because it will result in a logon and log-off process for every function call for your SAP system from this Universe connection.

19. Select the KEEP THE CONNECTION ACTIVE FOR option and leave the default value for POOL TIMEOUT (see Figure 4.11).

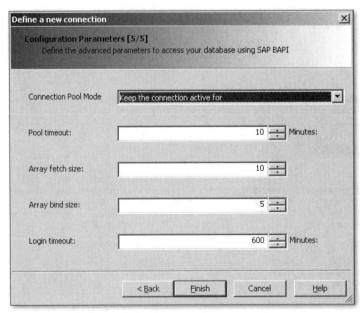

Figure 4.11 Configuration Parameters

20. Click FINISH.

21. Navigate to the CONTROLS tab from UNIVERSE PARAMETERS and make sure you uncheck all of the options (see Figure 4.12).

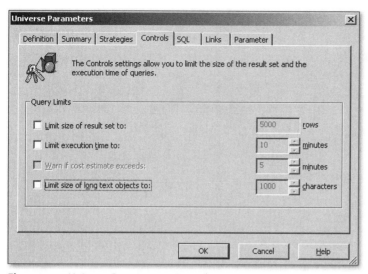

Figure 4.12 Universe Parameters - Controls

22. Navigate to the DEFINITION tab.

23. Enter a name for the new Universe into the field NAME.

24. Click OK.

25. Now the Universe designer connects with the SAP NetWeaver BW system and retrieves the metadata from the BW query that we selected.

26. After retrieving the metadata, the Universe is created following the logic presented in Table 4.1.

27. Your Universe should look similar to Figure 4.13 and Figure 4.14.

Figure 4.13 OLAP Universe Based on BW Query

Figure 4.14 OLAP Universe Based on BW Query

▶ As you can see, each characteristic has been created as a dimension object with a Level 00 and a Level 01 object where the Level 00 object represents the aggregated view of all members for the characteristic (for example, Distribution Channel).

▶ Each key figure has been created with up to three objects representing the numeric value, the unit, and the formatted value following the user preferences (for example, Billed Quantity).

▶ Display attributes — for example, the PRODUCT GROUP shown in Figure 4.14 — are incorporated into the Universe even though the Display attributes were not part of the BW query (for example, Product Price per UM).

▶ Filters and List of values have been created based on the variables in the BW query. Each List of values for a Filter based on a variable is created with a key and a description for the values shown in the list of values.

28. Follow the FILE • SAVE menu path to save the Universe.

29. Follow the FILE • EXPORT menu path to export the Universe to your BusinessObjects Enterprise system (see Figure 4.15).

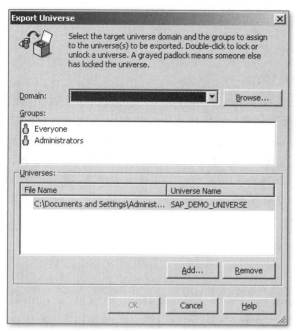

Figure 4.15 Export Universe

30. Click BROWSE.

31. Select a folder for the Universe and click OK.

32. Click OK.

You created a new Universe on top of a BW query and exported the Universe to your BusinessObjects Enterprise system, so now your end-users can create a new Web Intelligence report using the Universe that you just created.

4.3.6 Customize Your OLAP Universe

Before we continue and use the newly created OLAP Universe in conjunction with Web Intelligence, let's look at some common tasks for customizing the OLAP Universe. Let's look at how you can change the descriptions and organizational structure of your Universe, how you can add calculations, create your own hierarchies, create your own filter, and configure delegated measures.

First, let's create all of the customizations in the Universe and then use the Universe and the customizations later on in Web Intelligence.

Descriptions and Organizational Structure

All objects in the Universe have been created based on the metadata derived from SAP NetWeaver BW. In addition, you'll notice that the characteristics have been prefixed with L00 and L01 to indicate which level the selected object represents. In the first step, we'll remove the prefix and the L00 objects. Keep in mind that the L00 objects represent the aggregated level for all members of the characteristics and that you could use it for a drill down operation. If you don't need the L00 objects, you can skip to the next step.

1. In the Universe designer, follow the menu path: VIEW • REFRESH STRUCTURE.

2. Click BEGIN.

3. In the first screen with options, make sure you keep all of the default options selected and activate the DELETE OBSOLETE OBJECTS option instead of HIDE OBSOLETE OBJECTS (see Figure 4.16).

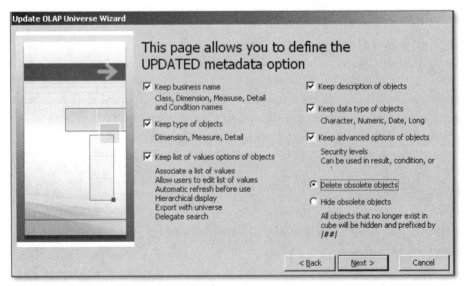

Figure 4.16   Update OLAP Universe Wizard

4. Click NEXT.

5. In the next screen, make sure you select the options as shown in Figure 4.17.

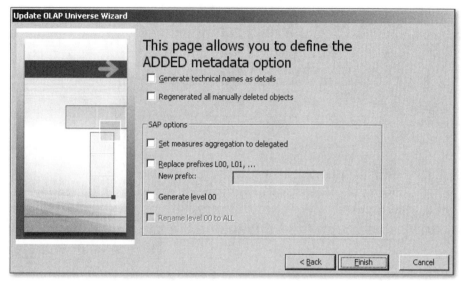

Figure 4.17   Update OLAP Universe Wizard — Additional Options

By removing the GENERATE LEVEL 00 option you are removing the Level 00 objects from your Universe. The REPLACE PREFIXES L00, L01, ... option might be tempting, but it will replace the prefix with a different string, for example, for L01 Distribution Channel, the object will be PREFIX01 Distribution Channel so the object still has a prefix, but it might not be what you are looking for.

OLAP Universe Options

The options listed in Figure 4.17 can also be preconfigured via the TOOLS • OPTIONS menu path on the OLAP tab. That way, you can preset these options for your installation of the Universe designer and the settings will be used for any new OLAP Universes.

6. The next screen contains a summary of the changes.

7. Click OK.

8. To remove the L01 prefix from the objects you need to manually change the descriptions of each object. You can reach the properties of each object by double-clicking (see Figure 4.18).

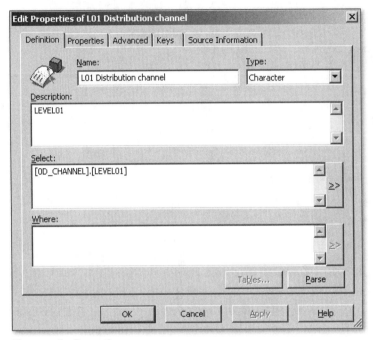

Figure 4.18   Properties

9. Edit the DESCRIPTION of the objects based on your needs.

10. Confirm the changes by clicking OK.

OLAP Universe Update Wizard

Remember, make sure the KEEP BUSINESS NAME and KEEP DESCRIPTION OF OBJECTS options are activated when you make changes in these areas and follow the VIEW • REFRESH STRUCTURE menu path to update the Universe, otherwise you will lose your changes.

Predefined Filter and Prompts

A predefined filter lets you create filter objects as part of the Universe so the user can use the filter and restrict the data set in the report without being prompted for a value. In the most simplistic way, the filter contains a set of fixed values. In our first example, we'll create a filter that lets the user filter data in the report to the months of the first quarter.

1. In the Universe designer navigate to the FILTER area in the Universe (see Figure 4.19).

Figure 4.19   Filter Area in the Universe

2. In our example, we want to create a predefined filter for the CALENDAR MONTH. Select the CALENDAR MONTH class folder.

3. Follow the menu path: INSERT • CONDITION.

4. The properties dialog for the new condition appears and a template for the syntax is shown in the WHERE box (see Figure 4.20).

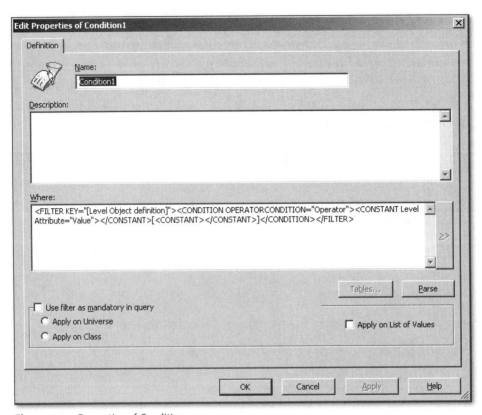

Figure 4.20 Properties of Condition

5. A filter in an OLAP Universe has the syntax:

```
<FILTER "[Level Object definition] >
    <CONDITION OPERATORCONDITION=Operator>
        <CONSTANT Level Attribute=Value></CONSTANT>
        [<CONSTANT></CONSTANT> …]
    </CONDITION>
</FILTER>
```

6. As you can see, the template syntax uses placeholders and Table 4.5 shows the options for these placeholders.

Template Element	Possible Values
Level Object Definition	Here, you need to enter the definition of the objects you want to use as part of the filter.
Operator	Equal
	Not equal
	Greater than
	Less than
	Greater than or equal to
	Less than or equal to
	Between
	Not between
	In list
	Not in list
	Matches pattern
	Different from pattern
	The Matches pattern and Different from pattern options result in client-side filtering.
Level Attribute	NAME
	CAPTION
	TECH_NAME
	DESCRIPTION
Value	Here you need to enter a value or a prompt syntax. You need to define one value per CONSTANT tag.

Table 4.5 Values for Filter Syntax Placeholders

7. Following the previous syntax, our example to filter the CALENDAR MONTH to the first quarter would look like the following:

```
<FILTER KEY="[0CALMONTH2].[LEVEL01].[TECH_NAME]">
<CONDITION OPERATORCONDITION="InList">
<CONSTANT TECH_NAME="[0CALMONTH2].[01]"></CONSTANT>
<CONSTANT TECH_NAME="[0CALMONTH2].[02]"></CONSTANT>
<CONSTANT TECH_NAME="[0CALMONTH2].[03]"></CONSTANT>
</CONDITION></FILTER>
```

8. In our example, we are using TECH_NAME as an attribute, which means we need to set the technical name of the value. The technical name consists of the name of the InfoObject (in our example, 0CALMONTH2) and the actual value with both of these values in brackets.

9. Enter the syntax into the WHERE box.

10. Enter Quarter 1 as the NAME.

11. Click the PARSE button to see if the syntax is correct.

12. Click OK.

13. The predefined filter can now be used as part of the Web Intelligence query panel, which we will do in Section 4.5, Web Intelligence — Quick Basics.

Index Awareness

It is important to make sure you are using the key value (NAME) or the full member name (TECH_NAME) as much as possible. Using a description as a filter value leads to situations where the description needs to be resolved to a key value before it is sent to the SAP NetWeaver BW system.

Time-based Filtering

People will often look for the option to filter the data based on the current date, month, or year. Typical examples are a filter showing the last 12 months, or the last full week, or the data from the current month. The problem is, as of Release XI 3.1 Service Pack 2, the OLAP Universes don't offer such functionality. Therefore, the recommendation in these cases is to either leverage Exit variables in the BW query filtering the data to the required timeframe or to use variables offering a time range in the BW query for cases where more flexibility is required.

In our second example, we'll create a filter for the CALENDAR MONTH, but this time we will not create a filter with a fixed list of values but a filter that includes a prompt instead. The steps are relatively similar and instead of the hardcoded values we will create a prompt allowing the user to select a start and an end value for the CALENDAR MONTH. To do this, we need to understand the syntax of the @ PROMPT option in the Universe designer.

```
@Prompt('message','type',[lov],Mono|Multi,
free|constrained|primary_key,persistent|not_persistent,[default_
values])
```

The @PROMPT syntax lets us create a prompt asking the user for a value and we can then use this value as part of our filter definition.

@PROMPT Syntax Placeholder	Possible Values
Message	Here, you enter the prompting text that the end user will see.
Type	This represents the data type for the list of values ▸ A for alphanumeric ▸ N for number ▸ D for date
LOV	This represents the list of values that are available. You have the option of using a list of values from an object in your Universe or you can create a hardcoded list of values.
Mono/Multi	Choose if the user can enter one value (mono) or multiple values (multi).
Free/constrained/ primary_key	If you select free, the user can enter values manually as well. If you select constrained, the user has to select a value from the list of values. When you use primary_key, the index awareness of the Universe is used and the value configured in the Index Awareness for the object is used as a filter.
persistent	When refreshing a document, the last value used in the prompt is displayed by default.
not_persistent	When refreshing a document, no values are displayed in the prompt by default.
Default_value	Here, you can create a default value for the prompt

Table 4.6 @PROMPT Syntax Placeholders

In the prompt for the starting month example, we can leverage the following @ PROMPT syntax:

```
"@Prompt('Select the starting month','A','Calendar month\L01 Calendar
month',Mono,primary_key)
```

We have to incorporate this into our filter syntax:

1. In the Universe designer, navigate to the FILTER area in the Universe (see Figure 4.19).

2. Navigate to the CALENDAR MONTH class folder.

3. In our example, we want to create a predefined filter for the CALENDAR MONTH that also includes prompts for the start and end month.

4. Follow the menu path: INSERT • CONDITION.

5. The properties dialog for the new condition appears and a template for the syntax is shown in the WHERE box (see Figure 4.20).

6. Remove the template syntax and enter the following syntax in the WHERE box:

```
<FILTER KEY="[0CALMONTH2].[LEVEL01].[TECH_NAME]">
<CONDITION OPERATORCONDITION="Between">
<CONSTANT TECH_NAME="@Prompt('Select the starting month','A','Calendar
month\L01 Calendar month',Mono,primary_key)"></CONSTANT>
<CONSTANT TECH_NAME="@Prompt('Select the ending month','A','Calendar
month\L01 Calendar month',Mono,primary_key)"></CONSTANT>
</CONDITION></FILTER>
```

7. If you want the filter to be optional, you can put an <OPTIONAL> tag in the beginning and a </OPTIONAL> tag at the end of the syntax.

8. Enter Quarter SELECTION WITH PROMPT as the NAME.

9. Click the PARSE button to see if the syntax is correct.

10. Click OK.

11. Save and export your Universe.

12. Now you've created two new filter objects in the Universe letting you filter all months for the first quarter or prompt for a start and end month for the timeframe.

Referencing the List of Values

As you can see in the previous syntax, we are only referencing the `Calendar month` dimension object with the class level above and not all class levels above the object. For the list of values, you only need to reference the object with the class that contains the objects.

Calculations

By creating a calculation in your Universe, you can use MDX functions to create objects such as a simple variance between two measures, a ranked measure or even more complex calculations. We'll look at some simple examples and the syntax for these objects. Uncovering all of the possibilities is beyond the scope of this book. There's a lot of material available that shows the possibilities of using MDX functions in conjunction with SAP NetWeaver BW. Each calculation you create needs to have the <EXPRESSION> </EXPRESSION> tags around the syntax, otherwise it will fail.

The first example we will create is a simple calculation for how much of our plan value we achieved. In our Universe, we have the BILLED QUANTITY and BILLED QUANTITY PLAN key figures (see Figure 4.13). The calculation will show the percentage value of the achievement of the plan number.

Custom Calculations and @Select

When creating custom calculations, it is recommended to leverage the `@Select` function to point to the objects instead of using the technical definition of the object because the `@Select` statement is resolved at query run time by Web Intelligence. In addition, the technical definition of the object might change and by using the `@Select` function such a change would not impact your custom calculation definition.

---

1. In the Universe designer, with the Universe open, select the KEY FIGURES class.

2. Follow the menu path: INSERT • OBJECT (see Figure 4.21).

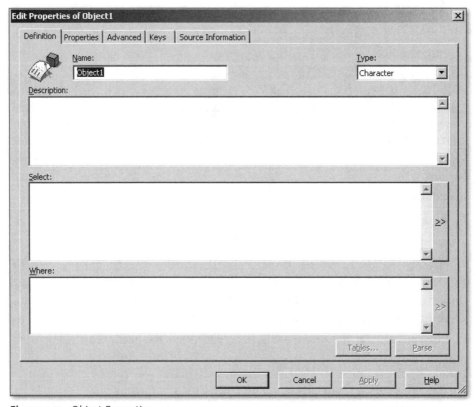

Figure 4.21 Object Properties

3. Enter `Billed Quantity Variance` as the NAME of the object.

4. Select NUMBER as TYPE.

5. Navigate to the PROPERTIES tab.

6. Select MEASURE as the QUALIFICATION.

7. Navigate back to the DEFINITION tab.

8. Click the button next to the SELECT box to open the editor.

9. Use the editor to create the following formula (see Figure 4.22):

```
@Select(Billed Quantity\Billed Quantity) / @Select(Billed Quantity
Plan\Billed Quantity Plan)
```

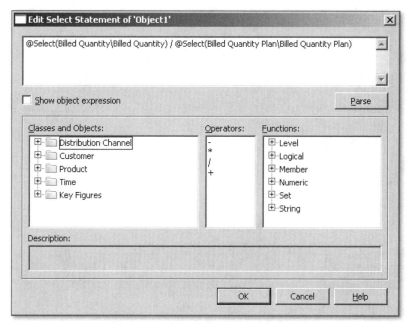

Figure 4.22 Select Statement Editor

10. Click OK.

11. The syntax from the editor is now shown in the SELECT box.

12. Put the <EXPRESSION> tag in front of the syntax and </EXPRESSION> at the end of the syntax (see Figure 4.23).

13. Click the PARSE button to see if the syntax is correct.

14. Navigate to the PROPERTIES tab.

15. Set the FUNCTION to DATABASE DELEGATED option.

16. Click OK.

17. The newly created object should be shown as an item in the KEY FIGURES class (see Figure 4.24).

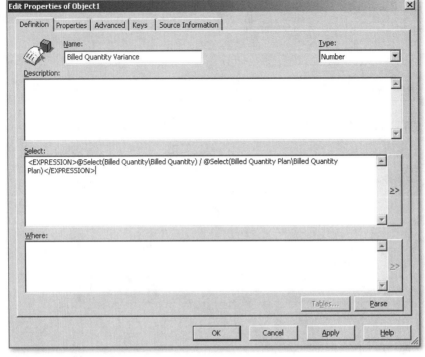

Figure 4.23 Objects Properties

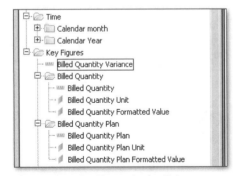

Figure 4.24 Key Figures in the Universe

<EXPRESSION> Syntax and Formula Editor

When you use the formula editor, you will notice that the formula editor is not going to create the <EXPRESSION> </EXPRESSION> tags for you. And when using the PARSE option in the editor, you will get an error message that the XML expression is incorrect. Make sure you include the Expression tags as part of the syntax.

18. Save the changes in the Universe and export the Universe to BusinessObjects Enterprise.

The second example we are going to create is a key figure, which is filtered to a specific set of values. This is very similar to a restricted key figure in your BW query. In the Universe we've been using up to this point, we also have a key figure called SALES PLAN. This shows the planned number for our sales revenue. Now we can create four new measure objects that show the Sales plan key figure for each quarter.

1. In the Universe designer, with the Universe open, select the KEY FIGURES class and navigate to the SALES PLAN subclass.

2. Follow the menu path INSERT • OBJECT.

3. Enter `Sales plan Quarter 1` as the NAME of the object.

4. Select NUMBER as the TYPE.

5. Navigate to the PROPERTIES tab.

6. Select MEASURE as the QUALIFICATION.

7. Navigate back to the DEFINITION tab.

8. We want to create a measure that aggregates the SALES PLAN key figure over a given set of members; therefore, we are using the MDX function AGGREGATE.

9. Enter the following syntax into the SELECT box:

```
<EXPRESSION>AGGREGATE(
{[0CALMONTH2].[01]:[0CALMONTH2].[03]},
@Select(Sales Plan\Sales Plan))
</EXPRESSION>
```

    The preceding syntax will aggregate the SALES PLAN key figure for the first three months representing the first quarter regardless of the year.

10. Click the PARSE button to see if the syntax is correct.

11. Click OK.

12. The newly created measure should now be shown in the SALES PLAN class.

13. Repeat the steps for the other three quarters with the change in the range for the CALENDAR MONTHS.

14. Save the changes to your Universe and export the Universe to your Business-Objects Enterprise system.

Supported MDX Functions

You can use Transaction SE37 with the BAPI_MDPROVIDER_GET_FUNCTIONS function on your SAP NetWeaver BW server to retrieve a list of supported MDX functions.

Custom Hierarchies

When you create a new OLAP Universe on top of SAP NetWeaver BW the available hierarchies are incorporated into the Universe automatically. If you prefer to create your own hierarchy based on the metadata that is available in the Universe, you can do so. The benefit of a custom hierarchy can be that your end users can now use the custom hierarchy for a drill down operation and you can use a custom hierarchy for a cascading list of values as well.

1. In the Universe designer, with the Universe open, follow the menu path: TOOLS • HIERARCHIES.

2. The HIERARCHY EDITOR will appear. On the left side you can see the DEFAULT HIERARCHIES and on the right side the CUSTOM HIERARCHIES.

3. Click NEW to create a new custom hierarchy top-level folder.

4. Enter `Custom Demo Hierarchy` as the name of your new hierarchy.

5. Now you can select dimension objects from the left side and make them members of your new hierarchy. In our example, we will add (see Figure 4.25).

    ▶ L01 REGION CODE

    ▶ L01 DISTRIBUTION CHANNEL

    ▶ L01 PRODUCT

6. Click OK.

7. Save the changes to your Universe and export it to your BusinessObjects Enterprise system.

8. When using Web Intelligence in the next chapter, we will use the custom hierarchy for a drill-down operation from the REGION CODE to the DISTRIBUTION CHANNEL.

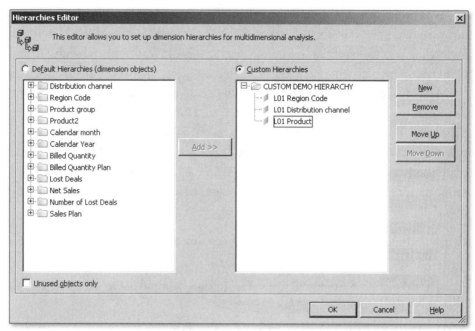

Figure 4.25 Hierarchies Editor

Cascading List of Values

A custom hierarchy can also be used to create a cascading list of values, which in our example would be a prompt that first shows the regions, then the distribution channels, then the product group, and, finally, allows the product. This can only work in situations where the Universe itself does not contain mandatory prompts on a Universe level, because otherwise the request of retrieving the list of values will fail because a prompt has to be filled first — especially for cases where the mandatory prompt is a mandatory variable in the underlying BW query.

Delegated Measures

In cases where you are using key figures that are not a standard aggregation like SUM, MAX, MIN, AVG, or COUNT, you may have to configure your measure in the Universe to become a delegated measure. When making a measure a delegated measure, the aggregation of values is transferred to the backend — in our case SAP NetWeaver BW.

As an example, consider a department head count of employees, which is not a measure that you want to summarize using the standard aggregation technique. Instead, it is most likely an exception aggregation in your cube already. If you don't configure such a measure as a delegated measure, then Web Intelligence uses the standard aggregation functions, and in the given example shows the wrong results. By making the measure a delegated measure, Web Intelligence delegates the aggregation to the underlying source system, which in most cases results in a two-step approach. In the first step, Web Intelligence asks for all of the data and dimension objects and in the second step, Web Intelligence asks for the aggregated numbers for the delegated measure of the needed aggregation level based on the report.

1. In the Universe designer, with the Universe open, navigate to the KEY FIGURES class.

2. Select a key figure from your Universe. In our example we're using the BILLED QUANTITY key figure.

3. Double-click on the key figure to open the PROPERTIES.

4. Navigate to the PROPERTIES tab (see Figure 4.26).

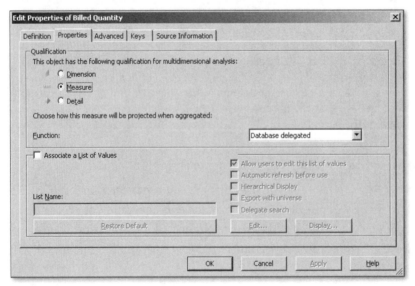

Figure 4.26 Properties

By setting the FUNCTION to DATABASE DELEGATED option, you configure the measure object to become a measure where Web Intelligence is not performing the aggregation but the underlying backend is.

In the last couple of sections, we customized our OLAP Universe and added our own calculations and objects. This book can only provide you with an overview and introduction to all of the capabilities that you can add using MDX functionality. If you are interested in further details on these options, the following literature is recommended. In Section 4.5, Web Intelligence — Quick Basics, we'll use the Universe that we created and Web Intelligence to get a better understanding of the capabilities of Web Intelligence as an ad hoc reporting tool.

OLAP Universe customizations

You can find additional information in the BusinessObjects section of the SAP community at *http://sdn.sap.com*. Look for a document named OLAP Universe Best Practices or use the following URL: *http://tinyurl.com/OLAPUniverse-Customization*.

With regard to the use of MDX functions in conjunction with SAP NetWeaver BW, the book *MDX Reporting and Analytics with SAP*, by Larry Sackett, is also recommended and available from SAP PRESS.

We will also discuss further customizations and Best Practices in Chapter 11, Best Practices for SAP BusinessObjects BI Tools.

4.3.7 Creating Your First Relational Universe on Top of SAP NetWeaver BW

In this section, we'll look at the process of creating a Universe on top of a data source exposed by Data Federator. The main difference between this approach and the OLAP Universe one is that Data Federator is exposing the InfoProvider as a relational Universe. For the following steps, we will assume that you installed and configured Data Federator and the SAP NetWeaver BW connectivity according to the Appendix.

First, we need to create the Data Federator source:

1. Follow the menu path: START • PROGRAMS • BUSINESSOBJECTS XI 3.0 • BUSINESS-OBJECTS DATA FEDERATOR • DATA FEDERATOR DESIGNER.

2. Log on to the Data Federator designer using the designer credentials we created during the installation and configuration.

3. Click ADD PROJECT (see Figure 4.27).

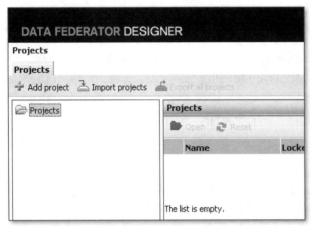

Figure 4.27 Data Federator Designer

4. Provide a name and description for your project (see Figure 4.28).

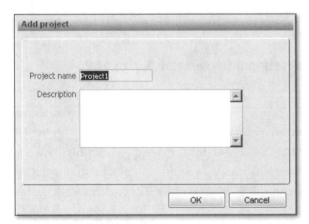

Figure 4.28 Add Project

5. Click OK.

6. Follow the ADD • ADD DATASOURCE menu path to add a new data source to your project (see Figure 4.29).

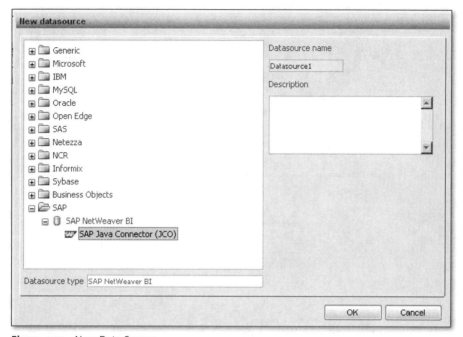

Figure 4.29 New Data Source

7. Select the SAP NETWEAVER BI connection.

8. Click OK.

9. The configuration screen appears and you need to provide the details from your SAP NetWeaver BW system (see Figure 4.30).

10. Select JCO.SAP.NETWEAVERBI as the DEFINED RESOURCE.

11. Enter the system details for your SAP NetWeaver BW system.

12. Set the AUTHENTICATION MODE to the USE THE DATA FEDERATOR LOGON option.

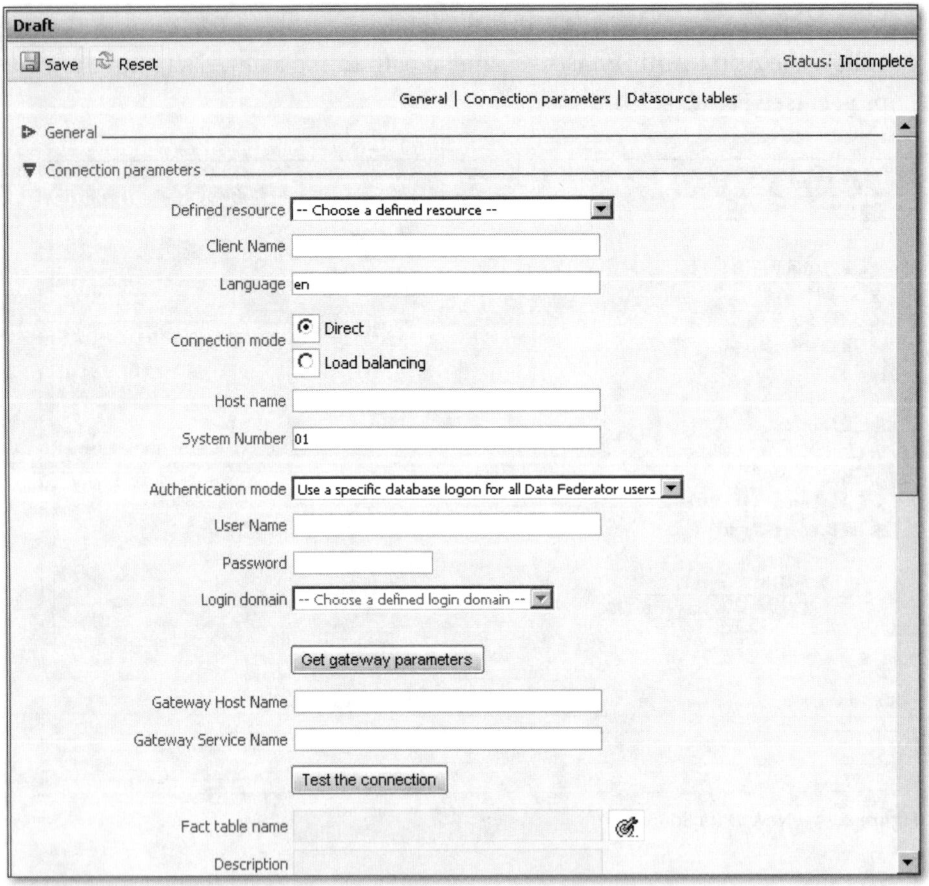

Figure 4.30 Data Source Configuration

Use the Data Federator Login

If you want to leverage the Authentication Mode USE THE DATA FEDERATOR LOGON you need to make sure the Data Federator credentials you are using also exist on the SAP NetWeaver BW system with the identical password.

13. Click GET GATEWAY PARAMETERS.

14. After the gateway parameters are retrieved, you can click CLOSE on the success message.

15. Click the TEST THE CONNECTION button to see if your configuration is correct.

16. Click the 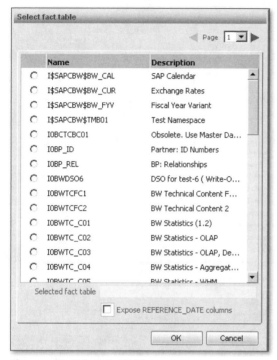 button next to the FACT TABLE NAME to select the fact tables for your InfoProvider (see Figure 4.31).

Figure 4.31 Select Fact Table

17. In our example, we will use InfoProvider 0D_NW_C01. The fact table is shown with a prefix "I" as for the technical name of the InfoProvider.

18. Select the fact table and click OK.

19. Data Federator now retrieves all of the information for the selected InfoProvider and then shows the tables in the lower screen (see Figure 4.32).

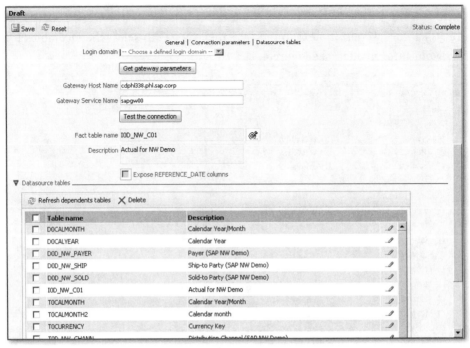

Figure 4.32 Data Federator Connection Configuration

20. Click SAVE.

SAP NetWeaver BW Star Schema

The following is basic information on the tables shown in the list of available tables and it is recommended to review the documentation on SAP NetWeaver BW for further details:

▶ The fact table of the InfoProvider is shown with a prefix "I"

▶ Master data tables are shown with a prefix "D"

▶ Text tables are shown with a prefix "T"

---

21. Select the folder for your data source on the left side (see Figure 4.33).

22. Click MAKE FINAL.

23. Now we need to send the project to the Data Federator server so we can create a Universe using our project as a data source. Click the ⊟ Deploy button to start the deploy process (see Figure 4.34).

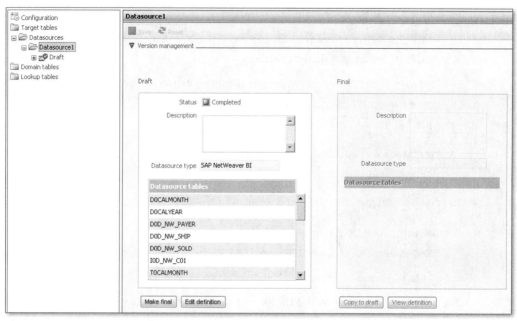

Figure 4.33 Data Source Configuration

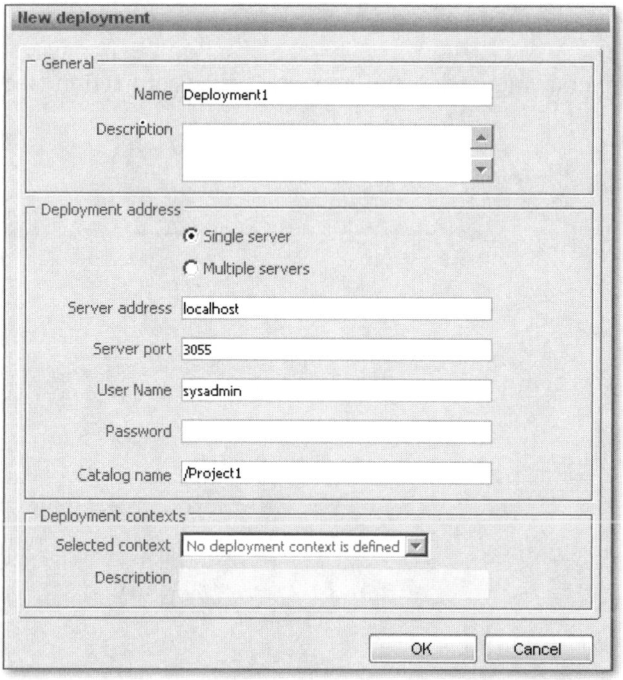

Figure 4.34 New Deployment

24. Enter a new NAME for the DEPLOYMENT.

25. Enter the designer credentials for the USER NAME and PASSWORD that we created during the installation process.

26. Define a CATALOG NAME, in our example, /Project1. Please make note of the name as you will need it when creating a Universe.

27. Click OK.

28. You have successfully deployed a Data Federator project using SAP NetWeaver BW as a data source.

Next, we'll create a new Universe on top of this Data Federator project.

1. Start the Universe designer by following the menu path: START • PROGRAMS • BUSINESSOBJECTS XI 3.1 • BUSINESSOBJECTS ENTERPRISE • DESIGNER.

2. Log on to your SAP BusinessObjects Enterprise system.

3. Click the 🔲 button in the toolbar to start the QUICK DESIGN WIZARD (see Figure 4.35).

4. Make sure the CLICK HERE TO CHOOSE STRATEGIES option is activated.

5. Click BEGIN.

6. Enter a name for the Universe and click NEW to create a new connection (see Figure 4.36).

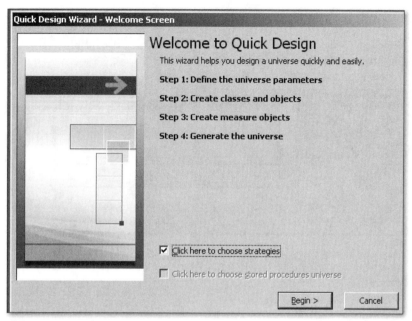

Figure 4.35   Quick Design Wizard

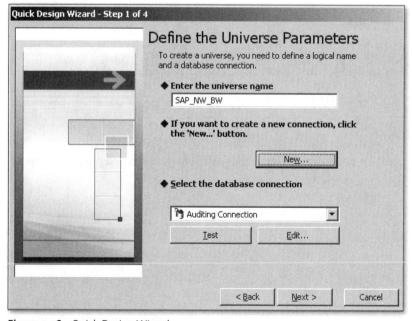

Figure 4.36   Quick Design Wizard

7. Click NEXT.

8. Enter a name for the connection and select THE JDBC DRIVER option for the DATA FEDERATOR SERVER (see Figure 4.37).

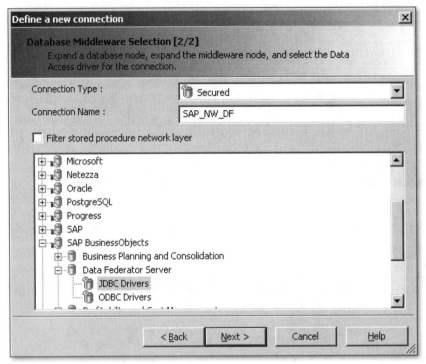

Figure 4.37 Define a New Connection

9. Click NEXT.

10. In the next screen, enter the Data Federator user we created during the installation (see Figure 4.38).

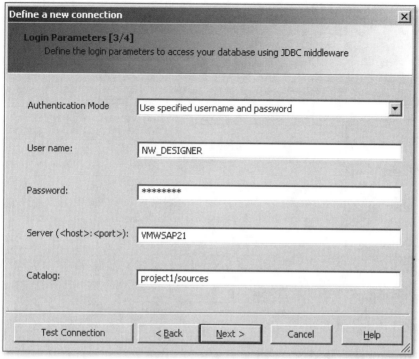

Figure 4.38 Define a New Connection

11. Enter the hostname of the Data Federator query server.

12. Enter the name of the CATALOG. The syntax follows the logic <Name of deployed project>/sources.

Authentication Mode

You can select between the Authentication mode USE SPECIFIED USERNAME AND PASS-WORD or the option USE BUSINESSOBJECTS CREDENTIAL MAPPING. In case you want to configure the connection with BusinessObjects credential mapping you need to logon to the Universe designer with the BusinessObjects Enterprise credentials with the mapped Data Federator credentials in place.

---

13. Click NEXT.

14. Click FINISH (see Figure 4.39).

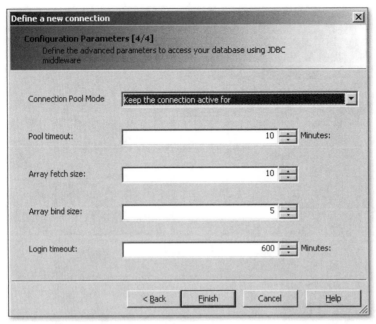

Figure 4.39 Configuration Parameters

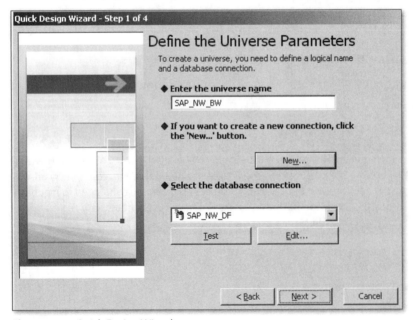

Figure 4.40 Quick Design Wizard

15. You're back at the QUICK DESIGN WIZARD. Continue the process by clicking NEXT (see Figure 4.40).

16. Set the OBJECT STRATEGY and JOIN STRATEGY to the value DATA FEDERATOR STRATEGY (see Figure 4.41).

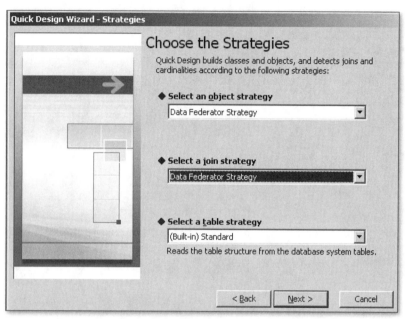

Figure 4.41 Quick Design Wizard — Strategies

17. Click NEXT.

18. Now you are presented with a list of classes, dimensions, and detail objects and you can decide what you want to include into your Universe (see Figure 4.42).

19. Select all of the objects and use the ADD button to move them to the UNIVERSE CLASSES AND OBJECTS list box (see Figure 4.43).

20. Click NEXT.

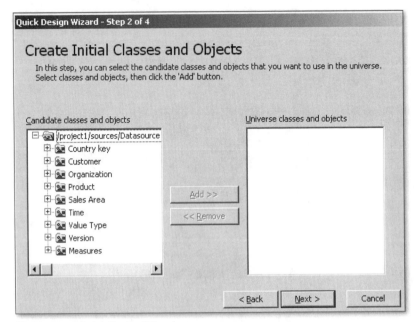

Figure 4.42 Quick Design Wizard

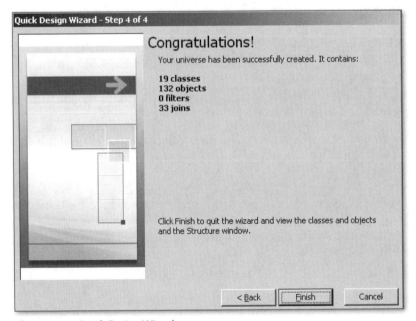

Figure 4.43 Quick Design Wizard

21. Click FINISH.

22. The Universe and the table schema for the selected InfoProvider appear (see Figure 4.44).

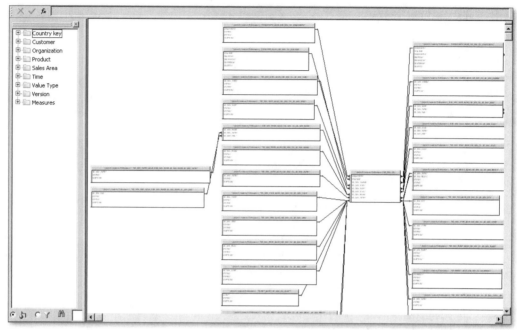

Figure 4.44 Relational Universe

23. Follow the FILE • EXPORT menu path to save and export your Universe to the SAP BusinessObjects Enterprise system.

After you export the Universe to the SAP BusinessObjects Enterprise system, we can create a Web Intelligence report based on this Universe. But before doing so, let's look at some customizations for our newly created Universe.

4.3.8 Customize Your Relational Universe

In this section, we'll create some objects based on the Data Federator approach that are not part of your basic Universe. We will create a calculation, a prompt, and a custom hierarchy.

Creating a Calculation

1. In the Universe designer, open the Universe we created in the previous section.

2. Open the MEASURES class in the Universe (see Figure 4.45).

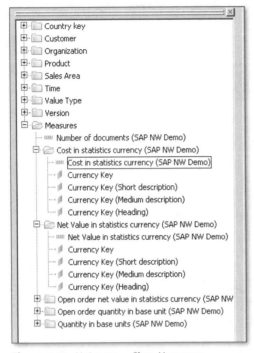

Figure 4.45 Universe — Class Measures

In our Universe, we obtained the COST IN STATISTICS CURRENCY (SAP NW DEMO) and NET VALUE IN STATISTICS CURRENCY (SAP NW DEMO) key figures. Now let's create a calculation for the Margin and the Margin in percent.

3. Navigate to the MEASURES class.

4. Follow the menu path: INSERT • OBJECT (see Figure 4.46).

5. Enter `Net Sales - Costs` as the NAME of the new measure.

6. Set the TYPE to NUMBER.

7. Click the button next to the SELECT area to start the editor.

8. Use the objects in the CLASSES AND OBJECTS list box to create a new calculation that subtracts costs from net value (see Figure 4.47).

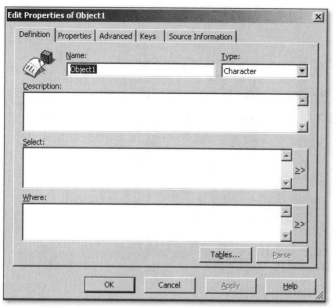

Figure 4.46 Object Properties

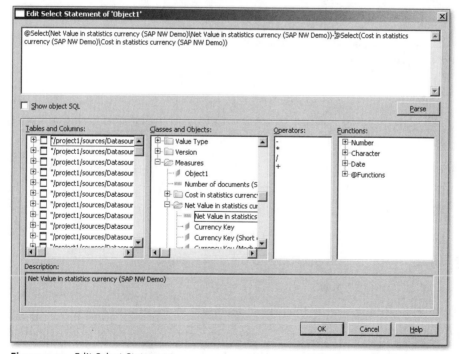

Figure 4.47 Edit Select Statement

9. Click OK.

10. Navigate to the PROPERTIES tab.

11. Select MEASURE as the QUALIFICATION (see Figure 4.48).

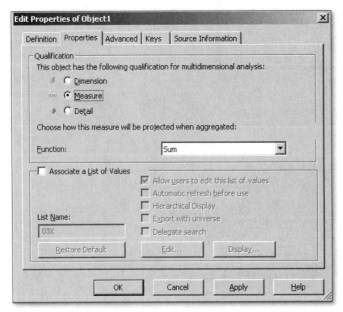

Figure 4.48 Edit Properties

12. Click OK.

13. The newly created measure is now part of the Universe and is shown in the MEASURES class (see Figure 4.49).

14. Save the changes to your Universe and export it to the SAP BusinessObjects Enterprise system.

15. Navigate to the MEASURES class.

16. Follow the menu path: INSERT • OBJECT.

17. Enter `Margin in %` as the NAME of the new measure.

18. Set the TYPE to NUMBER.

19. Click the button next to the SELECT definition to start the editor.

20. Use the objects in the CLASSES AND OBJECTS list box to create a new calculation that calculates the percentage value of the costs in relation to NET SALES.

Figure 4.49 Universe with Custom Measure

21. Click OK.

22. Navigate to the Properties tab.

23. Select Measure as the Qualification (see Figure 4.50).

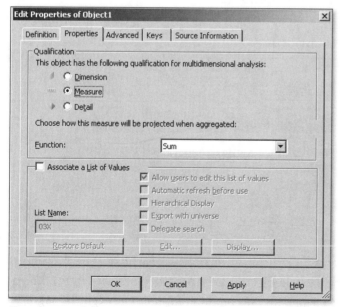

Figure 4.50 Edit Properties

24. Click OK.

25. Save the changes to your Universe and export it to the SAP BusinessObjects Enterprise system.

You have created two custom measures as part of your Universe and you can use them in Web Intelligence as part of your report.

Creating a Prompt

In this section, we'll create a prompt as part of our Universe so that the user can select a value and filter the data shown in the report. Creating a prompt in a relational Universe follows the same logic as in an OLAP Universe, which we described in Section 4.3.6, Customize Your OLAP Universe. We will create a condition in the Universe and leverage the @Prompt function to ask the user for a value.

1. In the Universe designer, with the previously created relational Universe open, navigate to COUNTRY KEY class folder.

   In our example, we want to create a predefined filter/condition with a prompt for the COUNTRY dimension object.

2. Follow the menu path: INSERT • CONDITION.

   The properties dialog for the new condition appears and you can prompt the editor for the WHERE clause of the CONDITION.

3. The @Prompt function follows the syntax shown here:

```
@Prompt('message','type',[lov],Mono|Multi,
free|constrained|primary_key,persistent|not_persistent,
[default_values])
```

   For our example, this results in the syntax shown here:

```
@Prompt('Please select a Country','A','Country key\Country (SAP NW
Demo)',multi,constrained,not_persistent)
```

   This syntax allows the user to select multiple values from a list, which is based on the COUNTRY dimension object.

4. You can use the elements in the CLASSES AND OBJECTS list box to ease the process of creating the syntax. Double-click on the COUNTRY (SAP NW DEMO) dimension object to add the element to the condition formula (see Figure 4.51).

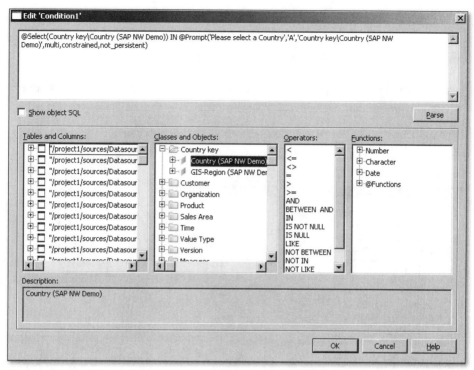

Figure 4.51 Condition Editor

5. Add the previously shown `@Prompt` syntax to the formula with the word `IN` in front of the `@Prompt` syntax. Your complete syntax should look similar to the following:

```
@Select(Country key\Country (SAP NW Demo)) IN @Prompt('Please select
a Country','A','Country key\Country (SAP NW
Demo)',multi,constrained,not_persistent)
```

6. Click OK to close the editor.

7. Click OK to close the object properties.

8. Save the changes to your Universe and export it to the SAP BusinessObjects Enterprise system.

9. You have now added a filter that also includes a prompt for the COUNTRY dimension object to your Universe, which lets the user select one or more values to restrict data volume.

Creating Custom Hierarchy

In the next step, we'll create a custom hierarchy as part of our Universe so that we can use it as part of our Web Intelligence report.

1. In the Universe designer, with the previously created relational Universe open, follow to the menu path: Tools • Hierarchies.

2. The Hierarchies Editor is shown. On the left side you can see the default hierarchies and on the right side the custom hierarchies (see Figure 4.52).

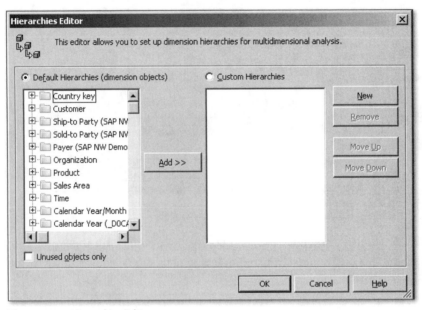

Figure 4.52 Hierarchies Editor

3. Click New to create a new custom hierarchy top-level folder.

4. Enter `Custom Hierarchy` as the Name of your new hierarchy.

5. Now you can select dimension objects from the left side and make them members of your new hierarchy. In our example, we will add (see Figure 4.53):

    ▸ Country (SAP NW Demo)

    ▸ Sales Organization (SAP NW Demo)

    ▸ Division (SAP NW Demo).

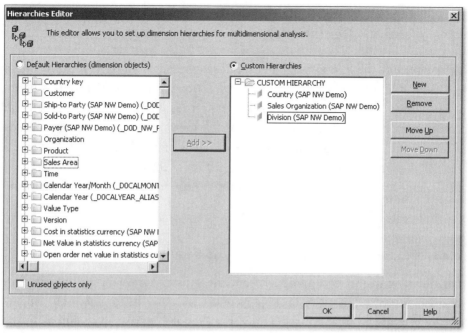

Figure 4.53 Hierarchies Editor

6. Click OK.

7. Save the changes to your Universe and export it to the SAP BusinessObjects Enterprise system.

You have created a custom hierarchy as part of your Universe and now you can leverage it as part of your Web Intelligence report.

In this section, you learned how you can use a relational Universe and an OLAP Universe to provide the metadata of your SAP landscape to Web Intelligence. You not only learned which elements are available in these Universes, but you also customized the Universes and created your own objects.

4.4 Customer Case Study — Ad Hoc Query and Analysis Requirements

In this section, we'll look into the overall requirements and see which of those we can fulfill with the ad hoc reporting tool Web Intelligence. Up to this point, we've learned the different options for data retrieval for Web Intelligence in an SAP landscape and we learned how we can use the Universe as a semantic layer to offer our end users a more business-oriented view of our data sources. Now we'll look at the requirements one by one and list those that we can't fulfill based on the overall list of requirements in Chapter 2, Section 2.2.1, Financial Reporting and Analysis Requirements.

4.4.1 Financial Reporting and Analysis Requirements

Let's start with the requirements from the financial area. From the previous chapter, we know that Crystal Reports is a very good fit for the requirements from the financial area. We also know that Crystal Reports can't fulfill all of the requirements. The following is a list of requirements that we can't fulfill with Web Intelligence:

Unfulfilled Financial Reporting Requirement

▶ For specific content (such as an income statement or a balance sheet) that's being created, the design needs to be layout focused with the actual print of the report a very high priority.

▶ The reporting and analysis tools need to allow the use of hierarchies and navigation along those hierarchies in the actual content.

As you can see, we have two main requirements that we can't fulfill with Web Intelligence. The first requirement on our list, the focus on the layout of the report, is not a surprise because a detailed layout is not the strength and focus of Web Intelligence. The second requirement, the usage of hierarchies, is listed because it is also not a major strength of Web Intelligence. Several enhancements have been made in the BusinessObjects XI 3.1 Service Pack 2 Release to improve the handling of hierarchies and the navigation within hierarchies in the report, but hierarchy handling is always a topic that needs to be carefully considered when selecting a reporting tool for your end users. We'll use a hierarchical report for the financial area in a later section so that you can learn these new enhancements.

Looking at these two requirements, you already know that the first requirement — layout-based reporting — is better suited for Crystal Reports. The second requirement — the navigation along hierarchies — is better suited for Pioneer.

4.4.2 Sales Reporting and Analysis Requirements

Next, we're going to look at all of the requirements from our sales area and see which ones we can't fulfill. The following represents the requirements that we can't fulfill:

> **Unfulfilled Sales Reporting Requirements**
>
> ▸ Users should be able to perform scenario-based analysis, where the user can see the data and influence certain factors to see their impact on the overall numbers, for example, a what-if analysis in a sales planning workflow.

As you can see, only one requirement from the sales area is listed as a requirement that we can't fulfill. All of the other requirements can be fulfilled with Web Intelligence. It should not be a surprise that the requirement to create a what-if analysis is listed; such a requirement is more suited by far for a data visualization created with Xcelsius, which we'll see in a later chapter.

4.4.3 Human Resource (HR) Reporting and Analysis Requirements

For the HR area, the following represents a list of requirements that Web Intelligence can't fulfill:

> **Unfulfilled HR Reporting Requirements**
>
> ▸ The content needs to present highly textual information in a layout-focused format.
> ▸ Some of the content (such as employee appraisals or performance reviews) will be used as official documents and therefore need to follow strict layout rules.

It's clear that the requirements regarding the layout and textual information — similar to the requirements from the financial area — are better suited for Crystal Reports. It is important, especially for the HR area, that these requirements are fully met and that the reports can be used as actual paper-based documents (for example, appraisal documents). Web Intelligence is capable of creating a report that will provide the necessary information, but Crystal Reports is much more suited for such a requirement.

4.4.4 Executive Leadership and Management Reporting and Analysis Requirements

The following requirements from the list for our leadership and management team are not the best suited for Web Intelligence:

> **Unfulfilled Executive Leadership and Management Reporting Requirements**
>
> ► The data needs to be shown in a highly visualized manner and the main Key Performance Indicators (KPIs) need to be presented in a single dashboard.
> ► The reports and analytics need to be easy to use and critical information needs to be easily identifiable.

The two main requirements that are not best suited for Web Intelligence are the request for a highly visualized reporting solution and the request to easily identify critical KPIs. With regard to the second, we would like to add a little bit more context, as Web Intelligence offers a great user experience and is a tool end users can learn very fast. The reason why the requirement is listed here is not because Web Intelligence is a difficult tool to use or not capable of offering highlighting or alerts as part of a report. The reasoning is the combination of highly visualized data and easily identifiable information with an executive and leadership management team audience.

If the audience were business analysts, Web Intelligence would be a great fit. However, because our audience is an executive and leadership team, this requirement is better satisfied by using Xcelsius to create an executive overview dashboard.

Web Intelligence could provide pretty much the same information, but it could become an "overload" on the tool side for an audience that needs critical information in a simple and easy-to-use manner.

Before we go into more detail and create a report to fulfill these requirements, let's look at some basic steps in Web Intelligence so that you can gain a basic understanding and overview of the tool.

4.5   Web Intelligence — Quick Basics

Similar to the approach for Enterprise Reporting, we'll first provide you with an overview of the basic functionality of Web Intelligence before we create the reports and analytics to fulfill our requirements.

4.5.1   Creating Your First Web Intelligence Report

Before we start a new Web Intelligence report based on the OLAP Universe we created and customized in the previous section, we need to look at some of the settings and preferences you can select as part of your user profile.

1. Launch InfoView via the menu path START • PROGRAMS • BUSINESSOBJECTS XI 3.1 • BUSINESSOBJECTS ENTERPRISE • BUSINESSOBJECTS ENTERPRISE JAVA INFOVIEW (see Figure 4.54).

2. As an alternative, you can enter the following URL directly into your browser: *http://<servername>:<port>/InfoViewApp*. The <servername> placeholder needs to be replaced with the name of your application server that is being used for BusinessObjects Enterprise and the <port> placeholder with the corresponding port.

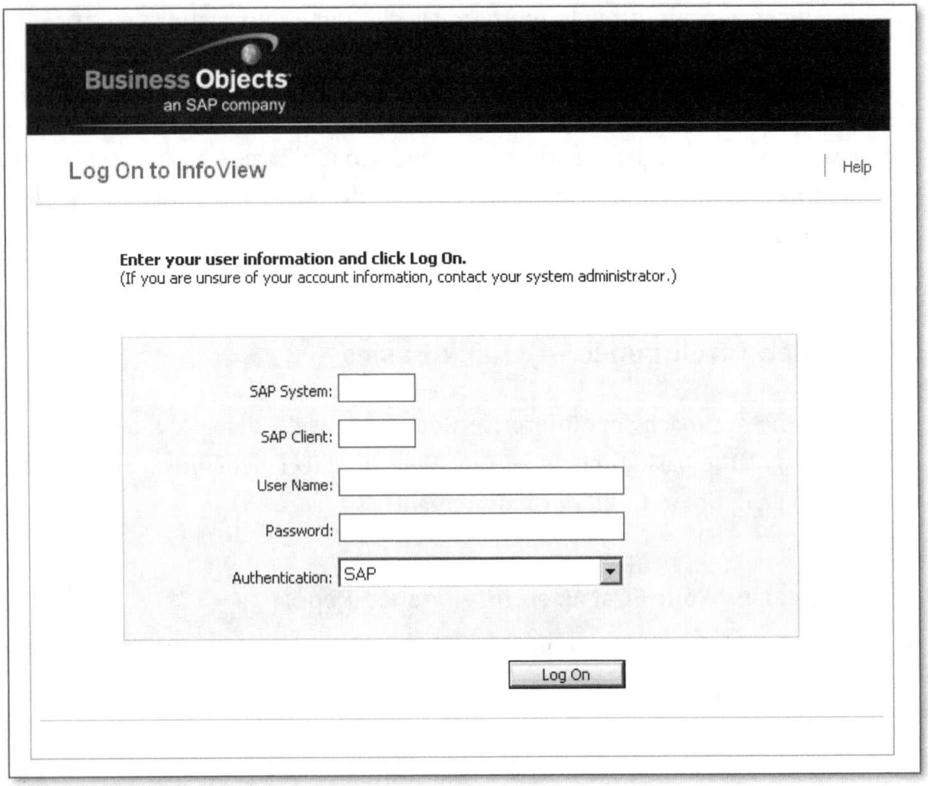

Figure 4.54 InfoView Logon Page

3. Use your SAP credentials to authenticate for the SAP system. Keep in mind that this requires the SAP authentication to be configured for your BusinessObjects Enterprise system. If the SAP authentication has not been configured, you can continue with the exercise using the Enterprise authentication, but you will not be able to use SSO.

4. After authentication, you are presented with the standard entry page for Info-View (see Figure 4.55).

5. Select the PREFERENCES option.

6. In the first screen of the PREFERENCES, close the GENERAL section by clicking on the small triangle next to GENERAL.

7. Open the WEB INTELLIGENCE section (see Figure 4.56).

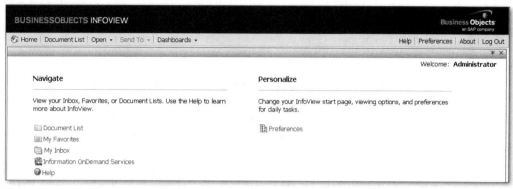

Figure 4.55 InfoView Start Page

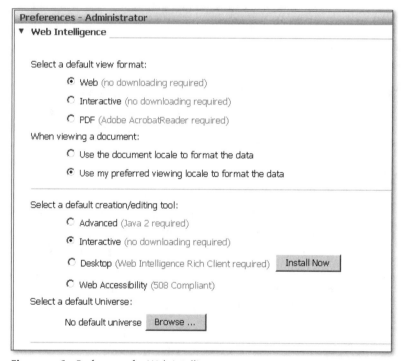

Figure 4.56 Preferences for Web Intelligence

8. As part of your user preferences you can select a default view format and a default creation/editing tool for Web Intelligence. Table 4.7 and Table 4.8 list more details on the different options.

Web Intelligence View Format	Details
Web	This option lets you view and print Web Intelligence documents. You can respond to prompts and perform drill operations.
Interactive	With the Interactive option you can view and print the Web Intelligence report. You can leverage filters, sorting, and calculations, and format objects in the report.
PDF	With this option, you can respond to prompts, view the document, and print the document.

Table 4.7 Web Intelligence View Formats

Web Intelligence Creation Tool	Details
Advanced	The Advanced editing tool is a Java-based reporting panel that lets you create and edit reports and underlying queries. With this option, you can also leverage multiple data sources, combine queries, and rank your data. This option offers you the most functionality.
Interactive	The Interactive option is an HTML-based query panel that lets you create and edit queries and documents.
Desktop	The Desktop option lets you download Web Intelligence Rich Clients and work in an offline environment.
Web Accessibility	The Web Accessibility option provides you with a step-by-step approach and lets you create a Web Intelligence document based on a single data source.

Table 4.8 Web Intelligence Creation and Editing Tools

9. For our activities, we'll use INTERACTIVE as the VIEW FORMAT and ADVANCED as the option to create new Web Intelligence reports (see Figure 4.57).

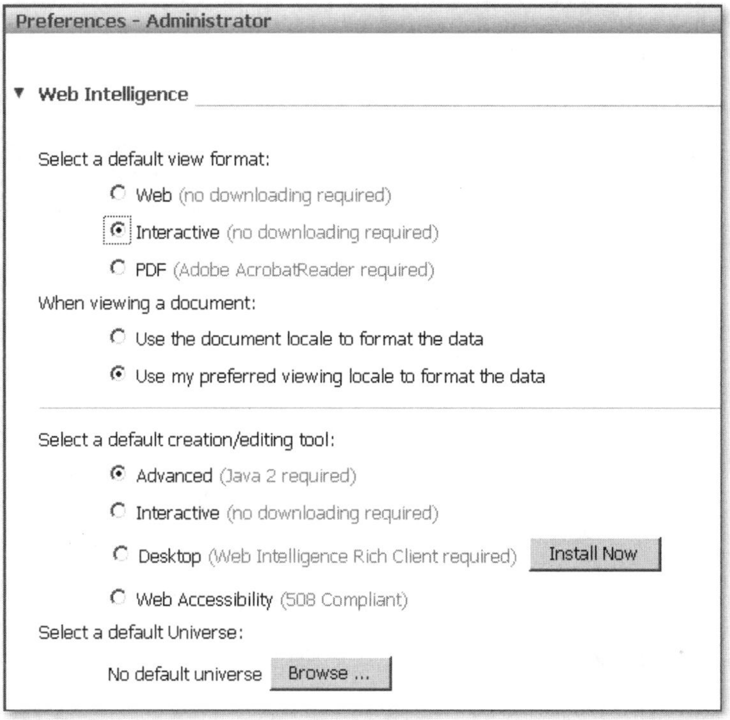

Figure 4.57 Web Intelligence Preferences

10. Click OK and you will be returned to the InfoView start page.

11. Click on DOCUMENT LIST.

12. You will be shown a folder structure and you can browse your Business-Objects Enterprise system for content.

13. In addition, you can now use the NEW menu to create a new Web Intelligence document.

14. Follow the menu path: NEW • WEB INTELLIGENCE DOCUMENT.

15. You will be presented with a list of Universes. Select the Universe we created in the previous section.

16. Because we chose the ADVANCED option for the creating and editing tool, we'll be asked to install Java components if this is the first time you are using Web Intelligence.

17. When the installation is finished, you will be presented with the Web Intelligence query panel (see Figure 4.58).

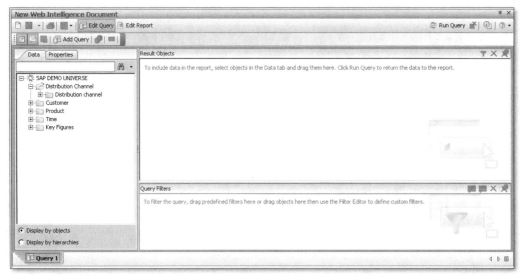

Figure 4.58 Web Intelligence Query Panel

18. The query panel consists of three major areas:

  ▶ The DATA and PROPERTIES panel provides you with the objects from your Universe.

  ▶ The RESULT OBJECTS panel, where you can include objects that you would like to offer to your end users and leverage in your report.

  ▶ The QUERY FILTERS panel, where you can — in addition to prompts in the Universe — create fixed filters and prompts for your report.

  In addition, you can see the two main views where you can use the EDIT QUERY button to influence data retrieval and the EDIT REPORT button, where you can create and edit the actual Web Intelligence report.

19. Add the following items to the RESULT OBJECTS panel: (see Figure 4.59)

  ▶ L01 REGION CODE

  ▶ L01 DISTRIBUTION CHANNEL

  ▶ L01 PRODUCT GROUP KEY

- L01 Product group

- L01 Product Key

- L01 Product

- L01 Calendar Year

- L01 Calendar month Key

- L01 Calendar month

- Billed Quantity

- Billed Quantity Plan

- Billed Quantity Variance

- Sales Plan

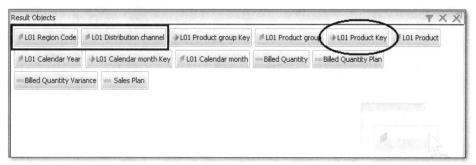

Figure 4.59   Result Objects

Detail Objects and Dimension Objects

In the Universe, the dimension objects (blue square symbol, surrounded by a box) represent, by default, the description of the characteristic and the detail objects (green diamond symbol, surrounded by an oval) represent the key value. It is especially important in cases where you would like to sort or group — like the Calendar month in our example — to include the key value to make sure you are sorting properly.

20. Click Run Query in the toolbar.

21. Because our BW query contains variables, we will be presented with a prompt dialog. In the dialog we can see that the prompts are optional and that we can click the Run Query button without providing any values (see Figure 4.60).

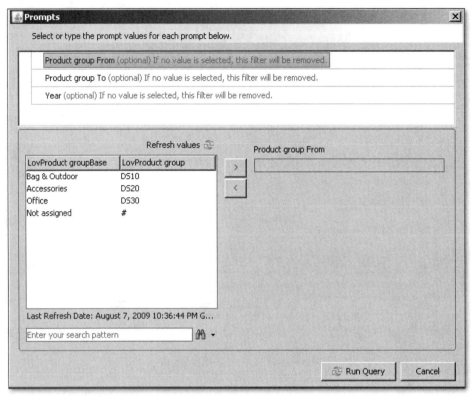

Figure 4.60 Web Intelligence Prompt Dialog

22. The query will be processed and because we didn't create a specific report layout a default table with all columns is presented to us.

23. Click RUN QUERY.

24. Because we didn't define any specific report layout, Web Intelligence gives us with a standard table that includes all of the columns that we included in the result objects (see Figure 4.61).

25. On the left side of your report, you can see the DATA panel and several others that you can leverage to change your report (see Figure 4.62).

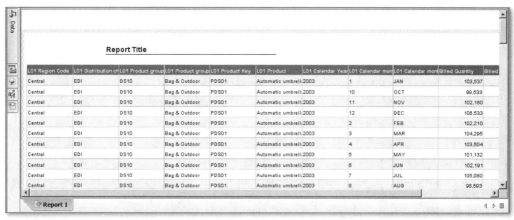

Figure 4.61 Web Intelligence Report

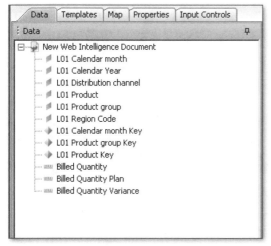

Figure 4.62 Data Panel

26. The DATA tab provides access to the elements of our query; the TEMPLATES tab lets you create tables, charts, and other elements; the MAP tab lets you navigate in the report; the PROPERTIES tab provides the properties for the selected object; and the INPUT CONTROLS tab lets you create items, like a list box, for elements of your report.

27. Make sure you can see the panel with the DATA tab selected.

28. Drag and drop the following column headers onto the DATA tab:

   ▶ L01 PRODUCT GROUP KEY

   ▶ L01 PRODUCT GROUP

   ▶ L01 PRODUCT KEY

   ▶ L01 PRODUCT

   ▶ L01 CALENDAR MONTH

   By dragging and dropping them onto the DATA tab you are removing the objects from the report. Keep in mind that the data is still collected, because the objects are part of your result object in the query panel (see Figure 4.63).

Report Title

L01 Region Code	L01 Distribution channe	L01 Calendar Year	L01 Calendar mon	L01 Calendar month	Billed Quantity	Billed Quantity Pla	Billed Quantity Variance
Central	EDI	2003	1	JAN	#TOREFRESH	5,974,659	#TOREFRESH
Central	EDI	2003	10	OCT	#TOREFRESH	5,705,640	#TOREFRESH
Central	EDI	2003	11	NOV	#TOREFRESH	4,656,874	#TOREFRESH
Central	EDI	2003	12	DEC	#TOREFRESH	4,878,449	#TOREFRESH
Central	EDI	2003	2	FEB	#TOREFRESH	5,825,700	#TOREFRESH
Central	EDI	2003	3	MAR	#TOREFRESH	6,014,092	#TOREFRESH
Central	EDI	2003	4	APR	#TOREFRESH	5,994,876	#TOREFRESH
Central	EDI	2003	5	MAY	#TOREFRESH	5,836,313	#TOREFRESH
Central	EDI	2003	6	JUN	#TOREFRESH	5,768,540	#TOREFRESH
Central	EDI	2003	7	JUL	#TOREFRESH	5,947,354	#TOREFRESH
Central	EDI	2003	8	AUG	#TOREFRESH	5,702,121	#TOREFRESH

Figure 4.63 Web Intelligence Report

29. You should now see that the custom calculation we created — BILLED QUANTITY VARIANCE — and the value for BILLED QUANTITY show the #TOREFRESH string.

30. We configured both of these key figures to be database-delegated key figures, which means that when you change the level of aggregation in your report (we removed PRODUCT GROUP and PRODUCT), Web Intelligence needs to receive the correct aggregated numbers from the underlying source system.

31. Click REFRESH DATA in the toolbar and refresh your report (see Figure 4.64).

Report Title							
L01 Region Code	L01 Distribution channel	L01 Calendar Year	L01 Calendar mont	L01 Calendar month	Billed Quantity	Billed Quantity Pla	Billed Quantity Variance
Central	EDI	2003	1	JAN	4,334,174	5,974,659	0.73
Central	EDI	2003	10	OCT	4,139,021	5,705,640	0.73
Central	EDI	2003	11	NOV	3,378,218	4,656,874	0.73
Central	EDI	2003	12	DEC	3,538,954	4,878,449	0.73
Central	EDI	2003	2	FEB	4,226,114	5,825,700	0.73
Central	EDI	2003	3	MAR	4,362,779	6,014,092	0.73
Central	EDI	2003	4	APR	4,348,841	5,994,876	0.73
Central	EDI	2003	5	MAY	4,233,814	5,836,313	0.73
Central	EDI	2003	6	JUN	4,184,649	5,768,540	0.73
Central	EDI	2003	7	JUL	4,314,366	5,947,354	0.73
Central	EDI	2003	8	AUG	4,136,467	5,702,121	0.73

Figure 4.64   Web Intelligence Report

32. Right-click the Billed Quantity Variance column and select Format Number.

33. Select Number as the Format type, scroll down the list of predefined options, and use the percentage format type (see Figure 4.65).

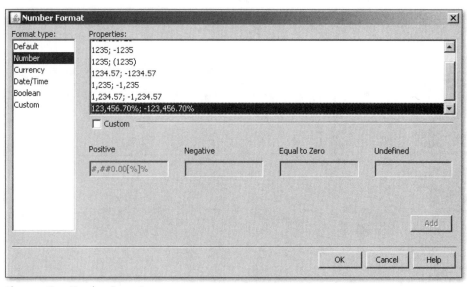

Figure 4.65   Number Format

34. Click OK.

> **Query Panel vs. Report Object**
>
> It is important to understand that Web Intelligence retrieves data based on the result objects defined in the underlying query. Even though you might only use a small part of the selected objects from the result objects in your report, the query will ask for all of the elements and data based on the defined list of objects in the result objects panel. It may be easier to remember by using the typical SAP Business Explorer terms, so remember that Web Intelligence does not have Free Characteristics that are leveraged on demand.

4.5.2 Using Filter and Prompts

So far, we have created a very basic table output from our underlying Universe. Let's build on this and leverage the filter and prompts that we created during the Universe customization.

1. Click EDIT QUERY in the toolbar.

2. Navigate to the CALENDAR MONTH class.

3. Drag and drop the QUARTER 1 filter that we created to the QUERY FILTER panel (see Figure 4.66).

Figure 4.66 Web Intelligence Query Panel

4. The QUARTER 1 filter object will limit the result set to the first three months of the selected year.

5. Click RUN QUERY and verify the filtered data in our example. You should only see data for the first three months — regardless of the calendar year.

6. Click EDIT QUERY in the toolbar.

7. Navigate to the CALENDAR MONTH class.

8. Remove the QUARTER 1 filter from the QUERY FILTER panel.

9. Drag and drop the QUARTER SELECTION WITH PROMPT filter to the QUERY FILTER panel. This filter includes two prompts asking for a start and an end month for the time interval.

10. Click RUN QUERY.

11. You will be prompted for the new time frame and asked to provide a starting and ending month (see Figure 4.67).

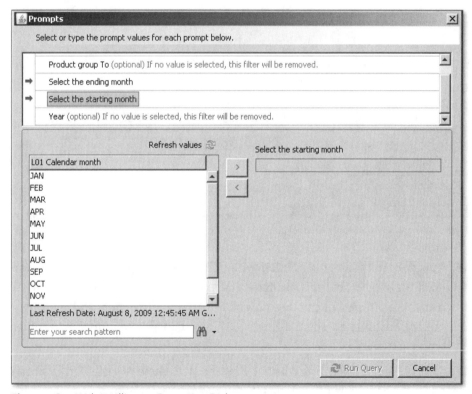

Figure 4.67 Web Intelligence Prompting Dialog

12. Select a time frame and click Run Query. You should now only see data for the selected time frame — regardless of the year.

13. Click Edit Query.

14. Remove the Quarter Selection with Prompt filter from the Query Filter panel.

15. Drag and drop the L01 Calendar month dimension object to the Query Filters panel (see Figure 4.68).

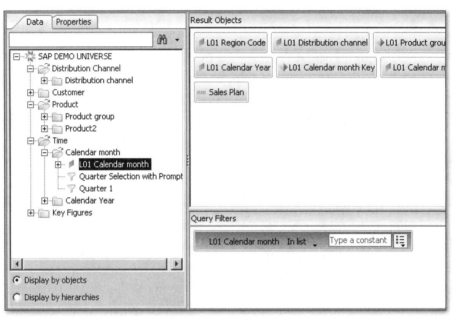

Figure 4.68 Web Intelligence Query Panel

16. Now we can create either a filter with a fixed list of values or a prompt. The main difference between the filter and prompt options we used before is, that the filter we are creating now is a filter for this report and the previous options were based on a Universe, which makes them reusable for other reports as well.

17. Click on the operator list, which, by default, will show In list. Here, you can select a broad range of operators. Select the Between option.

18. Now click on the properties symbol next to the value field (see Figure 4.69).

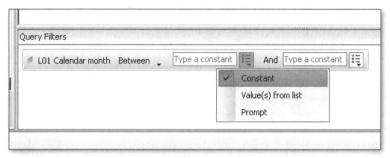

Figure 4.69   Query Filter Panel

19. Here, you can enter a constant value, select a value from the list, or create a prompt, which then lets the end user select a value.

20. Select the PROMPT option for the start and end value.

21. Now click on the 2 icon to configure the prompt options.

22. Configure both prompts as shown in Figure 4.70.

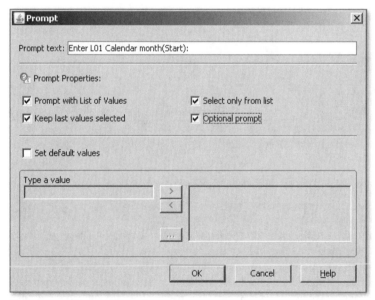

Figure 4.70   Prompt Properties

23. After you configure both prompts, click RUN QUERY to refresh your report.

24. You will be prompted with a list of values to select a starting and ending calendar month, but you can leave the values empty because we configured the prompt to be optional (see Figure 4.71).

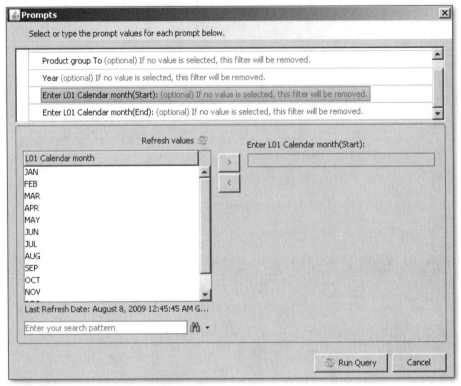

Figure 4.71 Web Intelligence Prompt Dialog

25. Click RUN QUERY to see the result of your report.

Prompts, Filters, and Index Awareness

When creating custom prompts, either in the Universe or in a Web Intelligence query panel, it is important to make sure that index awareness is leveraged in the Universe, otherwise you will send string descriptions as filter values to the underlying SAP NetWeaver BW system. Those string values then have to be resolved to key values, which is expensive with regard to performance, or even worse, the string values are language dependent and the filter might fail.

> ### Filtering in the Web Intelligence Report
>
> In addition to the options shown to filter the data, you can also leverage the Filter panel ⊞ and the Report Filter panel ⧉ from the toolbar when creating, editing, or viewing a report. Both options let you create filters based on the query.
>
> Starting with BusinessObjects XI 3.1 Service Pack 2, you can also leverage Input controls in your report to offer filtering.

4.5.3 Arranging Objects

Up to this point, we created a report that consists of a single table. In the following steps, we'll look at how to leverage different objects in a single report, how to ensure they are aligned, and how to influence the properties of the objects.

1. We'll continue using our report from the previous sections (see Figure 4.72).

					Billed Quantity	Billed Quantity Pla	Billed Quantity Variance
LO1 Region Code	LO1 Distribution channe	LO1 Calendar Year	LO1 Calendar mon	LO1 Calendar month			
Central	EDI	2003	1	JAN	4,334,174	5,974,659	72.54%
Central	EDI	2003	10	OCT	4,139,021	5,705,640	72.54%
Central	EDI	2003	11	NOV	3,378,218	4,656,874	72.54%
Central	EDI	2003	12	DEC	3,538,954	4,878,449	72.54%
Central	EDI	2003	2	FEB	4,226,114	5,825,700	72.54%
Central	EDI	2003	3	MAR	4,362,779	6,014,092	72.54%
Central	EDI	2003	4	APR	4,348,841	5,994,876	72.54%
Central	EDI	2003	5	MAY	4,233,814	5,836,313	72.54%
Central	EDI	2003	6	JUN	4,184,649	5,768,540	72.54%
Central	EDI	2003	7	JUL	4,314,366	5,947,354	72.54%
Central	EDI	2003	8	AUG	4,136,467	5,702,121	72.54%

Figure 4.72 Web Intelligence Report

2. Remove the REGION column from your table by dragging and dropping the column header to the DATA panel on the left side.

3. Remove the description for the CALENDAR MONTH from your table by dragging and dropping the column header to the DATA panel on the left side.

4. Navigate to the TEMPLATES tab (see Figure 4.73).

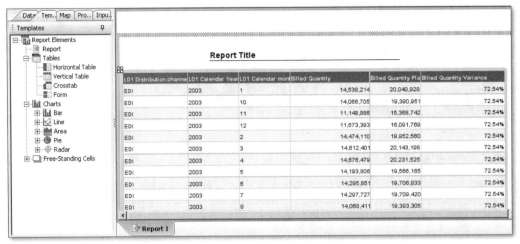

Figure 4.73 Templates

5. Drag and drop a CROSSTAB from the list of available templates on top of your table.

6. Your table is automatically turned into a cross tab report (see Figure 4.74).

	EDI 2003			EDI 2004			EDI 2005
1	14,538,214	20,040,928	72.54%	11,149,065	15,368,984	72.54%	14,538,214
10	14,066,705	19,390,951	72.54%	11,420,771	15,743,532	72.54%	14,066,705
11	11,148,886	15,368,742	72.54%	11,218,119	15,464,177	72.54%	11,148,886
12	11,673,393	16,091,769	72.54%	11,209,651	15,452,505	72.54%	11,673,393
2	14,474,110	19,952,560	72.54%	11,154,523	15,376,512	72.54%	14,474,110
3	14,612,401	20,143,198	72.54%	11,249,626	15,507,609	72.54%	14,612,401
4	14,676,479	20,231,525	72.54%	11,269,966	15,535,648	72.54%	14,676,479
5	14,193,806	19,566,165	72.54%	11,193,150	15,429,761	72.54%	14,193,806
6	14,295,851	19,706,833	72.54%	11,354,313	15,651,923	72.54%	14,295,851
7	14,297,727	19,709,420	72.54%	11,235,498	15,488,134	72.54%	14,297,727

Figure 4.74 Web Intelligence Crosstab

7. Remove the CALENDAR YEAR from the cross tab by dragging the column header outside of the report.

8. Remove the BILLED QUANTITY PLAN and BILLED QUANTITY VARIANCE key figures the same way.

As you can see, the calendar month is sorted based on a string, which is based on the fact that the data type NUMC from SAP NetWeaver BW is supported as a string (see Table 4.2). Because of this, we need to create a formula that converts the string to a number so that we then can sort the calendar month properly.

9. Click on the VARIABLE EDITOR icon in the toolbar.

10. Create a new formula according to Figure 4.75.

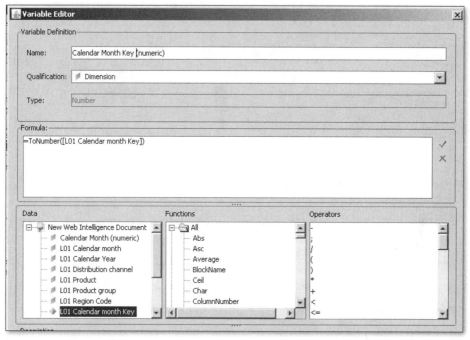

Figure 4.75 Variable Editor

11. Enter `Calendar Month KEY (numeric)` as the NAME and enter the following syntax as the FORMULA:

```
=ToNumber([L01 Calendar month key])
```

You can also use the listed objects and functions by double-clicking.

12. Click OK.

13. The new object will be listed in the DATA panel. Drag and drop the new object on top of the CALENDAR MONTH in the cross tab.

14. Now drag a BAR CHART from the TEMPLATE panel next to your cross tab (see Figure 4.76).

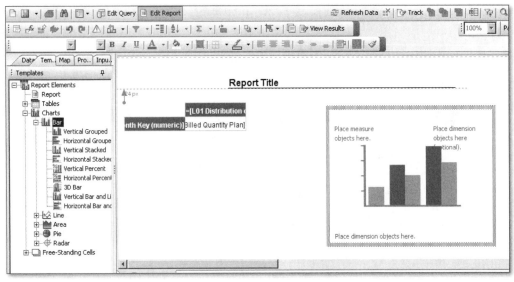

Figure 4.76 Structure of Our Web Intelligence Report

15. The report is shown in the structural view and we can now drag and drop objects from the DATA panel to the required objects for the chart.

16. Drag the L01 CALENDAR YEAR dimension object to the chart as a dimension object and drag the BILLED QUANTITY to the chart as a measure object.

17. In the structural view, right-click on the chart and follow the menu path: ALIGN • RELATIVE POSITION.

18. Set the values according to Figure 4.77. This way, the chart will always be shown on the top right hand of the cross tab, even when the number of distribution channel grows.

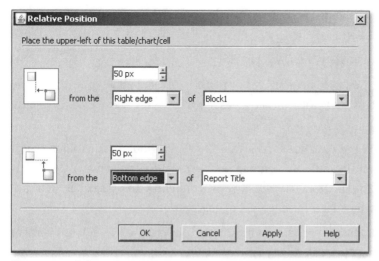

Figure 4.77 Relative Position

19. Click OK.

20. Click the VIEW RESULTS button in the toolbar; because you only changed the structure of the report there is no need to refresh the data of the report.

21. Using the PROPERTIES panel, you can now customize the chart.

Identifying Report Elements

If you are not sure what the identification of the report part that you selected is (for example Block1 for the crosstab in our report), there are two ways to find out:

▶ You can select the object in the report structure and the identity will be shown in the top-right corner.

▶ You can select the object, view the PROPERTIES panel, and look at the top entry called NAME.

4.5.4 Using Breaks, Sections, and Summaries

So far, our report shows a table and a chart without any groupings or summaries. In the next couple of steps, we'll continue using our report and create sections and summaries.

1. Our report shows the BILLED QUANTITY in a cross tab by CALENDAR MONTH and DISTRIBUTION CHANNEL.

2. Make sure you can view the DATA panel.

3. Drag and drop the L01 Calendar Year dimension object below your report title but above the cross tab. You will see a little tooltip saying DROP HERE TO CREATE A SECTION.

4. By just dragging the CALENDAR YEAR into the report you grouped your report based on the year. In addition, you will notice that the chart is now empty. This is because the BILLED QUANTITY key figure is configured to be database delegated and you now need a different level of aggregation.

5. Click REFRESH DATA and the chart will appear. Your cross tab and your chart are now showing data per Calendar year (see Figure 4.78).

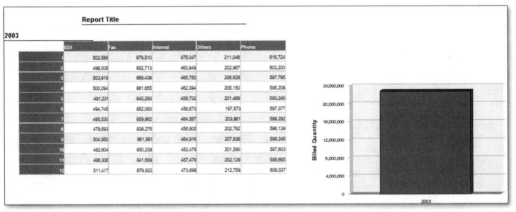

Figure 4.78 Web Intelligence Report

6. Now take a look at the MAP tab next to the DATA panel. For each section entry you will find an entry that the end user can use to navigate in the report (see Figure 4.79).

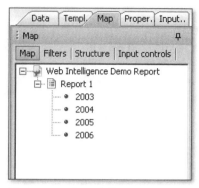

Figure 4.79 Report Map

7. Now drag and drop the L01 Region Code dimension object in front of the Calendar month column of your cross tab (see Figure 4.80).

Report Title				
2003				
		EDI	Fax	Internet	O
Central	1	142,726	242,897	138,321	
Central	2	140,896	241,542	136,578	
Central	3	143,771	241,061	137,982	
Central	4	142,680	239,586	132,292	
Central	5	139,410	234,078	136,360	
Central	6	140,870	235,952	133,308	
Central	7	144,853	239,827	138,855	
Central	8	135,910	231,169	132,463	
Central	9	142,872	242,635	135,799	
Central	10	137,206	235,751	131,011	
Central	11	140,828	233,952	135,435	

Figure 4.80 Web Intelligence Report

8. Select the column for L01 REGION CODE.

9. Use the INSERT/REMOVE BREAK ⊟ button from the toolbar to create a break per L01 REGION CODE (see Figure 4.81).

2003

Central		EDI	Fax	Internet	Others	Phone
	1	142,726	242,897	138,321	62,205	194,363
	2	140,896	241,542	136,578	61,755	190,636
	3	143,771	241,061	137,982	61,077	185,694
	4	142,680	239,586	132,292	62,373	184,421
	5	139,410	234,078	136,360	61,798	182,429
	6	140,870	235,952	133,308	59,810	187,563
	7	144,853	239,827	138,855	61,620	186,056
	8	135,910	231,169	132,463	60,424	182,665
	9	142,872	242,635	135,799	62,329	188,040
	10	137,206	235,751	131,011	62,995	186,020
	11	140,828	233,952	135,435	60,835	183,284
	12	146,856	242,843	139,903	63,751	192,138
Central						

Figure 4.81 Web Intelligence Report with Breaks

10. Select the BILLED QUANTITY key figure in the cross tab and use the INSERT SUMMARY Σ ▾ button to create totals per break (see Figure 4.82).

2003

Central		EDI	Fax	Internet	Others	Phone	Sum:
	1	142,726	242,897	138,321	62,205	194,363	780,512
	2	140,896	241,542	136,578	61,755	190,636	771,407
	3	143,771	241,061	137,982	61,077	185,694	769,585
	4	142,680	239,586	132,292	62,373	184,421	761,352
	5	139,410	234,078	136,360	61,798	182,429	754,075
	6	140,870	235,952	133,308	59,810	187,563	757,503
	7	144,853	239,827	138,855	61,620	186,056	771,211
	8	135,910	231,169	132,463	60,424	182,665	742,631
	9	142,872	242,635	135,799	62,329	188,040	771,675
	10	137,206	235,751	131,011	62,995	186,020	752,983
	11	140,828	233,952	135,435	60,835	183,284	754,334
	12	146,856	242,843	139,903	63,751	192,138	785,491
Central	Sum:	1,698,878	2,861,293	1,628,307	740,972	2,243,309	9,172,759

Figure 4.82 Web Intelligence Report with Totals

11. Now you can use the disk ▾ symbol in the toolbar to save your report to the BusinessObjects Enterprise system. You will be asked to select a folder for your report and you can decide if the report should be refreshed automatically when opened or if the report should show saved data (see Figure 4.83).

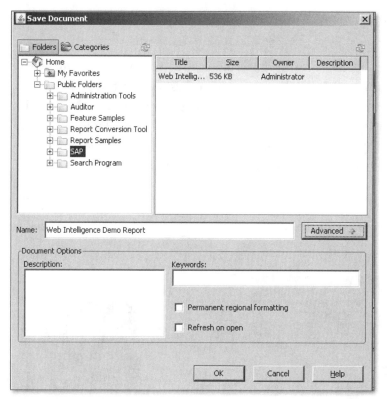

Figure 4.83 Save Document

After saving your report, you can view the report with the different viewing options in InfoView.

In this section, you learned the basics for how to use Web Intelligence for your reporting needs and how to create compelling analytics. We will use this knowledge in the next section, by fulfilling the requirements from the sales area using Web Intelligence.

4.6 Customer Case Study — Sales Reporting with Web Intelligence

Now we'll use Web Intelligence to deliver the reporting for our sales area. We'll focus on how we can use Web Intelligence and the Universe to provide the required reporting environment. We'll provide step-by-step instructions on how to create a report for our sales team.

We're going to create a report that shows our actual and planned sales in revenue and quantity based on different dimensions of the business, such as product group, product, region, and distribution channel. In addition, we'll provide the capability to drill down into more details, if required, and to filter the report based on dimensions. As part of the overall reporting, we will also deliver top and bottom performers and show some trending of the sales for the products (see Figure 4.84).

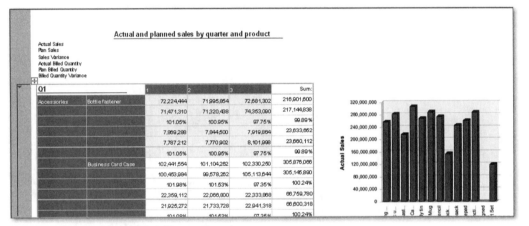

Figure 4.84 Web Intelligence Report

We'll leverage a BW query as the source for our reporting. This gives us the actual and planned sales revenue and quantity based on the SAP demo content cube 0D_DX_M01. The BW query that we are using contains the following Character-istics (see Figure 4.85):

- ▸ Calendar Month
- ▸ Distribution Channel
- ▸ Product Group
- ▸ Product
- ▸ Region Code

- ▸ QUARTER
- ▸ CALENDAR YEAR
- ▸ CUSTOMER
- ▸ REASON

and the following KEY FIGURES:

- ▸ ACTUAL SALES
- ▸ PLAN SALES
- ▸ ACTUAL BILLED QUANTITY
- ▸ PLAN BILLED QUANTITY
- ▸ LOST DEALS

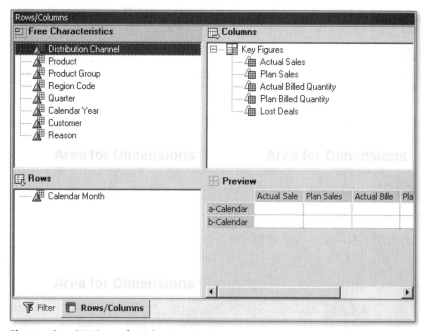

Figure 4.85 BW Query for Sales Reporting

Now we'll create the Universe and the Web Intelligence report for our sales reporting step by step.

1. Start the Universe designer via the menu path: START • PROGRAMS • BUSINESS-OBJECTS XI 3.1 • BUSINESSOBJECTS ENTERPRISE • DESIGNER.

2. The logon screen for the Universe designer appears and you need to provide the system name and your user credentials.

3. In our example, we'll use SAP authentication and our SAP credentials. For the system, we'll enter the name of the Central Management Server of our Business-Objects Enterprise system — VMWSAP20.

4. Because the Universe designer doesn't offer the SAP System ID and the SAP client number as explicit input fields as part of the logon mask, you need to enter your SAP credentials in the following format:

```
[SAP System ID]~800/[SAP user name]
```

For example:

```
CIM~800/DEMO
```

5. Click OK.

6. In the Universe designer, follow the menu path: FILE • NEW.

7. The UNIVERSE PARAMETERS dialog appears and you can use the NEW button to create a new connection to your SAP NetWeaver BW system.

8. Click NEXT to start the CONNECTION WIZARD.

9. Enter a name for the connection into the CONNECTION NAME field and scroll down to select the SAP BUSINESS WAREHOUSE connectivity type.

10. Click NEXT.

11. Enter the details to connect to your SAP system.

12. The LOGIN MODE lets us switch between an Application server and a Message server.

13. If you used your SAP credentials to log on to the Universe designer, you can set the AUTHENTICATION MODE to the USE SINGLE SIGN ON WHEN REFRESHING REPORTS AT VIEW TIME value. If SAP authentication is not configured on your BusinessObjects Enterprise system, you can continue with the USE SPECIFIED USERNAME AND PASSWORD setting and change the setting later on.

14. Click NEXT.

15. The list of available BW queries is shown in tree form with the InfoProvider listed at the top and the BW queries below each InfoProvider. $INFOCUBE lets us connect to all InfoCubes without a BW query.

16. In our example, we open the list of BW queries for InfoProvider 0D_DX_M01 and select the BW query that we created.

17. Click NEXT.

18. In the next screen, you can define connection parameters for the connection for your SAP NetWeaver BW system. The CONNECTION POOL MODE is especially important. Here, you define how long the connection will be kept active — the default value is 10 minutes. You can also select the DISCONNECT AFTER EACH TRANSACTION option, but you want to avoid doing so because it will result in a logon and log-off process for every single function call for your SAP system from this Universe connection.

19. Select the KEEP THE CONNECTION ACTIVE FOR option and leave the default value for POOL TIMEOUT.

20. Click FINISH.

21. Navigate to the CONTROLS tab from UNIVERSE PARAMETERS and make sure you uncheck all.

22. Navigate to the DEFINITION tab.

23. Enter a name for the new Universe into the NAME field.

24. Click OK.

25. Now the Universe designer connects with the SAP NetWeaver BW system and retrieves the metadata from the BW query that we selected.

26. After the Universe is presented to you, follow the menu path: FILE • SAVE to save the Universe.

27. Follow the FILE • EXPORT menu path to export the Universe to your Business-Objects Enterprise system.

28. Click Browse.

29. Select a folder for the Universe and click OK.

30. Click OK.

We just created a basic Universe and now we'll customize it to our needs.

1. The first thing we'll do is remove the Level 00 objects. Follow the menu path: View • Refresh Structure.

2. Click Begin.

3. Select the Delete obsolete Objects option and leave all of the other options with the default selection (see Figure 4.86).

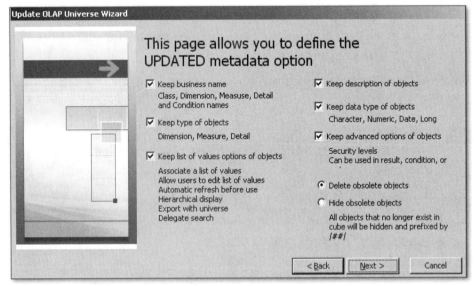

Figure 4.86 Update OLAP Universe Wizard

4. Click Next.

5. In the next screen, set the selections as shown in Figure 4.87.

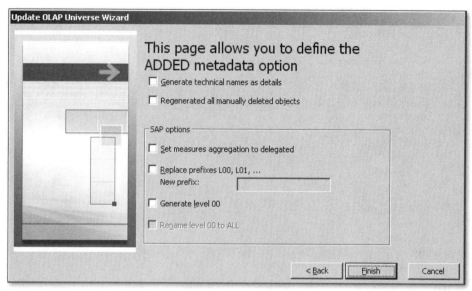

Figure 4.87 Update OLAP Universe Wizard

6. Click FINISH.

OLAP Universe Options

The options listed in Figure 4.87 can also be preconfigured via the TOOLS • OPTIONS menu path on the OLAP tab. That way, you can preset the options for your installation of the Universe designer and the settings can be used for any new OLAP Universes.

7. A list of changes will be presented to you.

8. Click OK.

9. In addition, we will remove the L01 prefix of the dimension objects and detail objects. This has to be done manually for each item.

10. Double-click on L01 DISTRIBUTION CHANNEL and remove prefix L01 from the NAME.

11. Repeat this step for the other objects in the Universe. Afterward, the Universe should look similar to Figure 4.88.

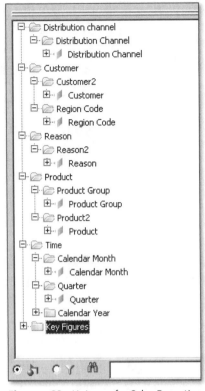

Figure 4.88 Universe for Sales Reporting

12. Next, we'll reorganize the structure of our Universe so that it's easier for our end users to leverage.

13. Select the top-level DISTRIBUTION CHANNEL class.

14. Follow the menu path INSERT • CLASS.

15. Enter `Product Sales` as the NAME.

16. Move all of the objects from your classes into the new PRODUCT SALES class (see Figure 4.89).

Reorganizing Universe Structure

Before you reorganize your universe structure into a different set of classes consider who your audience is and if the audience needs this. If your audience uses a set of prebuilt reports that they view and edit, then your audience will work on top of your Web Intelligence query and might not even see the actual Universe structure. If your audience creates their own reports on top of your Universes, then a restructuring of the classes might be appropriate to make the metadata more understandable.

In addition, keep in mind that if you are using Filters with a list of value objects (for example, a filter based on a BW variable), when you restructure the universe make sure the definition of the filter objects points to the right list of value objects.

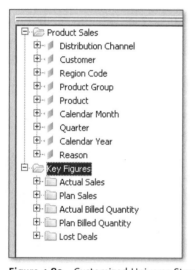

Figure 4.89 Customized Universe Structure

17. The next step in our customization is to create four filter objects that let the user filter down the report on each quarter.

18. In the previous section, you learned how to create a new filter object. First, we need the technical name of the CALENDAR MONTH. To find it, click on the dimension object.

19. You can see the technical name in the toolbar (see Figure 4.90).

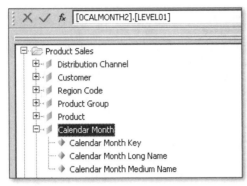

Figure 4.90 Calendar Month Definition

20. In our example, we need to know the first part of the definition [0CALMONTH2].

21. Select the PRODUCT SALES class.

22. Follow the INSERT • CONDITION menu path.

23. Enter the following syntax into the WHERE box for the definition of our Quarter 1 filter:

```
<FILTER KEY="[0CALMONTH2].[LEVEL01].[TECH_NAME]">
<CONDITION OPERATORCONDITION="InList">
<CONSTANT TECH_NAME="[0CALMONTH2].[01]"></CONSTANT>
<CONSTANT TECH_NAME="[0CALMONTH2].[02]"></CONSTANT>
<CONSTANT TECH_NAME="[0CALMONTH2].[03]"></CONSTANT>
</CONDITION></FILTER>
```

24. Enter `Calendar Year Quarter 1` as the Name of the filter.

25. Click OK.

26. Repeat the steps for the filters for Quarter 2 through Quarter 4 and change the values accordingly. Remember, you can copy and paste the filter objects.

27. The next step in our customization process is to create the variances for Actual Sales and Plan Sales, and Actual Billed Quantity and Plan Billed Quantity.

28. Select the KEY FIGURES class.

29. Follow the menu path: INSERT • OBJECT.

30. Select NUMBER as the TYPE.

31. Navigate to the PROPERTIES tab.

32. Select MEASURE as the QUALIFICATION.

33. Select DATABASE DELEGATED as the FUNCTION.

34. Navigate back to the DEFINITION tab.

35. Click the button next to the SELECT box to open the editor.

36. Use the editor to create the following formula:

    ```
    @Select(Actual Billed Quantity\Actual Billed Quantity) / @Select(Plan
    Billed Quantity\Plan Billed Quantity)
    ```

37. Click OK.

38. The syntax from the editor is now shown in the SELECT box.

39. Enter `Billed Quantity Variance` as the NAME.

40. Put the <EXPRESSION> tag in front of the syntax and the </EXPRESSION> tag at the end of the syntax.

41. Follow the steps as described earlier and create the variance for the Actual Sales and Plan Sales the same way.

42. Save and export your Universe to the BusinessObjects Enterprise system.

Now we are in a position to start building our report and share it with our sales force. Before we continue, we should clarify what kind of report we want to create. The report should show the actual and planned number for the sales revenue and the quantity. The numbers should be broken down by month, product group, and product; in addition, the report user should be able to filter the report based on the available dimensions.

1. Launch InfoView via the START • PROGRAMS • BUSINESSOBJECTS XI 3.1 • BUSINESS-OBJECTS ENTERPRISE • BUSINESSOBJECTS ENTERPRISE JAVA INFOVIEW menu path or launch InfoView via its URL in your browser.

2. Click DOCUMENT LIST.

3. Follow the menu path: NEW • WEB INTELLIGENCE DOCUMENT.

4. Select the Universe that we created from the list of available Universes.

5. Add the following objects to the RESULT OBJECTS panel:

   ▶ REGION CODE

   ▶ DISTRIBUTION CHANNEL

   ▶ PRODUCT GROUP

   ▶ PRODUCT

   ▶ CALENDAR MONTH (KEY)

   ▶ CALENDAR MONTH

   ▶ CALENDAR YEAR

   ▶ QUARTER

   ▶ REASON

   ▶ ACTUAL SALES

   ▶ PLAN SALES

   ▶ SALES VARIANCE

   ▶ ACTUAL BILLED QUANTITY

   ▶ PLAN BILLED QUANTITY

   ▶ VARIANCE BILLED QUANTITY

   ▶ LOST DEALS

6. Click RUN QUERY to retrieve the data. The default table layout will appear.

> **Note**
>
> Because we want to ensure a proper sorting for the CALENDAR MONTH, we'll first cre-
> ate a new formula/variable that represents the actual numeric value of the CALENDAR
> MONTH.

7. Click the VARIABLE EDITOR ⬚ symbol in the toolbar.

8. Enter `Calendar Month (numeric)` as the NAME.

9. Enter the following formula:

   ```
   =ToNumber([Calendar Month Key])
   ```

10. Click OK.

11. Replace the CALENDAR MONTH with the newly created CALENDAR MONTH (NUMERIC) objects by dragging the objects from the data panel on top of the CALENDAR MONTH column.

12. Remove the following objects from the table:

   ▸ REGION CODE

   ▸ DISTRIBUTION CHANNEL

   ▸ CALENDAR MONTH DESCRIPTION

   ▸ QUARTER

   ▸ CALENDAR YEAR

   ▸ REASON

   ▸ LOST DEALS

> **Note**
>
> We're removing those items from the table because we won't need them for our report, but we will need them as filter objects and we want to offer them to our user as options to be leveraged in the report, therefore, we included them in our result objects panel.

13. Navigate to the TEMPLATES tab and drag a cross tab template onto your table.

14. Arrange the objects in your cross tab so that the cross tab shows the PRODUCT GROUP and PRODUCT in the rows, and the CALENDAR MONTH in the columns.

15. Drag and drop the QUARTER dimension from the data panel above your cross tab and look for the DROP HERE TO CREATE A SECTION tooltip.

16. Now all of the key figures are shown next to each other, which creates a very wide cross tab. Drag the key figures below each other in your cross tab (see Figure 4.91).

17. Our cross tab doesn't show which numbers we're using, so we need to add the descriptions of the key figures. Let's look at two options here — feel free to choose the one you prefer.

Q1

		1	2	3
Accessories	Bottle fastener	72,224,444	71,995,854	72,681,302
		71,471,310	71,320,438	74,353,090
		1.01	1.01	0.98
		7,869,288	7,844,500	7,919,864
		7,787,212	7,770,902	8,101,998
		1.01	1.01	0.98
Accessories	Business Card Case	102,441,554	101,104,262	102,330,250
		100,453,984	99,578,262	105,113,644
		1.02	1.02	0.97
		22,359,112	22,066,800	22,333,868
		21,925,272	21,733,728	22,941,318

Figure 4.91 Web Intelligence Report

18. Select the complete cross tab in your report and open the PROPERTIES tab.

19. Activate the SHOW OBJECT NAME option, which is an option in the DISPLAY area (see Figure 4.92).

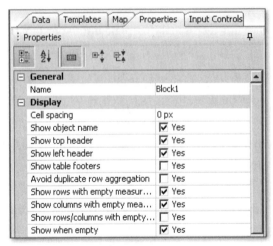

Figure 4.92 Cross Tab Properties

20. Your cross tab will look like Figure 4.93.

Q1

Product Group	Product		1	2	3
Accessories	Bottle fastener	Actual Sales	72,224,444	71,995,854	72,681,302
		Plan Sales	71,471,310	71,320,438	74,353,090
		Sales Variance	1.01	1.01	0.98
		Actual Billed Quantity	7,869,288	7,844,500	7,919,864
		Plan Billed Quantity	7,787,212	7,770,902	8,101,998
		Billed Quantity Variance	1.01	1.01	0.98
Accessories	Business Card Case	Actual Sales	102,441,554	101,104,262	102,330,250
		Plan Sales	100,453,984	99,578,262	105,113,644
		Sales Variance	1.02	1.02	0.97
		Actual Billed Quantity	22,359,112	22,066,800	22,333,868
		Plan Billed Quantity	21,925,272	21,733,728	22,941,318

Figure 4.93 Web Intelligence Report

Note

The alternative is to create a text block that shows the same information but doesn't repeat it as part of the cross tab.

21. Click on the VIEW STRUCTURE button in the toolbar.
22. Make sure you have enough space between your report title and the section for the quarter.
23. Now open the TEMPLATES tab and drag and drop a BLANK CELL template to the area between the REPORT TITLE and the quarter section.
24. Select the new object and click on the FORMULA EDITOR symbol in the toolbar. Next, use the NAMEOF function to create description fields for our six key figures.
25. For ACTUAL SALES the formula is `=NameOf([Actual Sales])`.
26. Repeat the steps for the other five key figures and format the fields (see Figure 4.94).

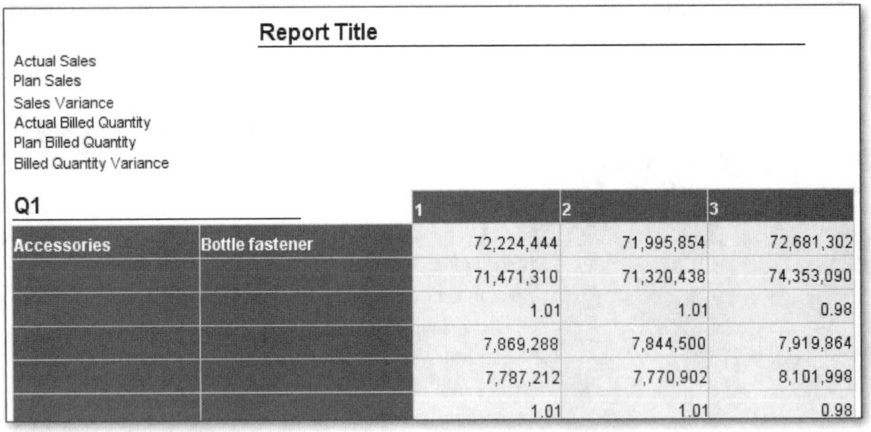

Figure 4.94 Web Intelligence Report

27. Select the PRODUCT GROUP column and click the INSERT/REMOVE BREAK [icon] button in the toolbar to create a break per PRODUCT GROUP; that way, we can create totals per PRODUCT GROUP and the description isn't repeated for each PRODUCT in the PRODUCT GROUP.

28. Right-click on the SALES VARIANCE key figure in the cross tab and select FORMAT NUMBER.

29. Select the FORMAT TYPE NUMBER and scroll down to select the percentage format style.

30. Repeat the steps for the BILLED QUANTITY VARIANCE.

31. Now select each key figure in the cross tab and use the INSERT SUM [Σ ▾] button in the toolbar to create summaries per PRODUCT GROUP.

32. You now have row totals and column totals for the PRODUCT GROUP and for the quarter.

33. Now navigate to the TEMPLATE tab.

34. Drag and drop a bar chart next to the cross tab.

35. The report is now shown in the structural view (see Figure 4.95).

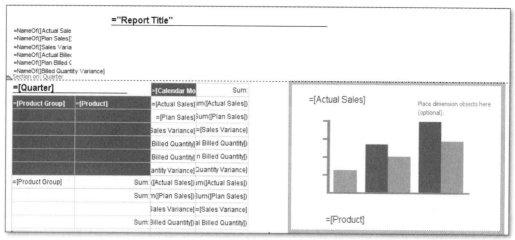

Figure 4.95 Structural View of the Web Intelligence Report

36. Drag the ACTUAL SALES key figure to the measure object and the PRODUCT dimension to the dimension object.

37. Right-click the chart and follow the menu path: ALIGN • RELATIVE POSITION.

38. Configure the chart to be 50px away from the RIGHT EDGE and 20px from the TOP EDGE.

39. Click REFRESH DATA in the toolbar.

40. Select the PRODUCT GROUP column of the cross tab.

41. Click the FOLD/UNFOLD [icon] button in the toolbar.

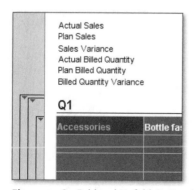

Figure 4.96 Fold and Unfold Option in Web Intelligence

42. Now you can fold and unfold the following items:

    ▶ The section, which in our example will then let you switch between the section header and the cross tab.

    ▶ The product group in the cross tab, which lets you show either the totals per PRODUCT GROUP or per quarter.

    ▶ The PRODUCT itself, which lets you switch between a summarized level on PRODUCT GROUP and PRODUCT level.

43. Now enter a REPORT TITLE for your report.

44. For this part of our report, the only step that is left is to incorporate the functionality to filter the report in specific dimensions. To do this, there are two options:

    ▶ You can use the ⊞ button to show the REPORT FILTER TOOLBAR and drag and drop a dimension onto it.

    ▶ You can use the new INPUT CONTROLS to provide the filter capabilities.

45. In our example, we'll use the INPUT CONTROLS to include the filter capabilities.

46. Navigate to the INPUT CONTROLS tab (see Figure 4.97).

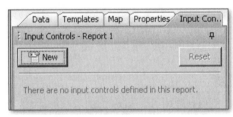

Figure 4.97 Input Controls

47. Click NEW.

48. Select the DISTRIBUTION CHANNEL dimension object.

49. Click NEXT

50. Select the RADIO BUTTONS option (see Figure 4.98).

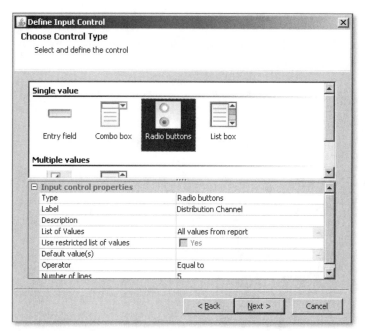

Figure 4.98 Define Input Control

51. Click NEXT.

52. Select the chart and table as elements that will be assigned to the input control. By assigning an element to the input control, the element will be filtered based on the selection (see Figure 4.99).

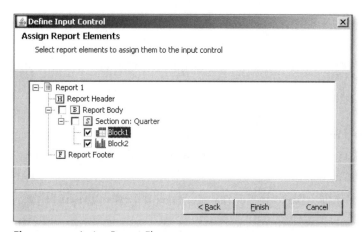

Figure 4.99 Assign Report Elements

53. Click FINISH.

54. Now you can selec the value from the list and filter you report to a single DIS-TRIBUTION CHANNEL (see Figure 4.100).

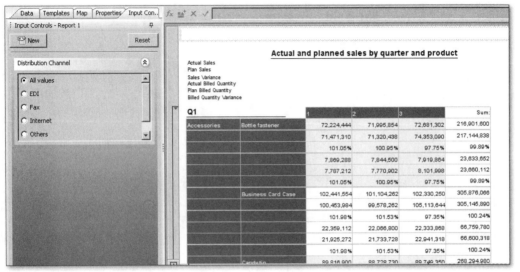

Figure 4.100 Web Intelligence Report with Input Controls

55. Save the report to your BusinessObjects Enterprise system.

56. In addition to the information we have so far, we should also show the amount of LOST DEALS and the reasons behind them as well.

57. To do so, let's create a second report tab. Right-click on the REPORT1 tab and select INSERT REPORT.

58. Navigate to the TEMPLATE tab and drag and drop a cross tab to your new report.

59. Navigate to the DATA tab.

60. Drag the REASON dimension objects into the rows from our cross tab and drag the CALENDAR MONTH into the columns. For a cell we'll use the LOST DEALS key figure.

61. Drag and drop a BLANK CELL from the TEMPLATE tab and enter a report title.

62. Drag and drop a PIE CHART from the TEMPLATE tab to your report. Use the LOST DEALS key figure as the measure and the REASON object as the dimension.

63. Drag and drop a BAR CHART next to the PIE CHART and use the CALENDAR MONTH as the dimension and the LOST DEALS key figure as the measure (see Figure 4.101).

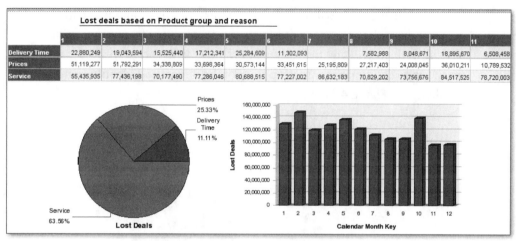

Figure 4.101 Web Intelligence Report

64. Right-click on the REPORT1 tab and select RENAME REPORT. Enter `Actual and planned sales by quarter` as the new report name.

65. Right-click on the REPORT2 tab and select RENAME REPORT. Enter `Lost sales revenue by reason and month` as the new report name.

66. Save your report to your BusinessObjects Enterprise system.

As you can see, we reused the data that we retrieved in two reports to show different views of the same information, which was the reasoning behind the last couple of steps. Just as we added an additional report, you can also add an additional query based on the same or a different Universe to your Web Intelligence document, allowing you to store data from several sources in a single document.

Next, we'll continue to work with Web Intelligence and focus on the requirements for the financial department.

4.7 Customer Case Study — Financial Reporting with Web Intelligence

In this section, we'll look at how we can use Web Intelligence to fulfill the requirements for our financial area. We'll create a report on top of a BW query showing a cost center hierarchy and the details broken down by cost elements. With regard to the key figures, we will leverage the actual and plan amounts and show the variance as an absolute value and as a percentage value. In addition, we'll enable alerting in the report and the tracking of changes with each refresh to make it easy for the cost center manager to keep track of the budget and identify changes in the numbers (see Figure 4.102).

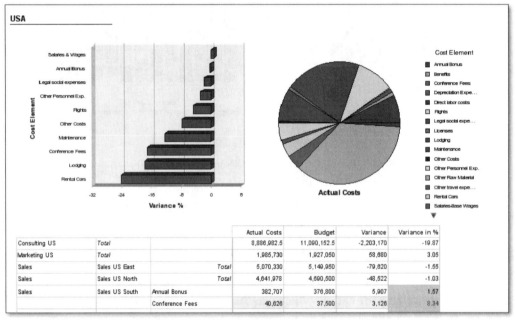

Figure 4.102 Web Intelligence Financial Report

We'll use a BW query based on InfoProvider 0CCA_M20 from the Cost Center Accounting area as the source for this Web Intelligence report. Our BW query contains the following elements (see Figure 4.103):

▶ Free Characteristics:

  ▶ Cost Center

    ▶ Cost Element

    ▶ Fiscal year

      ▶ Fiscal year/period

▶ Key Figures:

  ▶ Actual Costs

  ▶ Planned Costs

  ▶ Variance

  ▶ Variance %

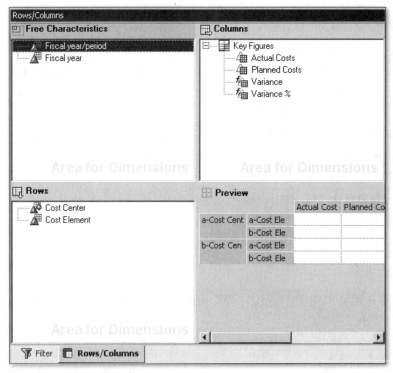

Figure 4.103 BW Query for Financial Report

Currency Conversion and Selections

In currency-sensitive reports, like the report we're creating in this section, it is highly recommended to either ensure the query will only return a single currency per key figure, or offer the user the option to use a variable from the BW query to select the currency. The reporting tools do not offer an automatic functionality to split the totals per currency, and therefore you might summarize numbers from different currencies.

In the following steps we continue without a variable, which is only done to keep the example simple because some of our readers may be new to this topic.

Just as we did for our sales-oriented report, now we will create and customize the Universe and then leverage Web Intelligence to create the report.

1. Start the Universe designer via the menu path: START • PROGRAMS • BUSINESS-OBJECTS XI 3.1 • BUSINESSOBJECTS ENTERPRISE • DESIGNER.

2. You will see the logon screen for the Universe designer and you need to provide the system name and you user credentials.

3. In our example, we'll use SAP authentication and our SAP credentials. For the system, we'll enter the name of the Central Management Server of our Business-Objects Enterprise system — VMWSAP20.

4. Because the Universe designer doesn't offer the SAP System ID and the SAP client number as input fields in the logon mask, you need to enter your SAP credentials in the following format:

`[SAP System ID]~800/[SAP user name]`

For example:

`CIM~800/DEMO`

5. Click OK.

6. This time we'll set the options before we create a new Universe so that we'll have less to customize.

7. Follow the TOOLS • OPTIONS menu path and navigate to the OLAP tab (see Figure 4.104).

Figure 4.104 OLAP Options

8. Make sure you set the options as shown in Figure 4.104.

9. Click OK.

10. In the Universe designer, follow the menu path: FILE • NEW.

11. The UNIVERSE PARAMETERS dialog appears and you can use the NEW button to create a new connection to your SAP NetWeaver BW system.

12. Click NEXT to start the CONNECTION WIZARD.

13. Enter a name for the connection in the CONNECTION NAME field and scroll down to select the SAP BUSINESS WAREHOUSE connectivity type.

14. Click NEXT.

15. Enter the details to connect to your SAP system.

16. The LOGIN MODE lets us switch between an Application server and a Message server.

17. If you used your SAP credentials to log on to the Universe designer, you can set the Authentication Mode to the Use Single Sign on when refreshing reports at view time value. If SAP authentication is not configured on your BusinessObjects Enterprise system, you can continue with the Use specified username and password setting and you can change the setting later on.

18. Click Next.

19. The list of available BW queries is shown in tree form with the InfoProvider listed at the top and the BW queries below each InfoProvider. $INFOCUBE lets us connect directly to all of the InfoCubes without a BW query.

20. In our example, we open the list of BW queries for InfoProvider 0CCA_M20 and select the BW query that we created.

21. Click Next.

22. In the next screen, you can define connection parameters for the connection for your SAP NetWeaver BW system. The Connection Pool Mode is especially important. Here, you define how long the connection will be kept active — the default value is 10 minutes. You can also select the Disconnect after each Transaction option, but you want to avoid doing so because it will result in a logon and log-off process for every single function call for your SAP system from this Universe connection.

23. Select the Keep the connection active for option and leave the default value for Pool Timeout.

24. Click Finish.

25. Navigate to the Controls tab from the Universe Parameters and make sure you uncheck all.

26. Navigate to the Definition tab.

27. Enter a name for the new Universe into the Name field.

28. Click OK.

29. Now the Universe designer connects to the SAP NetWeaver BW system and retrieves metadata from the BW query that we selected.

30. After the Universe is presented to you, follow the File • Save menu path to save the Universe.

31. FOLLOW THE FILE • EXPORT menu path to export the Universe to your Business-Objects Enterprise system.

32. Click BROWSE.

33. Select a folder for the Universe and click OK.

34. Click OK.

We just created a basic universe and now we'll customize it to our needs.

1. First, remove the L01 prefix from all of our objects — except from the COST CENTER dimension objects. To do so, we need to double-click on the object and then edit the NAME.

2. For the COST CENTER dimension objects we'll leave the prefix as part of the objects. In this case, the prefix represents the level of the hierarchy.

3. Next, we'll reorganize the structure of our Universe a little bit so that it is easier for our end users to leverage.

4. Follow the menu path: INSERT • CLASS.

5. Enter `Financial Elements` as the NAME.

6. Move all of the objects from your classes into the new FINANCIAL ELEMENTS class (SEE Figure 4.105).

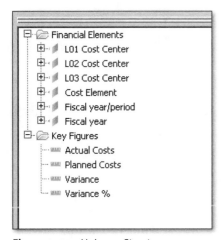

Figure 4.105 Universe Structure

7. Double-click the Variance % key figure and navigate to the Properties tab.

8. Configure the Function to be Database delegated.

For our financial reporting part, that's all we need to customize for now. Now let's start building the Web Intelligence report. In our example, we want to create a report that shows the Actual Costs and Budget Costs key figures along the Cost Center hierarchies with the information broken down by Cost Elements.

1. Launch InfoView via the Start • Programs • BusinessObjects xi 3.1 • Business-Objects Enterprise • BusinessObjects Enterprise Java InfoView menu path or launch InfoView via its URL in your browser.

2. Click Document List.

3. Follow the menu path: New • Web Intelligence Document.

4. Select the Universe that we created from the list of available Universes.

5. Add the following objects to the Result Objects panel (see Figure 4.106):

   ▶ L01 Cost Center

   ▶ L02 Cost Center

   ▶ L03 Cost Center

   ▶ Cost Element

   ▶ Actual Costs

   ▶ Budget Costs

   ▶ Variance

   ▶ Variance %

Figure 4.106 Web Intelligence Query Panel

6. Click RUN QUERY.

7. Right-click on the column for the top-level of our Cost Center hierarchy and select SET AS SECTION.

8. Click VIEW STRUCTURE in the toolbar.

9. Remove the table from your report.

10. Drag and drop a cross tab from the tab TEMPLATES to your report.

11. Drag and drop the following objects into your cross tab (see Figure 4.107):

   ▶ L02 COST CENTER as a row item

   ▶ L03 COST CENTER as a row item

   ▶ COST ELEMENT as a row item

   ▶ ACTUAL COSTS as a cell item

   ▶ BUDGET COSTS as a cell item

   ▶ VARIANCE as a cell item

   ▶ VARIANCE % as a cell item

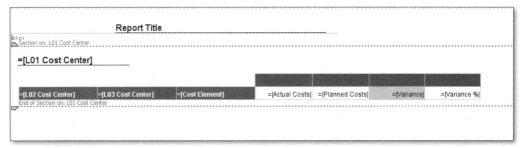

Figure 4.107 Web Intelligence Report

12. Click VIEW RESULTS.

13. Double-click on the column headers for the key figures and enter the proper column headers.

14. Double-click on the REPORT TITLE and enter Cost Center & Cost Elements – Actual/Budget comparison as the title.

15. Select the L02 COST CENTER column and click the INSERT/REMOVE BREAK button in the toolbar to create a break per level 2 of our Cost Center hierarchy.

16. Repeat the steps for the L03 COST CENTER column.

17. Click VIEW STRUCTURE in the toolbar (see Figure 4.108).

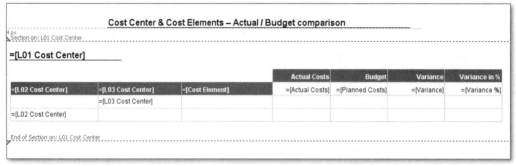

Figure 4.108 Web Intelligence Report

18. Insert the formula for L02 COST CENTER into the empty cell in front of the L03 Cost Center cell (see Figure 4.109).

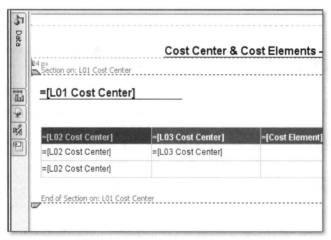

Figure 4.109 Web Intelligence Report

19. Select the complete cross tab. You will notice that there is an empty row at the bottom of your cross tab.

20. Right-click on the empty row and follow the menu path: REMOVE • REMOVE ROW.

21. Select each key figure in the cross tab (one by one) and use the INSERT SUM Σ ▾ button to create totals for the cross tab.

22. Remove the row totals created for the cross tab.

23. Remove the text Sum: in all of the Total rows of the cross tab.

24. Select the cross tab and navigate to the PROPERTIES tab (see Figure 4.110).

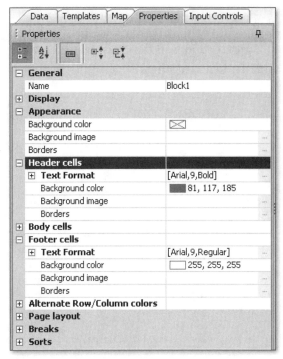

Figure 4.110 Properties

25. Remove the BACKGROUND COLOR from the HEADER CELLS.

26. Enter Total into your cross tab as shown in Figure 4.111.

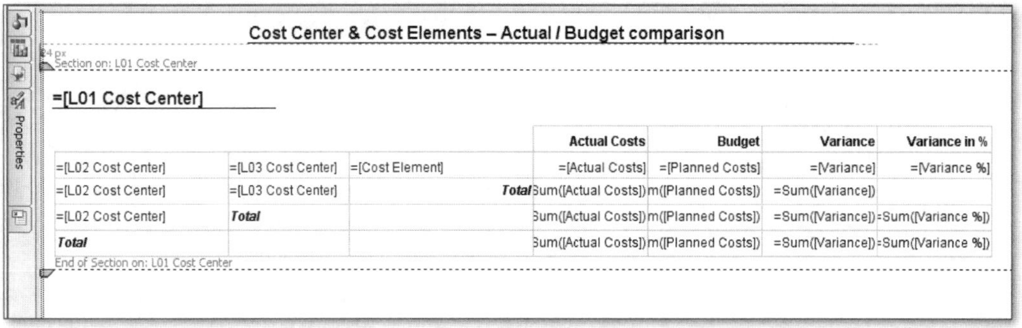

Figure 4.111 Web Intelligence Report

27. Click VIEW RESULTS.

28. Click the FOLD/UNFOLD ⊞ button in the toolbar.

29. Now you can use the FOLD and UNFOLD options in the cross tab to show different levels of the hierarchy with the totals (see Figure 4.112).

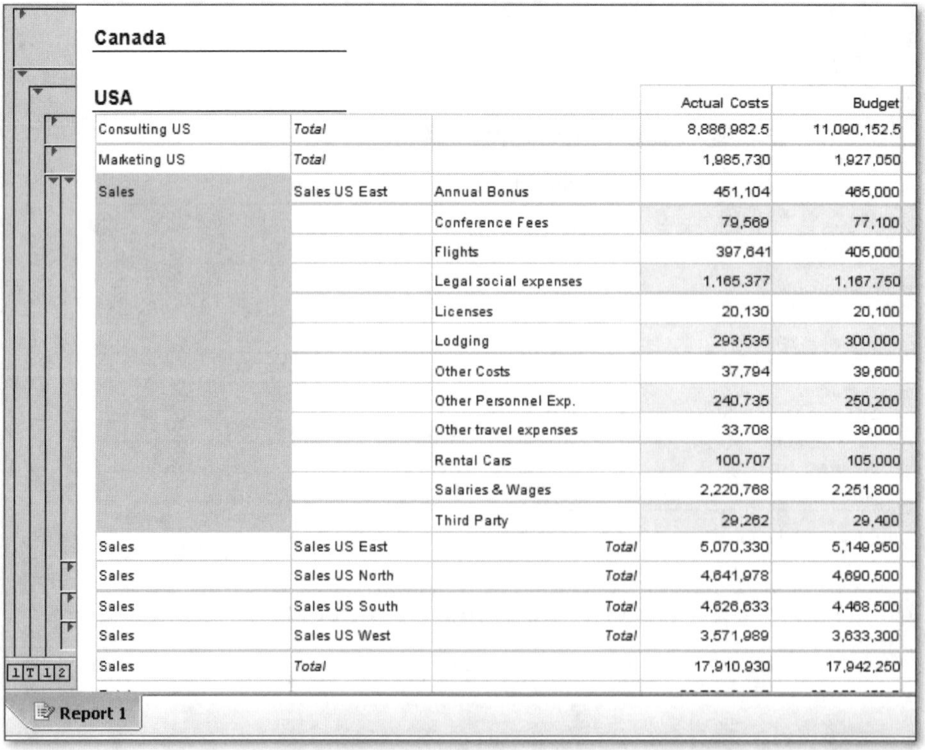

Figure 4.112 Web Intelligence Report with Fold and Unfold

In addition to the information and navigation that is already possible, we want to add alerts and highlighting to the report with some additional charts visualizing the most important information per country.

30. Click VIEW STRUCTURE in the toolbar.

31. Increase the size of the L01 COST CENTER section by moving the section lines.

32. Move the table further down so that you have enough space for two charts.

33. Drag and drop a BAR CHART from the tab TEMPLATES above your cross tab.

34. Drag and drop the COST ELEMENT dimension from the DATA tab to the bar chart as for the dimension, and use the VARIANCE % key figure for the measure.

35. Select the BAR CHART, click the APPLY/REMOVE RANKING ⊞▾ button, and define a TOP 10 RANKING for your chart (see Figure 4.113).

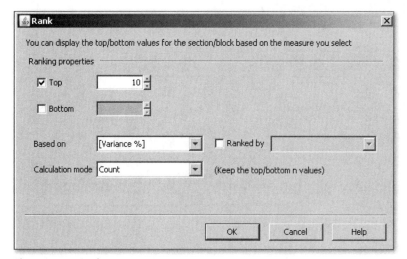

Figure 4.113 Ranking

36. Click OK.

37. Add another chart to your report, but this time use a pie chart.

38. Use the COST ELEMENT dimension and the ACTUAL key figure for the pie chart.

39. After adding the two charts, we can now add highlighting to our cross tab. We would like to highlight cost center or cost elements that are 5% or higher above budget.

40. Select the VARIANCE % key figure in the cross tab.

41. Click the ALERTERS ⚠ button in the toolbar to create a new alert for our report.

42. Click NEW.

43. Enter your description for the new alert and configure the alert to evaluate the VARIANCE % key figure above or equal to the value 5 as shown in Figure 4.114.

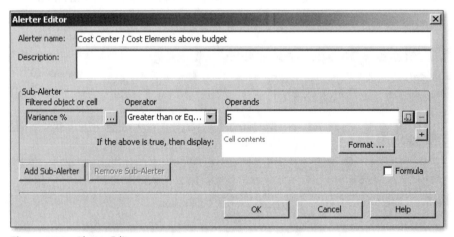

Figure 4.114 Alerter Editor

44. Click FORMAT.

45. Configure the formatting with a yellow background and red font as shown in Figure 4.115.

46. Click OK.

47. Now make sure you select each total in the cross tab for the VARIANCE % key figure and activate the newly created ALERTER by clicking the ⚠ button and set it by setting the checkbox (see Figure 4.116).

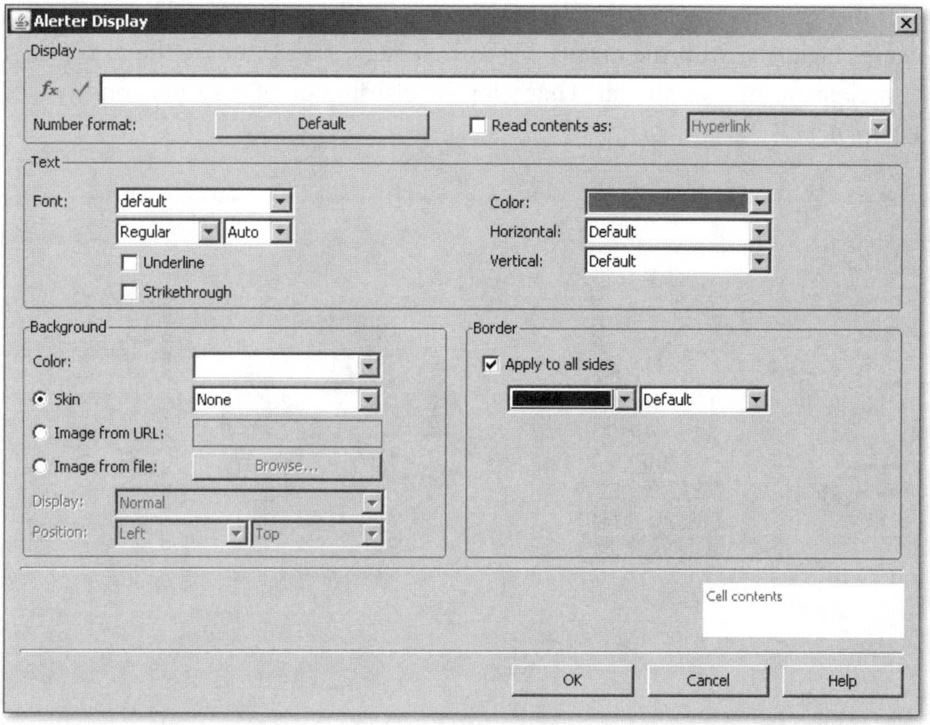

Figure 4.115 Alerter Display

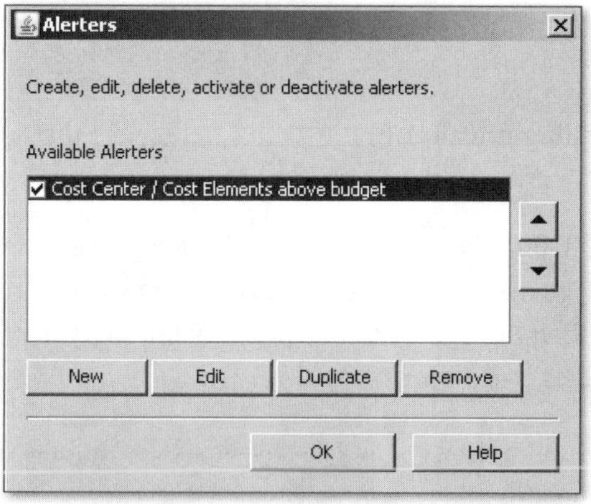

Figure 4.116 Activating Alerters

You just created a report that shows the actual and planned costs along a cost center hierarchy with the details per cost element. Users can see the top-ranked cost elements per country and charts for the distribution of costs per country (see Figure 4.117).

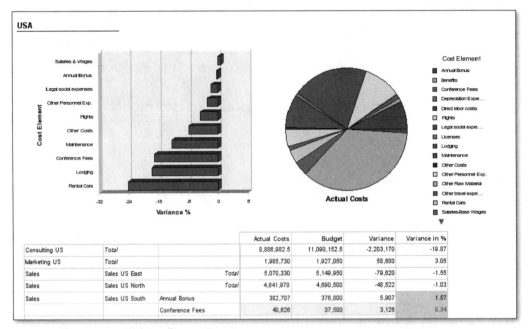

Figure 4.117 Web Intelligence Report

Next, we'll highlight a very compelling functionality in Web Intelligence that is very useful in the financial reporting area. It's the TRACK function.

In the Web Intelligence toolbar, you'll find the ☐ Track button, which lets you enable tracking of changes in your report. The user can configure a baseline for the report and each change in the report can then be highlighted, depending on the type of change in the DATA TRACKING OPTIONS (see Figure 4.118).

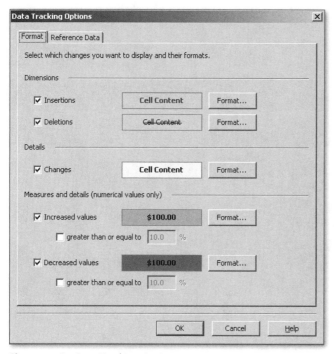

Figure 4.118 Data Tracking Options

By using these options, your user can quickly visualize and analyze any changes in his report that happened since the last time the report was refreshed. This will save the user a lot of time and effort. This functionality is especially helpful in cases where you're also using a key date variable as part of the underlying SAP NetWeaver BW query to ask for the date to resolve a time-dependency, such as a time-dependent hierarchical structure. In such cases, the Data Track Options visualize the changes based on a different key date in the report and users can quickly identify those changes.

4.8 Summary

In this chapter, we learned about the data connectivity options for Universes and Web Intelligence on top of our SAP data source. We also evaluated Web Intelligence as an ad hoc reporting tool against our requirements from different areas and then created reports for the sales and finance areas to fulfill parts of their requirements.

Use Xcelsius to create data visualization based on SAP data.

5   Dashboarding and Data Visualization

In this chapter, we'll look at how you can use Xcelsius for your data visualization and dashboarding requirements. We'll take a look at the required components, the data connectivity, and how to fulfill the requirements from different areas.

5.1   Installation and Deployment Overview

In this section, we'll focus on the installation and deployment of the necessary components to leverage Xcelsius for data visualization. To leverage Xcelsius against your SAP data you need the Xcelsius Designer tool and SAP frontend components installed on your client system.

Technical Prerequisites

Xcelsius offers several ways to connect to the data in your SAP system, but if you want to leverage the latest integration with SAP NetWeaver Business Warehouse (BW) as a datasource, you need to at least be running the following versions:

► SAP NetWeaver BW 7.01 (7.0 Enhancement Package 01) Service Pack 05
   or
► SAP NetWeaver BW 7.02.
► Xcelsius Enterprise 2008 Service Pack 02.
► SAP frontend 7.x installed on the client system with Business Intelligence (BI) add-ons.

Xcelsius Client-Side Installation

Before you install the Xcelsius designer, make sure you're using the Xcelsius Enterprise edition so that you can leverage the SAP NetWeaver BW connectivity.

1. Just as with the installation routine for the client side of Crystal Reports, you need to choose a setup language at the beginning of the Xcelsius designer installation.

2. After you accept the license agreement and provide the license key code, you can select the languages for the software. In our installation we select ENGLISH.

3. You can then select the folder for your Xcelsius installation. If Xcelsius is not the first SAP BusinessObjects product installed on the system, the suggested path will be the path from the already-installed SAP BusinessObjects products (see Figure 5.1).

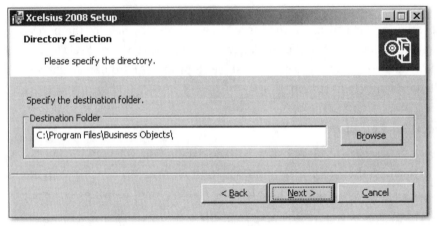

Figure 5.1 Xcelsius 2008 Setup

4. After you confirm the installation folder you can move to the next screen, where you will start the actual installation routine.

5. After this screen the installation will begin and you can leverage Xcelsius shortly thereafter.

As mentioned previously, to leverage the new Xcelsius connectivity for SAP NetWeaver BW you need to apply Service Pack 2 on top of the Xcelsius installation.

Xcelsius and Live Office

When you install Live Office and Xcelsius on the same system, Xcelsius will ask to configure the Live Office compatibility on the first start of Xcelsius.

You can configure the compatibility by following the FILE • PREFERENCES • EXCEL OPTIONS menu path. If you prefer to work with Live Office inside of Xcelsius, you need to activate the compatibility modes. If you disable the compatibility modes you need to work with Live Office outside of Xcelsius in a separate Microsoft Excel spreadsheet.

Next, we'll look at a more detailed overview on the connectivity options.

5.2 SAP Data Connectivity for Xcelsius

With regard to the data connectivity for Xcelsius, we will separate the view into SAP ERP and SAP NetWeaver BW.

If you'd like to leverage SAP ERP data for your Xcelsius dashboard, your options are somewhat limited. Xcelsius can leverage Live Office as a data source. That way, Xcelsius can leverage Crystal Reports via Live Office to connect directly to the SAP ERP system (see Figure 5.2). These are the options that you can leverage for direct connectivity to your SAP ERP system. There are also indirect options to connect to your ERP system, in combination with SAP NetWeaver BW, and leverage the data from your ERP system in real time (for example, a connection via Transient Provider).

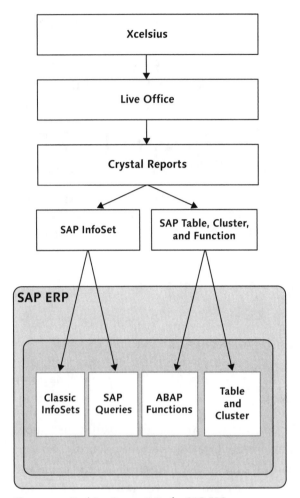

Figure 5.2 Xcelsius Connectivity for SAP ERP

You have a much broader range of choices with the connectivity for Xcelsius on top of SAP NetWeaver BW (see Figure 5.3).

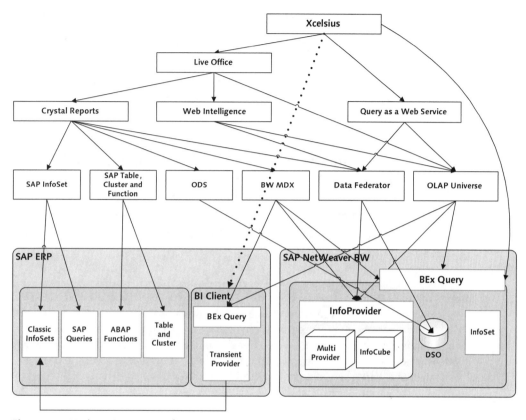

Figure 5.3 Xcelsius Connectivity for SAP NetWeaver BW

As you can see in Figure 5.3, Xcelsius can leverage a broad range of connectivity from Crystal Reports, Universes, and Web Intelligence via Live Office. In addition, you can leverage the Query as a Web Service tool and create your own web services on top of Universes and then leverage those web services in your Xcelsius dashboards to provide data.

There are two data connectivity options worth noting in Figure 5.3:

▶ Xcelsius can connect directly to the SAP NetWeaver BW queries without any additional middleware as of Xcelsius Enterprise Service Pack 02 (see Section 5.3.1, "Technical Pre-Requisites").

▸ Xcelsius can leverage the Transient Provider as part of SAP NetWeaver BW to connect to classic InfoSets in your ERP data and provide real-time ERP data as part of your dashboard.

In the next section, we will provide a detailed view on the new direct connectivity for SAP NetWeaver BW.

5.3 Xcelsius and SAP NetWeaver BI — Connectivity Details

In this section, we will look at the new option to leverage a BW query directly in the Xcelsius designer. We will look at the technical prerequisites for this new capability and how to leverage a BW query directly with Xcelsius, and how to offer the dashboard to your users.

Xcelsius Connectivity Options

As shown in the previous section, Xcelsius offers several ways to connect to your SAP data. In this book, we're focused on the new data connectivity for how Xcelsius connects to the BW query without any additional middleware. If you're interested in more details on other options, please read the book, *Integrating BusinessObjects XI 3.1 BI Tools with SAP NetWeaver,* from SAP PRESS.

5.3.1 Technical Prerequisites

The new connectivity for Xcelsius requires the following product releases:

▸ Xcelsius Enterprise 2008 Service Pack 02

▸ SAP NetWeaver 7.0 Enhancement Package 01 Service Pack 05 for ABAP and Java

▸ SAP frontend 7.10 with BI 7.x add-on

This new connectivity requires the BI Advanced Business Application Programming (ABAP) and BI Java usage types. This connectivity leverages the BI Consumer Services (BICS) as data interfaces (see Figure 5.4).

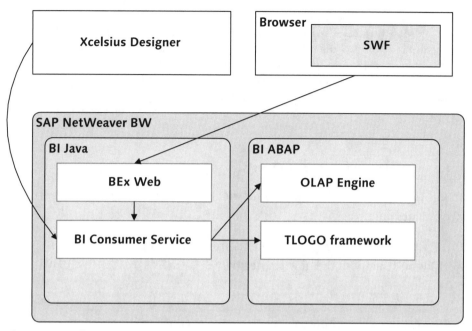

Figure 5.4 Xcelsius Connectivity for SAP NetWeaver BW

As you can see in Figure 5.4, the dashboards are using the Business Explorer (BEx) web runtime environment. This means that this integration does not require a BusinessObjects Enterprise environment like some connectivities do.

Deployment Considerations for Xcelsius Connectivity

With this new connectivity, you need to consider the overall picture of your BusinessObjects landscape and consider the different options and benefits of each approach.

Using Live Office provides you access to Crystal Reports, Web Intelligence, and Universes. It also allows you to leverage direct ERP connectivity; but it does require a BusinessObjects Enterprise landscape.

The new SAP NetWeaver BW connectivity for Xcelsius lets you cut out the middleware and does not require a BusinessObjects Enterprise system. On the other hand, it means you're now using two landscapes for your reporting needs (SAP NetWeaver BW for Xcelsius and BusinessObjects Enterprise for Crystal Reports, Web Intelligence, and BusinessObjects Explorer).

SAP NetWeaver BW Connectivity and BusinessObjects Enterprise

As shown in Figure 5.4, the new connectivity for Xcelsius does not require a BusinessObjects Enterprise landscape. Based on the Service Pack 02 release of BusinessObjects XI 3.1, an Xcelsius dashboard leveraging this new SAP NetWeaver BI connectivity will not work when hosted inside BusinessObjects Enterprise. This capability is on the product roadmap and you should check for more recent updates of the roadmap for further details.

5.3.2 Connecting to a BW Query

In this section, we will look at how the elements of a BW query are supported in Xcelsius designer.

In Table 5.1, you can see how elements from a BW query are supported in the Xcelsius designer with the new connectivity.

BW Query Element	Xcelsius Designer Element
Characteristic	Each characteristic in the actual dataset is retrieved based on the settings in the BW query (e.g., key, short text, medium text, and long text). In addition, each characteristic is also available with a list of members that can be used for filtering or providing values for variables.
Hierarchy	Each level of the hierarchy will be presented as a column in the data set. The depth of the hierarchy depends on the configured number of levels in the BW query designer.
Key Figure	Each key figure can be shown as a plain numeric value or as a formatted value based on user preferences. This choice can be made for each SAP NetWeaver BW connectivity configured in Xcelsius designer.
Calculated and Restricted Key Figures	Each calculated/restricted key figure is treated like a key figure. The user does not have access to the underlying definition in Xcelsius designer.
Filter	Filters will be applied to the underlying query. The user has access to the configured filter values and can use those values for display purposes. In addition, the user can set additional filter values for characteristics from the underlying BW query.

Table 5.1 SAP NetWeaver BW Metadata Mapping for Crystal Reports

BW Query Element	Xcelsius Designer Element
Navigational Attribute	Navigational Attributes are treated just as characteristics.
Display Attribute	Display attributes can be used for a list of values and can become part of the overall dataset. In the actual dataset, a display attribute can only be shown in combination with the actual characteristic.
SAP Variables	Variables from the BW query are transferred to Xcelsius as part of the connection and will be shown as variables in the Input Values.

Table 5.1 SAP NetWeaver BW Metadata Mapping for Crystal Reports (Cont.)

Now that we know how to support the BW metadata, let's look at some examples on how the metadata is supported in the Xcelsius designer. The focus here is to understand how you can leverage the metadata from SAP NetWeaver BW as part of your Xcelsius dashboard. We'll focus on the basics of Xcelsius as well, but we'll first clarify how we can use the metadata.

The first example we'll use is a simple BW query (see Figure 5.5) based on the Info-Provider 0D_DX_M01, which contains the following characteristics in the rows:

▸ Customer

▸ Product Group

The following characteristics in the free characteristics:

▸ Product

The following key figures:

▸ Billed Quantity

▸ Net Sales

1. Start the Xcelsius designer via the START • PROGRAMS • XCELSIUS • XCELSIUS 2008 menu path.

2. Follow the DATA • CONNECTIONS menu path.

3. Click the ADD button.

4. Select the SAP NETWEAVER BI CONNECTION option (see Figure 5.6).

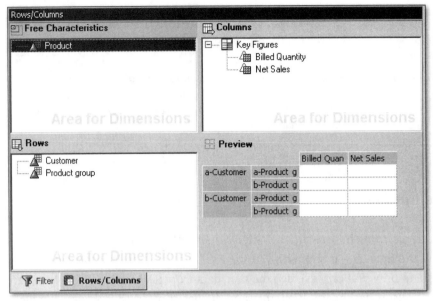

Figure 5.5 BW Query

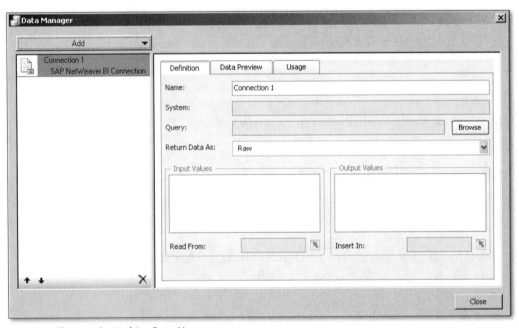

Figure 5.6 Xcelsius Data Manager

5. Click BROWSE.

6. Log on to your SAP system and select the BW Query.

7. The metadata from the BW query is shown in INPUT VALUES and OUTPUT VALUES according to the categories shown in Figure 5.7.

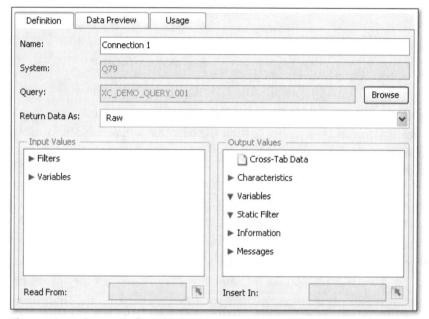

Figure 5.7 Xcelsius — Definition Tab

INPUT VALUES includes the option to set values as FILTER values for the characteristics that are included in the BW query. You can use Xcelsius components, such as a list box or a selector, to pass values to these filters and set additional filter values for the BW query. The VARIABLES category includes the option to set values for the VARIABLES. For our example, the details look like Figure 5.8.

Figure 5.8 Xcelsius Data Definition Details

For our example, we don't have any variables, but we can use the FILTERS for all of the characteristics and key figures to filter the data that will be used in the Xcelsius dashboard.

In OUTPUT VALUES we open up the details for the PRODUCT GROUP characteristic (see Figure 5.9). As you can see, for each characteristic you receive the LABEL, the DISPLAY STRING, and the INPUT STRING. The LABEL and the DISPLAY STRING represent the description and technical name of the characteristic. The INPUT STRING can be used to show the current filter selection for the characteristic. The options available under MEMBERS VALUE HELP depend on the InfoObject itself and represent the options for the descriptions and all available display attributes for the characteristic. These items can be used to give the dashboard user a list of values from a list box, for example.

Figure 5.9 Output Values per Characteristic

The INFORMATION category (see Figure 5.10) provides additional information for the BW query, such as when the BW query was last changed or when the data was last updated. This information can also be used in the dashboard.

Figure 5.10 Output Values — Information

The MESSAGES category (see Figure 5.11) gives you the option of including possible error messages as part of your dashboard.

Figure 5.11 Output Values — Messages

Now when you navigate to the DATA PREVIEW tab you can click the REFRESH DATA PREVIEW button and see a preview of the actual data set that you will retrieve (see Figure 5.12).

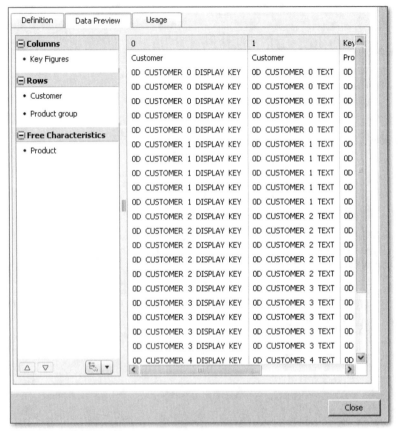

Figure 5.12 Data Preview

DATA PREVIEW is probably the most important part of the connectivity. The default view will show the elements of the BW query as you defined it in the BW query designer. All of the elements in the ROWS and COLUMNS from your BW query will become part of the result set and all of the elements from the FREE CHARACTERIS-TICS will, by default, not be part of the result set.

The real power of the DATA PREVIEW is on the left side, where you can move characteristics between ROWS, COLUMNS, and FREE CHARACTERISTICS and actually define the result set that will be returned to Xcelsius based on all of the elements in your BW query.

In addition, the actual display settings configured in the BW query for the characteristic will have an impact on your data set layout. As you can see in Figure 5.12, the CUSTOMER characteristic will be represented in our dataset with two columns; one column for the key and one for the description. This option can be set in the BW query designer for each characteristic.

Now when you navigate to the USAGE tab in DATA MANAGER, (see Figure 5.13) you have the option of configuring the connectivity to REFRESH ON LOAD, which means each time the dashboard is loaded the data will be refreshed. More importantly, you can also configure the USE DEFAULT QUERY DATA option. This lets you configure the first/initial run to be based on default values you might have configured in the BW query.

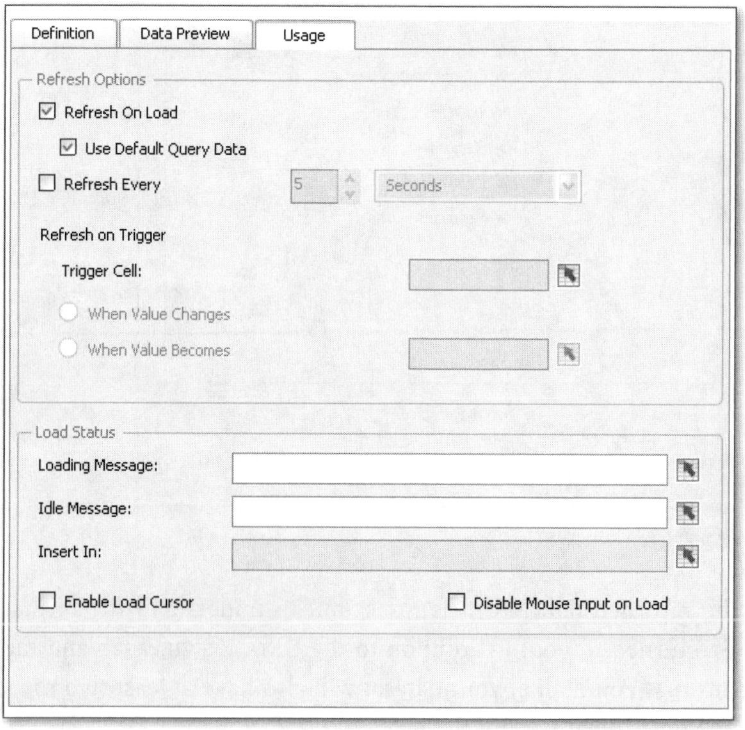

Figure 5.13 Data Manager — Usage

When you navigate back to the DEFINITION tab (see Figure 5.14), you will notice that the CROSS-TAB DATA entry is part of OUTPUT VALUES, which represents the data set you defined in the DATA PREVIEW tab.

In addition, you can use the RETURN DATA AS option to decide if the numbers should be returned as pure numeric numbers (RAW option) or you can select the FORMATTED option to return the numbers as a formatted string based on user preferences.

Figure 5.14 Data Manager — Definition

With regard to the returned data set, it is important to understand the format of the data that is returned to you. In addition to the DATA PREVIEW tab and the number of columns that you define, your dataset will also have at least two rows of data that provide more details about the data.

As shown in Figure 5.15, the first two rows of data contain additional information about the dataset by providing not only labels, but information about the unit and the actual scaling of the key figure. Keep in mind when creating your Xcelsius dashboards that at least these first two rows will always be there in addition to the actual results.

Key Figures	Billed Quantity	Net Sales
Product	ST	* 1.000 USD
PDS01	106282	132657.301
PDS02	126389	115240.45
PDS03	99792	124532.786
PDS12	33237	170818.32
Overall Result	365700	543248.857

Figure 5.15 Xcelsius — Sample Data Set

In addition, as you can see in Figure 5.15, the result set includes a row representing the OVERALL RESULT. This might not always be what you want to retrieve for your actual dashboard. If you want to avoid this row, you need to configure the RESULT ROWS option to the ALWAYS SUPPRESS option for each characteristic in the BW query designer.

Next, we'll change the BW query to also contain a set of fixed filters and a variable. In our example, we included a fixed filter for the CALENDAR MONTH and we added a variable for the PRODUCT GROUP (see Figure 5.16).

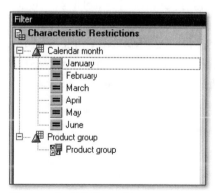

Figure 5.16 BW Query Changes

After we went back to Data Manager in Xcelsius and used the Browse option to reselect the BW query so that the changes will appear in Xcelsius, we can now identify the changes we made.

As shown in Figure 5.17, we now have the Input Value for the Variable we added to the BW query.

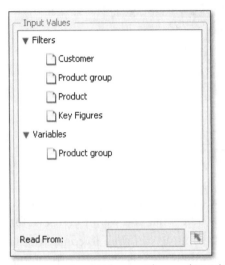

Figure 5.17   Input Values — Filters and Variables

We can also retrieve the values from the filter we added (see Figure 5.18) and we can use the Variable category in Output Values to create a list of possible members so that the user can select a value (see Figure 5.19).

At this point you should have a good understanding of how the Xcelsius designer is leveraging the metadata from the underlying BW query and where you can find which elements from the BW query. In the next section, we will look at the options for translating the text strings so that your dashboard can be viewed in different languages and then continue with the basics of the Xcelsius designer.

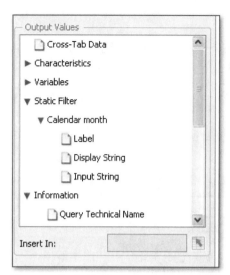

Figure 5.18 Static Filter

Figure 5.19 Variable

5.3.3 Integrating Translated Strings

In this section, we will look at how you can integrate translated strings as part of your dashboard. In the SAP menu you will find a menu item called TRANSLATION SETTINGS (see Figure 5.20).

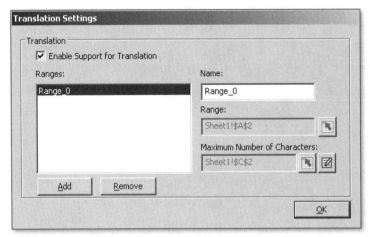

Figure 5.20 Translation Settings

In this dialog, you can use the ADD and REMOVE buttons to create or remove definitions of strings to be translated. These strings will then be transferred to the SAP NetWeaver BW system and you can use Transaction SE63 to translate them.

Let's go through the definition of such text strings:

1. In the Xcelsius designer, insert an additional sheet into your spreadsheet by right-clicking on the SHEET1 tab and select INSERT. The reason for inserting another sheet is that you can separate all of your translation strings from the data in your dashboard.

2. Create a table in your new sheet with two columns:

   ▶ String

   ▶ Maximum number of characters

   The maximum number of characters is helpful for the translation system so that the person translating the string has an indication of the string's maximum length.

> **Maximum Number of Characters**
>
> The maximum number of characters is not leveraged from the underlying SAP system as of SAP NetWeaver 7.0 Enhancement Package 01 Service Pack 05. However, this is on the list of future capabilities and therefore it's good practice to design the dashboards with this functionality in mind.

3. Enter the string labels you want to leverage for your dashboard and enter the maximum number of characters in the second column. For our example, see Figure 5.21.

	A	B
1	String	Maximum number of characteris
2	Sales	10
3	Revenue	15
4	Profit	10
5	Costs	10
6		
7		
8		

Figure 5.21 Translation Table

4. Follow the SAP • TRANSLATION SETTINGS menu path.

5. Now we need to add a definition per string that we would like to be translated.

6. Click ADD.

7. Click the 🔲 button next to RANGE and select the first string in our table.

8. Click the 🔲 button next to MAXIMUM NUMBER OF CHARACTERS and select the second column cell for the string.

9. Repeat the steps for our four strings.

Now you can use the strings in this table as labels or descriptions for any Xcelsius component and in that way provide a dashboard with language-dependent objects.

Now when you publish your Xcelsius dashboard to the SAP NetWeaver BW system, the strings will be transferred to the SAP system and you can use transaction

SE63 to translate those strings. Keep in mind that the underlying table in the Xcelsius designer will always show the strings that you entered and will not show the translated strings. The translated strings will be leveraged at runtime when you launch the Xcelsius dashboard.

5.3.4 Launching of dashboards

As shown in Figure 5.4, the Xcelsius dashboard is hosted and launched by the BEx web runtime. After you save an Xcelsius object into the role menu from your SAP NetWeaver BW, you will notice that the entry in the role menu looks similar to the following syntax:

```
<prt_protcl>://<prt_server>/<bi_launcher>?DASHBOARD=<Technical name of
the dashboard>.
```

This URL is very similar to the launching URL of a BW query for BEx web reporting, except that the parameter used in the URL is not QUERY (used to launch a BW query in web reporting) but DASHBOARD instead.

The placeholders `<prt_protcl>` and `<prt_server>` are dynamically resolved with the values from your system. The placeholder `<bi_launcher>` is a standard BEx web reporting iView launching the actual content.

5.3.5 Internationalization of Dashboards

Xcelsius offers limited support when it comes to the internationalization of your dashboard, which means showing a region-dependent number format or date format.

The following items are relevant to internationalization:

- Number format (for example, decimal point vs. decimal comma)
- Currency/Quantity
- Date format (for example, Day.Month.Year vs. Month/Day/Year)
- Time format

For the number format in the connectivity on top of SAP NetWeaver BI you have two options. You can either use the option of formatted numbers directly in the connection, which will provide you with the formatted number based on user preferences (Transaction SU3) as an actual string; or you can use the raw number format. In cases where you do use the formatted number option in the connection you need to keep in mind that you then retrieve an actual string and not a numeric value. If you do use the option to retrieve the raw number, the format of the number is decided based on the settings of the Xcelsius designer, which means if you design a dashboard with the regional settings for the Xcelsius designer set to English, your dashboard will show the English number format to all of your end users and if you create a dashboard with regional settings set to German your dashboard will show German number formats to everyone.

With regard to the currency and quantity information, the SAP NetWeaver BI connection provides you the correct currency and the correct quantity as part of the data retrieval and you can make use of it in your Xcelsius design (see Figure 5.12).

For date formats, you want to ensure that date values are being formatted in the underlying spreadsheet in a way that is not misleading. An example is the date 12/08/2009, which in some countries, for example, Germany, will be seen as 12th of August 2009 and in other countries, such as Canada, it would be seen as 8th of December 2009. When your dashboard displays dates, you want to be sure that the format is very clear by showing — as an example — the abbreviation of the month. In our example, this would mean 8 Dec 2009 instead of 12/08/2009. You can ensure this by formatting the corresponding spreadsheet cells.

When using timestamps, the problem is very similar to that of date formats. Some countries use a 24-hour timestamp — for example, 16:00 for 4:00 p.m. — and others use a 12-hour time stamp with a.m. and p.m. You should ensure that your dashboard design keeps a consistent format and that you show the complete time format, and not, for example, 4:00, without including a.m. or p.m.

In the next section we'll look at the requirements from our departments and evaluate which ones we can fulfill using Xcelsius.

5.4   Customer Case Study — Dashboarding Requirements

We will now look at the requirements from different areas and evaluate the ones that can be fulfilled best by using Xcelsius. We will — similar to previous chapters — list those requirements that we don't think we can fulfill with Xcelsius or that are better suited for another tool.

Financial Area Requirements — NOT Fulfilled by Xcelsius

The following represents a list of requirements we don't think can be fulfilled with Xcelsius or where we would use a different tool to best fulfill the requirement.

> **Unfulfilled Financial Area Requirement**
>
> ▸ For specific content (like an income statement or a balance sheet) that is being created, the design needs to be layout focused with the actual print of the report being a high priority.
> ▸ The reporting and analysis tools need to let the user create new calculations and formulas and share those with other consumers of the content.
> ▸ The reporting and analysis tools need to allow the use of hierarchies and navigation along those hierarchies in the actual content.

As you can see, the requirements we cannot fulfill from the financial area have to do with layout-based reports, such as a balance sheet or an income statement, and the capability to create on-demand calculations and formulas in the report.

The third requirement listed here is the visualization of the data along hierarchies.

Looking at these requirements, it's clear the first requirement is better suited by Crystal Reports — and we already provided the proof for that. The second requirement is better suited by Web Intelligence or Pioneer allowing the user to create calculations and formulas on-demand. The consumption of hierarchies is limited in Xcelsius (as outlined earlier), but it is possible, and we will leverage a hierarchy in our example. However, it is important to recognize the differences in how the user would like to leverage the hierarchies.

> **Xcelsius and SAP NetWeaver BW Hierarchies**
>
> With Xcelsius Enterprise 2008 Service Pack 02, you can directly leverage SAP NetWeaver BW connectivity. You can leverage hierarchies on a level based solution, where each level is presented as a single column. Right now there are no standard Xcelsius visualization components for hierarchies. There are several partner solutions for such visualization and you might want to look at the Xcelsius marketplace at *http://www.ondemand. com/information/xcelsius.asp.*

Sales Reporting Requirements — NOT Fulfilled by Xcelsius

The following is a list of requirements from the sales area that we think are better suited for another tool or cannot be fulfilled using Xcelsius.

> **Unfulfilled Sales Reporting Requirements**
>
> ▶ Distribution of content via email might be required.
> ▶ Users need the ability to change the view of the actual content. For example, changing a weekly sales statistics broken down by country into a weekly sales statistics broken down by sales region and quarter.
> ▶ Ideally, users should be able to modify existing reports or create new reports ad hoc.

The preceding requirements are those that we think are better suited for other tools or cannot be fulfilled by Xcelsius at all. Especially the capability to make Xcelsius dashboards available offline or distribute an Xcelsius dashboard via email, which are not standard functionalities offered as part of the BusinessObjects platform out of the box.

The requirement to change the view of the data in the report can be fulfilled with Xcelsius, to a certain degree, for those cases that are known when designing the dashboard, but Xcelsius cannot fulfill the requirement if this was not be considered when creating the dashboard.

The requirement to modify reports or create new reports is not something the Xcelsius tool can do and is better suited for Web Intelligence and Pioneer.

> **Xcelsius "Offline" and SAP BusinessObjects Innovation Center**
>
> You can see the Xcelsius publishing plug-in from the SAP BusinessObjects Innovation center at *https://www.sdn.sap.com/irj/boc/innovation-center.* This plug-in lets you create Xcelsius dashboards and update them with data on a regular basis.

HR Reporting Requirements — NOT Fulfilled by Xcelsius

The following list represents the requirements that we think are better suited for another tool or that cannot be fulfilled by Xcelsius.

Unfulfilled HR Reporting Requirements
▸ The content needs to leverage data from several different sources (SAP and non-SAP) and present it in a single report.
▸ It needs to present highly textual information and present it in a layout-focused format.
▸ Some of the content (such as employee appraisal or performance reviews) will be used as official documents and, therefore, need to follow strict layout rules.

The requirements that we can't fulfill with Xcelsius should come as no surprise, because these are requirements that we already thought were best suited for Crystal Reports.

Executive and Leadership Reporting Requirements — NOT Fulfilled by Xcelsius

There are no requirements that we can't fulfill with Xcelsius in the executive and leadership management area. This is not surprising as Xcelsius is a tool created for highly interactive and highly visualized dashboards, which is what the executive and leadership requirements are looking for.

Let's continue by looking at an overview of some of the basic steps in the Xcelsius designer.

5.5   Xcelsius Designer — Quick Basics

In the following sections, we'll look at some basic steps in the Xcelsius designer and how you can leverage Xcelsius to create data visualizations. The purpose of these sections is not to make you an Xcelsius expert but instead give you a basic understanding of how you can use Xcelsius with your SAP data.

5.5.1   Xcelsius Designer Overview

When you start the Xcelsius designer for the first time you will notice that your Xcelsius designer environment has five major areas (see Figure 5.22):

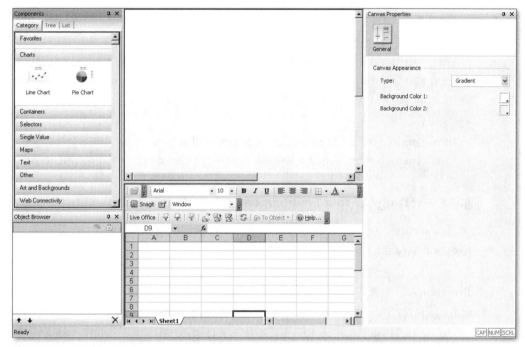

Figure 5.22   Xcelsius Designer

▶ **Components**
   With the VIEW • COMPONENTS menu path, you can enable or disable a list of components that you can leverage in your Xcelsius file. The COMPONENTS browser lets you view the list of components by CATEGORY, TREE control, or an alphabetical LIST.

▶ **Object Browser**
   With the VIEW • OBJECT BROWSER menu path, you can enable or disable the OBJECT BROWSER as part of the Xcelsius designer environment. The OBJECT BROWSER shows you all of the components that you can include into your Xcelsius visualization and you can select the objects, hide the objects, and lock the objects using the OBJECTS BROWSER; hiding components is especially helpful during the design of an Xcelsius file.

▶ **Canvas Properties**

The CANVAS PROPERTIES window is one of the most used windows in the Xcelsius designer when creating an Xcelsius dashboard. You can follow the VIEW • PROPERTIES menu path to activate the properties window. Or, you can right-click on the component and select PROPERTIES. The PROPERTIES window will show the properties and configuration options depending on the component.

▶ **Embedded Spreadsheet**

This embedded spreadsheet lets you define the area of data that is being leveraged and you can use it to create further calculations. We will look at this in more detail in Section 5.5.3, "Role of Microsoft Excel."

▶ **Canvas**

In the middle of the Xcelsius designer you will see an empty area. This is your canvas, which represents the area that you can use to create your Xcelsius file.

5.5.2 Setting Up Your Environment

In this section, we will look at some options for customizing your environment for your needs.

Preferences

Follow the FILE • PREFERENCES menu path to configure the global preferences that are being leveraged every time you create a new Xcelsius file for your design environment (see Figure 5.23).

▶ At DOCUMENT PREFERENCES, you can configure the size of your canvas based on either a list of preconfigured sizes or a custom size.

▶ In addition, you can preselect a DEFAULT THEME for your Xcelsius canvas. We will look at this in more detail in Section 5.5.5, "Common Look and Feel."

▶ At GRID PREFERENCES (see Figure 5.24), you can activate a grid for your canvas and configure if components should snap to the grid or not. The WIDTH and HEIGHT are entered in pixels.

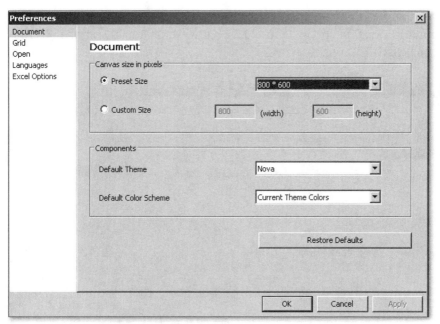

Figure 5.23 Xcelsius Designer Preferences

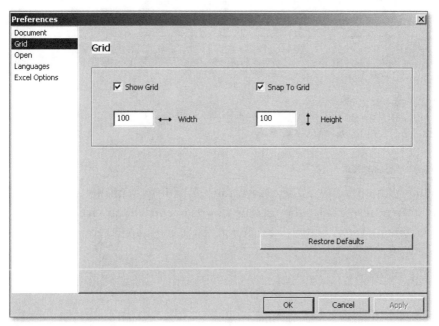

Figure 5.24 Grid Preferences

▶ EXCEL OPTIONS allows you to activate the LIVE OFFICE COMPATIBILITY, which is important when planning to use Live Office functionality in the Xcelsius designer (see Figure 5.25).

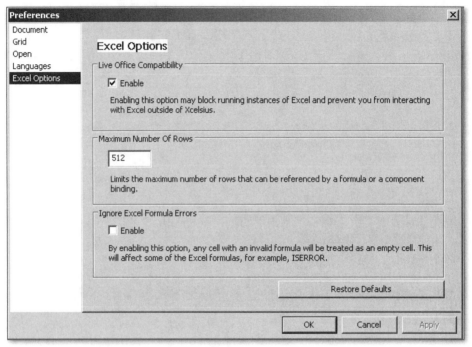

Figure 5.25 Excel Options

▶ You can set the MAXIMUM NUMBER OF ROWS that can be leveraged for components. The default value is 512 rows.

Document Properties

Follow the FILE • DOCUMENT PROPERTIES menu path to configure some of the global preferences specific to the Xcelsius file you opened in the Xcelsius designer and, if required, overwrite the global preferences (see Figure 5.26).

Figure 5.26 Document Properties

As you can see in Figure 5.26, you can change the size of the canvas and you can configure a standard font for the Xcelsius file.

Saving vs. Exporting

In the Xcelsius designer you can follow the menu paths FILE • SAVE AS and FILE • SAVE TO ENTERPRISE, and the FILE • EXPORT menu path, which offers several export options. The Xcelsius designer distinguishes between saving the actual design of your Xcelsius as an XLF file, which can be done using the FILE • SAVE AS or the FILE • SAVE TO ENTERPRISE menu path, and the option to export your Xcelsius file and generate a flash file (SWF) for end users to view your dashboard, which can be done with FILE • EXPORT.

5.5.3   Role of Microsoft Excel

Those who are new to Xcelsius often ask why they need the embedded spreadsheet in the Xcelsius designer. Therefore, the following list provides more details on the role of the embedded spreadsheet:

▶ In the most simplistic case, the embedded spreadsheet provides an option for entering data directly into the spreadsheet and visualizing it with Xcelsius. This can be helpful for cases where you don't have an underlying database or data warehouse.

▶ The embedded spreadsheet also lets you leverage formulas and calculations done in the spreadsheet so you can add calculations and possibly even aggregation to your data and use them in your Xcelsius visualization.

▶ The third part is the eventing that you can leverage from the spreadsheet. Each time the value of a cell or a range changes, you can leverage this as an event for your Xcelsius dashboard and use it, for example, to hide or unhide components from the dashboard.

The first two roles of the embedded spreadsheet are irrelevant, especially for the SAP NetWeaver BW case, because you have an actual datasource and data aggregation engine. In this case, the benefit you gain is the eventing model from the embedded spreadsheet that you can use to drive the interactive parts of your dashboard.

Because you need to use the embedded spreadsheet as a source for your components, it's important that you build some Best Practices regarding the usage of the spreadsheet. As an example, you can have multiple tabs in your embedded spreadsheet so that you can organize the data in a logical way. A second, very common practice is to color code the areas in the embedded spreadsheet used by the components and to employ different colors for different purposes, for example:

▶ Yellow: Data Retrieval

▶ Blue: Input Values

▶ Green: Embedded Formulas

▶ Red: Dynamic Visibility Flags

At this point, you have a good understanding of the Xcelsius designer environment. Let's move on to the next section and build the first Xcelsius dashboard on top of an SAP NetWeaver BW query.

5.5.4 Creating Your First Xcelsius Dashboard

In this section, we'll focus on some simple steps in the Xcelsius designer to get used to the data connectivity from SAP NetWeaver BW. This will also help you get familiar with the design of a dashboard using the Xcelsius designer.

Defining the Dashboard Scope

Before we start building the dashboard with Xcelsius it's always good practice to have a clear understanding of the scope and goal of the actual dashboard we're going to create. In our case, for the first dashboard we'll focus on some simple steps but try to cover all of the major concepts in Xcelsius.

Our dashboard should offer the sales revenue and sales costs broken down either by product or month — this should be the user's choice. In addition, the dashboard should show details broken down by month when the user selects a single product from the chart and it should show details broken down by product when the user selects a month in the chart.

In addition, we would like to see a set of critical Key Performance Indicators (KPIs) on the right-hand side, which would include the overall revenue, costs, and margin.

Defining the Data Connectivity

In our dashboard, we want to show the numbers broken down by month and by Product Group, and show some critical KPIs on an overall level. For our BW query this means we need to have the Calendar Month and Product Group as part of the BW query and we need to have all of the critical KPI in the BW query as well.

In the BW query shown in Figure 5.27, we have the PRODUCT characteristic and the CAL. YEAR/MONTH characteristic in the rows and several key figures in the columns. The key figures represent the NET SALES, PRODUCT COSTS, TRANSPORT COSTS,

TOTAL COSTS, PROFIT, and PERCENTAGE where as the last three key figures are formulas created in the BW query. The BW query is based on the NetWeaver Demo model InfoProvider 0D_NW_M01.

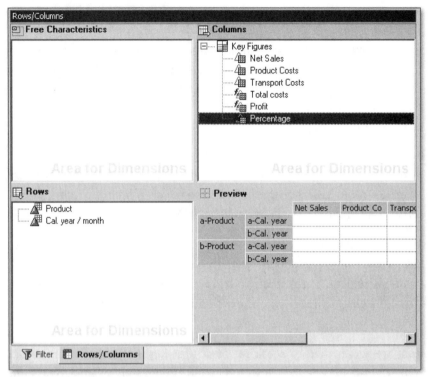

Figure 5.27 BW Query

In the BW query, make sure you configure both characteristics to be displayed with the key and description when available and configure both characteristics to suppress the result rows. Both of these configurations are done as part of the properties for each characteristic in the BW query designer.

SAP NetWeaver Demo Model

If you are interested in leveraging the SAP NetWeaver demo model for some simple exercises, you can find more information at *http://www.sdn.sap.com/irj/sdn/nw-demo-model*.

1. Start the Xcelsius Designer via the START • PROGRAMS • XCELSIUS • XCELSIUS 2008 menu path.

2. Follow the DATA • CONNECTIONS menu path.

3. Click ADD.

4. Select SAP NETWEAVER BI CONNECTION.

5. Click BROWSE.

6. Log on to your SAP system.

7. Select the newly created BW query (see Figure 5.28).

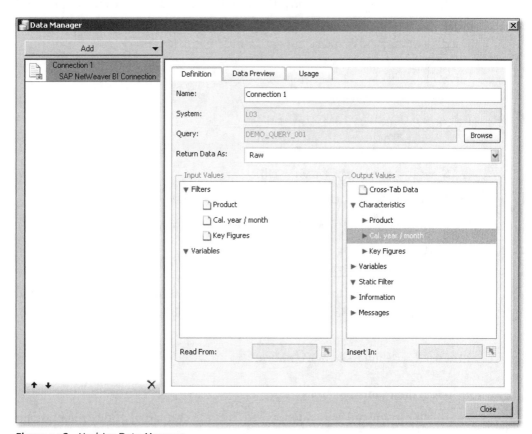

Figure 5.28 Xcelsius Data Manager

8. Navigate to the DATA PREVIEW tab.

9. Move the CAL. YEAR/MONTH characteristic to the FREE CHARACTERISTICS area.

10. Click REFRESH DATA PREVIEW to see a preview of the resultset.

11. Navigate back to the DEFINITION tab and enter `Data by Product` as the name for the connection.

12. Repeat these steps to add a second connection based on the same query with the same data preview configuration and name the connection `Data by Product (Drill)`.

In our case, we would like to show the data summarized once by the products and by the calendar month as an alternative, therefore, we need a second connection based on the same BW query but with a different data view.

13. Click ADD.

14. Select SAP NETWEAVER BI CONNECTION.

15. Click BROWSE.

16. Select the newly created BW query.

17. Navigate to the DATA PREVIEW tab.

18. Move the PRODUCT characteristic to the FREE CHARACTERISTICS area.

19. Click REFRESH DATA PREVIEW to see a preview of the resultset.

20. Navigate back to the DEFINITION tab and enter `Data by Calendar Month` as the name for the connection.

21. Repeat these steps to add a fourth connection based on the same query with the same data preview configuration and name the connection this time `Data by Calendar Month (Drill)`.

22. Click CLOSE in the DATA MANAGER.

Including Chart and Selectors

Now we'll prepare the embedded spreadsheet to organize all of the elements better. We have four connections for the data, and we need a way to select the option for summarizing the data by Product or Calendar Month and we will need an area to store the selections made by the user. This means we might need six sheets in our spreadsheet and four connections to organize things.

23. Navigate to the embedded spreadsheet.

24. Right-click on the Sheet 1 tab.

25. Select Insert and select a worksheet.

26. Repeat these steps to add another four sheets so that you have six sheets overall in the embedded spreadsheet.

27. Change the names of the sheets as follows:

    ▶ Sheet 1: Settings

    ▶ Sheet 2: Sales by Product

    ▶ Sheet 3: Sales by Month

    ▶ Sheet 4: Sales by Product (Drill)

    ▶ Sheet 5: Sales by Month (Drill)

    ▶ Sheet 6: Summary

28. In our first sheet (Settings) enter the following text:

    ▶ Cell A1 :Summarized by:

    ▶ Cell A2: Product

    ▶ Cell A3: Calendar month

    ▶ Cell B2: 1

    ▶ Cell B3: 2

29. Follow the View • Components menu path.

30. Drag and drop the Radio Buttons component from the selectors category to the top left corner of your canvas.

31. Right-click the new components and select properties (see Figure 5.29).

32. Click the ▣ button next to Title and set it to cell A1 in our sheet Settings.

33. Click the ▣ button next to Labels and select cells A2 and A3 in our Settings sheet.

34. Set the Insertion Type to Value.

35. Click the ▣ button next to Source Data and select cells B2 and B3 in our sheet Settings.

36. Click the  button next to DESTINATION and select cell B6 for our sheet SETTINGS.

37. Enter `Selected value` in cell A6 in our sheet SETTINGS.

38. Mark the value B6 in our SETTINGS sheet with a yellow highlight.

Figure 5.29   Properties for Radio Buttons

You just created two radio buttons that will use text stored in the embedded spreadsheet for display purposes and the values as the selected value. The user selection will be stored in a cell as well so that we can use it later on to hide or unhide a chart depending on the choice the user made.

39. Drag and drop a COLUMN CHART from CHARTS to your canvas and resize it so that it uses about half of the height of your canvas and three quarters of the width.

This chart will be showing the Net sales per product. But before we configure the properties we need to configure the data retrieval.

40. Follow the DATA • CONNECTIONS menu path.

41. Select the DATA BY PRODUCT connection we created and navigate to the DATA PREVIEW tab.

42. Click the REFRESH DATA PREVIEW button to verify the structure of the data set. You should see two columns for the product and six columns for the key figures.

43. Now navigate to the DEFINITION tab.

44. In OUTPUT VALUES, select CROSS-TAB DATA.

45. Click the ▣ button next to INSERT IN to select a range of eight columns and fifty rows (8x50) in our SALES BY PRODUCT sheet in the embedded spreadsheet.

46. Click OK.

47. Navigate to the USAGE tab.

48. Select the REFRESH ON LOAD option.

49. Click CLOSE in the DATA MANAGER.

50. Navigate to SALES BY PRODUCT in the embedded spreadsheet and highlight the area we just used green.

51. Right-click on the column chart in the canvas and select PROPERTIES.

52. Enter a title for the chart and remove the subtitle.

53. Select the BY SERIES option for the DATA and use the "+" symbol to add a series.

54. Enter Net sales as the NAME of the series.

55. Click the ▣ button next to VALUES (Y) and select the range C3 to C50 in our SALES BY PRODUCT sheet. Remember, the first two columns were PRODUCT KEY and PRODUCT DESCRIPTION and that the first two rows contain metadata (see Figure 5.15).

56. Click the ▣ button next to CATEGORY LABELS (X) and select the range B3 to B50 for the product descriptions (see Figure 5.30).

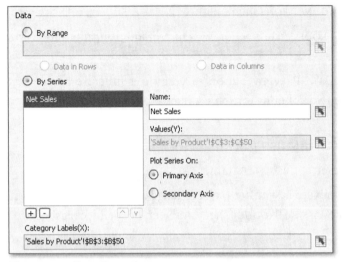

Figure 5.30 Chart Properties

57. Navigate to the Behavior tab of Properties. Select the Common tab.

58. Activate both options — In Series and In Values — for the Ignore Blank Cells option.

59. Navigate to the Scale tab from Behavior.

60. Activate the option Fixed Label Size to shorten the numbers on the Y-Axis.

61. Navigate to the Common tab from the Behavior area.

62. Click the ▣ button next to Status for Dynamic Visibility and from our Settings sheet, select cell B6, which is the cell where we store the user selection from the radio buttons.

63. Set the Key to the value 1, so that when the user selects the summary by product the chart will be shown; otherwise it will be hidden (see Figure 5.31).

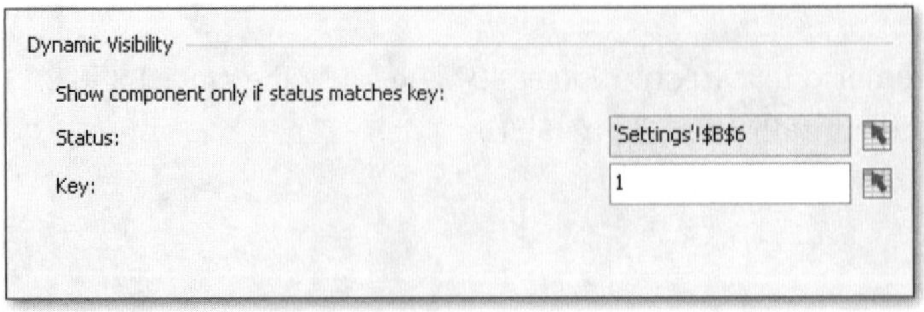

Figure 5.31 Dynamic Visibility

At this point we have an Xcelsius dashboard that allows us to select between a summary by PRODUCT or CALENDAR MONTH, and if we select the PRODUCT it shows the chart.

Now let's add the second chart to our canvas and we will use the OBJECT BROWSER to hide the current chart.

64. Follow the VIEW • OBJECT BROWSER menu path.

65. Select the option to hide the chart from your canvas (see Figure 5.32).

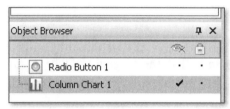

Figure 5.32 Object Browser

66. Drag and drop a COLUMN CHART from the CHARTS category to your canvas and resize it so that it uses about half of the height of your canvas and three quarters of the width, and overlaps with the chart we created previously. Here, you can also select both charts in the OBJECT BROWSER and use the FORMAT • MAKE SAME SIZE menu path to align the size of both charts.

67. Follow the DATA • CONNECTIONS menu path.

68. Select the DATA BY CALENDAR MONTH connection and navigate to the DATA PREVIEW tab.

69. Click the REFRESH DATA PREVIEW button to verify the structure of the data set. You should see one column for the Calendar month and six columns for the key figures.

70. Now navigate to the DEFINITION tab.

71. In OUTPUT VALUES, select CROSS-TAB DATA.

72. Click the button next to INSERT IN to select a range of seven columns and fifty rows (7x50) in our SALES BY MONTH sheet in the embedded spreadsheet.

73. Click OK.

74. Navigate to the USAGE tab.

75. Select the REFRESH ON LOAD option.

76. Click CLOSE in the DATA MANAGER.

77. Navigate to the SALES BY MONTH sheet in the embedded spreadsheet and highlight the area we just used green.

78. Right-click on the column chart in the canvas and select PROPERTIES.

79. Enter a title for the chart and remove the subtitle.

80. Select the BY SERIES option for the DATA and use the "+" symbol to add a series.

81. Enter NET SALES for the NAME of the series.

82. Click the button next to VALUES (Y) and select the range B3 to B50 in our sheet SALES BY MONTH. Remember that the first column is the Calendar month and the first two rows contain metadata (see Figure 5.15).

83. Click the button next to CATEGORY LABELS (X) and select the range A3 to A50 for the Calendar month descriptions.

84. Navigate to the BEHAVIOR tab of the properties. Select the COMMON tab.

85. Activate both options — IN SERIES and IN VALUES — for the IGNORE BLANK CELLS option.

86. Navigate to the SCALE tab from BEHAVIOR.

87. Activate the FIXED LABEL SIZE option to shorten the numbers on the y-axis.

88. Navigate to the COMMON tab from the BEHAVIOR area.

89. Click the button next to STATUS for DYNAMIC VISIBILITY and from our SETTINGS sheet, select cell B6, which is the cell where we store the user selection from the radio buttons.

90. Set the KEY to the value 2, so that when the user selects the summary by calendar month the chart will be shown; otherwise it will be hidden.

91. Follow the SAP • PUBLISH menu path to save the Xcelsius dashboard to your SAP NetWeaver BW system.

92. Enter a description and technical name for your Xcelsius dashboard (see Figure 5.33).

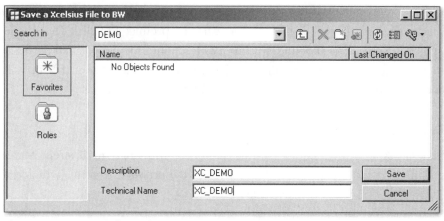

Figure 5.33 Saving Xcelsius File

93. Click SAVE.

94. Follow the SAP • LAUNCH menu path to launch the BEx web runtime and show your dashboard.

95. Enter the credentials for the BI Java part of your SAP system.

96. Your dashboard should appear and you should be able to switch between a view by product and calendar month (see Figure 5.34).

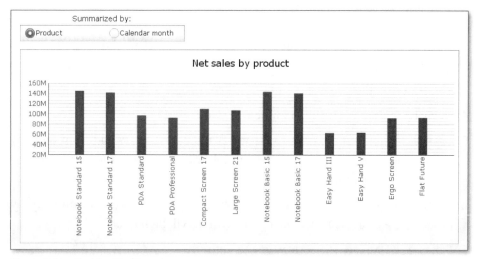

Figure 5.34 Xcelsius Dashboard

In the next step, we will add two additional charts to show the details of the opposite chart; so that when you show the net sales by product and click on a single bar, you will see a chart showing the net sales by month for the selected product. If you show the net sales by month and select a single month in the chart, you will see a chart showing the net sales by product for a single month.

Setting Up Drill Down

Up to this point, we created an Xcelsius dashboard showing two different charts based on our selection for either the month or the product. Now we will add a drill down chart for both of these charts.

In our example, we would like to show the numbers broken down by month in the lower level chart while the upper level chart shows the number broken down by product.

1. Drag and drop a new column chart to the canvas and place it below the existing two charts.

Naming of Elements

In the OBJECT BROWSER, you can right-click on a context menu for each element of your canvas and use RENAME to configure a name for each object. In that way it is easy to differentiate each object from the others.

---

2. This chart should only be displayed when the upper chart shows the Net sales by Product, so we need to configure the DYNAMIC VISIBILITY property.

3. Right-click on the new chart and select PROPERTIES.

4. Navigate to the COMMON tab in the BEHAVIOR area.

5. Click the ▣ button next to STATUS for DYNAMIC VISIBILITY and from our SETTINGS sheet, select cell B6, which is the cell where we store the user selections from the radio buttons.

6. Set the KEY to the value 1, that way, when the user selects the summary by product, the chart will be shown; otherwise it will be hidden.

7. Follow the DATA • CONNECTIONS menu path.

8. Select the DATA BY CALENDAR MONTH (DRILL) connection we created and navigate to the DATA PREVIEW tab.

9. Click the REFRESH DATA PREVIEW button to verify the structure of the data set. You should see one column for the calendar month and six columns for the key figures.

10. Now navigate to the DEFINITION tab.

11. In OUTPUT VALUES, select CROSS-TAB DATA.

12. Click the 🔳 button next to INSERT IN and select a range of seven columns and fifty rows (7x50) in our SALES BY MONTH (DRILL) sheet in the embedded spreadsheet.

13. Click OK.

14. Navigate to the USAGE tab.

15. Select the REFRESH ON LOAD option.

16. Click CLOSE in the DATA MANAGER.

17. Navigate to SALES BY MONTH (DRILL) sheet in the embedded spreadsheet and highlight the area we just used green.

18. Right-click on the chart and open the PROPERTIES.

19. Navigate to the GENERAL area.

20. Enter a title and remove the subtitle.

21. Select the BY SERIES option for the DATA and use the "+" symbol to add a series.

22. Enter Net sales as the NAME of the series.

23. Click the 🔳 button next to VALUES (Y) and select the range B3 to B50 in our SALES BY MONTH (DRILL) sheet. Remember, the first column is the Calendar month and the first two rows contain metadata (see Figure 5.15)

24. Click the 🔳 button next to CATEGORY LABELS (x) and select the range A3 to A50 from the SALES BY MONTH (DRILL) sheet for the Calendar month descriptions.

25. Navigate to the BEHAVIOR tab of the properties. Select the COMMON tab.

26. Activate both options — IN SERIES and IN VALUES — for the IGNORE BLANK CELLS option.

27. Navigate to the SCALE tab from BEHAVIOR.

28. Activate the FIXED LABEL SIZE option to shorten the numbers on the y-axis.

29. Without doing anything further, the lower chart would show the data for the month, but we want to show the Net sales for a single product, which is selected in the upper level chart and, therefore, we need to configure the drill down.

30. Right-click on the upper level chart showing the Net Sales by Product and select PROPERTIES, or you can also select the chart in the OBJECT BROWSER.

31. Navigate to the DRILL DOWN area.

32. Activate the ENABLE DRILL DOWN option (see Figure 5.35)

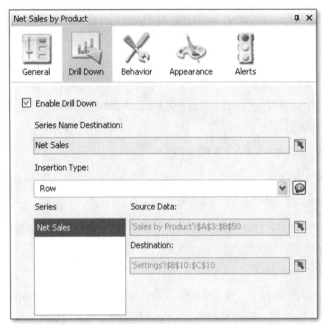

Figure 5.35 Drill Down Properties

33. Set the INSERTION TYPE to ROW.

34. Click the ▨ button next to SOURCE DATA and from our SALES BY PRODUCT sheet, select cells A3 to B50, which represent the key and description of our characteristic Product.

35. Use the ▨ button next to DESTINATION and set it to cells B10 to C10 in our sheet SETTINGS.

We configure the upper-level chart to store the first two columns of each selected element of the bar chart into cells B10 and C10. The reason for using the key and description value is to ensure that we send the actual key value as a filter for our BW query and not the description value, because the description value can be language dependent and is not unique.

Now we need to configure the data connectivity filter to only retrieve the values for a single product. If the user is setting a drill down, but we also want to see the values for all of the products, then when the user shows the net sales by month we can put in a small condition with a formula to define the correct filter in our spreadsheet.

36. Follow the DATA • CONNECTIONS menu path and select the NetWeaver BI connection DATA BY CALENDAR MONTH (DRILL).

37. Navigate to the DEFINITION tab and open the FILTER in the INPUT VALUES area.

38. Select PRODUCT.

39. Click the ▣ button next to READ FROM and select cell B10 in our SETTINGS sheet.

40. Navigate to the USAGE tab .

41. Click the ▣ button and select cell B10 as the TRIGGER CELL.

42. Activate the WHEN VALUE CHANGES option (see Figure 5.36).

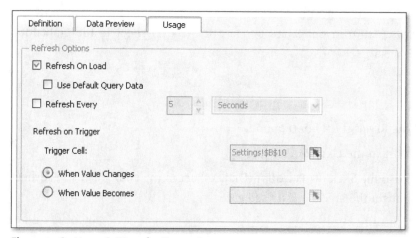

Figure 5.36 Usage Settings for Connection

43. Click CLOSE in DATA MANAGER.

44. Right-click on the lower level chart showing Net Sales by Month and select PROPERTIES.

45. Navigate to the GENERAL area.

46. Click the ▦ button next to the SUBTITLE property and select cell C10 from our SETTINGS sheet; this way, the chart will show the product description for each drill down.

47. Now we need to repeat these steps and create the drill down chart for the drill down from the calendar month showing each product.

48. Drag and drop a new column chart to the canvas.

49. Resize the chart so that it has a size similar to the first lower level chart.

50. Follow the DATA • CONNECTIONS menu path.

51. Select the DATA BY PRODUCT (DRILL) connection we created previously and navigate to the DATA PREVIEW tab.

52. Click the REFRESH DATA PREVIEW button to verify the structure of the data set. You should see two columns for the product and six columns for the key figures.

53. Now navigate to the DEFINITION tab.

54. In OUTPUT VALUES, select CROSS-TAB DATA.

55. Click the ▦ button next to INSERT IN and select a range of eight columns and fifty rows (8x50) in our SALES BY PRODUCT (DRILL) sheet in the embedded spreadsheet.

56. Click OK.

57. Navigate to the USAGE tab.

58. Select the REFRESH ON LOAD option.

59. Click CLOSE in the DATA MANAGER.

60. Navigate to the SALES BY PRODUCT (DRILL) sheet in the embedded spreadsheet and highlight the area we just used green.

61. Right-click on the newly created chart and select PROPERTIES.

62. Enter a title and remove the subtitle.

63. Navigate to the GENERAL area.

64. Select the BY SERIES option for the DATA and use the "+" symbol to add a series.

65. Enter Net Sales as the NAME of the series.

66. Click the ▣ button next to VALUES (Y) and select the range C3 to C50 in our SALES BY PRODUCT (DRILL) sheet. Remember, the first two columns are the product key and description and the first two rows contain metadata (see Figure 5.15).

67. Click the ▣ button next to CATEGORY LABELS (X) and select the range B3 to B50 from the SALES BY PRODUCT (DRILL) sheet for the product.

68. Navigate to the BEHAVIOR tab of the properties. Select the COMMON tab.

69. Activate both options — IN SERIES and IN VALUES — for the IGNORE BLANK CELLS option.

70. Navigate to the SCALE tab from BEHAVIOR.

71. Activate the FIXED LABEL SIZE option to shorten the numbers on the y-axis.

72. Navigate to the COMMON tab in the BEHAVIOR area.

73. Click the ▣ button next to STATUS for the DYNAMIC VISIBILITY and from our SETTINGS sheet, select cell B6, which is the cell where we store the user selections from the radio buttons.

74. Set the KEY to the value 2, that way, when the user selects the summary by Calendar month, the chart will be shown; otherwise it will be hidden.

75. Right-click on the upper level chart showing the Net Sales by month and select PROPERTIES.

76. Navigate to the DRILL DOWN area.

77. Activate the ENABLE DRILL DOWN option.

78. Set the INSERTION TYPE to ROW.

79. Click the ▣ button next to Source Data and from our Sales by Month sheet, select cells A3 to A50, which represent the key from our characteristic calendar month.

80. Click the ▣ button next to Destination and set it to cell B11 in our Settings sheet.

81. Follow the Data • Connections menu path and select the Data by Product (Drill) SAP NetWeaver BI connection.

82. Navigate to the Definition tab and open the Filter in the Input Values area.

83. Select Cal. Year / Month.

84. Click the ▣ button and select cell B11 in our Settings sheet.

85. Navigate to the Usage tab.

86. Click the ▣ button and select cell B11 as the Trigger Cell.

87. Activate the When Value Changes option (see Figure 5.36).

88. Click Close in the Data Manager.

89. Right-click on the lower level chart showing Net Sales by Product and select Properties.

90. Navigate to the General area.

91. Enter Net sales by product as the chart title.

92. Click the ▣ button next to the Subtitle property and select cell B11 from our Settings sheet; this way, the chart will show the calendar month for each drill down.

93. Follow the SAP • Publish menu path to save all of your changes back to the SAP NetWeaver BW repository.

94. Follow the SAP • Launch menu path to launch the Xcelsius dashboard (see Figure 5.37).

You created an Xcelsius dashboard that lets you not only select a different chart on the highest level, but also allows you to drill down into more details depending on the chart type you selected in the beginning.

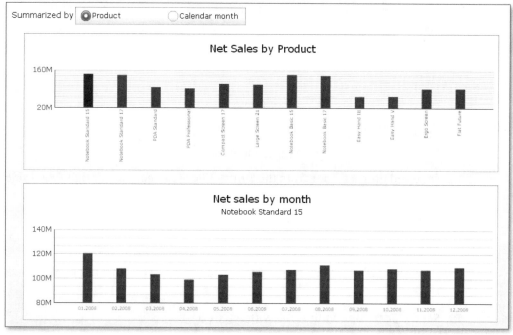

Figure 5.37 Xcelsius Dashboard

Adding Overall KPI

In the following steps, we will add some gauges to the dashboard to show overall revenue and cost.

1. Follow the DATA • CONNECTIONS menu path.
2. Click the ADD button to create a new SAP NetWeaver BI connection.
3. Click the BROWSE button to select the query we used previously.
4. Navigate to the DATA PREVIEW tab .
5. Move the PRODUCT and CAL YEAR / MONTH characteristics to the FREE CHARAC-TERISTIC area.
6. Click REFRESH DATA PREVIEW. You should now see a structure that only contains the key figures.
7. Now navigate to the DEFINITION tab.
8. In OUTPUT VALUES, select CROSS-TAB DATA.

9. Click the 🔳 button next to INSERT IN and select a range of seven columns and three rows (7x3) in our SUMMARY sheet in the embedded spreadsheet.

10. Click OK.

11. Navigate to the USAGE tab.

12. Select the REFRESH ON LOAD option.

13. Click CLOSE in the DATA MANAGER.

14. Follow the VIEW • COMPONENTS menu path.

15. Drag and drop a GAUGE from the SINGLE VALUE category to the right-hand side of the canvas.

16. Right-click the new gauge and select the menu item PROPERTIES.

17. Enter Net Sales as the TITLE.

18. Click the 🔳 button next to DATA and select the cell B3 from our SUMMARY sheet.

19. Set the SCALE option to AUTO with VALUE BASED.

20. Navigate to the ALERTS area.

21. Activate the ENABLE ALERTS option.

22. Use the AS PERCENT OF TARGET option and enter 2000000000 as the target value. You might have to adjust this value to your data in the system.

23. Select the HIGH VALUES ARE GOOD option for the COLOR ORDER option.

24. Navigate to the APPEARANCE area and select the TEXT tab.

25. Select VALUE and configure the number with a thousand separator and no decimals.

26. Drag and drop a second GAUGE from the SINGLE VALUE category to the right-hand side of the canvas, below the first gauge.

27. Right-click the new gauge and select PROPERTIES.

28. Enter Total Cost as the TITLE.

29. Click the 🔳 button next to DATA and select the cell E3 from our SUMMARY sheet.

30. Set the SCALE option to AUTO with VALUE BASED.

31. Navigate to the ALERTS area.

32. Activate the ENABLE ALERTS option.

33. Use the AS PERCENT OF TARGET option.

34. Click the  button and select cell B3 to represent Net Sales from our SUM-MARY sheet.

35. Select the LOW VALUES ARE GOOD option for the COLOR ORDER option.

36. Navigate to the APPEARANCE area and select the TEXT tab.

37. Select the VALUE and configure the number with a thousand separator and no decimals.

38. Follow the SAP • PUBLISH menu path to save your changes to the SAP NetWeaver BW system.

39. Use the SAP • LAUNCH menu path to view your dashboard (see Figure 5.38).

Figure 5.38 Xcelsius Dashboard

You created an Xcelsius dashboard that has several ways of interacting with and showing data in different ways. All of this is based directly on top of SAP NetWeaver BW data. In the next section, we'll take a look at how you can ensure a common look and feel for your dashboards. We'll then look at the requirements and how to realize them with Xcelsius.

5.5.5 Common Look and Feel

After working with Xcelsius for a while you will notice that there is a need for a common look and feel for your dashboards. A common look and feel can mean anything from the actual placement of a component, like a chart or gauge, to the color. Xcelsius offers several options to address this, so let's look at the three most common ones next.

Templates

From the FILE • TEMPLATES menu path you can find a list of predefined templates and samples based on certain tasks (see Figure 5.39).

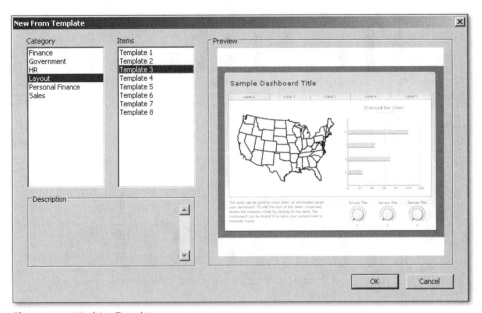

Figure 5.39 Xcelsius Templates.

Xcelsius delivers a set of templates that represent more complex dashboards and demonstrate the use of several components. These are worth spending some time with to see what you can do with Xcelsius. In addition, you will find a category called LAYOUT, where you will find a set of templates for specific tasks.

More importantly, you can create your own templates and make them company specific and offer them to all of your users.

To create a new template, all you have to do is:

1. Create the Xcelsius design in the Xcelsius designer.
2. Follow the FILE • SAVE AS menu path and save the XLF file to the template folder. If you used a standard installation, you will find the templates at *Program Files\Business Objects\Xcelsius\assets\template*.
3. Follow the FILE • EXPORT • FLASH (SWF) menu path and save the SWF file to the template folder.

After completing these steps, your Xcelsius design will be available in the list of templates. If you would like to create your own category, you can create a subfolder in the template folder and store your Xcelsius files there; the subfolder's name will be used as the name of the category.

Themes

Themes are a collection of properties; think of them as a style sheet for a web page. Follow the FORMAT • THEME menu path to select a theme for your Xcelsius design and it will be applied to all of your components.

It's important to note that the themes have different components and that switching between themes can influence the look and feel of your components, because it could be that a component you used before is not available in the new theme. In such cases, Xcelsius will replace the component with one from the newly selected theme.

Color Schemes

Follow the FORMAT • COLOR SCHEME menu path to leverage a set of predefined color schemes and create your own custom color schemes. The main difference between the color scheme and the theme is that you can customize the colors in the color scheme, whereas in the themes you can't.

Because you can't create your own themes in the current version of the product, your best option is to create a custom color scheme, with some templates that you can share.

In the next section, we will put this newly gained knowledge to work and use Xcelsius to fulfill parts of the requirements from the sales department.

5.6 Customer Case Study — Sales Management Dashboard with Xcelsius

In this section, we'll look at how we can fulfill the requirements from the sales area with Xcelsius. In Section 5.4, "Customer Case Study — Dashboarding Requirements," we noted that the following list of requirements can't be fulfilled with Xcelsius:

Unfilled Sales Management Reporting Requirements

▶ Distribution of content via email might be required.
▶ Users need the ability to change the view of the actual content. For example, changing a weekly sales statistics broken down by country into a weekly sales statistics broken down by sales region and quarter.
▶ Ideally, users should be able to modify existing reports or create new reports ad hoc.

But we also noted that the following requirements were well suited for Xcelsius:

▶ Content has to be available online and offline (for sales representatives on the road).

▶ Content has to leverage real-time data in most of the reports. Historical data might be required for comparisons.

▶ The content often needs to show a comparison of data along different time series.

▶ Users should be able to drill down or navigate to more detail-oriented data.

- Users should be able to perform a scenario-based analysis, where the user can see the data and influence certain factors to see the impact on the overall numbers. For example, a what-if analysis in a sales planning workflow.

For the purpose of our example, we will create a sales pipeline dashboard in form of a top customer scoreboard, showing the sales pipeline based on the sales cycle. The requirement that this dashboard is not covering — and that is based purely on scope of this book and not product capabilities — is the what-if analysis.

The first BW query that we are going to use is a BW query based on InfoProvider 0CRM_C04 (see Figure 5.40).

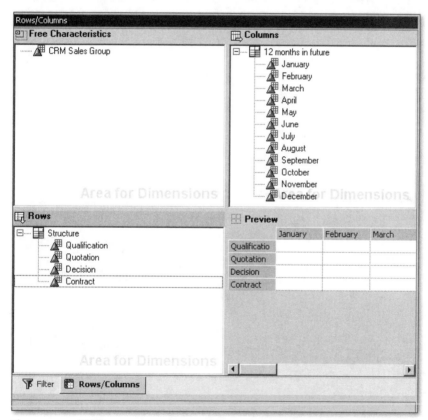

Figure 5.40 BW Query

The BW query contains a structure in the rows breaking down the Analysis Phase characteristic into four items (QUALIFICATION, QUOTATION, DECISION, and CONTRACT) in the rows and the CRM SALES GROUP characteristic in FREE CHARACTERISTICS. In the columns, the expected sales volume is broken down into a structure with twelve months. Overall, the BW query is retrieving the data for the current year via a SAP EXIT variable.

The second query for our overall scorecard is also based on InfoProvider 0CRM_C04, but it will retrieve a different set of data (see Figure 5.41).

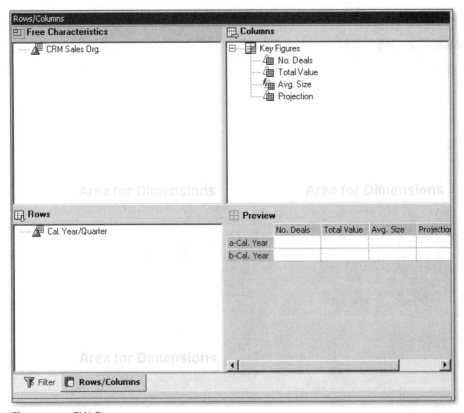

Figure 5.41 BW Query

This query shows a set of key figures broken down by the quarter and offering the CRM SALES ORG. as a FREE CHARACTERISTICS. The key figures shown are: NO. DEALS, TOTAL VALUE, AVG SIZE, and PROJECTION.

1. Start the Xcelsius designer.

2. Follow the DATA • CONNECTION menu path and click the ADD button to add two SAP NetWeaver BI connections.

3. Navigate to the first connection and enter `Sales Pipeline` as the name of the connection.

4. Click BROWSE.

5. Authenticate towards the SAP system and select the first query (as shown in Figure 5.40)

6. Navigate to the DATA PREVIEW tab and preview the data. Set the ANALYSIS PHASE structure into the rows, the CRM SALES ORG characteristic into FREE CHARACTERISTICS, and the key figures into the columns (see Figure 5.42).

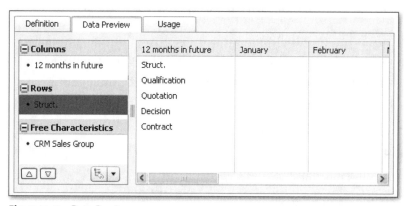

Figure 5.42 Data Preview

7. Navigate to the USAGE tab and activate the REFRESH ON LOAD option.

8. Select the second connection in the DATA MANAGER.

9. Enter `Sales Scorecard` as the NAME.

10. Click BROWSE.

11. Select the second query as shown in Figure 5.41.

12. Navigate to the DATA PREVIEW tab and preview the data. Set the CAL. YEAR/ QUARTER characteristic into the rows, the CRM SALES ORG characteristic into FREE CHARACTERISTICS, and the key figures into the columns (see Figure 5.43).

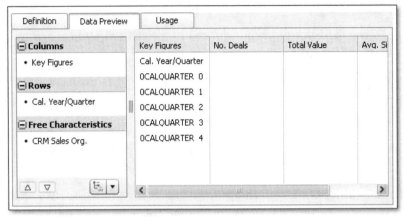

Figure 5.43 Data Preview

13. Navigate to the Usage tab and activate the Refresh on Load option.

14. Click Close in the Data Manager.

15. Right-click on Sheet1 in our embedded spreadsheet and use the Insert menu to add a second spreadsheet.

16. Repeat the step to add a third spreadsheet.

17. Name the spreadsheets as follows:

    ▸ Sheet 1: Settings

    ▸ Sheet 2: Sales pipeline

    ▸ Sheet 3: Sales scorecard

18. Follow the Data • Connections menu path and select the Sales Pipeline connection.

19. In Output Values, select Cross-tab data.

20. Click the ⬛ button next to Insert In and select cells A1 to M6 (a matrix of thirteen columns and six rows).

21. Click OK.

22. Select the second connection in the Data Manager called Sales scorecard.

23. In Output Values, select Cross-tab data.

24. Click the ⬛ button next to Insert IN and select cells A1 to E50 (a matrix of five columns and fifty rows).

25. Click OK.

26. Close the DATA MANAGER.

27. Follow the VIEW • COMPONENTS menu path.

28. Drag and drop a TAB SET component from the CONTAINERS area to your canvas.

29. Resize the component so that it fills the canvas.

30. Click on the first TAB1 tab in the component and use the "+" symbol to add a second tab.

31. Enter Sales Scorecard as the name of the tab and click OK.

32. Select TAB1 and then click on the empty space below the tab; that way, the PROPERTIES show the properties for the first tab.

33. In the PROPERTIES for TAB1, navigate to the GENERAL area and enter Sales Pipeline as LABEL.

34. Drag and drop four column charts to the first SALES PIPELINE tab and place them in the form of a matrix (see Figure 5.44).

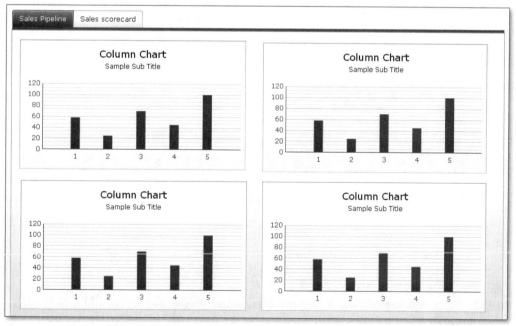

Figure 5.44 Xcelsius Design View

35. Right-click on the top-left column chart and select Properties.

36. Enter Qualification Phase as the Title.

37. Select the Data by Series option and use the "+" symbol to add a new series.

38. Enter Sales Volume as the Name.

39. Click the 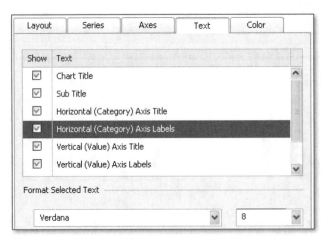 button next to Values(y) and select cells B3 to M3 from our Sales Pipeline sheet. Remember, our BW query retrieves a structure in the rows with Qualification being the first entry.

40. Click the ▨ button next to Category Labels (x) and select cells B1 to M1.

41. Navigate to the Behavior area and activate the Ignore Blank Cells In Series and In Values options.

42. Navigate to the Scale area and activate the Fixed Label Size option.

43. Navigate to the Appearance area and select the Text tab.

44. Navigate to each item in the list of text objects and set the font size to 8 (see Figure 5.45).

Figure 5.45 Text Properties

45. Right-click on the top-right column chart and select Properties.

46. Enter Quotation Phase as the Title.

47. Select the Data by Series option and use the "+" symbol to add a new series.

48. Enter Sales Volume as the Name.

49. Click the ▣ button next to Values(y) and select cells B4 to M4 from our Sales Pipeline sheet. Remember, our BW query retrieves a structure in the rows with Quotation being the second entry.

50. Click the ▣ button next to Category Labels (x) and select cells B1 to M1.

51. Navigate to the Behavior area and activate the Ignore Blank Cells In Series and In Values options.

52. Navigate to the Scale area and activate the Fixed Label Size option.

53. Navigate to the Appearance area and select the Text tab.

54. Navigate to each item in the list of text objects and set the font size to 8.

55. Right-click on the bottom-left column chart and select Properties.

56. Enter `Decision Phase` as the Title.

57. Select the Data by Series option and use the "+" symbol to add a new series.

58. Enter `Sales Volume` as the Name.

59. Click the ▣ button next to Values(y) and select cells B5 to M5 from our Sales pipeline sheet. Remember, our BW query retrieves a structure in the rows with Decision being the third entry.

60. Click the ▣ button next to Category Labels (x) and select cells B1 to M1.

61. Navigate to the Behavior area and activate the Ignore Blank Cells In Series and In Values options.

62. Navigate to the Scale area and activate the Fixed Label Size option.

63. Navigate to the Appearance area and select the Text tab.

64. Navigate to each item in the list of text objects and set the font size to 8.

65. Right-click on the bottom-right column chart and select Properties.

66. Enter `Contract Phase` as the title.

67. Select the Data by Series option and use the "+" symbol to add a new series.

68. Enter `Sales Volume` as the Name.

69. Click the ▣ button next to Values(y) and select cells B6 to M6 from our Sales pipeline sheet. Remember, our BW query retrieves a structure in the rows with Contract being the fourth entry.

70. Click the ▣ button next to Category Labels (x) and select cells B1 to M1.

71. Navigate to the Behavior area and activate the Ignore Blank Cells In Series and In Values options.

72. Navigate to the Scale area and activate the Fixed Label Size option.

73. Navigate to the Appearance area and select the Text tab.

74. Navigate to each item in the list of text objects and set the font size to 8.

75. Follow the View • Components menu path.

76. Drag and drop a Combo Box from the Selectors area above the tab set onto your canvas.

77. Right-click the new Combo Box and select properties.

78. Enter `Sales Organization` as the title.

79. Navigate to the Appearance area and select the Text tab.

80. Select Title and set the value for the Position option to Left (see Figure 5.46).

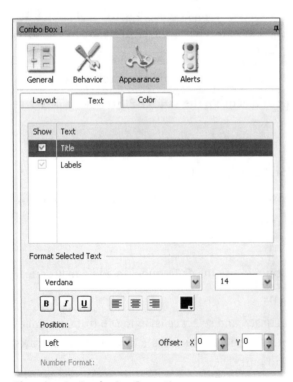

Figure 5.46 Combo Box Properties

81. Follow the DATA • CONNECTIONS menu path.

82. Select the SALES PIPELINE connection.

83. Navigate to OUTPUT VALUES and open the list of characteristics.

84. Open CRM SALES GROUP (see Figure 5.47).

Figure 5.47 Output Values

85. Select KEY in MEMBERS VALUE HELP.

86. Click the ■ button next to INSERT IN and select cells A2 to A20 in our SETTINGS sheet.

87. Select MEDIUM TEXT in MEMBERS VALUE HELP.

88. Click the ■ button next to INSERT IN and select cells B2 to B20 in our SETTINGS sheet.

89. Close the DATA MANAGER.

90. Navigate to the embedded sheet and select the SETTINGS sheet.

91. Enter the value ALL into cell B1.

We configured the CRM SERVICE ORG. characteristic to put values into cells A2 to B20 and now we can configure our combo box to pick up the values from there and use them as a filter for the charts. In addition, we added the text All with no key value, which lets us show the charts for all of the sales organizations together.

92. Right-click on the combo box and select PROPERTIES.

93. Click the ⊞ button next to LABELS and select cells B1 to B20 in our SETTINGS sheet.

94. Set the INSERTION TYPE to VALUE.

95. Click the ⊞ button next to SOURCE DATA and select cells A1 to A20 in our SETTINGS sheet.

96. Click the ⊞ button next to DESTINATION and select cell D1 in our SETTINGS sheet.

97. Follow the DATA • CONNECTIONS menu path and select SALES PIPELINE.

98. Select CRM Sales group in FILTERS of INPUT VALUES.

99. Click the ⊞ button next to READ FROM and select cell D1 in our SETTINGS sheet (see Figure 5.48).

Figure 5.48 Data Connection

100. Navigate to the Usage tab.

101. Click the 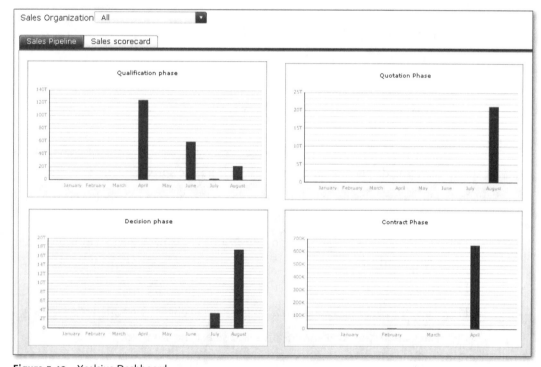 button next to Trigger Cell and select cell D1 in our Settings sheet.

102. Set the When Value Changes option.

103. Click Close to close the Data Manager.

104. Follow the SAP • Publish menu path to store your Xcelsius dashboard to SAP NetWeaver BW.

105. Follow the SAP • Launch menu path to see a preview of your Xcelsius dashboard (see Figure 5.49).

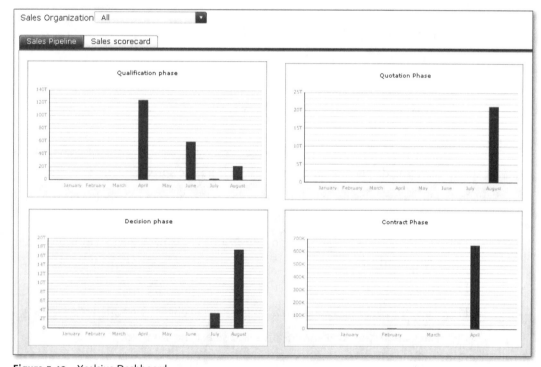

Figure 5.49   Xcelsius Dashboard

In the Sales scorecard tab, we will show the data by quarter from our BW query and we can add Trend icons, which will be shown per quarter, depending on the growth of the total sales value and the average deal size.

Our Sales scorecard BW query returns the quarter and 4 key figures in the following order: No. Deals (column B), Total Value (column C), Avg. Size (column D), Projection (column E).

106. Navigate back to the Xcelsius designer.

107. Navigate to the embedded spreadsheet and select the Sales Scorecard sheet.

108. In cell F1, enter the text `Total Value growth`.

109. In cell G1, enter the text `Avg. Deal size growth`.

110. Enter the following formula into cell F4:

    ```
    IF(A4="","",((C4/C3)-1))
    ```

111. Enter the following formula into cell G4:

    ```
    IF(A4="","",( (D4/D3)-1))
    ```

    By using the IF condition to check if there's a value for the quarter, we are avoiding displaying an error message from the spreadsheet.

112. Fill the other cells in column F and G with the same formula via copy and paste so that the relative pointer will be used.

113. Drag and drop a Grid component from the Other category into the Sales Scorecard tab.

114. Right-click the grid and select Properties.

115. Click the ▓ button next to Data and select cells A1 to A20.

116. Navigate to the Appearance area and select the Text tab.

117. Select the item Value and set the Number Format to General.

118. Make sure the text is left aligned.

    The reason for splitting up the numbers and the descriptions for the calendar year into two grid components is that the current grid component is only able to provide a single formatting for the values and we want to ensure that the descriptions and values are treated different.

119. Drag and drop a Grid component from the Other category onto the Sales Scorecard tab.

120. Right-click the grid and select Properties.

121. Click the ▣ button next to Data and select cells B1 to E20.

122. Navigate to the Appearance area and select the Text tab.

123. Select Value and set the Number Format to currency and make sure the number of decimal places is set to 2.

124. Make sure the text is right aligned.

125. Select both grids on your canvas and follow the Format • Align • Top menu path to make sure the two grids are perfectly aligned.

126. Save and launch your Xcelsius dashboard (see Figure 5.50).

At this point, all that is left to do is add the Trend icons for the growth of the Total Value and Avg. Size.

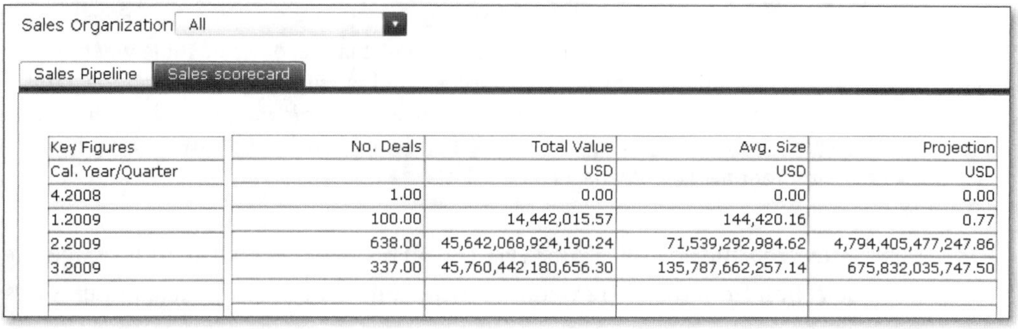

Key Figures	No. Deals	Total Value	Avg. Size	Projection
Cal. Year/Quarter		USD	USD	USD
4.2008	1.00	0.00	0.00	0.00
1.2009	100.00	14,442,015.57	144,420.16	0.77
2.2009	638.00	45,642,068,924,190.24	71,539,292,984.62	4,794,405,477,247.86
3.2009	337.00	45,760,442,180,656.30	135,787,662,257.14	675,832,035,747.50

Sales Organization All

Sales Pipeline | Sales scorecard

Figure 5.50 Xcelsius Dashboard

127. Drag and drop a Label component onto your canvas as a label for the first Trend icon. Place the Label component next to the table on the right-hand side.

128. Right-click the Label object and select properties.

129. Select the Link to cell option and point to cell F1 in our Settings sheet.

130. Drag and drop a second LABEL component onto your canvas as a label for the second TREND icon. Place the LABEL component next to the table on the right-hand side.

131. Right-click the LABEL object and select PROPERTIES.

132. Select the LINK TO CELL option and point to cell G1 in our SETTINGS sheet.

133. Drag and drop two TREND icons from the OTHER category to your canvas and place them next to each other and next to our fourth row of data.

134. Right-click the first TREND icon and select PROPERTIES.

135. Click the 🔳 button next to DATA and select cell F4 in our SALES SCORECARD sheet.

136. Repeat the steps and point the second TREND Icon to cell G4.

137. Repeat the steps to display as much data as you want in your dashboards. The pointer to the data moves on a row-by-row basis.

Real Data vs. "Fake" Data

The TREND icon is a good example of a component that becomes invisible when there is no actual data in the embedded spreadsheet and might make the actual design difficult for some people. Feel free to just use some sample numbers in the embedded spreadsheet during the design; at runtime the numbers will be overwritten with your definitions from the Data Manager.

---

138. After you include all of the TREND icons, all that is left is to leverage the selection from the SALES ORGANIZATION combo box for the data in our SALES SCORECARD.

139. Follow the DATA • CONNECTION menu path.

140. Select the SALES SCORECARD connection.

141. Select the DEFINITION tab .

142. Select CRM SALES GROUP in the FILTERS of INPUT VALUES.

143. Click the 🔳 button next to READ FROM and select cell D1 in our SETTINGS sheet.

144. Navigate to the Usage tab.

145. Click the button next to Trigger Cell and select cell D1 in our Settings sheet.

146. Set the When Value Changes option .

147. Click Close to close the Data Manager.

148. Publish your changes to the SAP NetWeaver BW system and launch your dashboard.

You should now have a dashboard that shows the sales pipeline broken by sales cycle phase on the first tab and a sales scorecard with sales pipeline numbers per quarter and trend indications on the second tab. In our next section, we will use Xcelsius to fulfill the requirement for a sales planning scenario.

5.7 Customer Case Study — Sales Planning Dashboard with Xcelsius

In our second example, we will look at how to use Xcelsius to not only show the numbers from your sales organization, but also offer a planning scenario where people can influence the planned numbers by using sliders in the dashboard. In the next couple of steps, we'll create an Xcelsius dashboard that provides the information about our sales revenue by product and regions, and also provide us the planning scenario where we can see the impact of reducing or increasing our product costs or our sales forecast.

Both queries that we'll use are based on InfoProvider 0D_NW_M01 from the SAP NetWeaver demo model. The first query shows the key figures Product Costs, Transports Costs, Number of deals, and Net Sales along with the characteristics Region, Product Category, and Cal. Year/Month (see Figure 5.51).

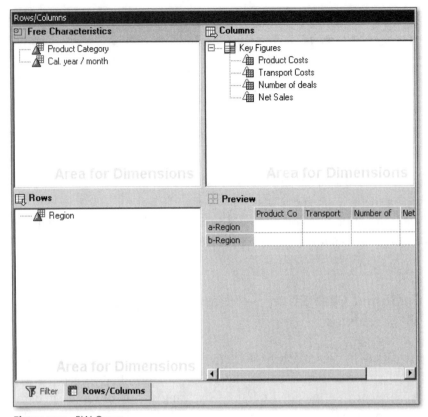

Figure 5.51 BW Query

The second query we will use for the planning scenario shows the identical key figures broken down by a structure that aggregates the key figures into quarters (see Figure 5.52).

In both BW queries, make sure that you configure the characteristics to show key and text and to suppress any result rows.

1. Start the Xcelsius designer.

2. Follow the DATA • CONNECTION menu path and click the ADD button to add four SAP NetWeaver BI connections.

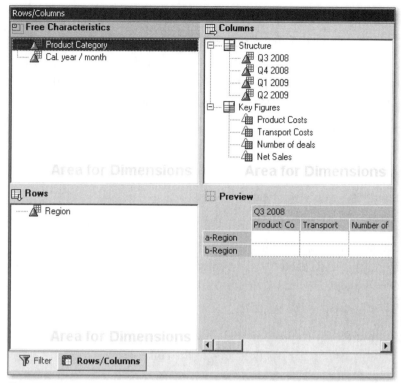

Figure 5.52 BW Query

3. Navigate to the first connection and enter `Current Sales Data by Region` as the name of the connection.

4. Click Browse.

5. Select the first BW query that we created (see Figure 5.51).

6. Navigate to the Usage tab and activate the Refresh on Load option.

7. Navigate to the Data Preview and make sure you can see the data in the preview. Make sure the Region characteristic is shown in the rows and any other characteristics are shown in Free Characteristic.

8. Navigate to the second connection in the list and enter `Current Sales Data by Product Category` as the name.

9. Click Browse.

10. Select the first BW query that we created.

11. Navigate to the Usage tab and activate the Refresh on Load option.

12. Navigate to Data Preview and make sure you can see the data in the preview. Make sure that the Product Category characteristic is shown in the rows and that any other characteristics are shown in Free Characteristics.

13. Navigate to the third connection and enter `Current Sales Data by Month (Region filter)` as name of the connection.

14. Click Browse.

15. Select the first BW query we created.

16. Navigate to the Usage tab and activate the Refresh on Load option.

17. Navigate to Data Preview and make sure you can see the data in the preview. Make sure that the Cal. Year / Month characteristic is shown in the rows and that any other characteristic are shown in the Free Characteristic.

18. Click Close in the Data Manager.

19. Navigate to the fourth connection and enter `Current Sales Data by Month (Product Category Filter)` as the name of the connection.

20. Click Browse.

21. Select the first BW query that we created.

22. Navigate to the Usage tab and activate the Refresh on Load option.

23. Navigate to Data Preview and make sure you can see the data in the preview. Make sure that the Cal. Year/Month characteristic is shown in the rows and that any other characteristics are shown in Free Characteristics.

24. Navigate to the embedded spreadsheet and add five more sheets to it. Name the sheet as follows:
    - Settings
    - Sales by Region
    - Sales by Product Category

- Sales by Month (Region Filter)
- Sales by Month (Product Filter)
- Sales planning

25. Add the following text to the sheet SETTINGS:

    - Cell A1: Revenue shown by
    - Cell A2: Product Category
    - Cell A3: Region
    - Cell B2: 1
    - Cell B3: 2

26. Drag and drop a TAB SET component from the CONTAINERS category to your canvas and resize it so that it uses all of the canvas space.

27. Select the first tab and enter `Sales Revenue` into the LABEL property.

28. Select the TAB SET component and use the "+" symbol to add a second tab.

29. Enter `Sales Planning` as the LABEL for the tab.

30. Drag and drop a RADIO BUTTON component from the SELECTORS category to the top left of our first tab.

31. Right-click the new RADIO BUTTON component and select PROPERTIES.

32. Click the ▨ button next to TITLE and select cell A1 in our SETTINGS sheet.

33. Click the ▨ button next to LABELS and select cells A2 to A3 in our SETTINGS sheet.

34. Set the INSERTION TYPE to VALUE option.

35. Click the ▨ button next to SOURCE DATA and select cell B2 to B3 in our sheet SETTINGS.

36. Click the ▨ button next to DESTINATION and select cell B5 in our sheet SETTINGS (see Figure 5.53).

37. Set the option ORIENTATION to HORIZONTAL.

38. Navigate to the APPEARANCE area and select the TEXT tab.

39. Select TITLE and set the POSITION option to the value LEFT.

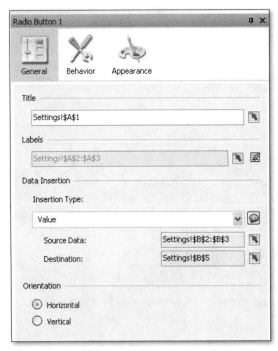

Figure 5.53 Radio Button Properties

40. Drag and drop a line chart to the first tab and size it so that it uses the complete width but about half of the height from the tab set.

41. Right-click on the Line Chart and select Properties.

42. Enter Net Sales Revenue into cell A20 in our Settings sheet.

43. Click the button next to Title and select cell A20 in our sheet Settings and remove the subtitle.

44. Follow the Data • Connections menu path and select Current Sales Data by Month (Region Filter).

45. Select Cross-Tab Data in Output Values. Click the button next to Insert In and select a matrix of 5 columns and 50 rows in the sheet Sales by Month (Region Filter).

46. Click Close in the Data Manager.

47. Right-click on the Line Chart and open the Properties.

48. Select the General area.

49. Select the BY SERIES option for the DATA.

50. Use the "+" symbol to add a new series.

51. Enter the text Net Sales into cell A21 in our SETTINGS sheet.

52. Click the ▣ button next to NAME for your series and select cell A21 in our sheet SETTINGS.

53. Click the ▣ button next to VALUES (Y) and select cells B3 to B50 in our SALES BY MONTH (REGION FILTER) sheet. These cells represent the NET SALES key figure, which you can also verify in the DATA PREVIEW of the data connection.

54. Click the ▣ button next to CATEGORY LABELS (X) and select cells A3 to A50 in our SALES BY MONTH (REGION FILTER) sheet.

55. Navigate to the BEHAVIOR area and set the IN SERIES and IN VALUES options on the COMMON tab.

56. Click the ▣ button next to STATUS for DYNAMIC VISIBILITY and select cell B5 in our SETTINGS sheet and set the key to the value 2.

57. Drag and drop a COMBO BOX to the first tab next to the radio buttons.

58. Follow the DATA • CONNECTIONS menu path and select CURRENT SALES DATA BY MONTH (REGION FILTER).

59. Select the item KEY in the Region MEMBER HELP list from OUTPUT VALUES (see Figure 5.54).

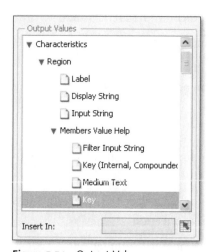

Figure 5.54 Output Values

60. Click the 🔳 button next to Insert In and select cells E2 to E50 in our Settings sheet.

61. Select Medium Text and click the 🔳 button next to Insert In and select cells F2 to F50 in our Settings sheet.

62. Close the Data Manager.

63. Enter ALL into cell F1 and leave cell E1 empty.

64. Right-click on the Combo Box and select Properties.

65. Click the 🔳 button next to Labels and select cell F1 to F50 in our Settings sheet.

66. Set the Insertion Type to the Value option.

67. Click the 🔳 button next to Source Data and select cells E1 to E50 in our Settings sheet.

68. Click the 🔳 button next to Destination and select cell B6 in our Settings sheet.

69. Navigate to the Behavior area and set the In Values option.

70. Click the 🔳 button next to Status for Dynamic Visibility, select cell B5 in our Settings sheet, and set the key to 2.

71. Follow the Data • Connections menu path and select the Current Sales Data by Month (Region Filter) connection.

72. Navigate to the Definition tab and select Region in the Filters area.

73. Click the 🔳 button next to Read From and select cell B6 in our Settings sheet.

74. Navigate to the usage tab, click the 🔳 button next to Trigger Cell, and select cell B6 in our sheet.

75. Activate the When Value Changes option.

76. Drag and drop a second Combo Box in the first tab so that it overlaps with the first combo box.

77. Follow the Data • Connections menu path and select the Current Sales Data by Month (Product Category Filter) connection.

78. Select Key in the Product Category Member help list from Output Values.

79. Click the ☒ button next to INSERT IN and select cells H2 to H50 in our SETTINGS sheet.

80. Select MEDIUM TEXT, click the ☒ button next to INSERT IN, and select cells I2 to I50 in our SETTINGS sheet.

81. Close the DATA MANAGER.

82. Enter the text ALL into cell I1 and leave cell H1 empty.

83. Right-click on the second COMBO BOX and select PROPERTIES.

84. Click the ☒ button next to LABELS and select cells I1 to I50 in our SETTINGS sheet.

85. Set the INSERTION TYPE to the VALUE option.

86. Click the ☒ button next to SOURCE DATA and select cell H1 to H50 in our SETTINGS sheet.

87. Click the ☒ button next to DESTINATION and select cell B7 in our SETTINGS sheet.

88. Navigate to the BEHAVIOR area and set the IN VALUES option.

89. Click the ☒ button next to STATUS for DYNAMIC VISIBILITY and select cell B5 in our SETTINGS sheet and set the key to 1.

90. Follow the DATA • CONNECTIONS menu path and select the CURRENT SALES DATA BY MONTH (PRODUCT CATEGORY FILTER) connection.

91. Navigate to the DEFINITION tab and select PRODUCT CATEGORY in the FILTERS area.

92. Click the ☒ button next to READ FROM and select cell B7 in our SETTINGS sheet.

93. Navigate to the USAGE tab, click the ☒ button next to TRIGGER CELL and select cell B7 in our SETTINGS sheet.

94. Activate the WHEN VALUE CHANGES option.

95. Drag and drop a second line chart into the first tab and size it so that it overlaps with the first line chart.

96. Right-click on the LINE CHART and select PROPERTIES.

97. Click the ▣ button next to TITLE and select cell A20 in our SETTINGS sheet and remove the subtitle.

98. Follow the DATA • CONNECTIONS menu path and select the CURRENT SALES DATA BY MONTH (PRODUCT CATEGORY FILTER) connection.

99. Select CROSS-TAB DATA in OUTPUT VALUES. Click the ▣ button next to INSERT IN and select a matrix of 5 columns and 50 rows in the SALES BY MONTH (PRODUCT FILTER) sheet.

100. Click CLOSE in the DATA MANAGER.

101. Right-click on the LINE CHART and open PROPERTIES.

102. Select the GENERAL area.

103. Select the BY SERIES option for the DATA.

104. Use the "+" symbol to add a new series.

105. Click the ▣ button next to NAME for your series and select cell A21 in our SETTINGS sheet.

106. Click the ▣ button next to VALUES (Y) and select cells B3 to B50 in our SALES BY MONTH (PRODUCT FILTER) sheet. These cells represent the NET SALES key figure, which you can also verify in the DATA PREVIEW of the data connection.

107. Click the ▣ button next to CATEGORY LABELS (X) and select cells A3 to A50 in our SALES BY MONTH (PRODUCT FILTER) sheet.

108. Navigate to the BEHAVIOR area and set the IN SERIES options and IN VALUE on the COMMON tab.

109. Click the ▣ button next to STATUS for DYNAMIC VISIBILITY, select cell B5 in our SETTINGS sheet and set the key to 1.

110. Drag and drop a PIE CHART in the first tab and size it so that it covers the lower left area below the line chart and half of the width.

111. Right-click on the PIE CHART and select PROPERTIES.

112. Enter `Revenue mix by region` into cell A23 in our SETTINGS sheet.

113. Click the ▣ button next to TITLE and select cell A23 in our SETTINGS sheet.

114. Select the GENERAL area of the properties.

115. Select the DATA IN COLUMNS option for the data.

116. Click the ▣ button next to VALUES and select cells C3 to C50 in our SALES BY REGION sheet.

117. Click the ▣ button next to LABELS and select cells B3 to B50 in our SALES BY REGION sheet.

118. Navigate to the BEHAVIOR area and set the IN VALUES option on the COMMON tab.

119. Click the ▣ button next to STATUS for DYNAMIC VISIBILITY, select cell B5 in our SETTINGS sheet, and set the key to 2.

120. Drag and drop a PIE CHART into the first tab so that it overlaps with the first pie chart.

121. Right-click on the PIE CHART and select PROPERTIES.

122. Enter `Revenue mix by product category` into cell A24 in our SETTINGS sheet.

123. Click the ▣ button next to TITLE and select cell A24 in our SETTINGS sheet.

124. Select the GENERAL area of the properties.

125. Select the DATA IN COLUMNS option for the data.

126. Click the ▣ button next to VALUES and select cells C3 to C50 in our SALES BY PRODUCT CATEGORY sheet.

127. Click the ▣ button next to LABELS and select cells B3 to B50 in our SALES BY PRODUCT CATEGORY sheet.

128. Navigate to the BEHAVIOR area and set the IN VALUES option on the COMMON tab.

129. Click the ▣ button next to STATUS for DYNAMIC VISIBILITY, select cell B5 in our SETTINGS sheet, and set the key to 1.

By now you should have a dashboard that lets you switch from a view of the data by product category to one by region. In addition, it lets you filter the top chart for a single region or product category. Next, we'll add a pie chart for cost distribution and then build the planning section.

130. Drag and drop a PIE CHART into the first tab and size it so that it covers the lower right area below the line chart and half of the width.

131. Right-click on the PIE CHART and select PROPERTIES.

132. Enter `Transport cost mix by region` into cell A25 in our SETTINGS sheet.

133. Click the ▣ button next to TITLE and select cell A25 in our SETTINGS sheet and remove the SUBTITLE.

134. Select the GENERAL area of the properties.

135. Select the DATA IN COLUMNS option for the data.

136. Click the ▣ button next to VALUES and select cells E3 to E50 in our SALES BY REGION sheet, which represents the TRANSPORT COSTS key figure. You can verify this in the DATA PREVIEW.

137. Click the ▣ button next to LABELS and select cells B3 to B50 in our SALES BY REGION sheet.

138. Navigate to the BEHAVIOR area and set the IN VALUES option on the COMMON tab.

139. Click the ▣ button next to STATUS for DYNAMIC VISIBILITY, select cell B5 in our SETTINGS sheet, and set the key to 2.

140. Drag and drop a PIE CHART into the first tab so that it overlaps with the previous pie chart.

141. Right-click on the PIE CHART and select PROPERTIES.

142. Enter `Cost mix by product category` into cell A26 in our sheet SETTINGS.

143. Click the ▣ button next to TITLE and select cell A26 in our sheet SETTINGS and remove the subtitle.

144. Select the GENERAL area of the properties.

145. Select the DATA IN COLUMNS option for the data.

146. Click the ▣ button next to VALUES and select cells F3 to F50 in our SALES BY PRODUCT CATEGORY sheet, which represents the PRODUCT COSTS key figure.

147. Click the ▣ button next to LABELS and select cells B3 to B50 in our SALES BY PRODUCT CATEGORY sheet.

148. Navigate to the BEHAVIOR area and set the IN VALUES option on the COMMON tab.

149. Click the 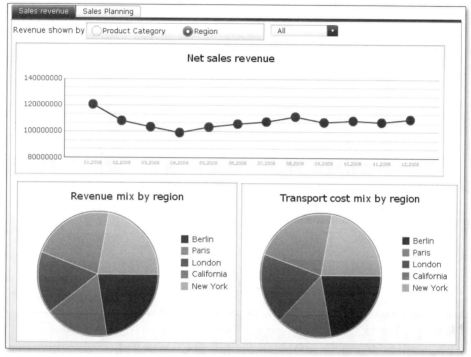 button next to STATUS for DYNAMIC VISIBILITY, select cell B5 in our SETTINGS sheet, and set the key to 1.

150. Publish and launch your dashboard (see Figure 5.55).

Figure 5.55 Xcelsius Dashboard

Your dashboard should now look like Figure 5.55. Now we will add the what-if analysis to our second tab.

1. Follow the DATA • CONNECTIONS menu path.

2. Click ADD to create a new SAP NETWEAVER BI connection.

3. Enter Sales Planning as the NAME for the connection.

4. Click BROWSE and select the second BW Query (see Figure 5.52).

5. Navigate to the DATA PREVIEW tab. Ensure the characteristic REGION is placed in the ROWS, the structure for the quarters and the key figures are placed in the COLUMNS, and all other characteristics are placed in FREE CHARACTERISTICS.

6. Click REFRESH DATA PREVIEW (see Figure 5.56).

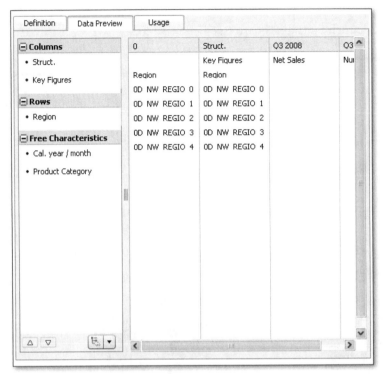

Figure 5.56   Data Preview

7. Look carefully at the data structure. Because we added the quarter structure into the columns, the actual data for our cross-tab object will not start in row 3 anymore — it will start in row 4.

   In the given scenario, we receive the data by Region and per quarter we receive four key figures. In our dashboard, we want to show the numbers from Q3 and Q4 2008 as they are, but be able to influence the numbers from Q1 and Q2 2009, therefore, we will have to use a set of formulas in our embedded spreadsheet.

8. Navigate to the DEFINITION tab.

9. Select the CROSS-TAB DATA entry in OUTPUT VALUES.

10. Click the 🖳 button next to INSERT IN and select a range of 18 columns and 50 rows (A1 to R50).

11. Click OK.

12. Navigate to the embedded spreadsheet. We now need to add several formulas that will allow us to create the planning scenario.

13. We will start with column S on our SALES PLANNING sheet. In cell S4, enter the following formula:

    ```
    =IF(K4="","",K4*(1+Settings!$B$9)).
    ```

14. Now copy and paste (or fill) column S up to row 50.

15. Now select cell T4 in the embedded spreadsheet and enter the following formula:

    ```
    =IF(M4="","",M4*(1-Settings!$B$10)).
    ```

16. Now copy and paste (or fill) column T up to row 50.

17. Now select cell U4 in the embedded spreadsheet and enter the following formula:

    ```
    =IF(N4="","",N4*(1-Settings!$B$11)).
    ```

18. Now copy and paste (or fill) column U up to row 50.

19. Now select cell V4 in the embedded spreadsheet and enter the following formula:

    ```
    =IF(O4="","",O4*(1+Settings!$B$9)).
    ```

20. Now copy and paste (or fill) column V up to row 50.

21. Now select cell W4 in the embedded spreadsheet and enter the following formula:

    ```
    =IF(Q4="","",Q4*(1-Settings!$B$10)).
    ```

22. Now copy and paste (or fill) column W up to row 50.

23. Now select cell X4 in the embedded spreadsheet and enter the following formula:

    ```
    =IF(R4="","",R4*(1-Settings!$B$11)).
    ```

24. Now copy and paste (or fill) column X up to row 50.

25. Navigate to the SETTINGS sheet.

26. Enter the following into the SETTINGS sheet:

  ▶ Cell A9: Forecast Increase

  ▶ Cell A10: Transport cost decrease

  ▶ Cell A11: Product cost decrease

  ▶ Cell B9: Enter the numeric value 0.05

  ▶ Cell B10: Enter the numeric value 0.05

  ▶ Cell B11: Enter the numeric value 0.05

We used Microsoft Excel functions in our embedded spreadsheet so we could use percentage values and increase or decrease the numbers in our Xcelsius dashboard. Now we can add the necessary components to our Xcelsius canvas.

1. Enter the text Net Sales by quarter into cell A27 in our SETTINGS sheet.

2. Drag and drop a BAR CHART to the SALES PLANNING tab and place it in the top-left corner.

3. Right-click the new chart and open PROPERTIES.

4. Click the button next to TITLE and select cell A27 from the SETTINGS sheet and remove the SUBTITLE.

5. Select the BY SERIES option and use the "+" symbol to add four series to the chart.

6. Enter Q3 2008 into the NAME for Series 1.

7. Click the button next to VALUES (X) and select cells C4 to C50 from the SALES PLANNING sheet.

8. Enter Q4 2008 into the NAME for Series 2.

9. Click the button next to VALUES (X) and select cells G4 to G50 from the SALES PLANNING sheet.

10. Enter Q1 2009 into the NAME for Series 3.

11. Click the button next to VALUES (X) and select cells S4 to S50 from the SALES PLANNING sheet.

12. Enter Q2 2009 into the NAME for Series 4.

13. Click the ⬛ button next to Values (X) and select cells V4 to V50 from the Sales Planning sheet.

14. Click the ⬛ button next to Category Labels (Y) and select cells B4 to B50 from the Sales Planning sheet.

15. Navigate to the Behavior tab and activate the In Series and In Values options.

16. Select the Common tab and activate the Fixed label size option.

17. Enter the text `Transport costs by quarter` into cell A28 in our Settings sheet.

18. Drag and drop a Bar Chart into the Sales Planning tab and place it in the top-right corner.

19. Right-click the new chart and open Properties.

20. Click the ⬛ button next to Title and select cell A28 from the Settings sheet and remove the Subtitle.

21. Select the by Series option and use the "+" symbol to add four series to the chart.

22. Enter `Q3 2008` into the Name for Series 1.

23. Click the ⬛ button next to Values (X) and select cells E4 to E50 from the Sales Planning sheet.

24. Enter `Q4 2008` into the Name for Series 2.

25. Click the ⬛ button next to Values (X) and select cells I4 to I50 from the Sales Planning sheet.

26. Enter `Q1 2009` into the Name for Series 3.

27. Click the ⬛ button next to Values (X) and select cells T4 to T50 from the Sales Planning sheet.

28. Enter `Q2 2009` into the Name for Series 4.

29. Click the ⬛ button next to Values (X) and select cells W4 to W50 from the Sales Planning sheet.

30. Click the ⬛ button next to Category Labels (Y) and select cells B4 to B50 from the Sales Planning sheet.

31. Navigate to the Behavior tab and activate the In Series and In Values options.

32. Select the Common tab and activate the Fixed label size option.

33. Enter the text Product costs by quarter into cell A29 in our Settings sheet.

34. Drag and drop a Bar Chart into the Sales planning tab and place it in the bottom-right corner.

35. Right-click the new chart and open Properties.

36. Click the ▣ button next to Title and select cell A29 from the Settings sheet and remove the Subtitle.

37. Select the by Series option and use the "+" symbol to add four series to the chart.

38. Enter Q3 2008 into the Name for Series 1.

39. Click the ▣ button next to Values (X) and select cells F4 to F50 from the Sales Planning sheet.

40. Enter Q4 2008 into the Name for Series 2.

41. Click the ▣ button next to Values (X) and select cells J4 to J50 from the Sales Planning sheet.

42. Enter Q1 2009 into the Name for Series 3.

43. Click the ▣ button next to Values (X) and select cells U4 to U50 from the Sales Planning sheet.

44. Enter Q2 2009 into the Name for Series 4.

45. Click the ▣ button next to Values (X) and select cells X4 to X50 from the Sales Planning sheet.

46. Click the ▣ button next to Category Labels (Y) and select cells B4 to B50 from the Sales Planning sheet.

47. Navigate to the Behavior tab and activate the In Series and In Values options.

48. Select the Common tab and activate the Fixed label size option.

49. Follow the View • Components menu path.

50. Drag and drop a Horizontal Slider from the Single Value area to the bottom-left area of the Sales Planning tab.

51. Right-click the new slider and open Properties.

52. Click the ▣ button next to Title and select cell A9 in our Settings sheet.

53. Click the ▣ button next to Data and select cell B9 in our Settings sheet.

54. Set the Maximum Limit to 0.5.

55. Select the Behavior area and set the value for the Increment to 0.025.

56. Select the Appearance area and select the Text tab. Select the entry Value in the list.

57. Set the Number Format to the value Percent and set the number of Decimal Places to 0.

58. Drag and drop an additional Horizontal Slider from the Single Value area to the bottom-left area of the Sales Planning tab.

59. Right-click the new slider and open Properties.

60. Click the ▣ button next to Title and select cell A10 in our Settings sheet.

61. Click the ▣ button next to Data and select cell B10 in our Settings sheet.

62. Set the Maximum Limit to 0.5.

63. Select the Behavior area and set the value for the Increment to 0.025.

64. Select the Appearance area and select the Text tab. Select the entry Value in the list.

65. Set the Number Format to the value Percent and set the number of Decimal Places to 0.

66. Drag and drop an additional Horizontal Slider from the Single Value area to the bottom-left area of the Sales Planning tab.

67. Right-click the new slider and open Properties.

68. Click the ▣ button next to Title and select cell A11 in our Settings sheet.

69. Click the ▣ button next to Data and select cell B11 in our Settings sheet.

70. Set the Maximum Limit to 0.5.

71. Select the area Behavior and set the value for the Increment to 0.025.

72. Select the Appearance area and select the Text tab. Select the entry Value in the list.

73. Set the Number Format to the value Percent and set the number of Decimal Places to 0.

74. Publish and launch your dashboard (see Figure 5.57).

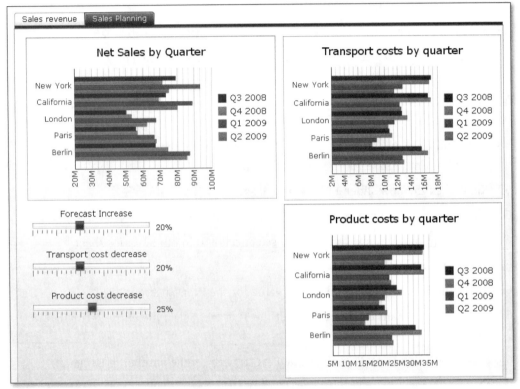

Figure 5.57 Xcelsius Dashboard

To finish off our dashboard design process, we'll now make use of the translation settings in Xcelsius and pass the string objects to the SAP NetWeaver BW system:

1. We put all of the strings that require translation, starting with the cell A20 up to cell A30, into our Settings sheet.

2. Add the numeric values behind each of the cells, where the numeric value represents the maximum number of characters (see Figure 5.58).

▶ The maximum number of characters is helpful for the translation system in that the person translating the string is receiving an indication of the string's maximum length.

Maximum Number of Characters

The maximum number of characters is not leveraged from the underlying SAP system as of SAP NetWeaver 7.0 Enhancement Package 01 Service Pack 05. However, this is on the list of future capabilities, and therefore it is a good practice to design dashboards with this functionality in mind.

	A	B	C
16			
17			
18			
19			
20	Net sales revenue	20	
21	Net Sales	10	
22	Revenue by Region	20	
23	Revenue mix by region	25	
24	Revenue mix by product category	35	
25	Transport cost mix by region	30	
26	Cost mix by product category	30	
27	Net Sales by Quarter	20	
28	Transport costs by quarter	30	
29	Product costs by quarter	30	
30			
31			

Figure 5.58 Translation Table

3. Follow the SAP • TRANSLATION SETTINGS menu path.

4. Activate the ENABLE SUPPORT FOR TRANSLATION option.

5. Click ADD.

6. Click the 🔲 button next to RANGE and select the first string in the table in SETTINGS sheet.

7. Click the 🔲 button next to MAXIMUM NUMBER OF CHARACTERS and select the second column cell for the string.

8. Repeat the steps for all of our strings.

Now, when you publish your Xcelsius dashboard to the SAP NetWeaver BW system, the strings will be transferred to the SAP system. You can use Transaction SE63 to translate those strings. Keep in mind that the underlying table in the Xcelsius designer will always show the strings that you entered and will not show the translated strings; the translated strings will be leveraged at runtime when you launch the Xcelsius dashboard.

You just created a dashboard that allows you to increase or decrease specific numbers and see the impact on your business right away. Remember, this only displays the information; this does not rewrite any information to SAP NetWeaver BW.

In this chapter, you learned how to use Xcelsius for your data visualizations needs, you also received an overview on the data connectivity options of Xcelsius as part of your overall SAP landscape. You then reviewed the requirements against the capabilities of Xcelsius as a data visualization and dashboarding tool, and you used Xcelsius to fulfill those requirements and create compelling dashboards.

You can use Live Office with your Business Intelligence (BI) content in a familiar Microsoft Office environment.

6 Integration with Microsoft Office

In this chapter, we will use Live Office to provide our users with content from our SAP BusinessObjects Enterprise system in Microsoft Office. We will learn how we can leverage live and refreshed data in Microsoft Office.

6.1 Installation and Deployment Overview

With Live Office you can leverage content from your BusinessObjects Enterprise system in Microsoft Excel, Microsoft Word, Microsoft PowerPoint, and Microsoft Outlook. With regard to installation, you need to install the Live Office plug-in on each client that will leverage such functionality.

6.1.1 Live Office Installation

Before you begin the installation process for Live Office, you should make sure Microsoft Office is installed on your client computer. The following steps outline the installation of Live Office:

1. Identical to the previous installation of client tools like Crystal Reports or the Xcelsius Designer, the first step in the installation routine will be the selection of the setup language. Remember that this selection does not influence the actual languages available for Live Office itself, but instead only influences the language for the installation routine.

2. After you accept the license agreement you can select the Language Packs for your Live Office deployment. In our installation, we chose ENGLISH.

3. In the next screen, you can set the destination folder for the installation (see Figure 6.1). You can use the BROWSE button to specify the location for the installation or you can accept the default path. If Live Office is not the first BusinessObjects product installed on the computer, the program will suggest the path you used for the other BusinessObjects products on your client system.

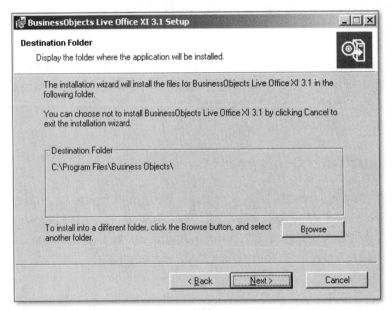

Figure 6.1 Live Office — Destination Folder

4. After confirming the folder location, you can start the actual installation routine in the next screen.

5. After this step, the installation routine will start and you should be able to leverage the Live Office functionality in Microsoft Excel, Microsoft PowerPoint, Microsoft Word, and Microsoft Outlook as soon as the installation is finished.

> **Live Office License Keys**
>
> You'll notice that the client-side installation routine of Live Office will not ask for a license key. The reason is that the license key has to be entered on the BusinessObjects Enterprise system. To do so, you need to log on to the Central Management Console, navigate to LICENSE KEYS, and enter the keycode for Live Office.

6.1.2   Live Office Configuration

To leverage Live Office we need to perform some simple configuration steps. These steps need to be done on each client and in each Microsoft Office product that will use Live Office (see Figures 6.2 and 6.3).

In the next couple of steps we will use Microsoft Excel as the example, but the steps are identical for the other Microsoft Office products:

1. Start Microsoft Excel.

2. Follow the LIVE OFFICE • OPTIONS menu path (see Figure 6.2).

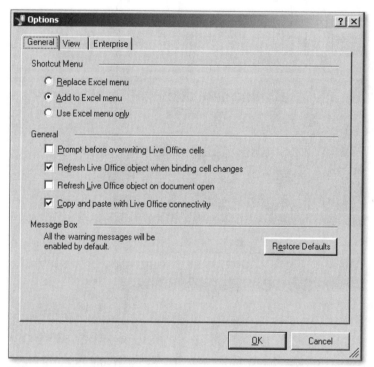

Figure 6.2   Live Office Options

3. Navigate to the ENTERPRISE tab.

4. Activate the USE SPECIFIC LOGON CRITERIA option.

5. Enter the URL for the web-services deployment of your BusinessObjects Enterprise system. In a default installation the URL would be (see Figure 6.3) :

http://<Application server>:<port>/dswsbobje/services/session.

Replace the placeholder `<Application server>` and the placeholder `<port>` with values from your BusinessObjects Enterprise system; in our example, the name of our application server is VMWSAP20 and the port is 8080.

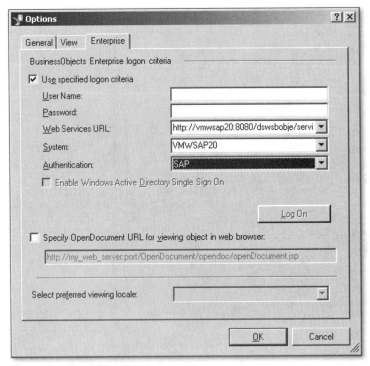

Figure 6.3 Live Office Options

6. As soon as the URL has been validated you can set AUTHENTICATION to SAP.

7. You can leave the USER NAME and PASSWORD empty, but you will then be asked for them each time you use Live Office to authenticate against the BusinessObjects Enterprise server.

8. Make sure that you uncheck the USE SPECIFIC LOGON CRITERIA option, otherwise Live Office will use the empty entries and try to log on to the system.

9. Click OK and you are now ready to use Live Office.

6.2   BusinessObjects Content and Microsoft Office

With Live Office you are able to leverage the content from different sources inside the Microsoft Office environment. As shown in Figure 6.4 you can recognize that Live Office is capable of retrieving content from Crystal Reports, Web Intelligence, and Universes. Important to be mentioned here is that Live Office is able to leverage all the investment you made into your reporting and analytics content; for example, you can leverage a well laid out chart from a Web Intelligence directly in Microsoft PowerPoint without having to reformat anything.

Not only can you leverage the actual reporting content from these reports, but you can also use the underlying data source, and with regard to your SAP landscape, this means that you can use data from your SAP NetWeaver Business Warehouse (BW) system and your SAP ERP system in Microsoft Office.

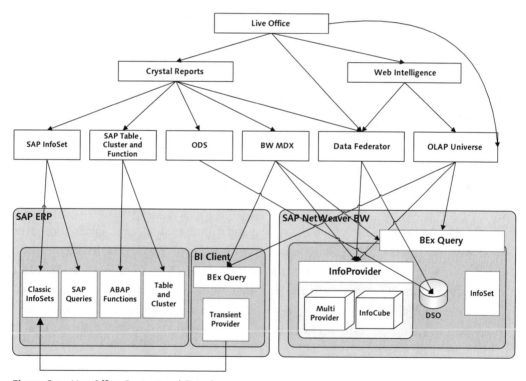

Figure 6.4 Live Office Content and Data Sources

In general, Live Office has two main uses:

1. You would like to provide information from your reporting and analysis environment to your end users and you would like to leverage Microsoft Office as the client tool for viewing and refreshing the content.

2. You would like to use Live Office as the "data engine" for pushing data into your Xcelsius dashboards. Xcelsius is capable of retrieving data from a Live Office document inside of Microsoft Excel and using the Live Office functionality directly inside the Xcelsius Designer. The benefit of using Live Office to provide data to Xcelsius is the ability to not only leverage live data but also pre-scheduled data from an instance or publication that you created with BusinessObjects Enterprise. (A publication of BusinessObjects is the counterpart to SAP NetWeaver BW Information Broadcasting).

6.3   Customer Case Study — Requirements for an Integration with Microsoft Office

In this section, we'll look at the requirements for the Live Office integration with Microsoft Office. If we look back at all of the requirements in Section 2.2 there are a couple that are relevant to Live Office:

▶ From the financial area, we received the requirement to make the data available in Microsoft Excel.

▶ From the sales area, we received the requirement that the reporting content needs to be available online and offline.

Let's elaborate a little bit on the online and offline requirement. Live Office gives you the option of providing information from your BusinessObjects Enterprise system in an offline manner, for example, via Microsoft Outlook or Microsoft PowerPoint. However, keep in mind that "offline" in this case means you providing a snapshot of the data to your user with the ability to refresh the data, if necessary; the refresh would then require a connection to the BusinessObjects Enterprise system and the underlying data source.

6.4   Live Office — Quick Basics

In this section, we will look at some simple steps for leveraging the information from our BusinessObjects Enterprise system inside Microsoft Office.

6.4.1   Live Office Environment

Before we start using Live Office with different content types, let's configure our environment and look at some of the common menus in Live Office.

1. Start Microsoft Excel.

2. Follow the LIVE OFFICE • OPTIONS menu path (see Figure 6.5).

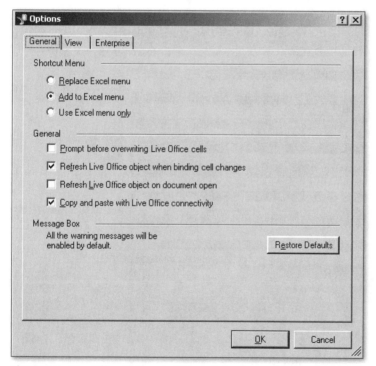

Figure 6.5   Live Office Options in Microsoft Excel

3. In the GENERAL tab in the SHORTCUT MENU area you can configure how the Live Office right-click menu is being presented to you. The Live Office menu will only be shown on Live Office relevant content.

4. In the GENERAL area on the GENERAL tab, you can configure several options:

▸ You can activate the PROMPT BEFORE OVERWRITING LIVE OFFICE CELLS option to prevent situations where you actually overwrite the content of a cell that is connected via Live Office to live data.

▸ You can use the REFRESH LIVE OFFICE OBJECT WHEN BINDING CELL CHANGES option to force a complete refresh of your Live Office–related data if the binding of a cell to Live Office data changes.

▸ You can use the REFRESH LIVE OFFICE OBJECT ON DOCUMENT OPEN option to force a refresh each time you open a document with Live Office content.

▸ You can use the COPY AND PASTE WITH LIVE OFFICE CONNECTIVITY option to keep the connectivity intact for when you copy and paste in Microsoft Office.

You will see that some of these options differ depending on which Microsoft Office product you are using.

5. Navigate to the VIEW tab (see Figure 6.6).

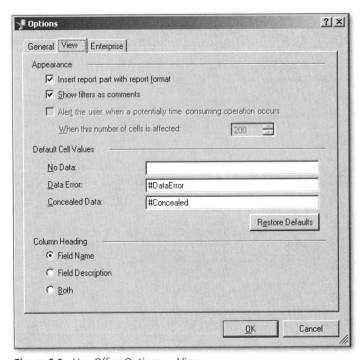

Figure 6.6 Live Office Options — View

6. In the Appearance area, please take note of the Insert Report Part with Report Format option. This option lets you insert (for example) a fully formatted Web Intelligence table into a Microsoft Office document with all of the formatting intact.

7. The Default Cell Values option lets you specify values for certain default cases, such as a field with no data.

8. The Column Heading option lets you specify how the fields in the menus and dialogs are shown to you and which option is used for the column header.

9. Activate the Field Description option in Column Heading.

In the following sections, we'll look at how you can leverage content from your BusinessObjects Enterprise system in different Microsoft Office products.

6.4.2   Using Live Office and Microsoft Excel

In this section, we'll look at how you can leverage Crystal Reports, Web Intelligence, and Universes in Microsoft Excel.

1. Start Microsoft Excel.

2. Follow the Live Office • Insert • Crystal Reports Content menu path.

3. You will be asked for your credentials. Remember, we configured Live Office to leverage SAP authentication, but here the Live Office screen is not providing the typical SAP logon dialog, therefore, you need to use the following syntax:

```
<SAP System ID>~<SAP Client Number>/<SAP User name>
```

For example:

```
ABC~800/DEMO
```

4. Enter your SAP credentials and password. If you haven't configured your BusinessObjects Enterprise system with the SAP authentication, you can continue with an Enterprise account but you won't be able to leverage Single Sign-On (SSO).

5. Click OK (see Figure 6.7).

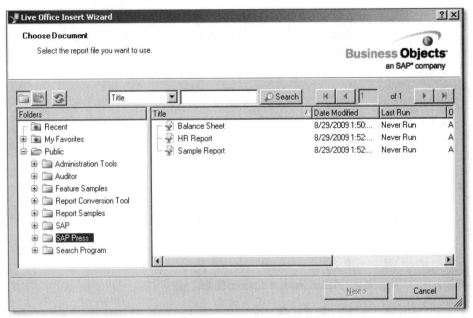

Figure 6.7 Live Office Insert Wizard

6. You will be presented with the repository from your BusinessObjects Enterprise system and you can navigate to the folder where you stored the objects.

7. In our case, we will use the Crystal Report object we created in Section 3.4, which was the first Crystal Report object we created in this book.

8. Select the report and click NEXT.

9. The Crystal Reports content is shown in the Crystal Reports viewer and you now can select content from the report. If you select content now, you can select parts of your report and leverage the report formatting (see Figure 6.8).

10. Use the SWITCH TO FIELDS option to see the complete list of available fields.

11. Select all of the fields from the DETAILS area and move them to the SELECTED FIELDS list by using the ⟩ button (see Figure 6.9).

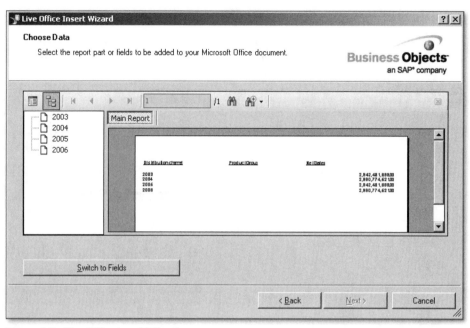

Figure 6.8 Live Office Insert Wizard

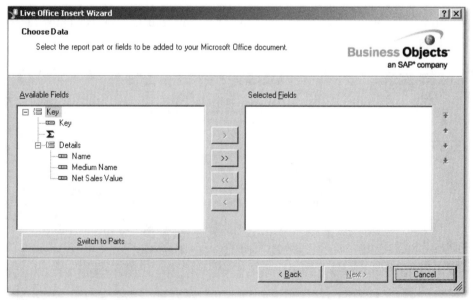

Figure 6.9 Live Office Insert Wizard

12. Click NEXT.

13. In the next screen, we can add a filter to our Live Office document, but for now we will skip this step (see Figure 6.10).

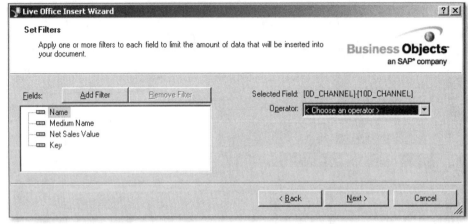

Figure 6.10 Live Office Insert Wizard

14. Click NEXT.

15. In the next screen, you can enter the name for your LIVE OFFICE OBJECT (see Figure 6.11).

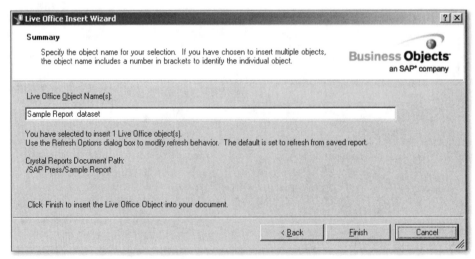

Figure 6.11 Live Office Insert Wizard

16. Click NEXT.

17. Click NEXT.

18. The content of the Crystal Report object is inserted into your Microsoft Excel sheet.

	A	B	C	
1	**Name**	**Medium Name**	**Net Sales Value**	
2	Internet	Bag & Outdoor	144230713	
3	Internet	Accessories	188404713	
4	Internet	Office	174020678	
5	Fax	Bag & Outdoor	270881630	
6	Fax	Accessories	348047077	
7	Fax	Office	332177231	
8	Others	Bag & Outdoor	66275851	
9	Others	Accessories	83644717	
10	Others	Office	78955705	
11	Phone	Bag & Outdoor	185807892	
12	Phone	Accessories	245339118	
13	Phone	Office	232029751	
14	EDI	Bag & Outdoor	170841470	
15	EDI	Accessories	215835601	
16	EDI	Office	205989552	
17	Internet	Bag & Outdoor	211184935	
18	Internet	Accessories	208231891	
19	Internet	Office	157070018	
20	Fax	Bag & Outdoor	336593498	
21	Fax	Accessories	328978177	
22	Fax	Office	254827544	
23	Others	Bag & Outdoor	87931877	
24	Others	Accessories	83535015	

Figure 6.12 Microsoft Excel with Crystal Reports Content.

In our first example using Microsoft Excel, as soon as you insert the content you can use the data inside the spreadsheet with all of the functionality and capabilities of Microsoft Excel; and you can refresh the data from the Live Office document at any time.

19. Follow the LIVE OFFICE • MODIFY OBJECTS menu path (see Figure 6.13).

20. The ADD/REMOVE FIELDS option will bring you back to the wizard and let you add or remove fields from your spreadsheet.

21. The FILTER SETTINGS option lets you create additional filters for your data.

22. Navigate to the PROPERTIES option (see Figure 6.14).

Figure 6.13 Live Office Menu

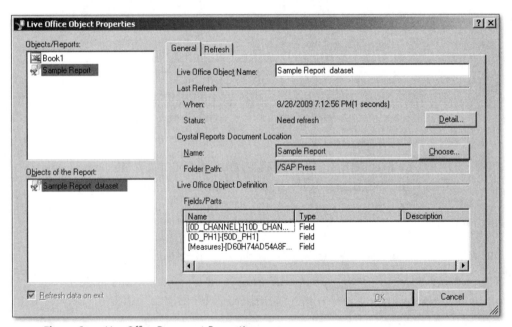

Figure 6.14 Live Office Document Properties

23. With the option Choose you can change to a different report or a different folder location in case the actual source document has been renamed or has been moved.

24. Navigate to the REFRESH tab (see Figure 6.15).

25. Click EDIT (see Figure 6.16).

26. With these REFRESH OPTIONS you can decide if your Live Office document should always refresh the data (On Demand) or use saved data or use a particular instance of the report that you prepared.

27. Close the dialogs and navigate back to the menu LIVE OFFICE.

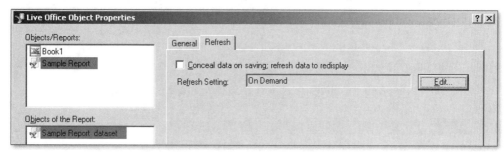

Figure 6.15 Live Office Document Properties

28. Select the menu item PUBLISH TO BUSINESSOBJECTS ENTERPRISE.

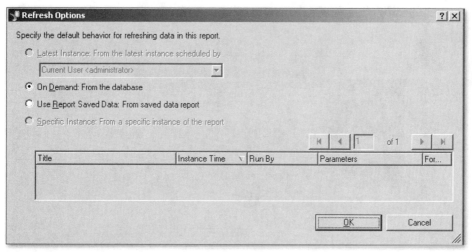

Figure 6.16 Refresh Options

29. With the option to store your Live Office document to BusinessObjects Enterprise you also have the option to secure your Live Office document, such as a Weekly Sales slide deck created with PowerPoint which contains data via Live Office, in your BusinessObjects Enterprise system.

30. Create a new empty sheet in our Microsoft Excel file.

31. Follow the LIVE OFFICE • INSERT • WEB INTELLIGENCE CONTENT menu path.

32. You will be presented with the repository from your BusinessObjects Enterprise system.

33. Navigate to the folder where you stored the Web Intelligence reports we created so far.

34. Select the Web Intelligence report from Section 4.5 (see Figure 6.17).

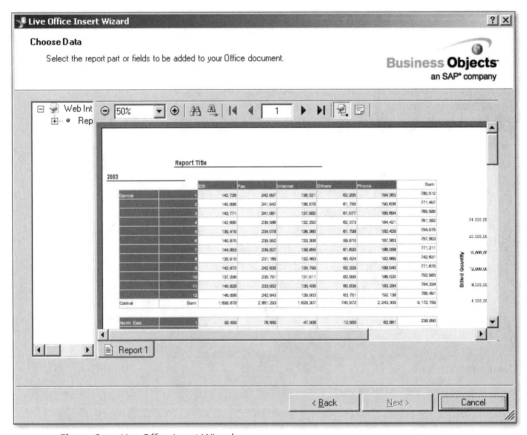

Figure 6.17 Live Office Insert Wizard

35. You will notice that Live Office does not offer an option to switch to the list of fields, which makes perfect sense because Live Office is offering the option to insert content based on a Universe as a separate menu item.

36. Select the cross tab object from the report. Keep in mind that the report includes a section, and when you select the cross tab object from the section you only insert the cross tab from this one section into the spreadsheet and no others, unless you select them as well.

37. Remember, this report had several parameters based on variables and therefore we will refresh the report and change these values.

38. Follow the LIVE OFFICE • REFRESH OBJECT menu path. The prompt screen will appear and you can select the values (see Figure 6.18).

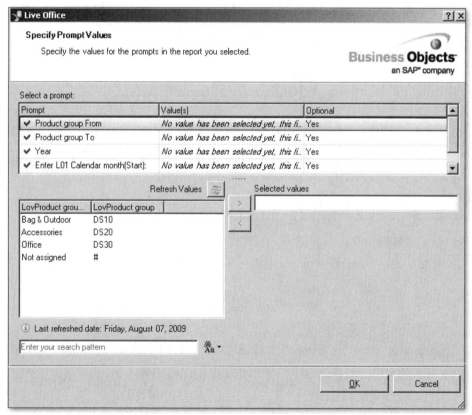

Figure 6.18 Live Office Prompting Screen

39. Based on the assumption that all of the parameters are optional, you can click OK and the report will run without any filtering.

40. After the refresh, follow the LIVE OFFICE • PROPERTIES FOR ALL OBJECTS menu path.

41. Select the Web Intelligence report in the list of available reports.

42. Navigate to the PROMPTS tab (see Figure 6.19).

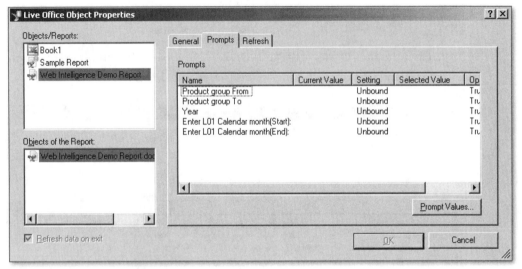

Figure 6.19   Live Office Object Properties

43. Click PROMPT VALUES (see Figure 6.20).

44. You now have three options:

   ▶ You can always get prompted for a value by using the ALWAYS ASK FOR VALUE option.

   ▶ You can specify a value by using the CHOOSE VALUES LIST option and selecting the values.

   ▶ You can bind the parameter to an Excel range by using the CHOOSE EXCEL DATA RANGE option.

45. The most flexible option is CHOOSE EXCEL DATA RANGE. Activate this option and use the ▨ button to specify a range on our spreadsheet (see Figure 6.21).

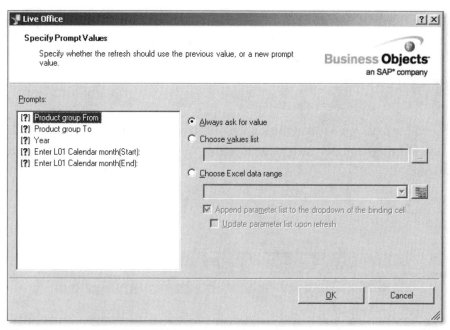

Figure 6.20 Live Office Prompt Values

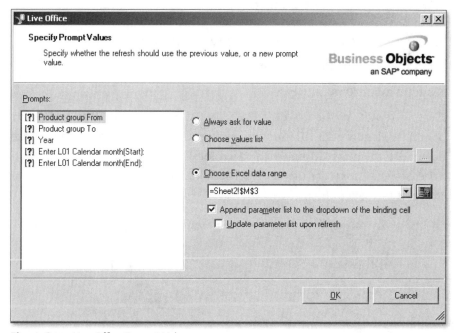

Figure 6.21 Live Office Prompt Values

46. Activate the APPEND PARAMETER LIST TO THE DROPDOWN OF THE BINDING CELL option.

47. Repeat the steps for all of the parameters and bind each of them to a cell range in the spreadsheet.

48. Click OK to close all of the dialogs.

49. You now have the option of using the cells that you defined as bounded cells to enter the values for each parameter and refresh your Live Office document (see Figure 6.22).

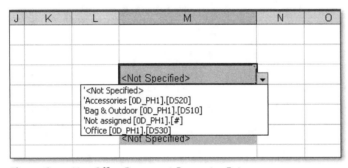

Figure 6.22   Live Office Document Parameter Entry

50. Follow the LIVE OFFICE • PROPERTIES FOR ALL OBJECTS menu path.

51. Select the Web Intelligence report.

52. Navigate to the REFRESH tab.

53. Please take note of the CONCEAL DATA ON SAVING; REFRESH DATA TO DISPLAY option (see Figure 6.23). This option lets you remove data from the Live Office document when the document is saved locally or to BusinessObjects Enterprise, so you can secure the data to a certain degree by removing the option to access the data offline.

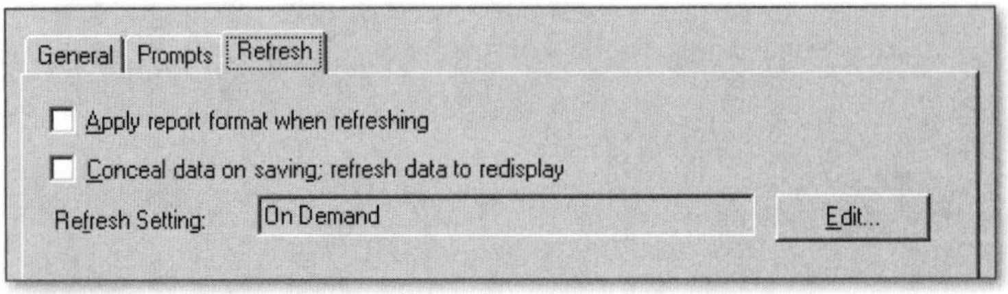

Figure 6.23   Refresh Options

Next, we'll take a look at how you can leverage a Universe in Microsoft Excel.

54. Close the dialogs and create a new empty sheet in our Microsoft Excel file.

55. Follow the LIVE OFFICE • INSERT • NEW QUERY menu path.

56. You will receive a list of Universes from your system, including the Universes we created in Section 4.3.5 (see Figure 6.24).

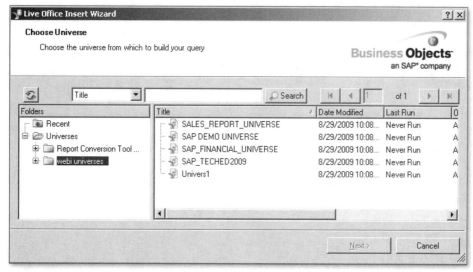

Figure 6.24 Live Office Insert Wizard

57. Select the first Universe we created and click NEXT.

58. You will see the query panel, which is similar to the Web Intelligence query panel, where you can define the objects you want to leverage (see Figure 6.25).

59. In our example, we'll use:

  ▸ L01 Distribution Channel

  ▸ L01 Product Group

  ▸ L01 Product

  ▸ Net Sales

  ▸ Billed Quantity

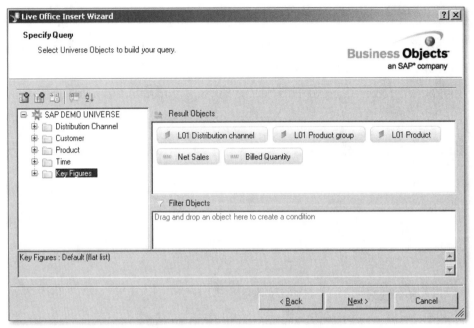

Figure 6.25 Live Office Insert Wizard

60. Click NEXT.

61. Because the Universe contains prompts, we'll have to provide values for them. If all of the prompts are optional, you can ignore them for now and click NEXT to run the query without any filtering.

62. In the next screen, click FINISH to load the data to the spreadsheet (see Figure 6.26).

When you leverage data form a Universe like this, you can use all of the functionality from Live Office the same way you use Crystal Reports and Web Intelligence–based content. The only exception is that you cannot leverage data from instances or from a publication. A Universe cannot be prescheduled, therefore, the data retrieved by a Universe-based query is always on demand.

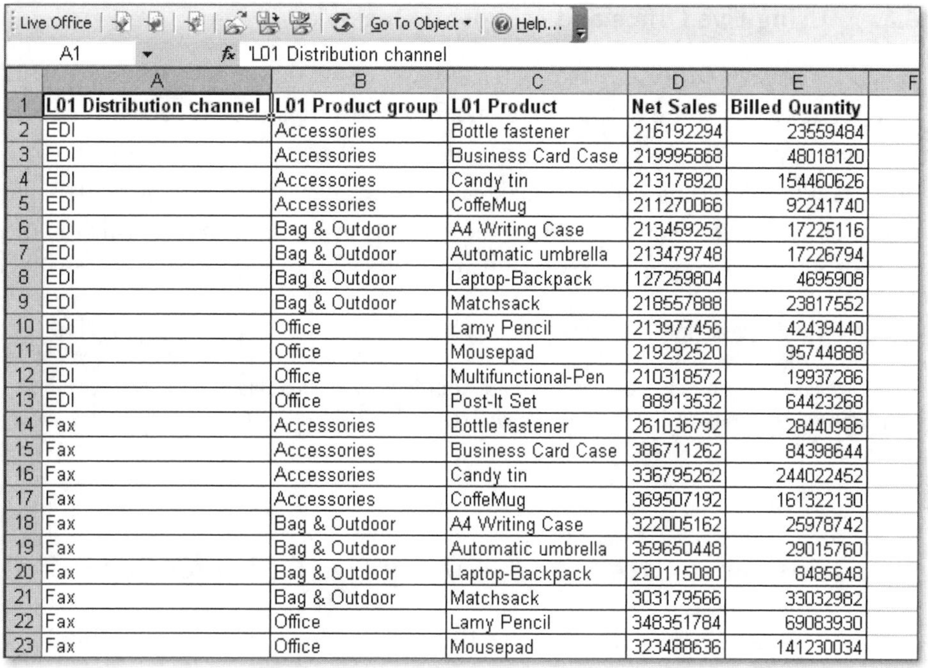

	A	B	C	D	E
1	L01 Distribution channel	L01 Product group	L01 Product	Net Sales	Billed Quantity
2	EDI	Accessories	Bottle fastener	216192294	23559484
3	EDI	Accessories	Business Card Case	219995868	48018120
4	EDI	Accessories	Candy tin	213178920	154460626
5	EDI	Accessories	CoffeMug	211270066	92241740
6	EDI	Bag & Outdoor	A4 Writing Case	213459252	17225116
7	EDI	Bag & Outdoor	Automatic umbrella	213479748	17226794
8	EDI	Bag & Outdoor	Laptop-Backpack	127259804	4695908
9	EDI	Bag & Outdoor	Matchsack	218557888	23817552
10	EDI	Office	Lamy Pencil	213977456	42439440
11	EDI	Office	Mousepad	219292520	95744888
12	EDI	Office	Multifunctional-Pen	210318572	19937286
13	EDI	Office	Post-It Set	88913532	64423268
14	Fax	Accessories	Bottle fastener	261036792	28440986
15	Fax	Accessories	Business Card Case	386711262	84398644
16	Fax	Accessories	Candy tin	336795262	244022452
17	Fax	Accessories	CoffeMug	369507192	161322130
18	Fax	Bag & Outdoor	A4 Writing Case	322005162	25978742
19	Fax	Bag & Outdoor	Automatic umbrella	359650448	29015760
20	Fax	Bag & Outdoor	Laptop-Backpack	230115080	8485648
21	Fax	Bag & Outdoor	Matchsack	303179566	33032982
22	Fax	Office	Lamy Pencil	348351784	69083930
23	Fax	Office	Mousepad	323488636	141230034

Figure 6.26 Universe Query Data in Microsoft Excel

Now let's look at how you can use Live Office in conjunction with Microsoft PowerPoint and what some of the differences between Live Office in Microsoft Excel and Microsoft PowerPoint are.

6.4.3 Using Live Office and Microsoft PowerPoint

When using Live Office in Microsoft PowerPoint all of the previously mentioned items and combinations with Microsoft Excel are possible — with one exception. You can't bind parameters from underlying sources, such as Crystal Reports, Web Intelligence, or a Universe, to an area in your PowerPoint slide deck to change the parameters. If you want to change the parameters you have to either configure the document to prompt you for the values or you can leverage the Live Office • Properties for all Objects menu path to specify the values that will be used.

6.4.4   Using Live Office and Microsoft Outlook

When using Live Office in Microsoft Outlook, all of the menu items and steps outlined for Microsoft Excel are the same for Microsoft Outlook. You will see that you can only use the Live Office menus when you create a new email and, more importantly, the receiver of the email can only refresh or modify the actual Live Office object in your message when the email is in the Edit mode, which is the case when the receiver of your email is using the Reply or Forward functionality.

> **Integrating BusinessObjects XI 3.1 BI Tools with SAP NetWeaver**
>
> With regard to using Live Office as a data source for Xcelsius dashboards, you can find the complete details in *Integrating BusinessObjects XI 3.1 BI Tools with SAP NetWeaver*, from SAP Press.

6.5   Customer Case Study — Using Live Office for Reporting

Based on the requirements we received earlier, we need Live Office to fulfill the following requirements:

- From the financial area, we received the requirement to make the data available in Microsoft Excel.
- From the sales area, we received the requirement that the reporting content needs to be available online and offline.

The request to provide financial data in a Microsoft Excel spreadsheet is not uncommon and we will use Live Office embedded in Microsoft Excel to provide this functionality.

The request for offline information to the sales force is also very common and we have the option of using Microsoft PowerPoint or Microsoft Outlook for this. The benefit of using Microsoft PowerPoint is that people can use the information right away. The benefit of using Microsoft Outlook is the tool itself, because we can use email to communicate the information to our sales force, but the downside is that the information is an email and can't be used for anything else.

First, let's use Microsoft Excel in combination with Live Office to provide the financial information.

1. Start Microsoft Excel.

2. Make sure you select cell A1 in the spreadsheet.

3. Follow the LIVE OFFICE • INSERT • NEW QUERY menu path.

4. From the repository, select the Universe for the financial report that we created in Section 4.7

> **Universe Query vs. Web Intelligence Report**
>
> When using Live Office on top of a Web Intelligence report that is leveraging the Fold/ Unfold feature, you will notice that the data shown in Live Office represents the Fold/ Unfold status that was active at that point in the Web Intelligence report. This could mean you are not showing all levels in the Live Office document, therefore, we will use a Universe query as the source for our Live Office report.

5. Click NEXT.

6. Add the following items to the RESULT OBJECTS panel (see Figure 6.27):

   ▸ L01 Cost Center

   ▸ L02 Cost Center

   ▸ L03 Cost Center

   ▸ Cost Element

   ▸ Actual

   ▸ Budget

   ▸ Variance

   ▸ Variance %

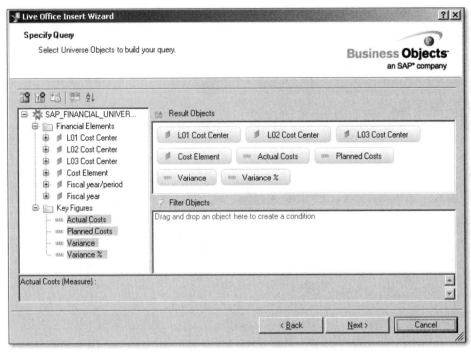

Figure 6.27 Live Office Insert Wizard

7. Click NEXT.

8. In the next screen, click FINISH to present the data in a Microsoft Excel spreadsheet (see Figure 6.28).

	A	B	C	D	E	F	G	H
1	L01 Cost Center	L02 Cost Center	L03 Cost Center	Cost Element	Actual Costs	Planned Costs	Variance	Variance %
2	Canada	Consulting Canada		Annual Bonus	364758	345000	19758	5.73
3	Canada	Consulting Canada		Benefits	237753	315000	-77247	-24.52
4	Canada	Consulting Canada		Conference Fees	53496	94500	-41004	-43.39
5	Canada	Consulting Canada		Depreciation Expenses	14580	41430	-26850	-64.81
6	Canada	Consulting Canada		Flights	848467.95	1335000	-486532.05	-36.44
7	Canada	Consulting Canada		Legal social expenses	1157202	1215000	-57798	-4.76
8	Canada	Consulting Canada		Licenses	76074	180000	-103926	-57.74
9	Canada	Consulting Canada		Lodging	1021213.62	1425000	-403786.38	-28.34
10	Canada	Consulting Canada		Maintenance	3588	9684	-6096	-62.95
11	Canada	Consulting Canada		Other Costs	28677	40500	-11823	-29.19
12	Canada	Consulting Canada		Other Personnel Exp.	300840	315000	-14160	-4.5
13	Canada	Consulting Canada		Other travel expenses	122102.61	279000	-156897.39	-56.24
14	Canada	Consulting Canada		Rental Cars	297327.75	531000	-233672.25	-44.01
15	Canada	Consulting Canada		Salaries-Base Wages	1046628	1395000	-348372	-24.97
16	Canada	Consulting Canada		Salaries & Wages	1792704	1740000	52704	3.03
17	Canada	Consulting Canada		Third Party	149799	285000	-135201	-47.44
18	Canada	Marketing Canada		Annual Bonus	198063	197400	663	0.34
19	Canada	Marketing Canada		Conference Fees	49626	46260	3366	7.28

Figure 6.28 Live Office Document in Microsoft Excel

9. Because we used the Universe query as the source for our spreadsheet, a filter would be needed to change the actual underlying Universe query, but we can also use Microsoft Excel functionality now.

10. Select the first four columns of our spreadsheets.

11. Follow the DATA • FILTER • AUTO FILTER menu path. Now the user can easily filter down the data in the spreadsheet.

12. In our report, we also included a pie chart showing the situation and we will add those to the Microsoft Excel spreadsheet now.

13. Select a cell on the right side next to the data from the Universe.

14. Follow the LIVE OFFICE • INSERT • WEB INTELLIGENCE CONTENT menu path.

15. Select the financial report from Section 4.7.

16. Select the pie charts we created. Remember, these pie charts are available per section, so you have to select them per section from the report (see Figure 6.29).

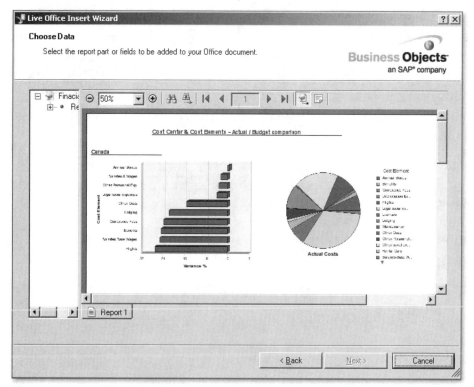

Figure 6.29 Live Office Insert Wizard

17. Click NEXT.

18. Click FINISH in the next screen to insert the pie charts into our Live Office document.

19. We've now created a Live Office document, which allows the user to see, sort, and filter the financial data; and use standard Microsoft Excel functionalities. We also added overview charts to give the user a quick summary (see Figure 6.30).

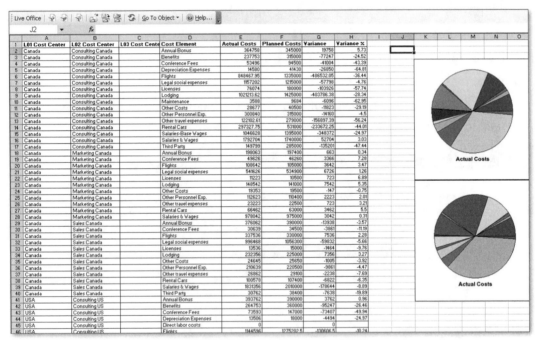

Figure 6.30 Live Office Document

20. Follow the LIVE OFFICE • PROPERTIES FOR ALL OBJECTS menu path.

21. Select the REFRESH tab.

22. Activate the CONCEAL DATA ON SAVING, REFRESH DATA TO REDISPLAY option (see Figure 6.31).

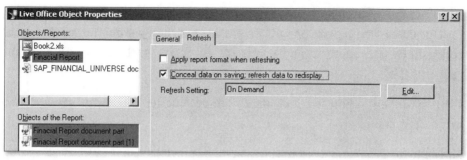

Figure 6.31 Live Office Objects Properties

23. By using this option, we ensure that the data is not stored in the Microsoft Excel file but refreshed instead, which also means the user must authenticate against the system to perform the refresh. It's important to note that, in our case, you have data from a Web Intelligence report and a Universe, so you need to set this property for the report and Universe in this dialog.

24. You have two options for storing the final Microsoft Excel file:

   ▶ You can store the file on every client computer that requires access to the information so that the user can open the file from their computer.

   ▶ You can store the Live Office document onto the BusinessObjects Enterprise system and uses can open it from the BusinessObjects system via the Live Office functionality.

25. Because this information is for the financial area and is not only sensitive information, but mainly used by users in the office, we'll store the Live Office document to the BusinessObjects system.

26. Follow the LIVE OFFICE • PUBLISH TO BUSINESSOBJECTS ENTERPRISE • SAVE TO BUSINESSOBJECTS ENTERPRISE menu path.

27. You will be presented with the folder structure of your BusinessObjects Enterprise system.

28. Select a folder and provide a name for the Live Office document.

29. Click OK.

In our second requirement, we will provide our sales force with offline content using Live Office and Microsoft PowerPoint.

We'll use the Web Intelligence report from Section 4.6 as the source document for Live Office. The report contains a cross tab and chart per quarter for the actual and planned sales numbers, and a cross tab and charts for the overall numbers on the lost deals.

For our "offline" report, we'll create a slide per quarter and a slide showing the lost deals measures.

Similar to the Fold/Unfold report situation in the previous activity, we have the same problem with our sales report where we're using the Fold/Unfold functionality, but we can't leverage it before showing the data in Live Office; therefore, we need to change the report slightly and then leverage the information in Live Office.

1. Log on to INFOVIEW.

2. Navigate to the Web Intelligence report from Section 4.6.

3. Right-click on the report and select the MODIFY option.

4. Now use the Fold/Unfold feature in Web Intelligence to show the cross tab on a level where the quarter and the product category is shown (see Figure 6.32).

Figure 6.32 Web Intelligence with Fold/Unfold Functionality

5. Save the changes to your report. Remember, this change is only changing the initial view of your report, the user can still leverage the Fold/Unfold feature and reach the details, but we can now leverage the aggregated information with Live Office.

6. Start Microsoft PowerPoint.

7. Make sure you have at least one empty slide in your presentation.

8. Follow the LIVE OFFICE • INSERT • WEB INTELLIGENCE CONTENT menu path.

9. From the repository, select the Web Intelligence report that we created in Section 4.6.

10. Select the cross tab and the chart from the section for the first quarter (see Figure 6.33).

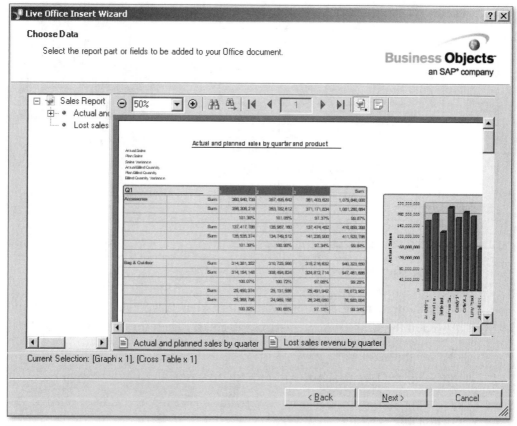

Figure 6.33 Live Office Insert Wizard

11. Click NEXT.

12. Click FINISH.

13. The cross tab and the chart will be inserted into the slide and you can then resize and format the objects as you wish (see Figure 6.34), but the data is still live and can be refreshed.

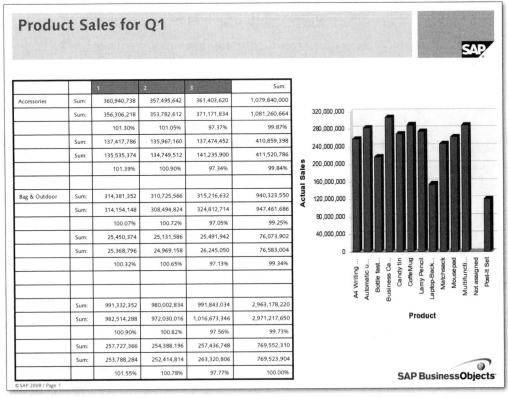

Figure 6.34 Live Office Document in Microsoft PowerPoint

14. Now insert three additional slides into your PowerPoint presentation and repeat the steps to show the cross tab and the chart for Q2, Q3, and Q4.

15. After this, add a fifth slide into your presentation.

16. Select the LIVE OFFICE • INSERT • WEB INTELLIGENCE CONTENT menu path.

17. From the repository, select the Web Intelligence report that we created in Section 4.6.

18. Select the tab for the second report.

19. Select the two charts in the second report and click NEXT (see Figure 6.35).

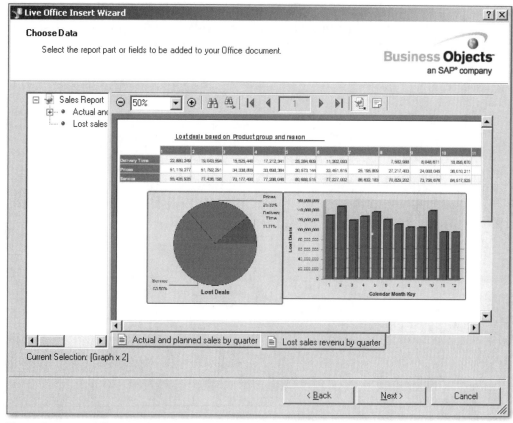

Figure 6.35 Live Office Insert Wizard

20. Click FINISH.

21. You can now resize the two charts on the slide deck and now your PowerPoint slide deck shows the Actual and Planned sales number for all four quarters and the lost revenue for the lost opportunities.

22. The data in the PowerPoint slide deck can be refreshed by each user who has access to the Live Office software.

23. You can now save the PowerPoint slide deck and send it to the sales force. Each recipient can refresh the data – assuming the person has access to the Live Office software and he has access to the underlying source system.

6.6   Summary

In this chapter, you learned how you can leverage Live Office to provide data from your BusinessObjects system to Microsoft Office. You also learned to leverage online data and provide your end users with a familiar environment, such as Microsoft Excel, but keep the data refreshable and secure.

SAP BusinessObjects Explorer offers a unique user experience by providing search and explore functionality. In this chapter, we will learn how to use SAP BusinessObjects Explorer with our SAP data.

7 Data Exploration and Searching

In this chapter, we will learn how to install and configure SAP BusinessObjects Explorer in conjunction with our SAP landscape, particularly with SAP NetWeaver BW Accelerator (BWA). We will use SAP BusinessObjects Explorer to provide a compelling user experience for users and offer a search and explore interface on top of our data warehouse.

7.1 Installation and Deployment Overview

In this section, we'll look at the installation and configuration steps for SAP BusinessObjects Explorer in conjunction with different data sources from your SAP landscape.

SAP BusinessObjects Explorer Service Pack 01

Please note that SAP BusinessObjects Explorer Service Pack 01 is not supported by Service Pack 02 for SAP BusinessObjects Enterprise. Service Pack 02 for SAP BusinessObjects Explorer is scheduled for release by the end of 2009.

SAP BusinessObjects Explorer vs. Polestar

SAP BusinessObjects Explorer is the rebranded version of Polestar. Polestar was the project codename for the actual product, and as of XI 3.1 it was rebranded as SAP BusinessObjects Explorer. You will notice that in some parts of the software the name Polestar still appears, but you can assume it is all the same product, SAP BusinessObjects Explorer.

7.1.1 Installation of SAP BusinessObjects Explorer

For this section, we will use the Release XI 3.1 Service Pack 01 of SAP Business-Objects Explorer. After you download the installation media from the SAP Service Marketplace (*http://service.sap.com/swdc*), start the installation for SAP BusinessObjects Explorer by running setup.exe (for a Windows environment).

SAP BusinessObjects Explorer vs. SAP BusinessObjects Explorer, Accelerated Version

There are two versions of SAP BusinessObjects Explorer:

▶ SAP BusinessObjects Explorer is available on standard hardware and platforms that support SAP BusinessObjects Enterprise and let you leverage Universes for data access.

▶ SAP BusinessObjects Explorer, Accelerated Version is delivered on preconfigured blades for the same hardware and platforms as SAP NetWeaver BWA.

---

1. After starting the installation, we will be asked to select the language for the installation routine. Just as with the previous installations of SAP BusinessObjects products, the selection of a language at this point does not impact the actual product, it only impacts the installation routine (see Figure 7.1).

Figure 7.1 SAP BusinessObjects Explorer — Setup Language

2. Set the language to ENGLISH and click OK.

3. Click NEXT in the upcoming dialog.

4. In the next dialog, accept the license agreement (see Figure 7.2).

5. Click NEXT.

6. In the next step (see Figure 7.3), we can select the list of LANGUAGE PACKS for the software. Select ENGLISH.

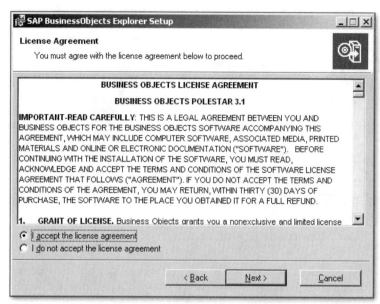

Figure 7.2 SAP BusinessObjects Explorer — License Agreement

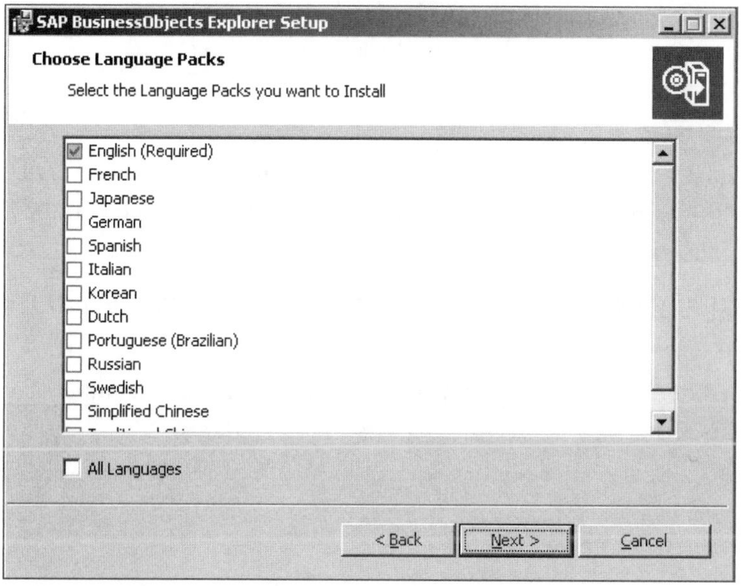

Figure 7.3 SAP BusinessObjects Explorer — Language Packs

7. Click NEXT.

8. In the next step (see Figure 7.4), the list of available components is shown. By default, all components are selected for installation. Leave the default selection.

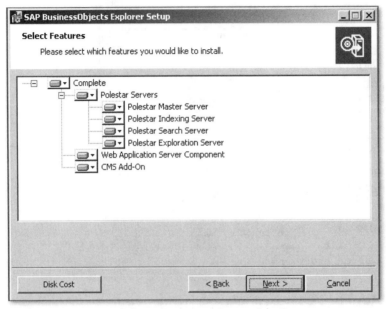

Figure 7.4 SAP BusinessObjects Explorer — Feature Selection

9. Click NEXT.

10. We now need to provide the details of our Central Management Service (CMS). Enter the name of your CMS into the CMS NAME field (see Figure 7.5). For our example, enter VMWSAP21.

11. Enter the port of your CMS into the CMS PORT field. For our example, the default port is 6400.

12. Provide the credentials for an administrative account. In our example, the user ADMINISTRATOR.

13. Click NEXT.

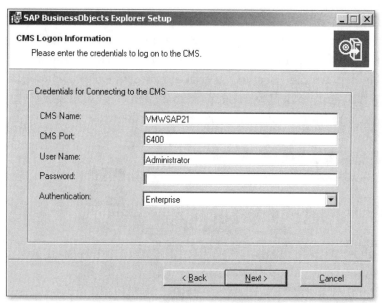

Figure 7.5 SAP BusinessObjects Explorer — CMS Logon Information

14. Next, you need to provide the NODE NAME of the SERVER INTELLIGENCE AGENT of your SAP BusinessObjects Enterprise server. In our example, it is a single server deployment and therefore the name of our SERVER INTELLIGENCE AGENT is VMWSAP21 (see Figure 7.6).

Figure 7.6 SAP BusinessObjects Explorer — Server Intelligence Agent

15. Enter the name of your SERVER INTELLIGENCE AGENT and click NEXT.

16. SAP BusinessObjects Explorer is a web-based Business Intelligence (BI) tool, and therefore the web applications need to be deployed on the application server. In this step, we can select to either automatically deploy the applications during the setup or deploy the applications manually (see Figure 7.7). Select the option YES, AUTOMATICALLY DEPLOY THE WEB APPLICATION.

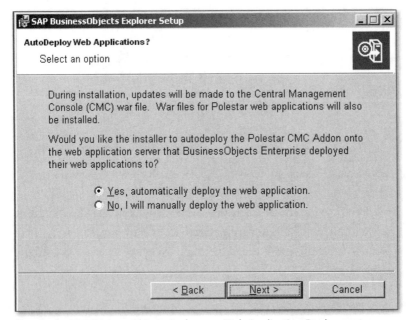

Figure 7.7 SAP BusinessObjects Explorer — Web Application Deployment

17. Click NEXT.

18. Because we chose to automatically deploy the web applications, we now need to provide the details of our web application server (WAS) (see Figure 7.8). Ensure that the details are correct for your system.

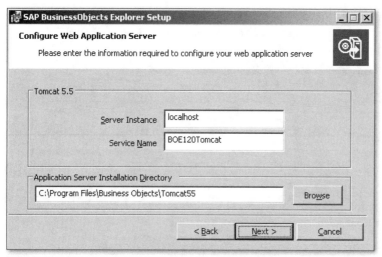

Figure 7.8 SAP BusinessObjects Explorer — WAS Details

19. Click NEXT.

After providing all of the details, the set up routine is ready to install the SAP BusinessObjects Explorer application (see Figure 7.9).

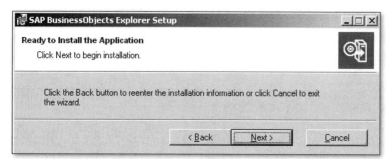

Figure 7.9 SAP BusinessObjects Explorer — Ready to Install Application

20. Click NEXT.

The installation process will start and after a few minutes the setup routine will deploy SAP BusinessObjects Explorer.

21. Click FINISH.

After you finish installing of SAP BusinessObjects Explorer, you will find a set of additional services as part of your SAP BusinessObjects Enterprise system.

1. Follow the menu path START • PROGRAMS • BUSINESSOBJECTS XI 3.1 • BUSINESS-
   OBJECTS ENTERPRISE • CENTRAL CONFIGURATION MANAGER (SEE Figure 7.10).

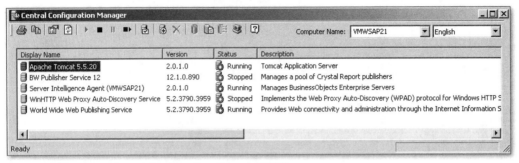

Figure 7.10   Central Configuration Manager (CCM)

2. Click the  button to review the list of available servers on your SAP Business
   Objects Enterprise system.

3. Authenticate towards the SAP BusinessObjects system.

4. Click CONNECT.

5. Review the list of available servers on your system. You will see four additional
   servers for SAP BusinessObjects Explorer (see Figure 7.11):

   ▶ POLESTAR.EXPLORATION

   ▶ POLESTAR.INDEXING

   ▶ POLESTAR.MASTER

   ▶ POLESTAR.SEARCH

VMWSAP21.PolestarExploration	Running	Enabled	VMWSAP21	1720	Explorer Exploration Server
VMWSAP21.PolestarIndexing	Running	Enabled	VMWSAP21	5812	Explorer Indexing Server
VMWSAP21.PolestarMaster	Running	Enabled	VMWSAP21	5144	Explorer Master Server
VMWSAP21.PolestarSearch	Running	Enabled	VMWSAP21	1652	Explorer Search Server

Figure 7.11   SAP BusinessObjects Explorer Servers

6. Close the CENTRAL CONFIGURATION MANAGER.

7. Open a browser window and enter the following URL:

```
http://<host name>:<port>/polestar/
```

Replace the `<host name>` placeholder with the name of your WAS, and `<port>` with the port of your WAS.

In our example:

```
http://vmwsap21:8080/polestar/
```

You can now leverage SAP BusinessObjects Explorer and create workspaces (see Figure 7.12). But before doing so, we'll configure the SAP authentication for SAP BusinessObjects Explorer and the connectivity to SAP NetWeaver BWA.

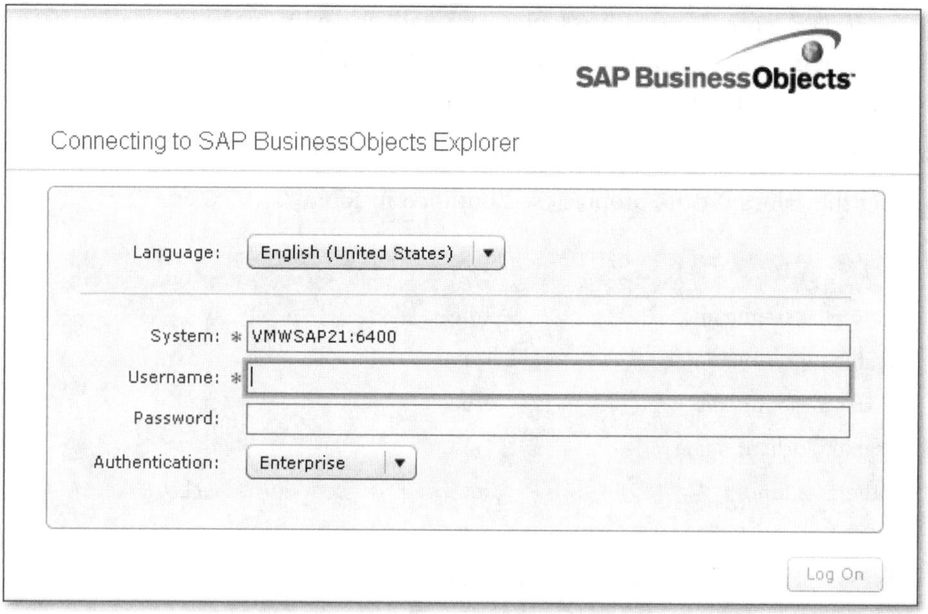

Figure 7.12 SAP BusinessObjects Explorer Logon Screen

SAP BusinessObjects Explorer and Flash Player

The user interface (UI) of SAP BusinessObjects Explorer is based on Flex/Flash, therefore, you need to install the Adobe Flash Player. You can download the latest version of Adobe Flash Player from *www.adobe.com*.

7.1.2 Configuration of SAP Authentication for SAP BusinessObjects Explorer

After you install SAP BusinessObjects Explorer on top of your SAP BusinessObjects Enterprise system, you will notice that the logon screen for SAP BusinessObjects Explorer is not offering SAP authentication as an authentication option. In order for the users to leverage their SAP credentials, we need to edit the default properties settings from the web applications of SAP BusinessObjects Explorer.

1. Navigate to the folder \Program Files\Business Objects\Tomcat55\webapps\polestar\ WEB-INF\classes. This path assumes an installation on Windows using Tomcat as the application server. If you are using a different application server, make sure you navigate to the web application folder of your application server.

2. Open the `default.settings.properties` file with an editor like notepad.

3. Set the values for the properties as outlined in Table 7.1.

Property	Value
show.sapsystem.name	True
disable.sapsystem.name	False
show.sapclient.name	True
disable.sapclient.name	False
authentications	secEnterprise, secWinAD, secLDAP, secSAPR3
hide.authentication.method	False
disable.authentication.method	False

Table 7.1 Property Settings

4. Restart your web application server.

5. Open the URL to start SAP BusinessObjects Explorer.

   After selecting SAP as the AUTHENTICATION method, your logon screen for SAP BusinessObjects Explorer should have the SAP SYSTEM ID and SAP CLIENT ID fields (see Figure 7.13) and users should be able to use the SAP credentials to log on to SAP BusinessObjects Explorer. The use of SAP authentication with SAP BusinessObjects Explorer requires that the SAP BusinessObjects Integration for SAP solutions is installed and deployed on the SAP BusinessObjects Enterprise system, and that SAP authentication is configured for the SAP NetWeaver Business Warehouse (BW) system.

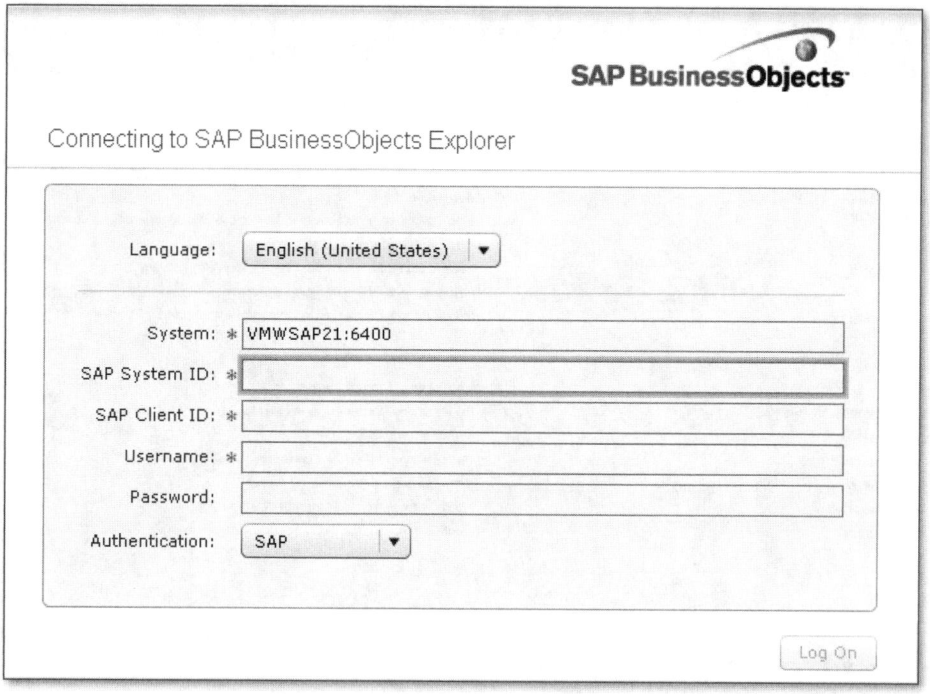

Figure 7.13 SAP BusinessObjects Explorer Logon Screen

7.1.3 Configuration of SAP BusinessObjects Explorer Combined with SAP NetWeaver BWA

In order for SAP BusinessObjects Explorer to leverage indices from BWA, we need to configure the SAP BusinessObjects Explorer application with the details of the Text Retrieval and Extraction (TREX) host and port, so that SAP BusinessObjects Explorer knows how to communicate to the BWA instance.

1. Follow the menu path: START • PROGRAMS • BUSINESSOBJECTS XI 3.1 • BUSINESSOBJECTS ENTERPRISE • BUSINESSOBJECTS ENTERPRISE CENTRAL MANAGEMENT CONSOLE.

2. Authenticate with an administrative account for your SAP BusinessObjects Enterprise system.

3. Select APPLICATIONS in the dropdown list (see Figure 7.14).

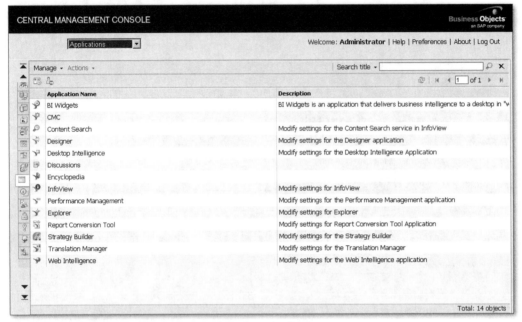

Figure 7.14   Central Management Console — Applications

4. Right-click EXPLORER and select PROPERTIES (see Figure 7.15).

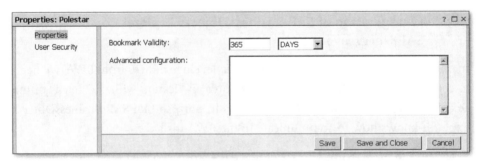

Figure 7.15   SAP BusinessObjects Explorer — Properties

5. We need to add the following parameters to the ADVANCED CONFIGURATION:

   ▸ com.businessobjects.datadiscovery.dataprovider.trex.host=

   ▸ com.businessobjects.datadiscovery.dataprovider.trex.port=

   The parameter TREX_HOST needs the name of the active name server of the BWA deployment and the parameter TREX_PORT needs the port number.

6. Enter these two parameters and their corresponding values from your SAP landscape into the ADVANCED CONFIGURATION field.

7. Click SAVE (see Figure 7.16).

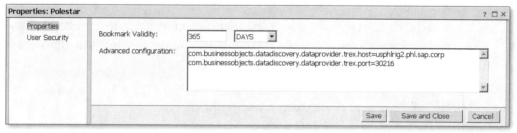

Figure 7.16 SAP BusinessObjects Explorer — Properties

8. Click SAVE AND CLOSE.

Backup Server and Higher Availability

The ADVANCED CONFIGURATION option lets you enter more than one server entry. You can enter multiple TREX index servers so that the SAP NetWeaver BWA connection can reach a higher availability.

7.1.4 User Security Configuration for SAP BusinessObjects Explorer

Before we can leverage SAP BusinessObjects Explorer with our users, we need to assign the necessary rights in the SAP BusinessObjects Enterprise system.

1. Log on to the CMC of your SAP BusinessObjects Enterprise system.

2. Select APPLICATIONS in the dropdown list.

3. Right-click EXPLORER and select USER SECURITY (see Figure 7.17).

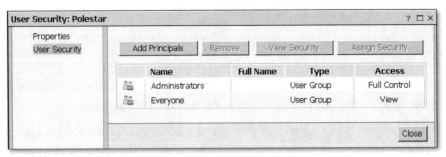

Figure 7.17 User Security

4. Click ADD PRINCIPALS.

5. Select the necessary user groups and users and move them to the list of SELECT-ED USERS/GROUPS (see Figure 7.18). In our example, the user BIR~003/I819882 has been imported via the SAP authentication.

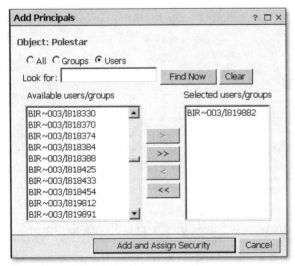

Figure 7.18 Add Principals

6. Click ADD AND ASSIGN SECURITY.

7. Navigate to the ADVANCED tab.

8. Click ADD/REMOVE RIGHTS.

9. Now you can grant or deny security to the user for the GENERAL area (see Figure 7.19) and the EXPLORER area (see Figure 7.20).

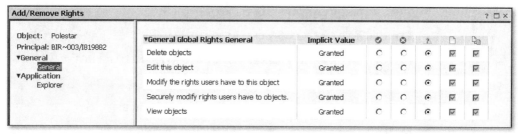

Figure 7.19 Security Area General

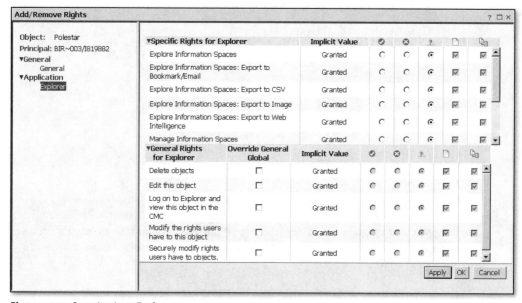

Figure 7.20 Security Area Explorer

10. Grant the following rights for the GENERAL area:

   ▸ EDIT THIS OBJECT

   ▸ VIEW OBJECT

11. Grant the following rights for the EXPLORER area :

   ▸ SPECIFIC RIGHTS FOR EXPLORER

      ▸ EXPLORE INFORMATION SPACES

      ▸ EXPLORE INFORMATION SPACES: EXPORT TO BOOKMARK/EMAIL

- ▸ EXPLORE INFORMATION SPACES: EXPORT TO CSV

- ▸ EXPLORE INFORMATION SPACES: EXPORT TO IMAGE

- ▸ EXPLORE INFORMATION SPACES: EXPORT TO WEB INTELLIGENCE

- ▸ MANAGE INFORMATION SPACES

- ▸ MANAGE INFORMATION SPACES: CREATE A NEW SPACE

- ▸ MANAGE INFORMATION SPACES: LAUNCH INDEXING

- ▸ MANAGE INFORMATION SPACES: MODIFY A SPACE

- ▸ MANAGE INFORMATION SPACES: SCHEDULE INDEXING

- ▸ GENERAL RIGHTS FOR EXPLORER

  - ▸ LOG ON TO EXPLORER AND VIEW THIS OBJECT IN THE CMC

  - ▸ EDIT THIS OBJECT

12. Click APPLY.

13. Click OK.

14. Click OK.

15. Click CLOSE.

> **User Security Assignment**
>
> The preceding assignments are for educational purposes and not for a real product deployment. In a real production deployment, you should consider a more detailed authorization concept.

7.1.5   SAP BusinessObjects Explorer Enablement

Before we can use SAP BusinessObjects Explorer in conjunction with SAP NetWeaver BWA and our SAP NetWeaver BW system, we need to enable the general usage of SAP BusinessObjects Explorer.

1. Log on to your SAP NetWeaver BW system.

2. Start Transaction SE38.

3. Enter `RSDDTREX_ADMIN_MAINTAIN` as the PROGRAM (see Figure 7.21).

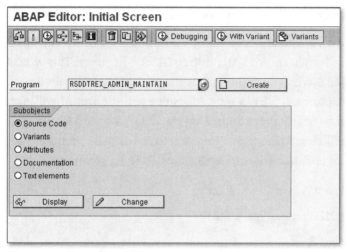

Figure 7.21 Transaction SE38

4. Follow the menu path PROGRAM • EXECUTE • DIRECT PROCESSING (or press [F8]).

5. Set the value for the OBJECT field to POLESTAR_SYSTEM.

6. Set the value for the VALUE field to X.

7. Use the INSERT option (see Figure 7.22).

Maintain BI Accelerator (BIA) Index Parameter

If you already configured the necessary parameters in Transaction SE38, you may have to use the UPDATE option for the program instead of INSERT.

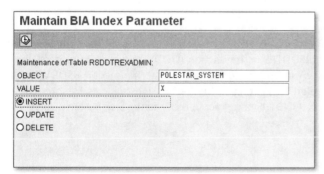

Figure 7.22 Maintain BIA Index Parameter

8. Follow the menu path: PROGRAM • EXECUTE (or press [F8]).

7.1.6 SAP NetWeaver BWA — Index Wizard

After we've configured all of the previous steps, we can now create an enhanced index using the BWA index wizard for SAP BusinessObjects Explorer. This wizard will leverage an existing BWA index and enhance it so that it can be used with SAP BusinessObjects Explorer. If a BWA index doesn't exist, the wizard will start the standard BWA index wizard after configuring the details of the SAP BusinessObjects Explorer–specific enhancements. This wizard is basically rebuilding an existing BWA index and enhancing it for SAP BusinessObjects Explorer.

1. Log on to your SAP NetWeaver BW system.

2. Start Transaction RSDDTPS (see Figure 7.23).

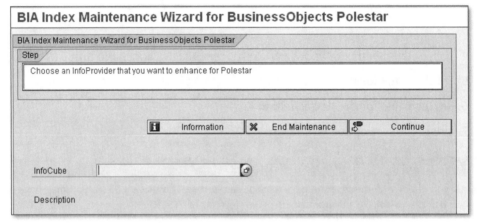

Figure 7.23 BIA Index Maintenance Wizard

Transaction RSDDTPS vs. Transaction RSDDV

You can leverage Transaction RSDDTPS or Transaction RSDDV to use SAP BusinessObjects Explorer on top of a BWA index. The difference is that Transaction RSDDV lets you create the BWA index before navigating to the SAP BusinessObjects Explorer enhancements, while Transaction RSDDTPS brings you directly to the SAP BusinessObjects Explorer enhancements.

BIA Index Maintenance Wizard

When you first start the wizard you need to specify the language and date format that will be used for the indexing for SAP BusinessObjects Explorer. You can't select different languages per user or a date format per user.

---

3. Select an InfoCube from the list of available InfoCube. In our example we will use InfoCube 0D_NW_C01 from the SAP NetWeaver demo model.

4. Click CONTINUE (see Figure 7.24).

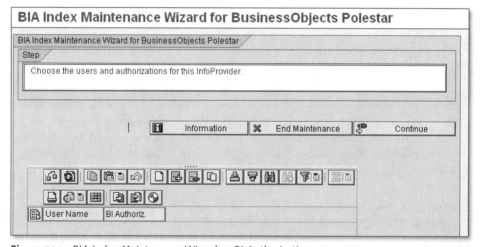

Figure 7.24 BIA Index Maintenance Wizard — BI Authorization

SAP BusinessObjects Explorer and BI Authorizations

As part of Release XI 3.1 Service Pack 01, you can only assign a single BI authorization maintained in Transaction RSECADMIN per user. This single authorization can include several data level restrictions and is not limited to a single characteristic.

---

5. Click the 🔲 button to add a new row to the list of users and authorizations.

6. Enter the users that need access to the index data.

7. For now, we will add authorization 0BI_ALL, which provides access to all data for the users (see Figure 7.25). If you leave the field empty, the system will automatically add 0BI_ALL as an authorization object for the user.

BIA Index Maintenance Wizard for BusinessObjects Polestar

BIA Index Maintenance Wizard for BusinessObjects Polestar

Step

Choose the users and authorizations for this InfoProvider.

| | Information | | End Maintenance | | Continue |

User Name	BI Authoriz.
i819882	0BI_ALL

Figure 7.25 BIA Index Maintenance Wizard — BI Authorization

SAP BusinessObjects Explorer and BI Authorizations

After you add the list of users with BI authorizations, an index with authorization information is created. Each added USER NAME can only be assigned a single BI Authorization. At this point (BusinessObjects Explorer XI 3.1 Service Pack 1), only "flat" BI Authorizations can be used, which means no hierarchy node authorizations can be used.

8. Click CONTINUE (see Figure 7.26).

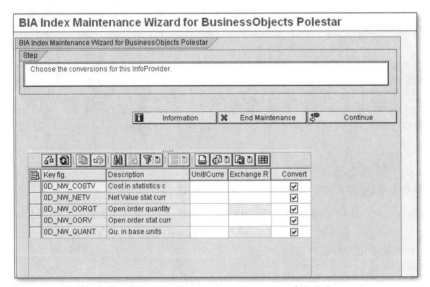

Figure 7.26 BIA Index Maintenance Wizard — Currency and Unit Conversion

You will be presented with the list of key figures that need a UNIT or CURRENCY conversion.

Unit and Currency Conversion

Before creating the index, you have to configure a target currency and unit for each key figure. The currency conversion rates are read from the TCUR* tables. The unit conversion details are read from the T006* tables.

SAP BusinessObjects Explorer only supports simple, common conversions, such as centimeter to meter or gram to kilogram. More complex conversions, for example, box to pallet, are not supported.

Exception Aggregation and Noncumulative Key Figures

Noncumulative key figures and key figures defined with exception aggregations can't be used in SAP BusinessObjects Explorer XI 3.1 Service Pack 1 because the required dependencies have not been resolved.

---

9. After you provide details for the currency and unit conversion, click CONTINUE.

10. You will be presented with a summary of your settings and any outstanding warnings, for example, missing currency translations (see Figure 7.27).

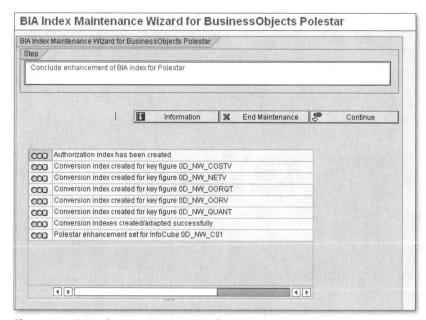

Figure 7.27 BIA Index Maintenance Wizard — Summary

11. Click CONTINUE (see Figure 7.28).

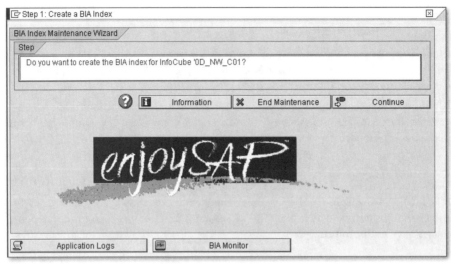

Figure 7.28 BIA Index Maintenance Wizard — Create BIA Index

12. Now you can use the CONTINUE button to create the BIA INDEX (see Figure 7.29).

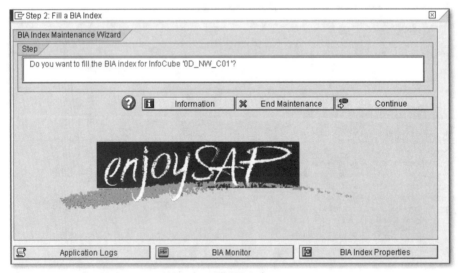

Figure 7.29 Index Maintenance Wizard — Fill BIA Index

13. Click CONTINUE to fill the BIA Index (see Figure 7.30).

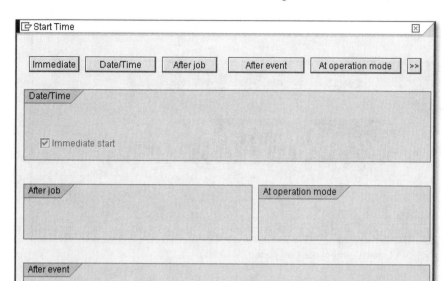

Figure 7.30 Index Maintenance Wizard — Start Time

14. Click IMMEDIATE.

15. Click SAVE.

   After the index has been created, the INDEX WIZARD displays the message STEP SUCCESSFULLY EXECUTED; END OF BIA MAINTENANCE (see Figure 7.31).

16. Click END MAINTENANCE.

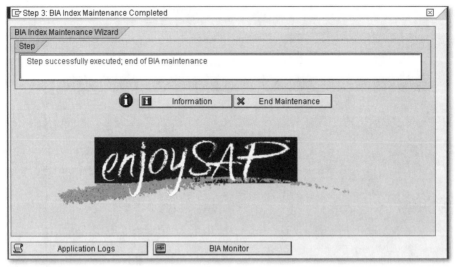

Figure 7.31 BIA Index Maintenance Completed

7.1.7 SAP BusinessObjects Explorer using BWA Index

Now that we created the BWA index, we are ready to use it in SAP BusinessObjects Explorer.

1. Log on to SAP BusinessObjects Explorer with your SAP credentials. Make sure the credentials were configured as part of the BWA Index wizard.

2. Select MANAGE SPACES (see Figure 7.32).

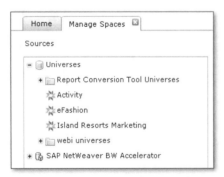

Figure 7.32 SAP BusinessObjects Explorer — Manage Spaces

3. Open the list of available BWA indexes (see Figure 7.33).

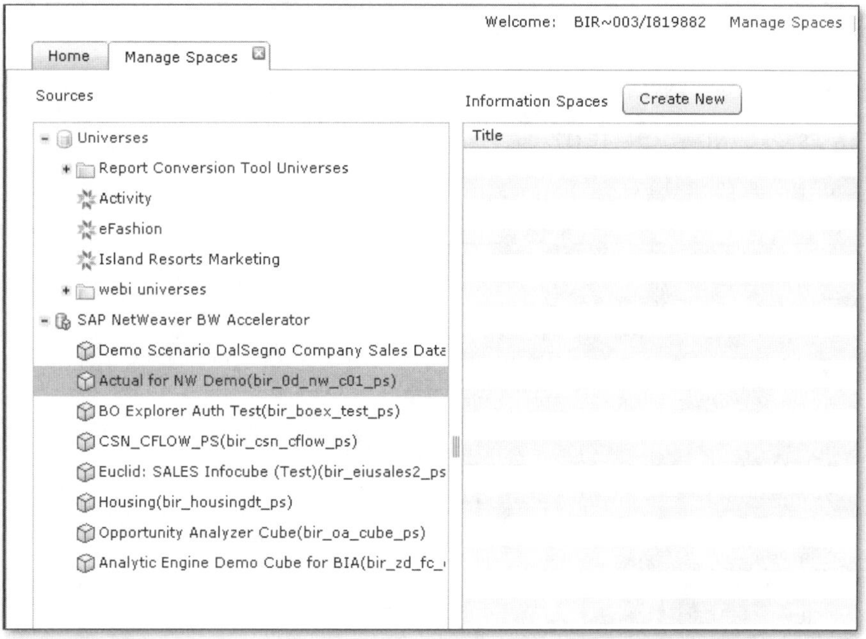

Figure 7.33 SAP BusinessObjects Explorer — BWA Indexes

4. Select ACTUAL FOR NW DEMO.

5. Click CREATE NEW.

6. Enter `Actual for NW Demo Information Workspace` as the Name.

7. Navigate to the OBJECTS tab.

8. Add all key figures to the list of MEASURES AND DIMENSIONS.

9. Add the following characteristics to the list of MEASURES AND DIMENSIONS (see Figure 7.34):

   ▶ CALENDAR YEAR/MONTH

   ▶ DISTRIBUTION CHANNEL (TEXT)

   ▶ COUNTRY (TEXT)

   ▶ DIVISION (TEXT)

► PLANT (TEXT)

► PRODUCT (TEXT)

► REGION (TEXT)

► SALES GROUP (TEXT)

► SALES ORGANIZATION (TEXT)

► CALENDAR YEAR (KEY)

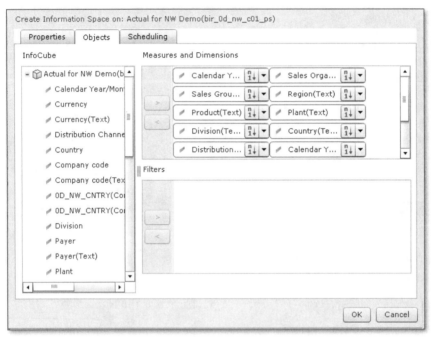

Figure 7.34 SAP BusinessObjects Explorer — Measures and Dimensions

Characteristic Key and Description

As you can see from the list of available objects, when creating an Information Space on top of a BWA index, you have the key and the description for characteristics. Which object you use depends on your preference. Please note, SAP BusinessObjects Explorer does not provide functionality that lets you switch between the key and the description in the SAP BusinessObjects Explorer tool itself.

10. Click OK (see Figure 7.35).

Figure 7.35   SAP BusinessObjects Explorer — Information Spaces

11. Use the INDEX NOW [icon] button to connect the INFORMATION WORKSPACE to the BWA index (see Figure 7.36).

Figure 7.36   SAP BusinessObjects Explorer — Information Spaces

After a short time, the status of the INFORMATION WORKSPACE will change to OK and you can use the INFORMATION WORKSPACE to explore the data from BWA (see Figure 7.37).

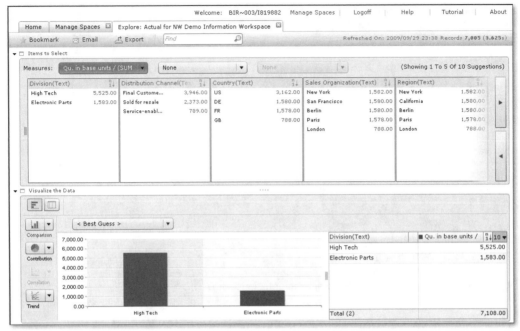

Figure 7.37 SAP BusinessObjects Explorer — Information Spaces

7.1.8 Deployment Options for SAP BusinessObjects Explorer

Before we go into more detail on the connectivity and the requirements for SAP BusinessObjects Explorer, let's look at the deployment options that are available.

Figure 7.38 shows the options for deploying SAP BusinessObjects Explorer, Accelerated Version, on preconfigured blades in conjunction with SAP BusinessObjects Enterprise and SAP BusinessObjects Integration for SAP Solutions.

Figure 7.39 shows an alternative, where you deploy SAP BusinessObjects Enterprise and SAP BusinessObjects Integration for SAP Solutions on SAP BusinessObjects Enterprise–supported hardware and operating systems. Please note that in such a scenario, SAP BusinessObjects Explorer, Accelerated Version, needs to be deployed on the same hardware and operating system combination as SAP NetWeaver BWA. In this case, it means SAP BusinessObjects Explorer, Accelerated

Version, is still deployed on the blade server. The benefit of the deployment on a preconfigured blade server is the performance-optimized deployment and the out-of-the-box deployment and configuration delivered to you. In this scenario, you can deploy the services from the SAP BusinessObjects Enterprise system and the web tier of your SAP BusinessObjects Enterprise system on standard supported hardware and operating systems, but SAP BusinessObjects Explorer needs to be deployed on the supported platforms and operating systems in conjunction with SAP NetWeaver BWA.

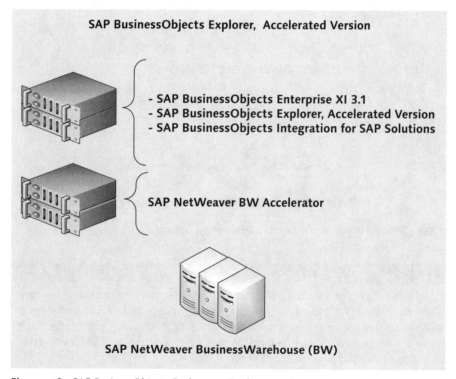

Figure 7.38 SAP BusinessObjects Explorer — Deployment Options

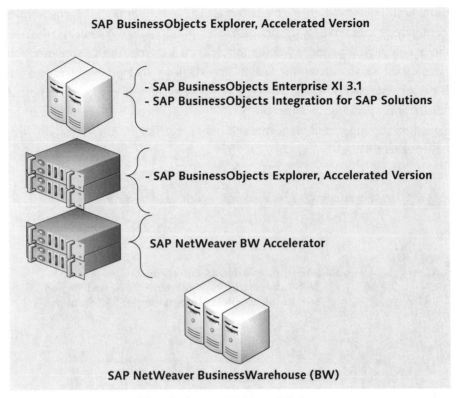

Figure 7.39 SAP BusinessObjects Explorer — Deployment Options

---

SAP BusinessObjects Explorer without SAP NetWeaver BWA

In a deployment scenario not using SAP NetWeaver BWA, you can install SAP BusinessObjects Explorer on a standard supported operating system and hardware. Based on the volume of data you might want to explore with SAP BusinessObjects Explorer, it is highly recommended to leverage SAP NetWeaver BWA, because only SAP NetWeaver BWA lets you index such large data volumes.

Now that we've configured our SAP BusinessObjects Explorer and SAP NetWeaver BW and BWA environments, let's get into more detail with data connectivity in the next section.

7.2   SAP Data Connectivity for SAP BusinessObjects Explorer

SAP BusinessObjects Explorer can leverage a Universe or an existing index from SAP NetWeaver BWA as a data source.

Figure 7.40 shows what this means for SAP BusinessObjects Explorer in conjunction with your SAP landscape. SAP BusinessObjects Explorer can leverage:

► A relational Universe using the integration with Data Federator based on an InfoProvider or a Data Store Object (DSO).

► An OLAP Universe using the SAP connectivity for SAP NetWeaver BW on top of a BW query or an InfoProvider.

► An existing index from SAP NetWeaver BWA.

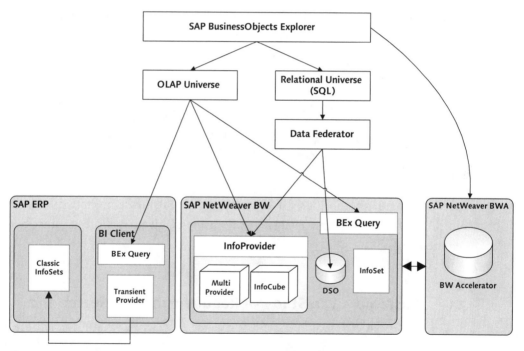

Figure 7.40   SAP BusinessObjects Explorer — Data Connectivity

For the first two connectivity options, SAP BusinessObjects Explorer would have to create and store its own index. With SAP NetWeaver BWA this is not necessary, and more importantly, SAP BusinessObjects Explorer can handle much larger data volumes.

As shown in Figure 7.40, the available sources that SAP BusinessObjects Explorer can use are:

- BW QUERY via OLAP UNIVERSE.
- BW INFOCUBE and MULTIPROVIDER via OLAP Universe.
- ERP data via TRANSIENT PROVIDER and BW QUERY using the OLAP UNIVERSE.
- INFOCUBE, MULTIPROVIDER, and DSOs via a RELATIONAL UNIVERSE using DATA FEDERATOR.
- BWA indexes based on INFOCUBES using a direct connectivity to BWA. These BWA indexes can be based on INFOCUBES and MULTIPROVIDER.

Looking at the different data sources you will see that — as of this writing — the only data sources that BWA can't leverage are the DSO objects and the ERP data via the Transient Provider. The recommended approach is to leverage a BWA instance for indexing because the amount of data that you can leverage with BWA compared to a non-BWA deployment is much larger.

Multiprovider Snapshot Solution

So far, BWA indexes are only based on InfoCubes, but a solution has been developed to create BWA indexes based on MultiProvider (see SAP Notes 1332090 and 1332392 for further details).

After looking at the options for connecting SAP BusinessObjects Explorer to our SAP data, we will now evaluate SAP BusinessObjects Explorer against our requirements.

7.3 Customer Case Study — Requirements for Search and Exploration

In this section, we'll use the requirements from the previous section and see which ones are a good fit for using SAP BusinessObjects Explorer as a BI tool. Before looking at the requirements, we need to note a major difference between SAP Business-

Objects Explorer and the other BI tools like Web Intelligence, Crystal Reports, and Xcelsius. SAP BusinessObjects Explorer is focused on the search and exploration user experience while the other tools are focused on providing well-structured answers to consumer questions (see Chapter 2, Reporting and Analysis — Customer Case Study). Based on the focus of SAP BusinessObjects Explorer, most of the requirements are not seen as a best fit for SAP BusinessObjects Explorer. This does not mean that SAP BusinessObjects Explorer can't fulfill some of the requirements. SAP BusinessObjects Explorer can be a great starting point for a consumer in situations where a report or analytics does not exist for a user's question. The user can leverage the information provided by SAP BusinessObjects Explorer and use it in Web Intelligence for further analysis. Based on these assumptions, let's look at the requirements.

7.3.1 Financial Reporting and Analysis Requirements

The following list represents the requirements for which SAP BusinessObjects Explorer is not the best fit.

> **Unfulfilled Financial Reporting Requirement**
>
> ▶ For specific content (such as an income statement or a balance sheet) that is being created, the design needs to be layout focused with the actual print of the report very high priority.
>
> ▶ The reporting and analysis tools need to let users create new calculations and formulas and share those with other consumers of the content.
>
> ▶ The reporting and analysis tools need to allow the use of hierarchies and allow navigation along those hierarchies in the actual content.
>
> ▶ The reporting and analysis tools need to leverage custom structures that have been defined on a BW query layer.
>
> ▶ The content needs to resolve the time dependency defined for the financial cost and profit center hierarchies.
>
> ▶ The content must be available in a web-based environment and in a Microsoft Office environment (especially Microsoft Excel).

As you can see, based on the preceding list of requirements, the functionality to create custom calculations or structures is not the best fit for SAP BusinessObjects

Explorer. The requirement to leverage hierarchies as part of the search and exploration workflow has been acknowledged and is planned for a future release. When it comes to integration with the Microsoft Office environment, it is important to mention that it is possible to export the data from SAP BusinessObjects Explorer to Microsoft Excel – but it is an export and not live data like Live Office.

7.3.2 Sales Reporting and Analysis Requirements

In the sales area of our requirements, based on the list below, we can see that we only have a few requirements that we cannot fulfill with SAP BusinessObjects Explorer.

Unfulfilled Sales Reporting Requirements

▶ Content has to be available online and offline (for sales representatives on the road).

▶ Users should be able to perform scenario-based analysis, where the user can not only see the data but can influence certain factors and see the impact on the overall numbers. For example, a what-if analysis in a sales planning workflow.

These two requirements are better suited for Live Office and Xcelsius, as we already acknowledged in the previous chapters.

7.3.3 Human Resource (HR) Reporting and Analysis Requirements

Based on the nature of the requirements for the HR area, there are some key deliverables that we think we can't fulfill using SAP BusinessObjects Explorer.

Unfulfilled HR Reporting Requirements

▶ The content needs to present highly textual information in a layout-focused format.

▶ Some of the content (such as employee appraisals or performance reviews) will be used as actual official documents, and therefore need to follow strict layout rules.

SAP BusinessObjects Explorer can't create highly textual reports or deliver official documents. These requirements are much better suited for Crystal Reports.

7.3.4 Executive Leadership and Management Reporting Requirements

There is only one requirement on the list for the executive leadership and management area that can't be fulfilled with SAP BusinessObjects Explorer.

Unfulfilled Executive Leadership and Management Reporting Requirements

▶ The content needs to present highly aggregated information with the necessary alerts for important Key Performance Indicators (KPIs).

SAP BusinessObjects Explorer can show and visualize highly aggregated information, but it can't provide alerts on specific KPIs in a proactive manner.

Overall, we highly recommend that you become familiar with SAP BusinessObjects Explorer as a BI tool and experience the different focus in the user experience yourself. Leverage all of the guidance and decision criteria that we discussed in Chapter 2, Reporting and Analysis — Customer Case Study, to ensure that you leverage the right tool for the job. SAP BusinessObjects Explorer is a very unique user experience, which can be a great help to your overall solution, but it can also be overwhelming for some users. SAP BusinessExplorer is meant to provide an easy-to-use BI experience, which it does. It is not meant for those looking to receive a structured answer to a repeatable question. SAP BusinessObjects Explorer provides a large volume of data to the consumer, who can then use common techniques and navigation steps to explore the data.

After reviewing how SAP BusinessObjects Explorer can help us fulfill some of our requirements, now we'll learn more about the tool itself.

7.4 SAP BusinessObjects Explorer — Quick Basics

In this section, we will learn how to use SAP BusinessObjects Explorer on an indexed data set created using SAP BusinessObjects Explorer without SAP NetWeaver BWA; we will focus on the UI instead. For these steps we will use the sample database and eFashion Universe. This Universe should be available as part of your SAP BusinessObjects Enterprise deployment, but if it is not you can find the Universe at: *\Program Files\Business Objects\BusinessObjects Enterprise 12.0\ Samples\en\UniverseSamples.*

1. Start SAP BusinessObjects Explorer by using the URL *http://<Host name>:<port>/ polestar*, where you replace the <Host name> placeholder with the name of your application server, and the <port> placeholder with the port of your application server.

2. Authenticate yourself for SAP BusinessObjects Explorer (see Figure 7.41).

Figure 7.41 SAP BusinessObjects Explorer

3. Click MANAGE SPACES in the menu bar (see Figure 7.42).

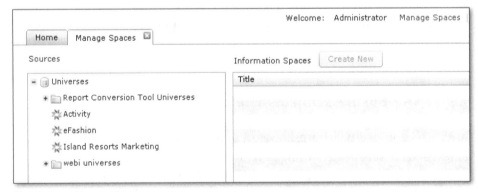

Figure 7.42 Manage Spaces

4. Select the EFASHION UNIVERSE NAME and click CREATE NEW (see Figure 7.43).

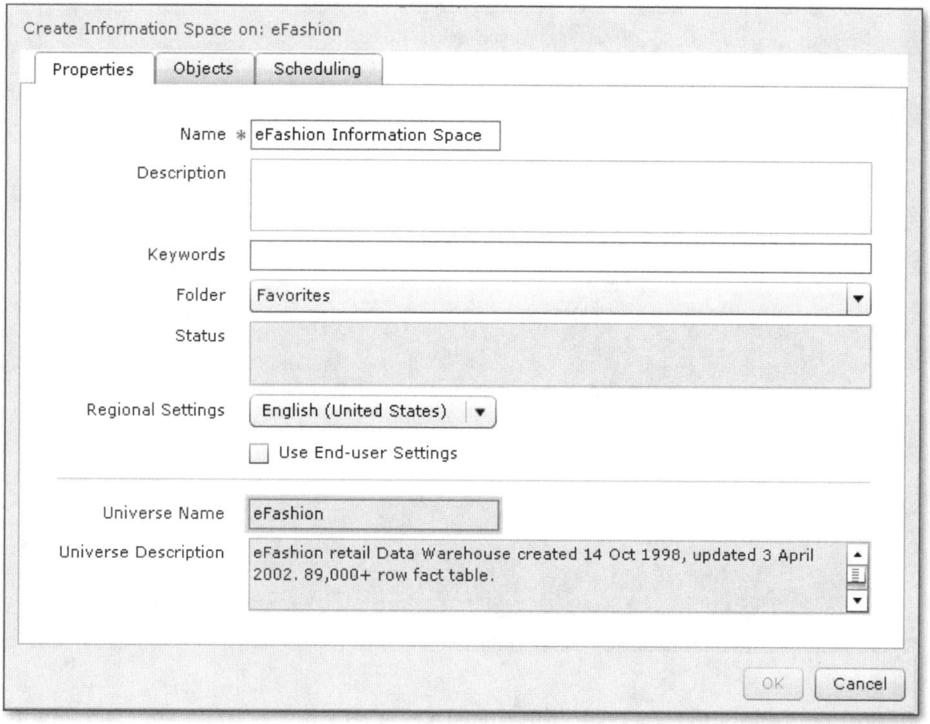

Figure 7.43 Create Information Space

5. Enter a NAME for the Information Space, in our example, EFASHION INFORMA-
TION SPACE.

6. Navigate to the OBJECTS tab (see Figure 7.44).

On the OBJECTS tab, we can select the elements from the Universe and add
them to either MEASURES AND DIMENSIONS or FILTERS. The elements in MEA-
SURES AND DIMENSIONS will be part of our indexed data set and the FILTERS
panel lets us create filter values limiting our data volume.

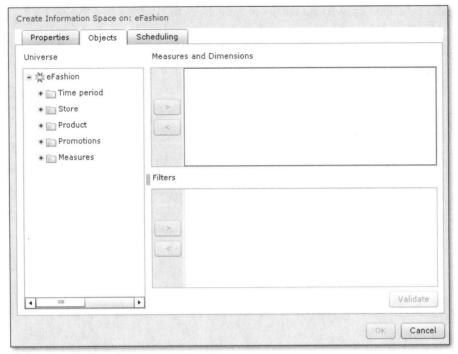

Figure 7.44 Create Information Space — Objects

7. Add the following objects to the MEASURES AND DIMENSIONS panel (see Figure 7.45) :

▸ Class Time Period

   ▸ Year

   ▸ Quarter

   ▸ Month

▸ Class Store

   ▸ State

   ▸ City

   ▸ Store Name

   ▸ Sub Class Store Details

      — Sales floor size group

      — Long opening hours

- ▸ Class Product
  - ▸ Lines
  - ▸ Category
  - ▸ Color
- ▸ Class Measures
  - ▸ Discount
  - ▸ Margin
  - ▸ Quantity Sold
  - ▸ Sales Revenue

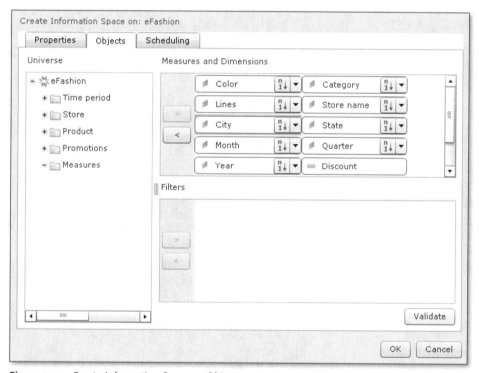

Figure 7.45 Create Information Space — Objects

8. Navigate to the SCHEDULING tab.

9. Select the ONCE option for the SCHEDULING MODE (see Figure 7.46).

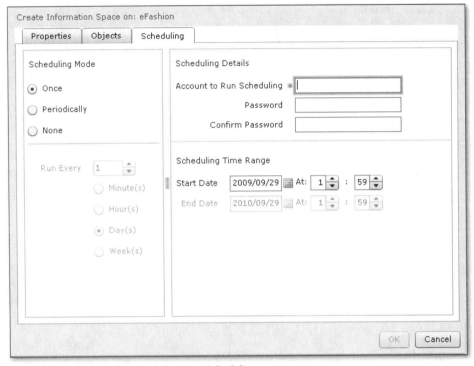

Figure 7.46 Create Information Space — Scheduling

10. Enter the user credentials.

11. Ensure the SCHEDULING TIME RANGE is set to a date and time in the future.

12. Click OK.

 After a period of time you should see your INFORMATION SPACE STATUS change to a green check symbol to indicate that the indexing was successful (see Figure 7.47).

Figure 7.47 SAP BusinessObjects Explorer — Information Space

13. Navigate to the HOME tab.

14. Click REFRESH.

15. Click on the EFASHION INFORMATION SPACE that we created previously (see Figure 7.48).

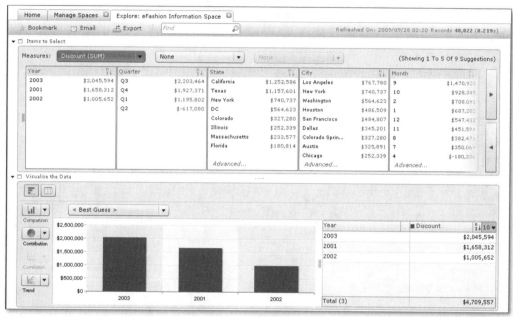

Figure 7.48 SAP BusinessObjects Explorer — Information Space

We are presented with a set of facets on the upper part of the screen. Each facet is based on a dimension object that we included in our Information Space and shows the members of each object that is available as part of the indexed data set. For example, in Figure 7.48 you can see the facet for the dimension object YEAR on the far left showing the values for the years 2001, 2002, and 2003. The lower part of the screen provides you access to a different set of types of charts, which we will explore in the next couple of steps. In addition, there is a representation in table form on the lower right of the screen, which also lets you specify a ranking, such as Top 10. You can use the facets and different chart options for navigation purposes, but you can also use the FIND option to start your data exploration.

16. Enter the following question into the FIND dialog: How many T-shirts did we sell in New York (see Figure 7.49).

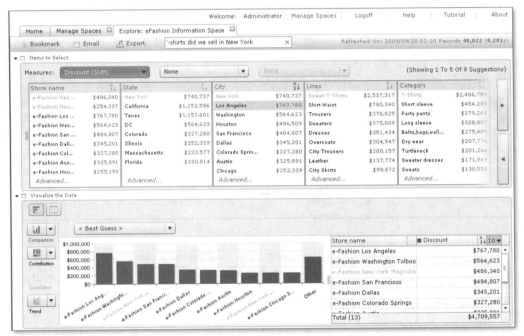

Figure 7.49 SAP BusinessObjects Explorer — Information Space

Now the information is presented to us with a focus on the possible answer to our question:

▸ The facets for the STORE NAME, STATE, CITY, and LINES have moved to the left side.

▶ Matching terms are highlighted in each of the facets, for example, NEW YORK is highlighted in the STATE and CITY facet.

17. As we are mostly interested in revenue, let's switch SALES REVENUE with DISCOUNT AS MEASURE.

18. Click on T-SHIRTS in the CATEGORY facet (see Figure 7.50).

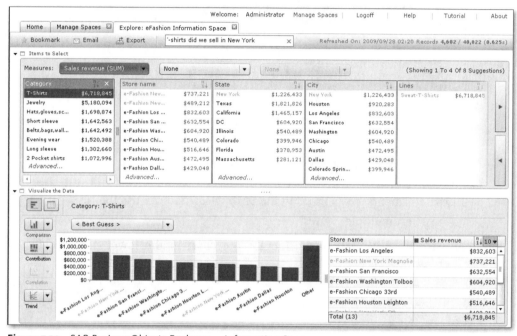

Figure 7.50 SAP BusinessObjects Explorer — Information Space

The CATEGORY facet has been moved to become the leading facet and T-SHIRT is used as a filter for the data set. For example, the LINES facet only includes SWEAT-T-SHIRTS, because it is the only matching member for the CATEGORY T-SHIRTS.

19. As we are mainly interested in revenue from New York, we can click on NEW YORK in the STATE facet.

20. Add MARGIN (SUM) as a second measure (see Figure 7.51).

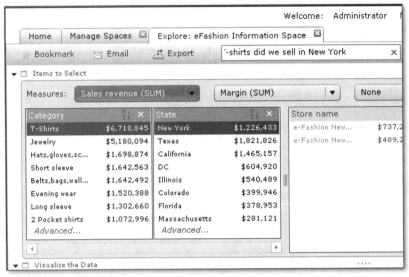

Figure 7.51 SAP BusinessObjects Explorer — Information Space

21. Select the first five entries in the STATE facet. You can use the ⌨Ctrl + ⌨Shift to select multiple entries.

22. Select the MONTH dimension for the chart in the lower part (see Figure 7.52).

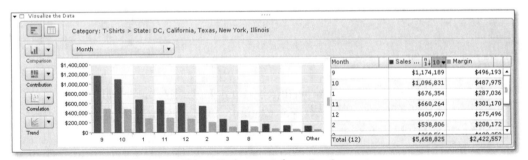

Figure 7.52 SAP BusinessObjects Explorer — Information Space

23. Use the ranking option in the table and set the value to 12. Uncheck the OTHER VALUES option (see Figure 7.53).

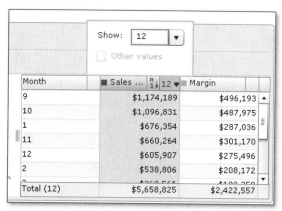

Figure 7.53 SAP BusinessObjects Explorer — Information Space

24. Click on the column heading MONTH to sort the data based on the MONTH.

25. Set the chart visualization to TREND (see Figure 7.54).

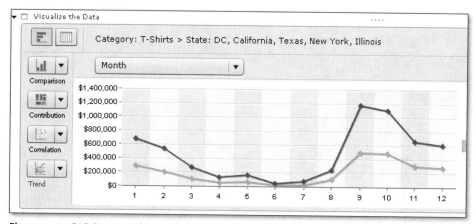

Figure 7.54 SAP BusinessObjects Explorer — Information Space

We can now see the trend in T-Shirt sales revenue and margin for the selected states. We can see that we had a huge peak in sales revenue in September and October.

26. Use the X symbol on the CATEGORY facet to remove it from the selection (see Figure 7.55). Because we removed the first (far left) facet, the STATE facet will also be removed from the selection.

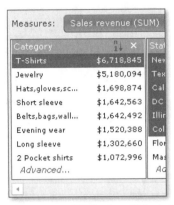

Figure 7.55 SAP BusinessObjects Explorer — Information Space

27. To find out more about the stores in New York, we need to select the two highlighted stores in the STORE NAME facet (see Figure 7.56).

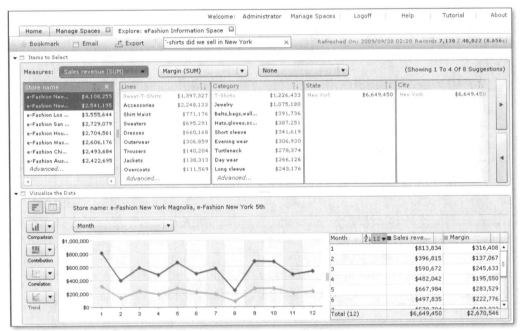

Figure 7.56 SAP BusinessObjects Explorer — Information Space

Like before, the other facets only show relevant entries for the two selected stores. Let's find out more about the products sold in these two stores.

28. Change the chart type for the visualization to Pie Chart from the Contribu-
    tion type .

29. Set the dimension for the visualization to Lines (see Figure 7.57).

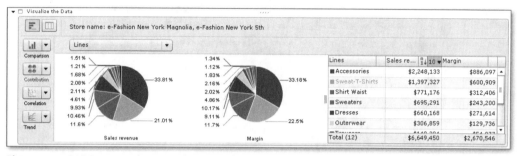

Figure 7.57 SAP BusinessObjects Explorer — Information Space

We are now looking at the sales revenue and margin contribution broken
down by product lines for our two stores in New York. In addition, the table
information shown on the right-hand side provides us with a very easy ranking, and we can identify the product lines Accessories and Sweat-T-Shirts as
the top 2 product lines in Sales revenue (see Figure 7.58).

Lines	Sales re... ⇅10 ▾	Margin	
■ Accessories	$2,248,133	$886,097	▲
■ Sweat-T-Shirts	$1,397,327	$600,909	
■ Shirt Waist	$771,176	$312,406	≡
■ Sweaters	$695,291	$243,200	
■ Dresses	$660,168	$271,614	
▨ Outerwear	$306,859	$129,736	
⬚ Trousers	$149,204	$54,077	▾
Total (12)	$6,649,450	$2,670,546	

Figure 7.58 SAP BusinessObjects Explorer — Information Space

We found the two most contributing product lines, but we want to know if
there is a relation between the sales revenue and the actual store size. The
easiest way to find out is to enter a new question into the Find dialog (see
Figure 7.59).

30. Enter the following question into the Find dialog: How does the store size
    relate to our sales revenue?

Our two stores in the STORE NAME facet haven't changed, but the SALES FLOOR SIZE GROUP facet has moved next to our selection and because we are only looking at the SALES REVENUE, MARGIN has been deselected.

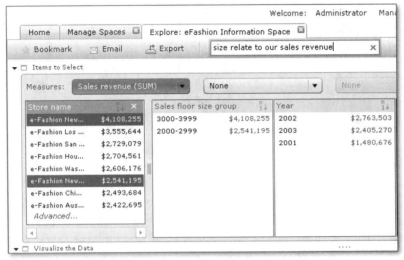

Figure 7.59 SAP BusinessObjects Explorer — Information Space

31. Remove the STORE NAME facet from the selection.

32. Select all entries in the SALES FLOOR SIZE GROUP facet (see Figure 7.60).

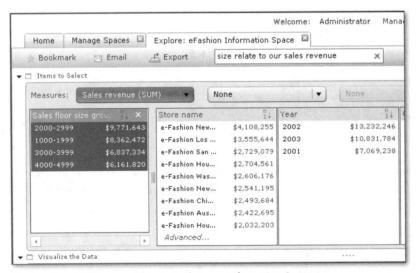

Figure 7.60 SAP BusinessObjects Explorer — Information Space

33. Add MARGIN back as a second measure.

34. Select SALES FLOOR SIZE GROUP for the lower part of the data visualization.

35. Select the COMPARISON visualization type.

36. Click on the MARGIN heading in the table shown at the bottom-right corner (see Figure 7.61).

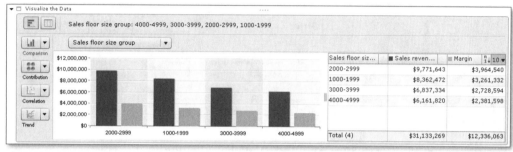

Figure 7.61 SAP BusinessObjects Explorer — Information Space

Now we can see that smaller stores are returning more revenue compared to larger stores, but the margin for the smaller stores is not much larger than the bigger stores.

37. Select STATE for the data visualization (see Figure 7.62).

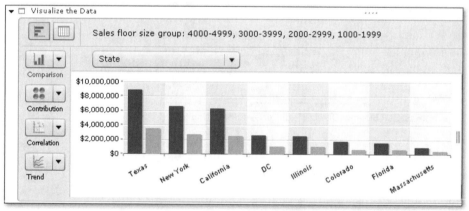

Figure 7.62 SAP BusinessObjects Explorer — Information Space

Here, we can see that TEXAS, NEW YORK, and CALIFORNIA contribute a huge amount of revenue with a small margin compared to other states.

38. Remove the SALES FLOOR SIZE GROUP facet from the selection.

39. Select TEXAS, NEW YORK, and CALIFORNIA from the STATE facet.

40. Select LINES for the data visualization (see Figure 7.63).

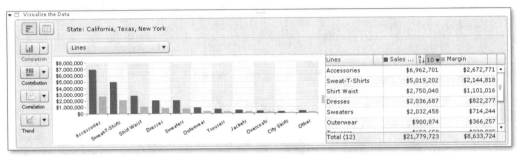

Figure 7.63 SAP BusinessObjects Explorer — Information Space

PRODUCT LINE SWEAT-T-SHIRTS provides a margin nearly as large as ACCESSO-RIES, but with much less revenue.

41. Select SWEAT-T-SHIRTS in the chart (see Figure 7.64).

Lines	Sales ... 10
Sweat-T-Shirts	$5,019,202
Shirt Waist	$2,750,040
Dresses	$2,036,687
Sweaters	$2,032,458
Outerwear	$900,874
Trousers	$653,650
Total (12)	$21,779,723

Figure 7.64 SAP BusinessObjects Explorer — Information Space

42. Now use the ZOOMING option at the bottom-right corner of the chart to use the selection in the chart to filter the data.

43. Set the dimension for the data visualization to CATEGORY.

44. Select CONTRIBUTION for the visualization (see Figure 7.65).

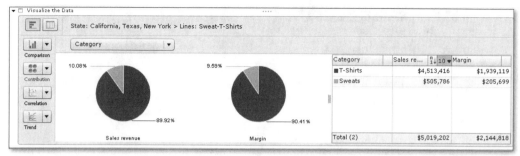

Figure 7.65 SAP BusinessObjects Explorer — Information Space

Here, we can see that over 90% of our MARGIN is contributed by the CATEGORY T-SHIRTS.

45. Set the dimension for the data visualization to COLOR (see Figure 7.66).

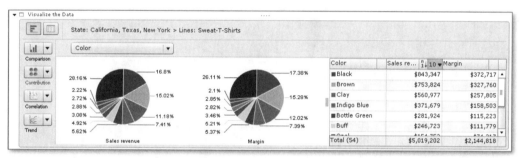

Figure 7.66 SAP BusinessObjects Explorer — Information Space

Now we can see that the colors BLACK, BROWN, and CLAY account for almost 50% of our sales revenue and margin.

46. Now we would like to share this information with our colleagues. Click on the ☒ Email symbol in the toolbar (see Figure 7.67).

After your configured email program starts, a bookmark link to our Information Space, including the navigation status, is included in a new email message.

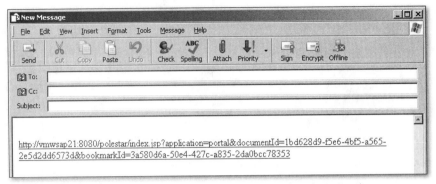

Figure 7.67 SAP BusinessObjects Explorer — Sharing a Bookmark via Email

47. Close the email message.

48. Click the ⚎ Export option in the toolbar (see Figure 7.68).

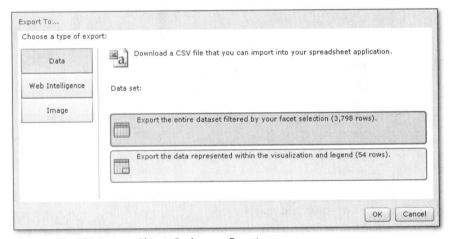

Figure 7.68 SAP BusinessObjects Explorer — Export

Now you can export the raw data to a CSV file, or create a Web Intelligence report based on the data, or create an Image file based on the data visualization.

49. Select the WEB INTELLIGENCE option.

50. Activate the REFRESH ON OPEN option.

51. Click OK.

52. After a short time, you will see the message shown in Figure 7.69 and you can click on the link to open the Web Intelligence document (see Figure 7.70).

The document eFashion Information Space has been sent to the Inbox folder.

Click on the link below to open it:

eFashion Information Space

Your browser's pop-up blocker may prevent new window from opening. In this case, deactivate it.

OK

Figure 7.69 SAP BusinessObjects Explorer — Transfer to Web Intelligence

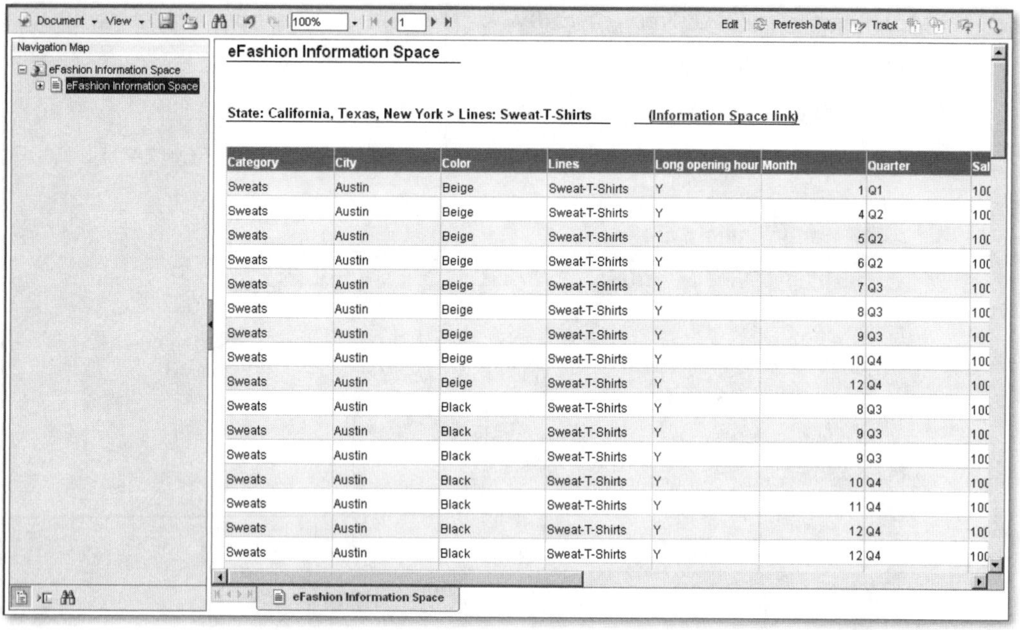

Figure 7.70 SAP BusinessObjects Explorer — Transfer to Web Intelligence

The Web Intelligence report opens and you can use the report with all of the features and functions of Web Intelligence. In addition, the report contains a link back to the SAP BusinessObjects Explorer Information Space.

In the next section, we'll look at the opportunity to leverage SAP BusinessObjects Explorer for the sales department.

7.5   Customer Case Study — Sales Analysis

Now that we've covered the basic steps using SAP BusinessObjects Explorer, we can set up SAP BusinessObjects Explorer to fulfill the requirements from our sales department. We will use the MultiProvider 0D_DX_M01 — SAP Demo Scenario Reporting Cube. Because we are using a MultiProvider, we first need to leverage the MultiProvider snapshot tool (see SAP notes 1332392 and 1332090 for details). In this case, because we are using the BWA index, there is no need for a BW query. We will use the Multiprovider snapshot tool and create an index on the MultiProvider.

1. Log on to the SAP NetWeaver BW system with an administrative account that can create BWA indexes.

2. Start Transaction SE38.

3. Enter RSDDTPS_MPRO_MAINTAIN as the PROGRAM name (see Figure 7.71).

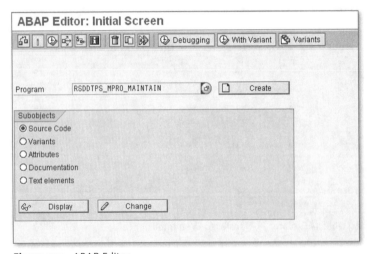

Figure 7.71 ABAP Editor

4. Follow the PROGRAM • EXECUTE • DIRECT PROCESSING menu path OR PRESS F8.

5. Enter 0D_DX_M01 as value for the MULTIPROVIDER field (see Figure 7.72)

6. Click EXPLORER PROPERTIES.

   The BIA Index Maintenance wizard will start and we need to configure the properties for the BWA index (seeFigure 7.73).

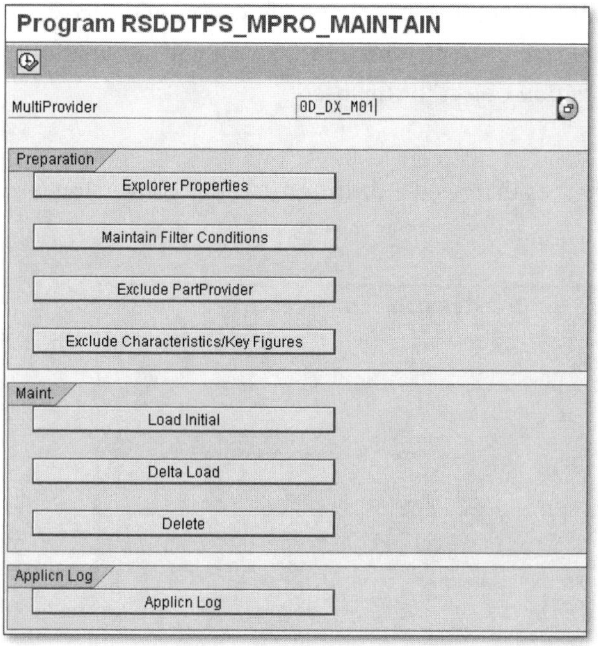

Program RSDDTPS_MPRO_MAINTAIN

MultiProvider .... 0D_DX_M01

Preparation

> Explorer Properties

> Maintain Filter Conditions

> Exclude PartProvider

> Exclude Characteristics/Key Figures

Maint.

> Load Initial

> Delta Load

> Delete

Applicn Log

> Applicn Log

Figure 7.72 Program RSDDTPS_MPRO_MAINTAIN

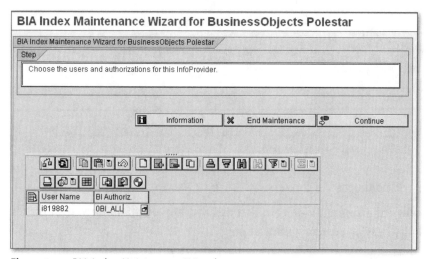

Figure 7.73 BIA Index Maintenance Wizard

7. Click the button to add a new row to the list of user and authorizations.

8. Enter the users that need access to the index data.

9. For now, we will add the authorization 0BI_ALL, which will provide access to all data for the users. If you leave the field empty the system will automatically add 0BI_ALL as the authorization object for the user.

10. Click CONTINUE.

   You will see a list of key figures that need a UNIT or CURRENCY conversion (see Figure 7.74)

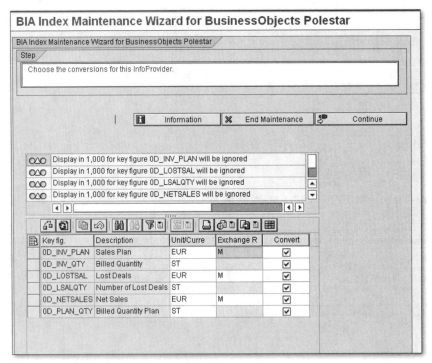

Figure 7.74 BIA Index Maintenance Wizard

11. After you complete the conversions, click CONTINUE.

12. You will see a summary of your settings and any outstanding warnings, for example, missing currency translations.

13. Click CONTINUE.

   You are then returned to the start of the program (see Figure 7.75).

14. Click LOAD INITIAL

15. Click IMMEDIATE (SEE Figure 7.76).

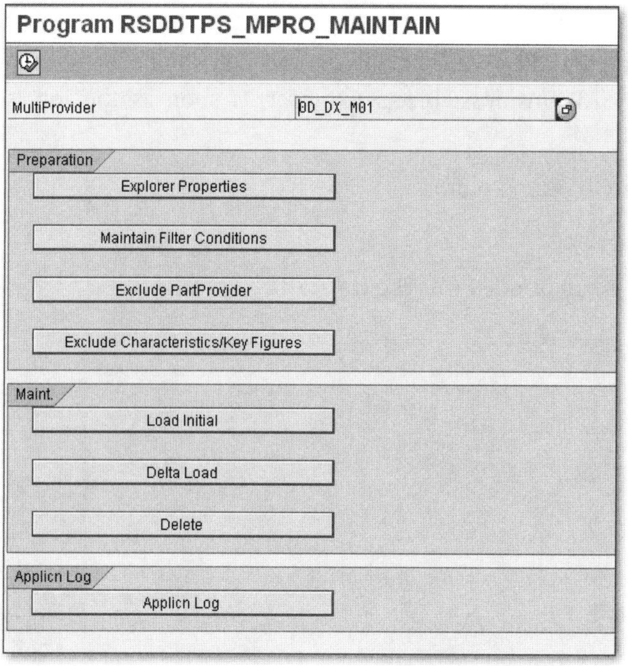

Figure 7.75 Program RSDDTPS_MPRO_MAINTAIN

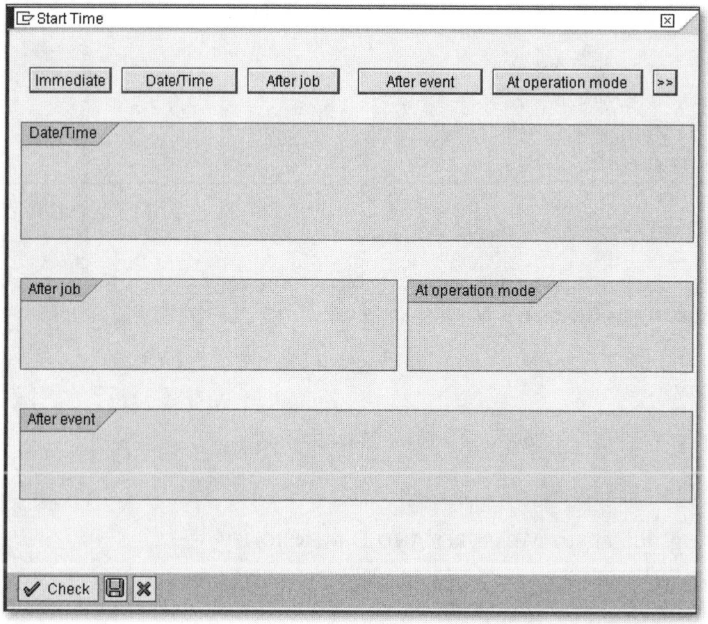

Figure 7.76 Start Time

16. Click SAVE.

    The BWA Indexing job should now be scheduled and you should be able to leverage the index in SAP BusinessObjects Explorer as soon as the job is finished.

17. Log on to SAP BusinessObjects Explorer.

18. Click MANAGE SPACES.

19. Navigate to the newly created index (see Figure 7.77).

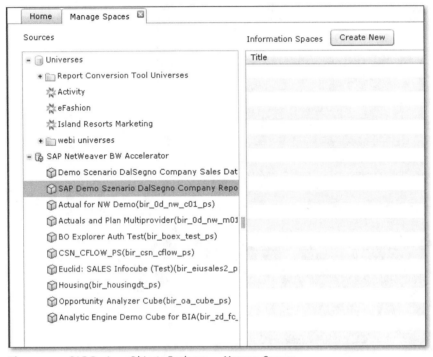

Figure 7.77 SAP BusinessObjects Explorer — Manage Spaces

20. Click CREATE NEW.

21. Enter `Demo Scenario MultiProvider` as the NAME.

22. Navigate to the OBJECTS tab.

23. Add the following objects to MEASURES AND DIMENSIONS:

    ▶ All key figures

    ▶ Calendar Year/Month

- ▸ Quarter (Text)
- ▸ Distribution Channel (Text)
- ▸ Customer (Text)
- ▸ Region Code (Text)
- ▸ Reason (Text)
- ▸ Product Group (Text)
- ▸ Product (Text)
- ▸ Calendar Year

24. Click OK.

25. Use the Index Now  button to leverage the BWA index.

    After a short time the status of your Information Space will be set to OK.

26. Navigate to the HOME tab.

27. Click REFRESH.

28. Select the newly created DEMO SCENARIO MULTIPROVIDER Information Space (see Figure 7.78).

Figure 7.78 Information Spaces

29. Select NET SALES as the MEASURE (SEE Figure 7.79).

30. Add SALES PLAN as a second MEASURE.

31. Select the current year in the CALENDAR YEAR (KEY) facet. Based on the demo data, the actual year value is 2006.

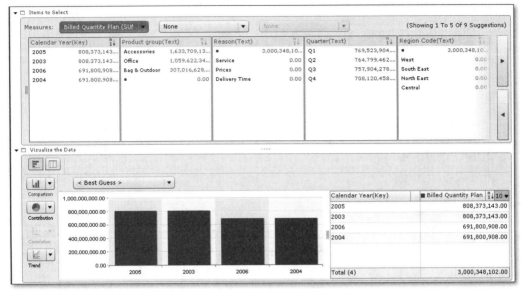

Figure 7.79 SAP BusinessObjects Explorer Sales Information Space

32. Set the dimension of the lower part of the visualization to CALENDAR YEAR/
MONTH (see Figure 7.80).

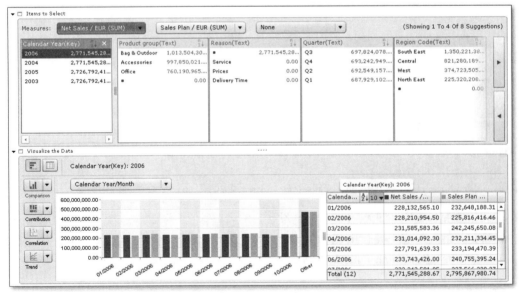

Figure 7.80 SAP BusinessObjects Explorer Sales Information Space

33. Set the visualization type to TREND.

34. Click on the TOP N option in the table for CALENDAR YEAR/MONTH and set the value to 12.

35. Uncheck the OTHER VALUES option (see Figure 7.81)

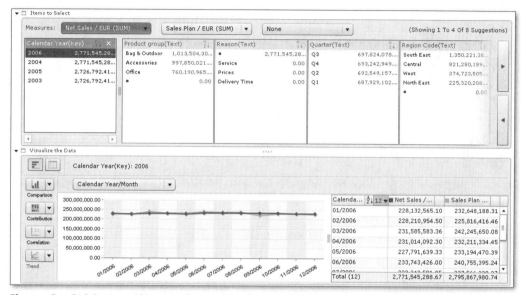

Figure 7.81 SAP BusinessObjects Explorer Sales Information Space

As you can see, our NET SALES is always pretty close to the SALES PLAN. Now let's look at the third measure, LOST DEALS.

36. Add the third measure, LOST DEALS.

37. Click on LOST DEALS so that the facets show the values for LOST DEALS.

38. Select the Top 3 entries in the REASON (TEXT) facet.

39. Set the first measure to be LOST DEALS.

40. Set the second measure to be NUMBER OF LOST DEALS.

41. Set the third measure to NONE.

42. Set the dimension for the lower data visualization to REGION (TEXT).

43. Set the visualization type to CONTRIBUTION.

Now we can easily see that more than 50% of our losses are occurring in the SOUTH EAST region (see Figure 7.82).

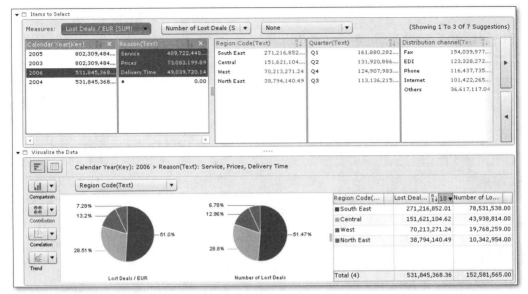

Figure 7.82 SAP BusinessObjects Explorer Sales Information Space

44. Select SOUTH EAST in the REGION (TEXT) facet.

45. Set the dimension for the lower part to REASON (TEXT).

46. Select the CONTRIBUTION visualization type (see Figure 7.83).

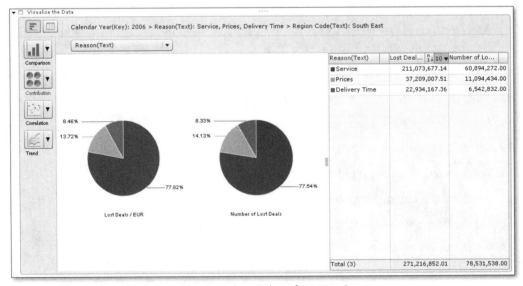

Figure 7.83 SAP BusinessObjects Explorer Sales Information Space

Close to 75% of our losses can be attributed to bad customer service. Now we need to find out if this is a general issue in the SOUTH EAST region or if this is related to a particular customer.

47. Select SERVICE in the REASON (TEXT) facet.

48. Set the dimension for the visualization to CUSTOMER (TEXT).

49. Set the visualization type to COMPARISON.

50. Click on the LOST DEALS column head in the table. Configure a Top 10 ranking and exclude OTHERS (see Figure 7.84).

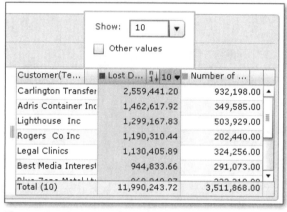

Figure 7.84 Top 10 Ranking

Now we are looking at the Top 10 customers for the LOST DEALS measure in the SOUTH EAST region (see Figure 7.85). We can quickly see that we have a small set of customers that cause this large amount of losses.

Now we can use this information and share it with sales management to ensure that the necessary steps are taken to improve customer satisfaction, especially for the list of customer that we just identified.

51. Click EXPORT in the toolbar.

52. Select the IMAGE option (see Figure 7.86).

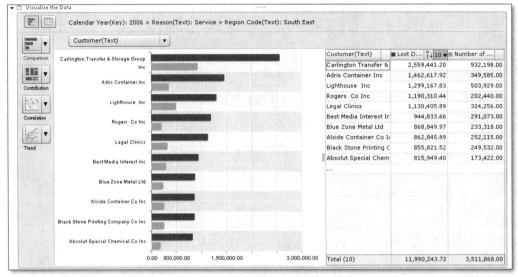

Figure 7.85 Top 10 Ranking — Data Visualization

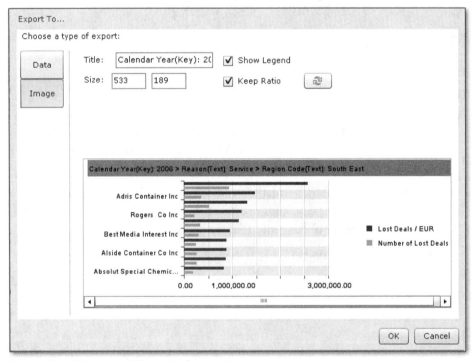

Figure 7.86 SAP BusinessObjects Explorer — Export

53. Click OK.

54. The data visualization is exported into a PNG file. Save the file to your desktop.

55. Click EMAIL in the toolbar.

56. Your email program will come up and you can share a bookmark pointing to the SAP BusinessObjects Explorer Information Space. In addition, you can include the image we exported to provide some information offline (see Figure 7.87).

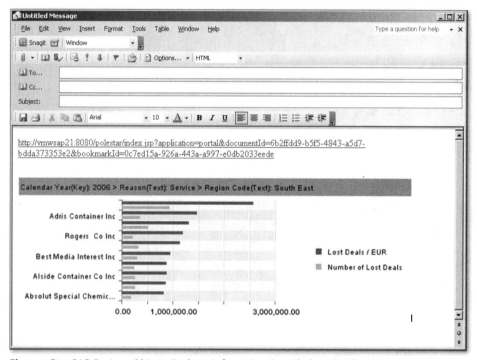

Figure 7.87 SAP BusinessObjects Explorer Information Provided via Email

In the next section, we'll look at the requirements from the financial area and how we can deliver a solution for those using SAP BusinessObjects Explorer.

7.6   Customer Case Study — Financial Analysis

In this section, we will use SAP BusinessObjects Explorer to create a solution for the requirements from the financial area. In this exercise, we will use an OLAP Universe on top of a BW query as the data source and create the index for SAP BusinessObjects Explorer without using BWA. The reason for using this approach is not related to the financial area, but purely to show both options with step-by-step instructions.

We will use a BW query based on the 0CCA_M20 InfoCube from the Cost Center Accounting (CCA) area. Our BW query contains the following elements (see Figure 7.88):

- ▶ ROWS
    - ▶ COST ELEMENT
    - ▶ COST CENTER
    - ▶ PROFIT CENTER
    - ▶ FISCAL YEAR
    - ▶ FISCAL YEAR / PERIOD
    - ▶ CONTROLLING AREA
    - ▶ VENDOR
- ▶ COLUMNS
    - ▶ KEY FIGURES
    - ▶ ACTUAL COSTS
    - ▶ PLANNED COSTS
    - ▶ VARIANCE
    - ▶ VARIANCE %

We don't have to worry about where we place the elements as we will create a Universe on top of the BW query and then use the Universe as a source for SAP BusinessObjects Explorer. Now let's create a Universe on top of the BW query.

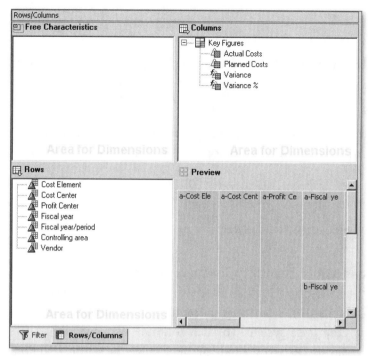

Figure 7.88 BW Query

1. Start the Universe designer via the menu path: START • PROGRAMS • BUSINESS-OBJECTS XI 3.1 • BUSINESSOBJECTS ENTERPRISE • DESIGNER.

2. You will be presented with the log on screen for the Universe designer and you need to provide the system name and you user credentials.

3. In our example, we will use SAP authentication and our SAP credentials. For the system we will enter the name of the CMS of our BusinessObjects Enterprise system — VMWSAP20.

4. Because the Universe designer doesn't offer the SAP System ID and the SAP client number as explicit input fields, as part of the log on mask you need to enter your SAP credentials in the format:

```
[SAP System ID]~800/[SAP user name]
```

5. For example,

```
CIM~800/DEMO
```

6. Click OK.

7. In the Universe designer, follow the menu path: FILE • NEW.

8. The UNIVERSE PARAMETERS dialog appears and you can use the NEW button to create a new connection to your SAP NetWeaver BW system.

9. Click NEXT to start the CONNECTION WIZARD.

10. Enter a name for the connection into the CONNECTION NAME field and scroll down to select the SAP BUSINESS WAREHOUSE connectivity type.

11. Click NEXT.

12. Enter the details to connect to your SAP system.

13. The LOGIN MODE lets us switch between an APPLICATION SERVER and a MESSAGE SERVER.

14. If you used your SAP credentials to log on to the Universe designer, you can set the AUTHENTICATION MODE to USE SINGLE SIGN ON WHEN REFRESHING REPORTS AT VIEW TIME. If the SAP authentication is not configured on your BusinessObjects Enterprise system, you can continue with the setting USE SPECIFIED USERNAME AND PASSWORD and you can change the settings later on.

15. Click NEXT.

16. The list of available BW queries is shown in tree form with the InfoProvider listed at the top and the BW queries below each InfoProvider. The $INFO-CUBE entry lets us connect to all of the InfoCubes directly without a BW query.

17. In our example, we open the list of BW queries for InfoProvider 0CCA_M20 and select the BW query that we created.

18. Click NEXT.

19. In the next screen, you can define connection parameters for the connection for your SAP NetWeaver BW system. The CONNECTION POOL mode is especially important. Here, you define for how long the connection will be kept active and the default value is 10 minutes. You also have the option to select the DISCONNECT AFTER EACH TRANSACTION option, which you want to avoid

because it will result in a log on and log off process for every single function call to your SAP system from this Universe connection.

20. Select the KEEP THE CONNECTION ACTIVE FOR option and leave the default value for POOL TIMEOUT.

21. Click FINISH.

22. Navigate to the CONTROLS tab from the UNIVERSE PARAMETERS and uncheck all.

23. Navigate to the DEFINITION tab.

24. Enter a name for the new Universe into the NAME field.

25. Click OK.

26. Now the Universe designer is connecting with the SAP NetWeaver BW system to retrieve the metadata from the BW query that we selected.

27. After the Universe is presented to you, select the menu FILE • SAVE to save the Universe.

28. Follow the FILE • EXPORT menu path to export the Universe to your BusinessObjects Enterprise system.

29. Click BROWSE.

30. Select a folder for the Universe and click OK.

31. Click OK.

Now that we have the Universe available in the SAP BusinessObjects Enterprise system, we can log on to SAP BusinessObjects Explorer and create the index for our data.

1. Log on to SAP BusinessObjects Explorer.

2. Click MANAGE SPACES.

3. Navigate to the newly created Universe (see Figure 7.89).

4. Click CREATE NEW.

5. Enter SAP Financial Information Space as the NAME.

6. Navigate to the OBJECTS tab.

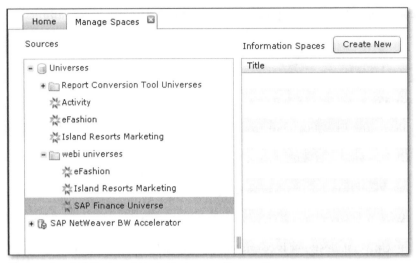

Figure 7.89 SAP BusinessObjects Explorer — Manage Spaces

7. Add the following objects to MEASURES AND DIMENSIONS:

   ▶ L01 COST CENTER

   ▶ L01 PROFIT CENTER

   ▶ L01 CONTROLLING AREA

   ▶ L01 COST ELEMENT

   ▶ L01 FISCAL YEAR/PERIOD

   ▶ L01 FISCAL YEAR

   ▶ All key figures

8. Click OK.

9. Use the INDEX NOW ⬛ button to create a new index based on the Unvierse data connection. After a short time, the status of your Information Space will be set to OK.

10. Navigate to the HOME tab.

11. Click REFRESH.

12. Select the newly created Information Space (see Figure 7.90).

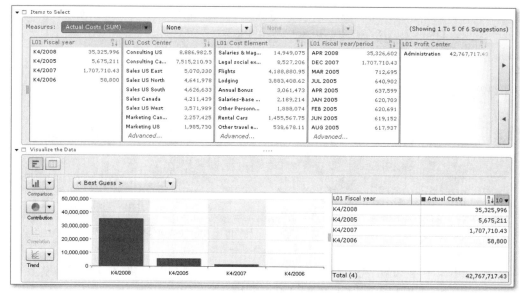

Figure 7.90 SAP BusinessObjects Explorer — Financial Information Space

13. Set the ACTUAL COSTS and PLANNED COSTS as measures.

14. Select the current year in the L01 FISCAL YEAR facet, in our example, 2008.

15. Now we are looking for COST CENTER and COST ELEMENTS that are above the planned budget. We are adding the Variance as a third measure.

16. Click on the VARIANCE column header in the table (bottom right) to sort the data by Variance (see Figure 7.91).

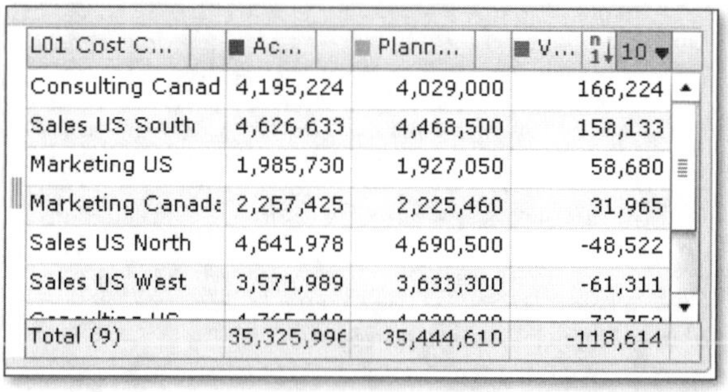

L01 Cost C...	▣ Ac...	▣ Plann...	▣ V...
Consulting Canad	4,195,224	4,029,000	166,224
Sales US South	4,626,633	4,468,500	158,133
Marketing US	1,985,730	1,927,050	58,680
Marketing Canada	2,257,425	2,225,460	31,965
Sales US North	4,641,978	4,690,500	-48,522
Sales US West	3,571,989	3,633,300	-61,311
Consulting US	4,765,249	4,838,000	72,752
Total (9)	35,325,996	35,444,610	-118,614

Figure 7.91 SAP BusinessObjects Explorer — Financial Information Space

We can now see that Consulting Canada and Sales US South are the two Cost Centers that are most over budget.

17. Select these two entries in the table (see Figure 7.92).

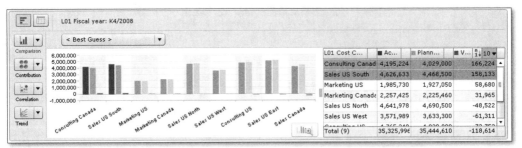

Figure 7.92 SAP BusinessObjects Explorer — Financial Information Space

18. Use the magnifying glass in the bottom-right corner of the chart to make your selection part of the actual navigation (see Figure 7.93).

Figure 7.93 SAP BusinessObjects Explorer — Financial Information Space

Now we are looking at the COST ELEMENT details for the selected COST CENTERS. We can see that the COST ELEMENTS SALARIES & WAGES and ANNUAL BONUS are way over budget. We can also see that COST ELEMENTS FLIGHTS, LODGING, and RENTAL CARS are also over budget. This might indicate more travel expenses than expected.

19. Select COST ELEMENTS: FLIGHTS, LODGING, and RENTAL CARS in the L01 COST ELEMENT facet.

20. Select COST CENTER for the dimension on the data visualization in the lower part (see Figure 7.94).

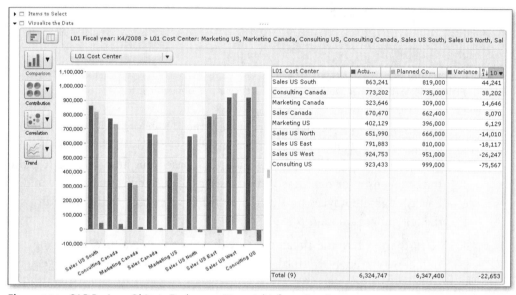

Figure 7.94 SAP BusinessObjects Explorer — Financial Information Space

Based on the information shown on the right-hand side of the table, we can see that the Cost Center in Canada is over budget, but the Cost Center in the U.S. is below.

21. Add the SALARIES & WAGES and ANNUAL BONUS cost elements to the L01 COST ELEMENTS facet (see Figure 7.95).

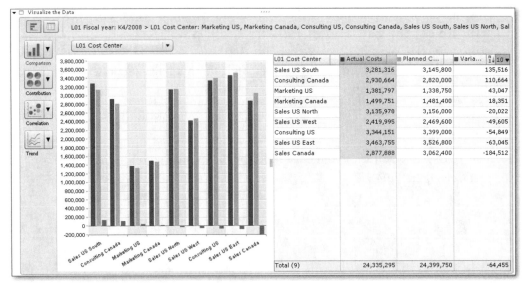

Figure 7.95 SAP BusinessObjects Explorer — Financial Information Space

Here, we can see a similar pattern, where the U.S.-based cost center is under budget, but the Canadian-based cost center is over budget. This could indicate that our consulting business sees more U.S.-based business, leading to more travel expenses for our Canadian teams, or it could indicate that we couldn't find enough employees for our U.S.-based business and therefore didn't use the full budget amount.

To further analyze the situation, we will export the data to Web Intelligence so that we can analyze it further and then share the report with management.

22. Click EXPORT in the toolbar.

23. Select the WEB INTELLIGENCE option (see Figure 7.96).

24. Activate the REFRESH ON OPEN option.

25. Click OK.

We will receive a message with a link to the Web Intelligence report (see Figure 7.97).

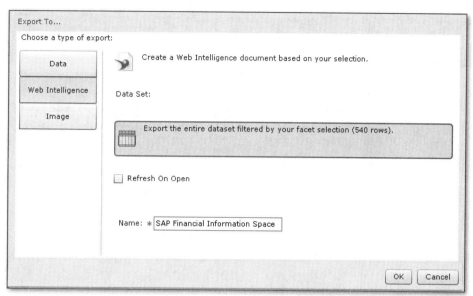

Figure 7.96 SAP BusinessObjects Explorer — Export to Web Intelligence

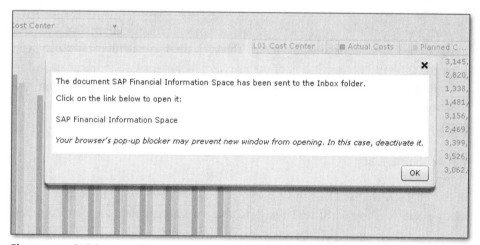

Figure 7.97 SAP BusinessObjects Explorer — Export to Web Intelligence

26. Click the link to open the Web Intelligence report (see Figure 7.98).

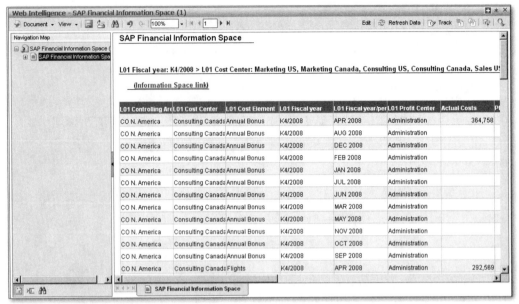

Figure 7.98 Web Intelligence Report

With the Web Intelligence report, we can now further analyze the data and share our findings with management. The Web Intelligence report has also been stored as a report in the Inbox of the user and includes a link to the actual Information Space in SAP BusinessObjects Explorer that was used to create the report.

7.7 Summary

In this chapter, we used SAP BusinessObjects Explorer to provide our users a very unique and easy-to-use BI tool that lets you explore the data and use common search workflows to "find" the answer. We discovered the different data connectivities for SAP BusinessObjects Explorer, started using basic steps, and fulfilled the requirements for the sales and finance departments.

Advanced Analysis is driven by the Pioneer project. Pioneer will replace Business Explorer (BEx) Analyzer, BEx web reporting, and Voyager. In this chapter, you will learn how Pioneer can help you fulfill the need for a user experience offering a rich Online Analytical Processing (OLAP) type of reporting client.

8   Advanced Analysis with Pioneer

In this chapter, we'll look into the future and provide you with a preview of the Pioneer project. Pioneer will replace BEx Analyzer, BEx web reporting, and Voyager according to the product integration roadmap. We will look at the deployment options, SAP-specific features and functions, and how we can use Pioneer to fulfill our requirements.

> **Pioneer — Disclaimer**
>
> As of this writing, Pioneer has not been released as an official product. The exact workflow, steps, and menu items shown in this chapter may change in the final product. These items are subject to change at any time without any notice and the author is not providing any warranty on these statements.

8.1   Deployment Overview

Pioneer is a project combining the technologies from BEx Analyzer, BEx web reporting, and Voyager into a new Business Intelligence (BI) client tool providing advanced OLAP analysis capabilities.

Pioneer will be available in two versions: Pioneer Office and Pioneer Web.

▶ Pioneer Web will be based on the SAP BusinessObjects Enterprise platform (see Figure 8.1) and leverage the repository service and lifecycle management services from the SAP BusinessObjects Enterprise platform.

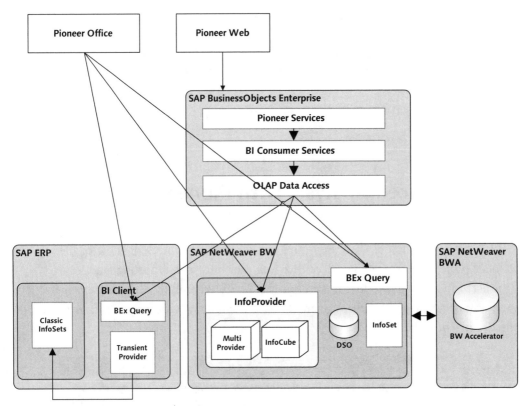

Figure 8.1 Pioneer Deployment Overview

- ▶ Pioneer Office will be available as an add-on to Microsoft Excel and Microsoft PowerPoint, and allows for a lean deployment and direct connectivity to the SAP NetWeaver Business Warehouse (BW) system (see Figure 8.1). In Pioneer Office, the workbooks will leverage the repository and life cycle management services from the SAP NetWeaver BW stack.

When using BEx Web Templates, customers will have the opportunity to leverage BEx Web Templates as part of a Pioneer workspace (see Figure 8.2) in the first release of Pioneer (planned for 2010). The long-term plan is to offer a rich Pioneer Software Development Kit (SDK) (planned for a future release), which will provide equivalent functionality to the BEx Web Templates (see Figure 8.3).

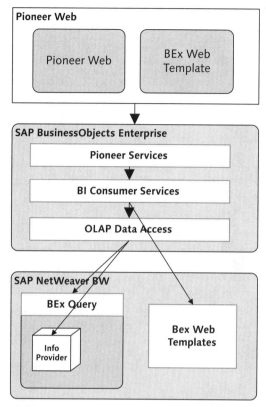

Figure 8.2 Pioneer and BEx Web Templates

Migration to Pioneer

The first release of Pioneer is supposed to offer a migration for Voyager customers to Pioneer Web (planned for 2010). A migration of BEx workbooks to Pioneer Office is scheduled for the second release of the Pioneer project in 2011.

SAP BusinessObjects Enterprise and Project Pioneer

When this chapter mentions SAP BusinessObjects Enterprise as a platform for Pioneer, please note that this is not a reference to the SAP BusinessObjects XI Release 3.1 platform. The Pioneer project is based on the next major version of the SAP BusinessObjects Enterprise platform planned for 2010.

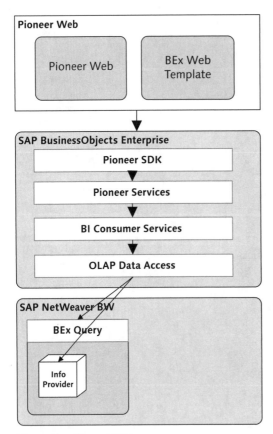

Figure 8.3 Pioneer SDK

In the next section, we'll look into the data connectivity options for Pioneer.

8.2 SAP Data Connectivity for Pioneer

In this section, let's look at the options for connecting Pioneer to your SAP data source.

As shown in Figure 8.4, Pioneer will be able to leverage BW queries and InfoProvider as data sources. Pioneer will be able to leverage BW queries, BW InfoProvider, Data Store Objects (DSO) via BW queries, and ERP data via the Transient Provider connected to a BW query.

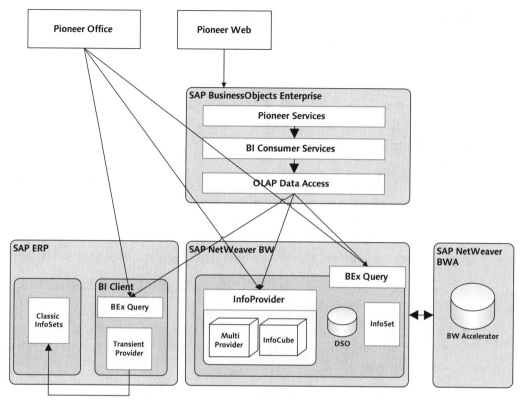

Figure 8.4 Pioneer Data Connectivity

The current plan for Pioneer is to support SAP NetWeaver BW 7.0 or higher. Based on SAP NetWeaver BW 7.0, Pioneer should be able to leverage BW 3.5 and BW 7.0 queries.

In the next section, we'll look at our requirements and see which one we can fulfill with Pioneer.

8.3 Customer Case Study — Requirements for Advanced Analysis

In this section, we'll look at our overall requirements and see which ones we can fulfill with Pioneer. We will start with requirements from the financial area.

8.3.1 Financial Area Requirements

There is only one requirement that we think we can't fulfill with Pioneer. This does not necessarily mean that Pioneer is the best choice for all of the requirements, because we also need to consider who and what type of user our audience is; it means that Pioneer is capable of delivering the requirements but that in some situations a different tool may be a better choice because it is more compelling to the consumer.

> **Unfulfilled Financial Area Requirements**
>
> ▸ For specific content (like an income statement or a balance sheet), the design needs to be layout focused, with the actual print of the report being a very high priority.

Some of the requirements that we can fulfill with Pioneer include the following:

▸ The content must be available in a web-based and Microsoft Office environment (especially Microsoft Excel).

▸ The user needs to navigate from aggregated data to more granular items. For example, navigating from a cost center aggregated value to the actual line items per cost element.

We already looked at the different deployment options and noted that Pioneer will come as an add-on for Microsoft Office. Most customers will expect a Microsoft Excel plug-in, which Pioneer will have, but Pioneer will also be available as a plug-in to Microsoft PowerPoint. This gives you a great new option to deliver compelling analytics into the Microsoft Office environment and use this feature even as "offline" option.

With regard to the navigation between different sets of data or even different sets of BI client tools, Pioneer will deliver a new client interoperability functionality that will let you leverage a Pioneer workspace and share this workspace and the data definition with Crystal Reports and Web Intelligence.

8.3.2 Sales Area Requirements

Just as with the financial area, only a single requirement is listed as not being fulfilled by Pioneer. Pioneer will deliver some predictive functionality, but an actual what-if analysis model is better suited for a tool like Xcelsius.

Unfulfilled Sales Area Requirements

▶ Users should be able to perform scenario-based analyses, where the user is able to see the data and can also influence certain factors and see the impact on the overall numbers. For example: What-if analysis in a sales planning workflow.

The new option to leverage Pioneer inside Microsoft PowerPoint is very relevant to the sales area and offers a new kind of offline type of reports that need to be shared with a large set of users that are unable to connect to the data.

8.3.3 Human Resources (HR) Area Requirements

There are two unfulfilled requirements for the HR area.

Unfulfilled HR Area Requirements

▶ The content needs to be able to present highly textual information in a layout-focused format.

▶ Some of the content (such as employee appraisals or performance reviews) will be used as actual official documents and therefore needs to follow strict layout rules.

Pioneer is an advanced analysis client; therefore, it should not be a surprise that Pioneer is unable to fulfill the highly textual-based requirements for the HR area.

8.3.4 Executive and Leadership Area Requirements

There are two unfulfilled requirements for the executive and leadership area

Unfulfilled Executive and Leadership Area Requirements

▶ The data needs to be shown in a highly visualized manner and the main Key Performance Indicators (KPIs) need to be presented in a single dashboard.

▶ The consumption of the reports and analytics needs to be easy to use and critical information needs to be easily identifiable.

In the next section, we'll take a look at some basic steps using Pioneer.

8.4   Pioneer — Quick Basics

In this section, we'll look at some simple steps using Pioneer to learn more about the tool and its functionality. We will use Pioneer Web for these steps and we'll use Pioneer Office later in the chapter.

> **Pioneer Project**
>
> Please note that the following steps have been conducted using an early version of the Pioneer project in conjunction with the next major release of SAP BusinessObjects Enterprise. The exact steps, user interfaces (UIs), and menus might change in the final release of the product.

For the following steps, we are using a BW query based on the SAP NetWeaver demo model InfoProvider 0D_NW_N01 (see Figure 8.5).

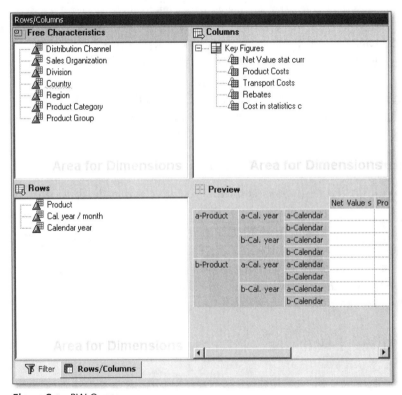

Figure 8.5 BW Query

1. Log on to the Central Management Console (CMC) of your SAP BusinessObjects Enterprise system.

2. Select the PIONEER CONNECTIONS option.

3. Select NEW CONNECTION.

4. You will be asked to provide the details of your SAP system (see Figure 8.6).

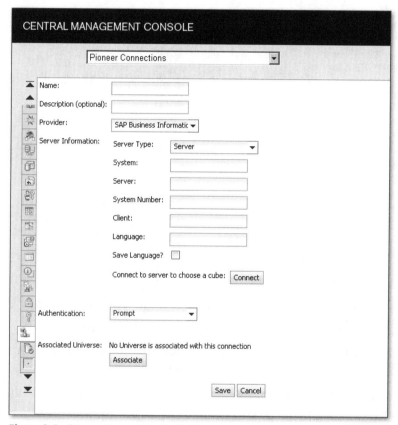

Figure 8.6 Pioneer Connection Definition

5. Provide the system details and click CONNECT.

6. You will be asked to provide your SAP credentials to authenticate for the SAP system.

7. After the authentication, you can select the BW query from the CUBE BROWSER (see Figure 8.7).

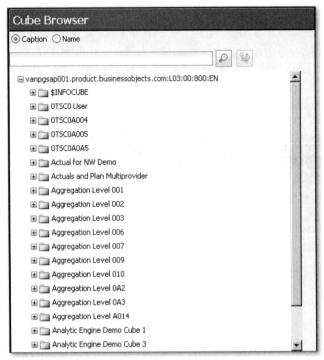

Figure 8.7 Pioneer Cube Browser

8. SELECT THE BW QUERY and click SELECT.

9. You can choose between the following AUTHENTICATION options:

   ▶ Prompt: In this case, the user always gets prompted for user credentials.

   ▶ Single Sign-On (SSO): In this case, the SAP authentication from your SAP BusinessObjects Enterprise system will be leveraged.

   ▶ User Specified: In this case, you can provide a single set of user credentials that will then be used for all users.

10. Set the AUTHENTICATION option to SSO.

11. Click SAVE.

The connection is now stored in the CMC and we can create a new Pioneer workspace based on this connection.

1. Log on to InfoView.

2. Select DOCUMENT LIST.

3. Follow the NEW • PIONEER WORKSPACE menu path.

4. You will be presented with a list of defined connections. Select the newly created connection and click OK (see Figure 8.8).

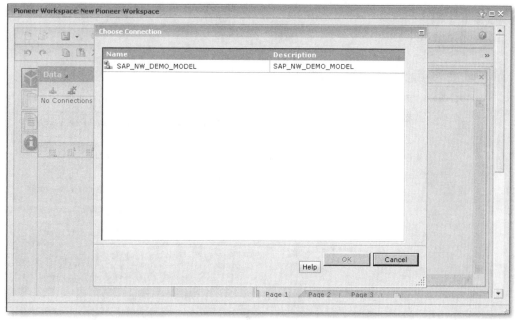

Figure 8.8 Pioneer Connection Selection

5. The PIONEER WORKSPACE is made up of five main areas (see Figure 8.9):

   ❶ The TASK PANEL TOOLBAR lets you switch between Data, Pages, Properties, and Information.

   ❷ The TASK PANEL provides access to objects based on your selection in the TASK PANEL TOOLBAR.

   ❸ The LAYOUT PANEL provides access to elements of your underlying data source, such as characteristics and key figures. In the LAYOUT PANEL, you define which elements are shown as part of the rows and columns and which elements are used as filters.

❹ The ANALYSIS WINDOW provides you with the actual data. You can include up to four components per window and you can include several pages into a single workspace.

❺ The LAYOUT, FORMAT, ANALYZE, and VISUALIZE tabs provide access to a set of menus for specific operations. For example, the LAYOUT tab lets you define the look, feel, and elements of your workspace.

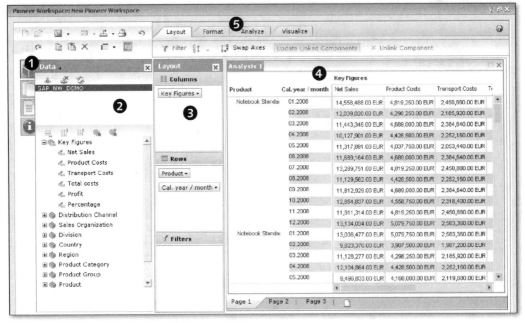

Figure 8.9 Pioneer Workspace

6. Select DATA in the TASK PANEL TOOLBAR. The TASK PANEL will show us all of the elements retrieved from the BW query (see Figure 8.10).

7. Now we can drag and drop the elements selected for the ROWS and COLUMNS in the LAYOUT PANEL.

8. In addition, we can use the ADD TO ROWS, ADD TO COLUMNS, and ADD TO SLICE options shown in the TASK PANEL (see Figure 8.11). The ADD TO SLICE option will add the select characteristic to the FILTERS section.

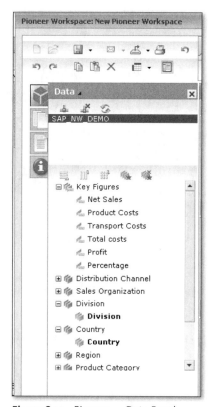

Figure 8.10 Pioneer — Data Panel

Figure 8.11 Pioneer — Data Panel

9. Drag and drop the CAL. YEAR/MONTH characteristic to the COLUMNS.

10. Drag and drop the key figures to the COLUMNS.

11. Drag and drop the PRODUCT characteristic to the ROWS (see Figure 8.12).

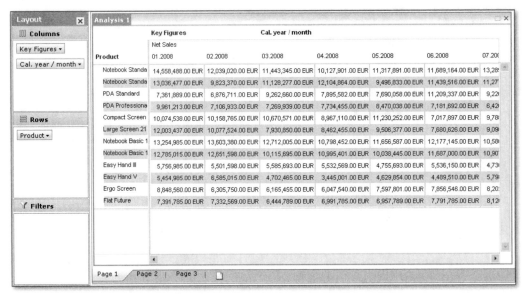

Figure 8.12 Pioneer Workspace

12. Click on the CAL. YEAR/MONTH characteristic shown in the COLUMNS (see Figure 8.13).

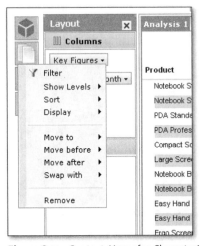

Figure 8.13 Context Menu for Characteristic

13. Select FILTER.

14. When the MEMBER SELECTOR dialog appears, select the twelve months for 2008 (see Figure 8.14).

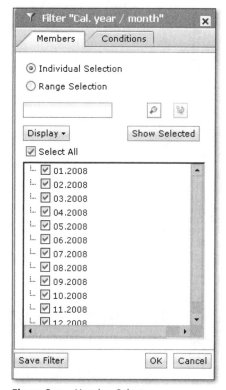

Figure 8.14 Member Selector

15. Drag and drop the COUNTRY characteristic to the ROWS so that it replaces PRODUCT.

16. Drag and drop the Net Sales key figure to the FILTERS section so that only NET SALES is shown in the workspace.

17. Select the VISUALIZE tab (see Figure 8.15).

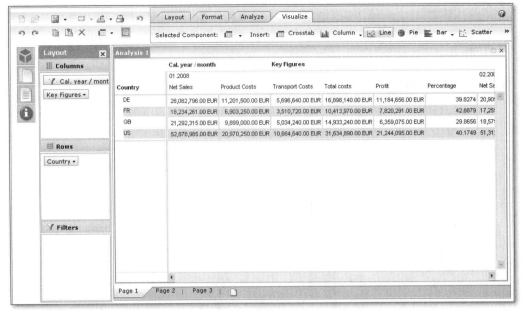

Figure 8.15 Pioneer — Tab Visualize

18. Select the LINE chart option (see Figure 8.16).

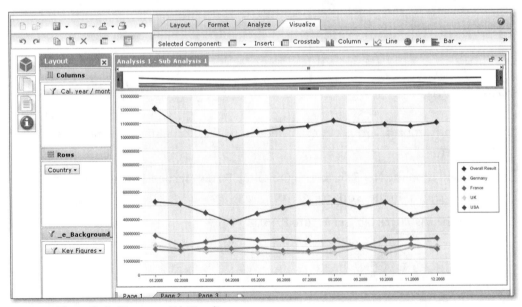

Figure 8.16 Pioneer — Tab Visualize

19. You can split the chart component to open a chart zoom control window on top of the actual chart to size the chart and allow for easier navigation for large volumes of data (see Figure 8.16). In addition, you can increase the size of the chart as part of your overall workspace.

20. Next, we want to highlight the number with a traffic light. Navigate to the ANALYZE tab.

21. Click on CAL. YEAR/MONTH in the column heading.

22. Click on EXCEPTION and select the NEW EXCEPTION HIGHLIGHTING option (see Figure 8.17).

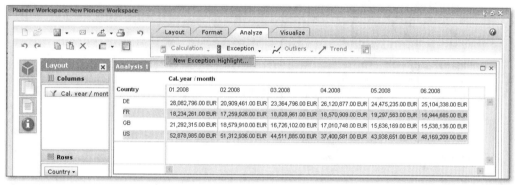

Figure 8.17 Pioneer — Exceptions

23. The EXCEPTION dialog is presented and you can define new exception highlighting using the dialog options (see Figure 8.18).

24. We are adding three exceptions:

   ▶ Exception 1 uses values from 0 to 25000000 and is set to Level 1

   ▶ Exception 2 uses values from 25000000 to 50000000 and is set to Level 2

   ▶ Exception 3 uses values from 50000000 to 100000000 and is set to Level 3

25. After defining the EXCEPTIONS, click OK (see Figure 8.19). The key figure is highlighted according to the defined rules.

Exception on Analysis 1
Rules
Name: Exception 1
Settings:
Based on measure: Format:
Net Sales
Cell Background
Definition:
Operator:
Between
1
and:
+
No exception rules have been set
Preview
Reset
OK
Cancel

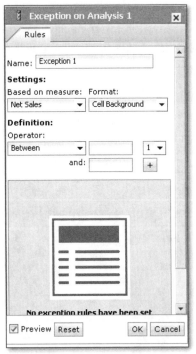

Figure 8.18 Exceptions Definition

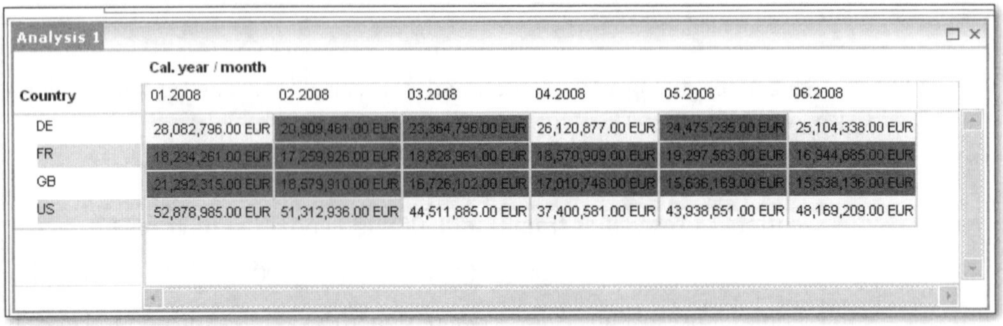

Analysis 1
Cal. year / month
Country
01.2008 02.2008 03.2008 04.2008 05.2008 06.2008
DE 28,082,796.00 EUR 20,909,461.00 EUR 23,364,796.00 EUR 26,120,877.00 EUR 24,475,235.00 EUR 25,104,338.00 EUR
FR 18,234,261.00 EUR 17,259,926.00 EUR 18,828,961.00 EUR 18,570,909.00 EUR 19,297,563.00 EUR 16,944,685.00 EUR
GB 21,292,315.00 EUR 18,579,910.00 EUR 16,726,102.00 EUR 17,010,748.00 EUR 15,636,169.00 EUR 15,538,136.00 EUR
US 52,878,985.00 EUR 51,312,936.00 EUR 44,511,885.00 EUR 37,400,581.00 EUR 43,938,651.00 EUR 48,169,209.00 EUR

Figure 8.19 Pioneer Exceptions

26. Now let's show the relevant numbers in relation to the Products and Product Groups and add a second page to our Pioneer Workspace.
27. Click on the PAGE 2 tab in your Pioneer Workspace. An empty page is presented to you.

28. Navigate to the LAYOUT tab.

29. In the menu bar select the NEW ANALYSIS option (see Figure 8.20).

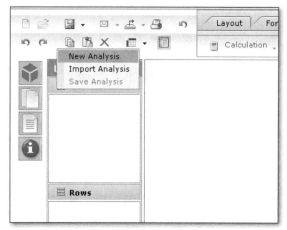

Figure 8.20 New Analysis

30. Open the DATA PANEL.

31. Move the Product characteristic to the ROWS.

32. Add the Product Group characteristic to the ROWS so that Product Group is shown first and Product is shown under Product Group.

33. Drag and drop the Net Sales and Product Costs key figures to the COLUMNS section.

34. Navigate to the FORMAT tab.

35. Click TOTAL AND PARENTS and uncheck the DISPLAY GRAND TOTALS and DISPLAY SUBTOTALS options (see Figure 8.21).

36. Navigate to the LAYOUT tab.

37. Right-click on the column header for PRODUCT COSTS and follow the menu path: SORT • DESCENDING (see Figure 8.22).

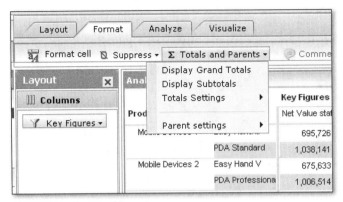

Figure 8.21 Total and Parents

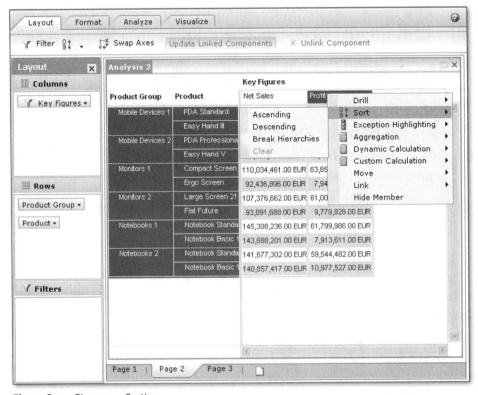

Figure 8.22 Pioneer — Sorting

38. In the LAYOUT tab, click the ⟦ Swap Axes ⟧ button to swap the axes from our CROSSTAB.

39. Navigate to the VISUALIZE tab.

40. Click SELECTED COMPONENT and switch the CROSSTAB to a CLUSTERED BAR Chart (see Figure 8.23).

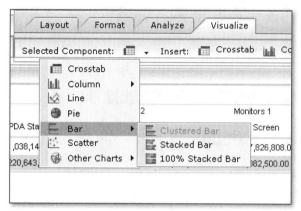

Figure 8.23 Switch Selected Components

In our example, the cross tab is turned into a bar chart and we can now compare NET SALES with PRODUCT COSTS (see Figure 8.24).

41. Select SELECTED COMPONENTS and choose the CROSSTAB option.

42. Navigate to the ANALYZE tab.

43. Select the Product Costs row.

44. Follow the OUTLIERS • FIND OUTLIERS menu path in the toolbar (see Figure 8.25).

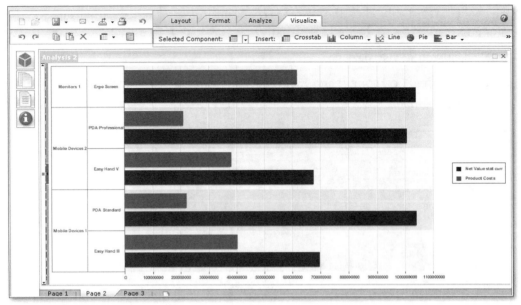

Figure 8.24 Pioneer Workspace — Visualize

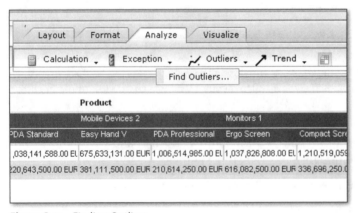

Figure 8.25 Finding Outliers

45. The FIND OUTLIERS screen appears (see Figure 8.26) and we can define the boundary conditions.

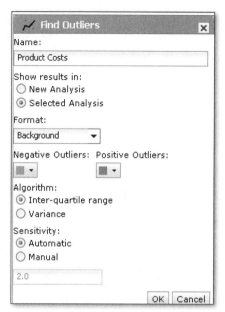

Figure 8.26 Find Outliers

The positive and negative outliers are highlighted (see Figure 8.27).

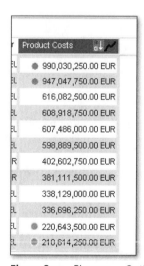

Figure 8.27 Pioneer — Outliers

46. Select the Properties tab in the toolbar (see Figure 8.28).

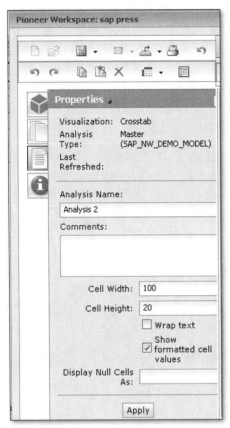

Figure 8.28 Pioneer Workspace — Properties

47. Enter an ANALYSIS NAME and COMMENTS for your workspace.

48. Use the SAVE option in the toolbar to save your workspace to the BusinessObjects Environment.

In the next section, we'll look at how Pioneer can fulfill the requirements for our finance and sales area.

8.5 Customer Case Study — Financial Analysis

In this section, we'll use Pioneer Office to provide our financial department with the required reporting and analysis environment.

1. Start Pioneer Excel.

2. Navigate to the Pioneer tab in the Microsoft Office ribbon.

3. Follow the menu path: INSERT SOURCE • USE SOURCE.

4. Select the SAP NetWeaver BW system from the list of available systems.

5. Enter the details to your SAP system (see Figure 8.29).

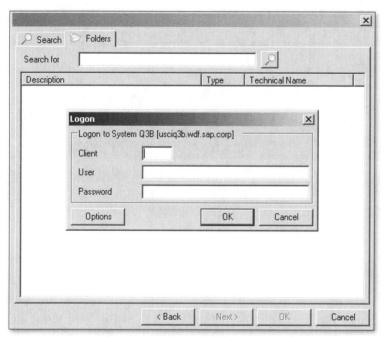

Figure 8.29   Pioneer Office — Logon Dialog

6. Select the query from the dialog box and click OK (see Figure 8.30).

   In the given example, we are using the BW query that we used for our financial reporting with Web Intelligence in Chapter 4, Section 4.7, Customer Case Study — Financial Reporting with Web Intelligence. Because we activated a hierarchy for the COST CENTER characteristic, Pioneer is showing us the first levels of the hierarchy.

7. Click on DISPLAY TASK PANEL in the Pioneer ribbon (see Figure 8.31).

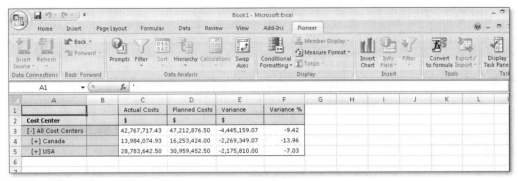

Figure 8.30   Pioneer Office

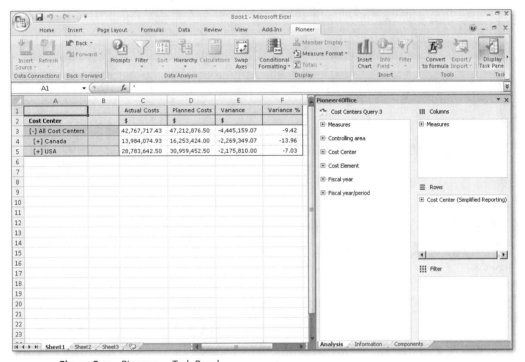

Figure 8.31   Pioneer — Task Panel

8. Collapse the node for Cost Center in the Task Panel (see Figure 8.32).

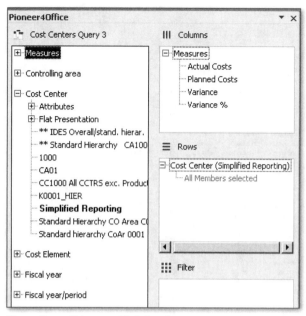

Figure 8.32 Pioneer — Task Panel

In our example, the selected hierarchy is highlighted in bold. We can use the TASK PANEL to select members and attributes, and move elements to the ROWS, COLUMNS, and FILTER sections.

9. Drag and drop the COST ELEMENTS characteristic to the cross tab so that you receive the COST CENTER hierarchy first, and for each element of the hierarchy you will then see the COST ELEMENTS (see Figure 8.33). You can drag and drop with the cross tab in the spreadsheet or you can drag and drop in the TASK PANEL.

10. Select the column for the VARIANCE % key figure.

11. Follow the FILTER • FILTER BY MEASURE menu path from the Pioneer ribbon (see Figure 8.34).

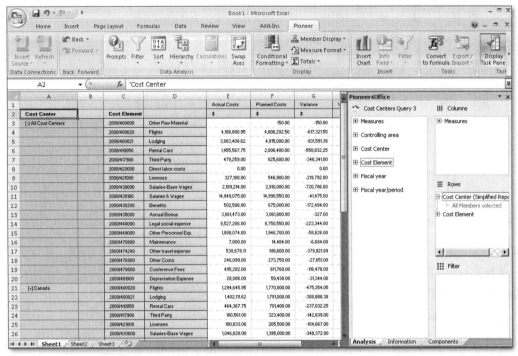

Figure 8.33 Pioneer Office

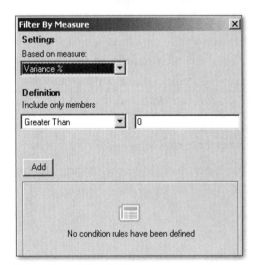

Figure 8.34 Filter By Measure

12. Set the GREATER THAN option and use the VALUE -10, which will then shows us all COST ELEMENTS that either have 10% of their budget left or are over budget (see Figure 8.35).

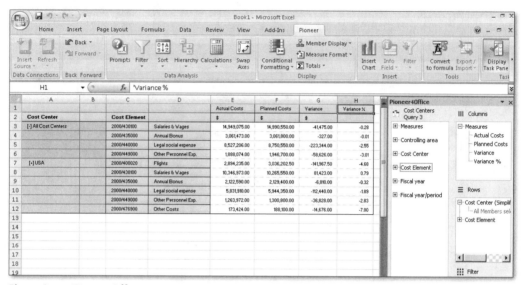

Figure 8.35 Pioneer Office

13. Right-click on the characteristic Cost Center.

14. Follow the HIERARCHY • LEVEL VISIBILITY menu path and uncheck all of the hierarchy levels so that only the hierarchy leaves are shown (see Figure 8.36).

> **Pioneer and Hierarchy Visibility**
>
> As shown in Figure 8.36, you can activate and deactivate the hierarchy levels display. It's important to note that Pioneer lets you enable or disable the hierarchy level displays independent of each other. For example, you could show LEVEL 01 and LEVEL 03 and hide LEVEL 02.

15. Right-click on the COST ELEMENT characteristic in the TASK PANEL.

16. Select FILTER BY MEMBER (see Figure 8.37).

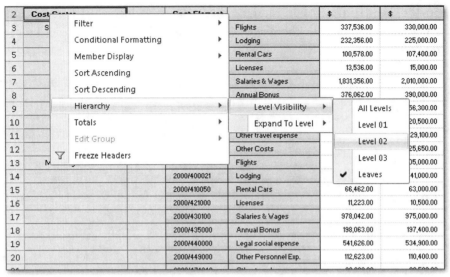

Figure 8.36 Hierarchy Level Visibility

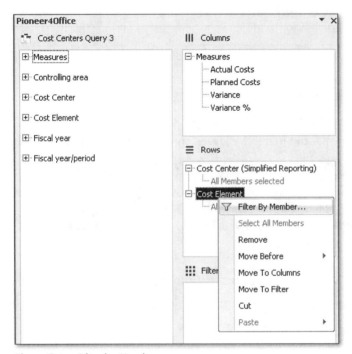

Figure 8.37 Filter by Member

17. Select the travel-related Cost Elements (see Figure 8.38).

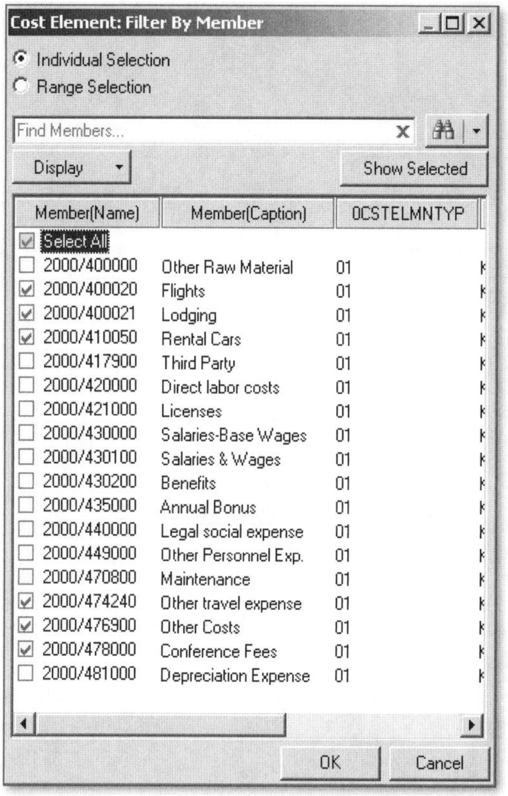

Figure 8.38   Filter by Member

18. Select the VARIANCE % column.

19. Follow the CONDITIONAL FORMATTING • NEW menu path in the Pioneer ribbon (see Figure 8.39).

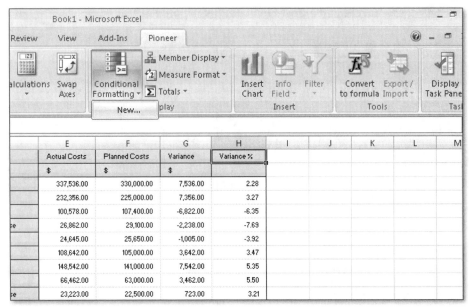

Figure 8.39 Conditional Formatting

20. Define a new condition for values larger than 0 to highlight those Cost Elements that have gone over budget (see Figure 8.40).

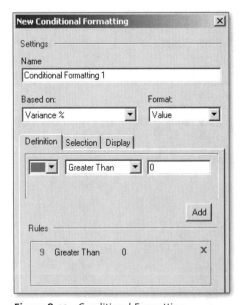

Figure 8.40 Conditional Formatting

21. Click OK. The numbers will be highlighted in the spreadsheet according to the defined rule (see Figure 8.41).

	A	B	C	D	E	F	G	H
1					Actual Costs	Planned Costs	Variance	Variance %
2	**Cost Center**		**Cost Element**		$	$	$	
3	Sales Canada		2000/400020	Flights	337,536.00	330,000.00	7,536.00	2.28
4			2000/400021	Lodging	232,356.00	225,000.00	7,356.00	3.27
5			2000/410050	Rental Cars	100,578.00	107,400.00	-6,822.00	-6.35
6			2000/474240	Other travel expense	26,862.00	29,100.00	-2,238.00	-7.69
7			2000/476900	Other Costs	24,645.00	25,650.00	-1,005.00	-3.92
8	Marketing Canada		2000/400020	Flights	108,642.00	105,000.00	3,642.00	3.47
9			2000/400021	Lodging	148,542.00	141,000.00	7,542.00	5.35
10			2000/410050	Rental Cars	66,462.00	63,000.00	3,462.00	5.50
11			2000/474240	Other travel expense	23,223.00	22,500.00	723.00	3.21
12			2000/476900	Other Costs	19,353.00	19,500.00	-147.00	-0.75
13			2000/478000	Conference Fees	49,626.00	46,260.00	3,366.00	7.28
14	Sales US North		2000/400020	Flights	340,626.00	345,000.00	-4,374.00	-1.27
15			2000/400021	Lodging	225,429.00	234,000.00	-8,571.00	-3.66
16			2000/410050	Rental Cars	85,935.00	87,000.00	-1,065.00	-1.22
17			2000/474240	Other travel expense	28,962.00	28,500.00	462.00	1.62
18			2000/476900	Other Costs	34,974.00	36,000.00	-1,026.00	-2.85
19	Sales US South		2000/400020	Flights	437,061.00	420,000.00	17,061.00	4.06
20			2000/400021	Lodging	298,638.00	285,000.00	13,638.00	4.79
21			2000/410050	Rental Cars	127,542.00	114,000.00	13,542.00	11.88

Figure 8.41 Conditional Formatting

22. Now you can use the FILTER option (see Figure 8.42) in the Pioneer ribbon to place some filter buttons onto our spreadsheet to provide an easy-to-use filter (see Figure 8.43).

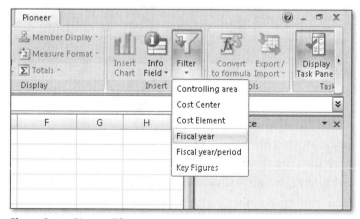

Figure 8.42 Pioneer Filter

	A	B	C	D	E	F
1						
2		Fiscal year/period				
3		Cost Element				
4		Cost Center				
5		Controlling area				
6						
7						
8						
9						
10			Actual Costs	Planned Costs	Variance	Variance %
11	**Cost Center**		$	$	$	
12	[-] All Cost Centers		42,767,717.43	47,212,876.50	-4,445,159.07	-9.42
13	[-] Canada		13,984,074.93	16,253,424.00	-2,269,349.07	-13.96
14	#	Consulting Canada	7,515,210.93	9,546,114.00	-2,030,903.07	-21.27
15	#	Sales Canada	4,211,439.00	4,481,850.00	-270,411.00	-6.03
16	#	Marketing Canada	2,257,425.00	2,225,460.00	31,965.00	1.44
17	[-] USA		28,783,642.50	30,959,452.50	-2,175,810.00	-7.03

Figure 8.43   Filter Placed on the Spreadsheet

23. You can also use INFO FIELD from the Pioneer ribbon to put information on the spreadsheet (see Figure 8.44).

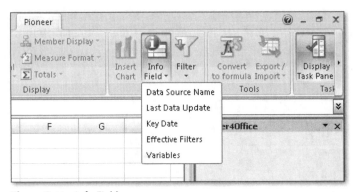

Figure 8.44   Info Field

We used Pioneer to create an overview of our actual and planned costs based on our cost center hierarchy showing the details of each cost element. We used conditional formatting and filtering to only show cost elements above the planned budget, and we provided additional options to filter the data and to retrieve information about the data itself.

8.6 Summary

In this chapter, you previewed the Pioneer project and learned about the possible deployment and data connectivity options that are planned for Pioneer. In addition, we used Pioneer to uncover some basic steps using Pioneer Web and then created a cost center report using Pioneer Office for our financial area.

In this chapter, we'll look at how you can use Dashboard Builder to combine content from your BusinessObjects Enterprise system into compelling dashboards.

9 Combining Content into Dashboards

Dashboard Builder is a tool that lets you build dashboards and analytics. In the following sections, you'll learn how you can leverage your SAP data in conjunction with Dashboard Builder. The focus of this chapter is analytics and dashboard functionality —not Predictive Analysis, Performance Manager, Set Analysis, or Process Analysis.

9.1 Installation and Deployment Overview

Dashboard Builder is part of your BusinessObjects Enterprise deployment and installation process. As part of the BusinessObjects Enterprise installation, you will find three configured servers: Dashboard Server, Dashboard Analytics Server, and PM Repository Server. There are several other servers as well, but for what we will cover in this chapter, these three servers are all that we need.

Performance Manager Repository

For the activities in this chapter, we will not need to configure a Performance Manager Repository because we are focusing on creating analytics and dashboards. However, we need the Performance Manager Repository Service because several tasks will verify to see if it is up and running. If you are planning to leverage more functionality from the Dashboard and Analytics capability other than creating dashboards and analytics — for example, metrics — it's recommended to review the *Dashboard and Analytics Setup and Administration Guide* at *http://help.sap.com*.

In addition to the servers for your BusinessObjects Enterprise system, we want to make sure that we can leverage all of the analytic templates, and therefore we need to deploy the Xcelsius-based templates for the analytics. These templates are included as part of your installation and you can manually upload them by following these steps:

1. Copy the file XCTEMPLATEUPLOADER.WAR from *\Program Files\Business Objects\ BusinessObjects Enterprise 12.0\java\applications* to the folder for your web applications; in case you used the default deployment with Tomcat as Java application server the path would be *\Program Files\Business Objects\Tomcat55\ webapps* (all paths are assuming a Windows-based deployment). In case you are using another Java application server please refer to the documentation for the Java application server to deploy the WAR file manually.

2. Restart the Java application Server. In case you are using Tomcat you can restart the service using the Central Configuration Manger via the menu START • PROGRAMS • BUSINESSOBJECTS XI 3.1 • BUSINESSOBJECTS ENTERPRISE • CENTRAL CONFIGURATION MANAGER.

3. After you deploy the .war file, you can call the Xcelsius Template publisher using the URL *http://<application server>:<port>/XCTemplateUploader/ (see* Figure 9.1).

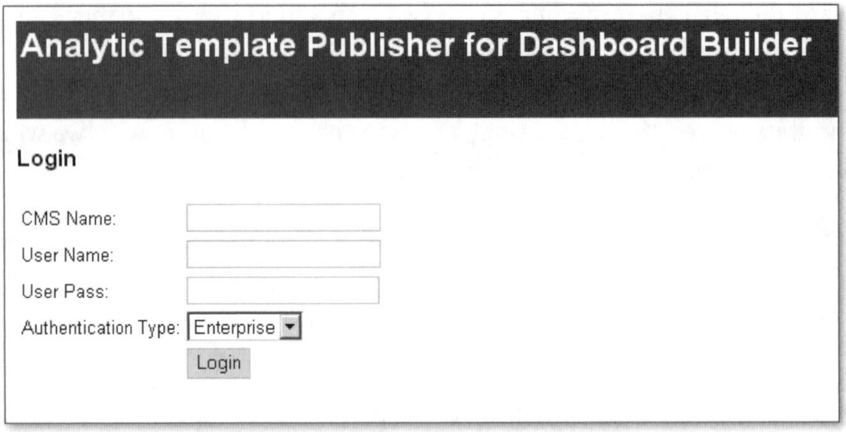

Analytic Template Publisher for Dashboard Builder

Login

CMS Name:
User Name:
User Pass:
Authentication Type: Enterprise ▾
Login

Figure 9.1 Analytic Template Publisher

4. Enter the name and port of your CMS into the CMS NAME field.

5. Enter an administrative USER NAME and USER PASSWORD.

6. Click LOGIN (see Figure 9.2).

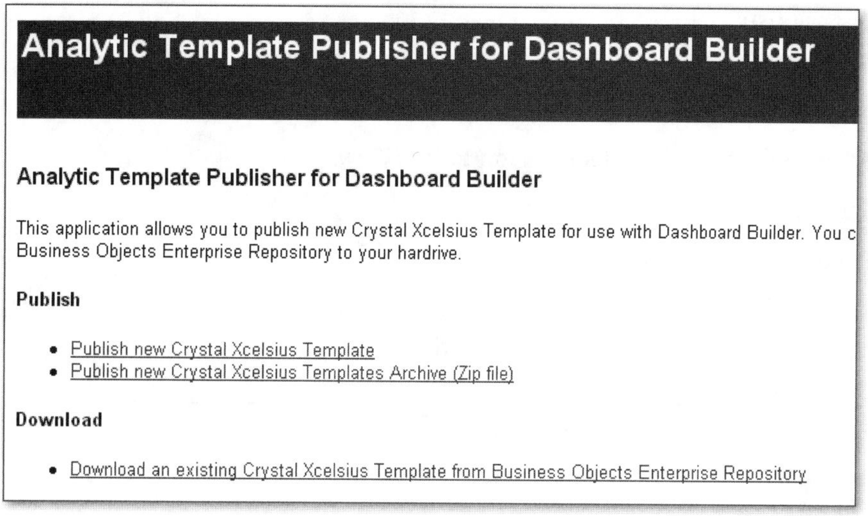

Figure 9.2   Analytic Template Publisher

7. Select the PUBLISH NEW CRYSTAL XCELSIUS TEMPLATES ARCHIVE (ZIP FILE) option.

8. Click BROWSE.

9. Select the first file from the default installation path *\Program Files\Business Objects\Dashboard and Analytics 12.0\setup* with the filename *templates.zip.*

10. Select the FORCE FOLDERS CREATION and FORCE OVERWRITE options (see Figure 9.3).

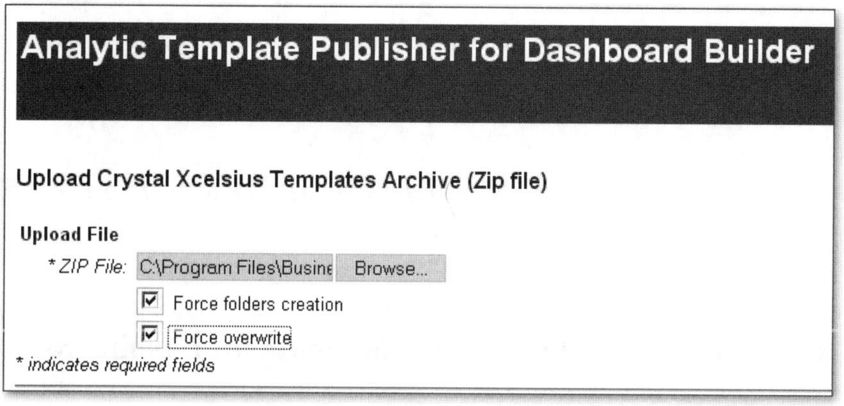

Figure 9.3   Upload Archive File

11. Click Finish.

12. Repeat the steps for the files samples.zip and data_exploration_templates. zip.

13. After you deploy these files, log on to InfoView.

14. Select Document List.

15. Follow the menu path: New • Analytic.

16. You should now see a list of four categories of analytics (see Figure 9.4). Each category offers several different analytics.

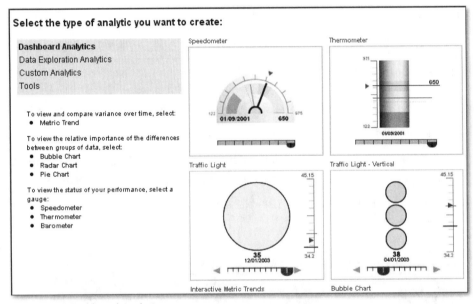

Figure 9.4 Dashboard Analytics

Now you can start using Dashboard Builder with the newly added templates and create compelling dashboards for your users.

9.2 Customer Case Study — Requirements for Dashboards

With regard to the overall requirements for the different areas and how Dashboard Builder can fulfill them, we need to look at the role Dashboard Builder plays in the overall reporting and analysis solution. Dashboard Builder provides you with the functionality to combine content from different tools, such as Crystal Reports, Web Intelligence, and Xcelsius, into dashboard-style pages. In addition, Dashboard Builder provides you with the functionality to create analytics based on a given set of templates as part of your dashboards. Dashboard Builder is not a typical reporting or analytics tool. It is a tool that lets you combine content from the tools that we looked at in the previous chapter.

Based on these capabilities, we will focus on using Dashboard Builder to fulfill the requirements for the executive and leadership team:

► The content needs to present highly aggregated information with the necessary alerts for important Key Performance Indicators (KPIs).

► The data needs to be shown in a highly visualized manner and the main KPIs need to be presented in a single dashboard.

► The consumption of the reports and analytics needs to be easy to use and critical information needs to be easily identifiable.

► The preceding requirements can be fulfilled using Dashboard Builder. The actual content that is shown in the dashboards will be created using Crystal Reports, Web Intelligence, and Xcelsius.

9.3   Dashboard Builder — Quick Basics

In this section, we'll look into the use of Dashboard Builder and how you can create dashboards and analytics based on your SAP data. First, we'll focus on the creation of dashboards, and then we'll focus on the use of the analytic templates and how we can use them in our dashboards.

9.3.1   Creating Dashboards

Dashboard Builder lets you create new dashboards and leverage the following content types from your BusinessObjects Enterprise system:

► Crystal Reports

► Xcelsius

- ▶ Web Intelligence
- ▶ Desktop Intelligence
- ▶ Analytics
- ▶ PDF documents
- ▶ Microsoft Excel spreadsheets, Microsoft Word documents, Microsoft Power-Point presentations
- ▶ Text files, Rich text files
- ▶ Hyperlinks

In general, you can separate your personal dashboards in the My Dashboard area from the dashboards that are available to all of your end users in the Corporate Dashboards area. You can't copy dashboards between these two categories, but you can leverage the identical content from each category.

In the following steps, we'll look at how you can create new dashboards and leverage the content for your BusinessObjects system.

1. Log on to InfoView with your SAP credentials using the SAP authentication mode.

2. Select the DOCUMENT LIST option.

3. In InfoView, follow the menu path: DASHBOARDS • MY DASHBOARD (see Figure 9.5).

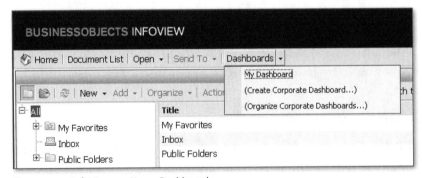

Figure 9.5 InfoView — Menu Dashboards

4. You will see the dashboard start page, because we haven't created any dashboards yet (see Figure 9.6).

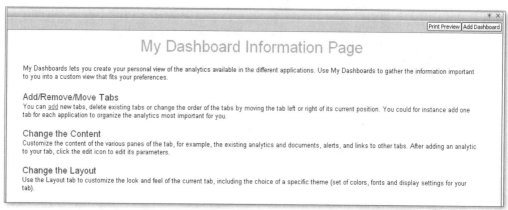

Figure 9.6 *My Dashboard Information Page*

5. Click the ADD DASHBOARD button.

6. Enter `My first dashboard` as the TITLE and select the FAVORITES folder as the storage LOCATION (see Figure 9.7).

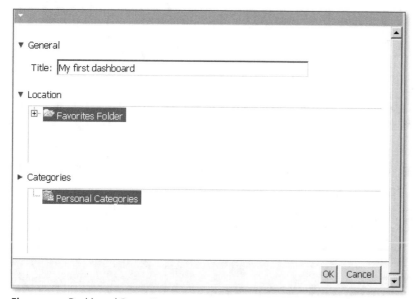

Figure 9.7 *Dashboard Properties*

7. Click OK.

8. Your newly created dashboard will be shown as a tab in the toolbar. Select the tab for your dashboard and click the EDIT DASHBOARD button.

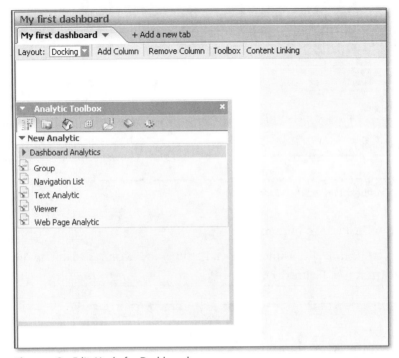

Figure 9.8 Edit Mode for Dashboards

9. Close the ANALYTIC TOOLBOX. We can always call the ANALYTIC TOOLBOX with the TOOLBOX menu item in the toolbar.

10. With the LAYOUT option, you can decide if your dashboard is based on a FREE-FORM placement of the content, based on a TEMPLATE, or based on the DOCK-ING option (see Figure 9.9).

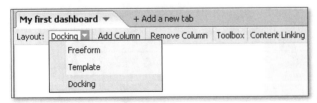

Figure 9.9 Layout Options

11. Select LAYOUT TEMPLATE (see Figure 9.10).

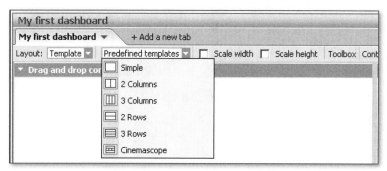

Figure 9.10   Layout Template with Predefined Templates

12. When selecting the TEMPLATE option you select how the content of your dashboard is going to be displayed from a range of predefined templates.

13. Select the 2 COLUMNS option.

14. The SCALE WIDTH and SCALE HEIGHT options are only available in the LAYOUT TEMPLATE option. These two options let you configure your dashboard to scale with regard to height and width when the browser window is resized.

15. Activate the SCALE WIDTH and SCALE HEIGHT options.

16. Select the left column in the dashboard and click on the header (see Figure 9.11).

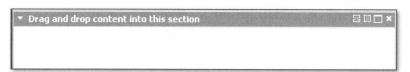

Figure 9.11   Header Bar

17. The icons on the right-hand side let you split the column horizontally or vertically, if required.

18. Next, we need to select the content that we want to display.

19. Click on the TOOLBOX option in the toolbar (see Figure 9.12).

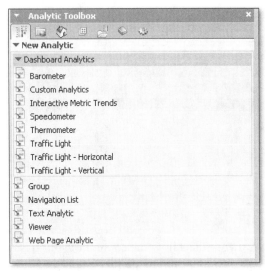

Figure 9.12   Analytic Toolbox

20. The ANALYTIC TOOLBOX provides you with several options (from left to right):

   ▶ The NEW ANALYTIC option provides you with a set of predefined analytics that you can leverage to create new analytics as part of your dashboard. In addition, this option contains a list of preconfigured analytics, such as the NAVIGATION LIST and VIEWER.

   ▶ The CORPORATE ANALYTICS option provides you with access to the Business-Objects Enterprise repository and you can select content from your BusinessObjects system (see Figure 9.13).

   ▶ The PERSONAL ANALYTICS option contains all of the analytics used in dashboards from the MY DASHBOARD category.

   ▶ The EXISTING ANALYTICS option contains all of the analytics used in CORPORATE DASHBOARDS.

   ▶ The LIST OF ANALYTICS option shows all of the analytics stored as part of your Inbox in the BusinessObjects system and as part of the folders you are allowed to access.

   ▶ The ANALYTIC CATALOG option contains predefined analytics that you can apply to your data.

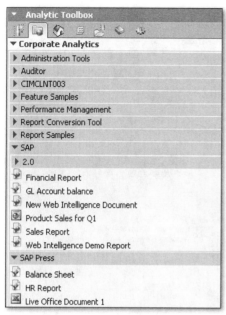

Figure 9.13 Corporate Analytics

21. Navigate to the CORPORATE ANALYTICS option.

22. Navigate to the folder we stored the content we created so far.

23. Select the Web Intelligence sales report we created in Chapter 4, Section 4.6, Customer Case Study — Sales Reporting with Web Intelligence.

24. Drag and drop the sales report from the ANALYTIC TOOLBOX to the left column for our dashboard (see Figure 9.14).

25. You will notice a heading with the note RIGHT-CLICK ON THIS REPORT TO SELECT/ UNSELECT A PART. You can select specific parts of the Web Intelligence report as part of your dashboard. Simply select the part and right-click on the part of your report (see Figure 9.15).

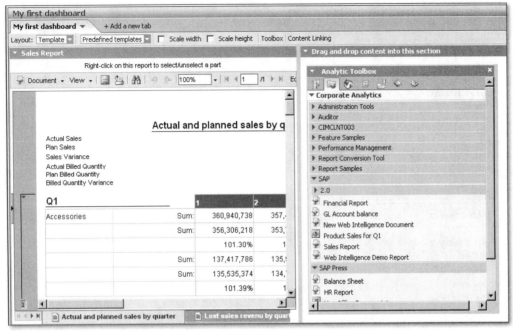

Figure 9.14 Web Intelligence Report Shown in Dashboard

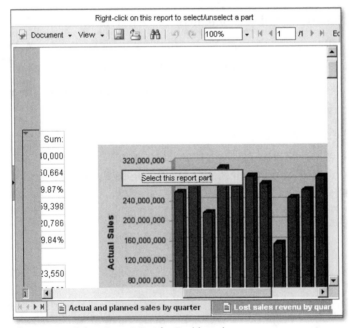

Figure 9.15 Select Report Part for Dashboard

26. For now, we'll select the complete report. We will leverage this functionality in a later exercise.

27. Click the 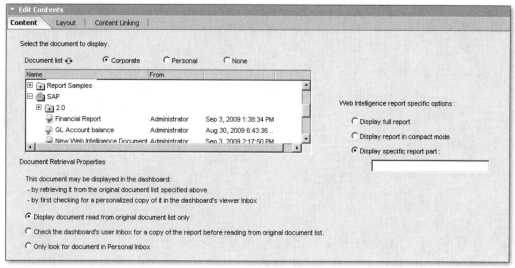 symbol in the heading of the analytic in your dashboard to open up the Properties (see Figure 9.16).

Figure 9.16 Edit Content — Tab Content

28. In the Content tab, you can select the report that is being displayed and configure if the report should be shown fully, in a compact mode, or if only a specific part should be shown. The compact mode will leverage a toolbar based on user-specific rights and thereby save some display space.

29. In addition, you can configure if the report should be retrieved from the original location or the personal inbox.

30. Set the Display Report in Compact Mode option and navigate to the Layout tab (see Figure 9.17).

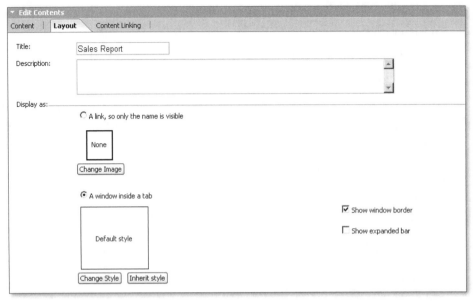

Figure 9.17 Edit Content — Tab Layout

31. In the LAYOUT tab you can change the title and description, and you can configure how the content is displayed. You can decide whether the content is displayed as a link or inside a tab.

32. Select the A WINDOW INSIDE A TAB option.

33. Click OK.

34. We will return to the CONTENT LINKING tab in a later section.

35. Now use the ANALYTIC TOOLBAR and the Corporate Analytics category and select the G/L ACCOUNT BALANCE report, which we created with Crystal Reports in Chapter 3, Section 3.5,Customer Requirements — Financial Reporting with Crystal Reports, and drag the report to the right side of our dashboard (see Figure 9.18).

36. Click the ☑ symbol in the heading of the analytic showing the Crystal Reports content to open the properties (see Figure 9.19).

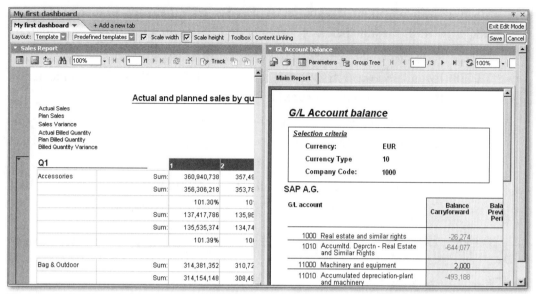

Figure 9.18 Dashboard with Two Columns

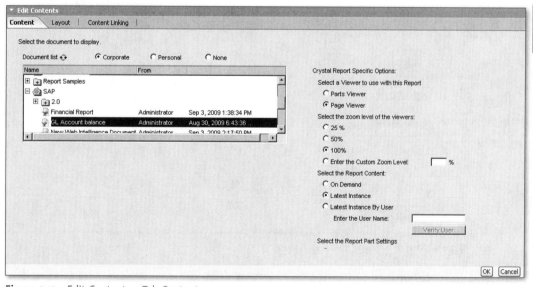

Figure 9.19 Edit Content — Tab Content

37. The CONTENT tab lets you select the VIEWER for the report to specify the zoom level of the initial view of the report, decide if you want to view the report on demand, or view the latest or a specific instance.

38. If you select the PARTS VIEWER, the report will be shown with the initial report part that has been configured in the report itself.

39. If you want to leverage the Report PARTS VIEWER in conjunction with Crystal Reports, REPORT PART SETTINGS lets you specify the OBJECT NAME and the DATA CONTEXT.

40. The LAYOUT tab lets you — similar to the Web Intelligence part — specify a TITLE and DESCRIPTION, and the type of DISPLAY (see Figure 9.20).

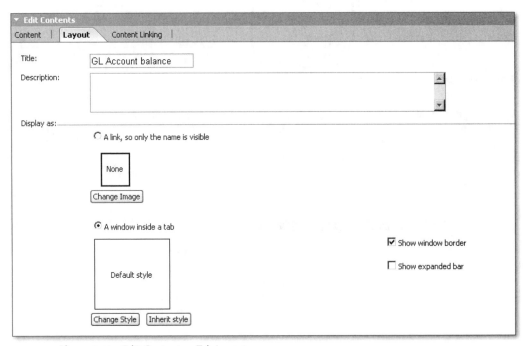

Figure 9.20 Edit Content — Tab Layout

41. Click OK.

42. Click SAVE in the toolbar to save your dashboard.

43. Click EXIT EDIT MODE (see Figure 9.21).

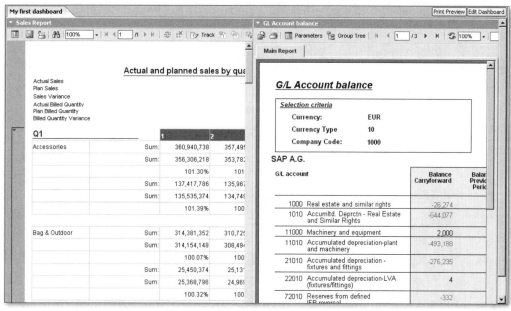

Figure 9.21 Dashboard Display

44. The dashboard is displayed as configured with two columns and the content is displayed. You can click the ▼ button in the top-left corner of each content frame to open or close the display and you can click the ▢ symbol in the top-right corner to switch between a full-screen display and the configured size of the column.

45. Click the EDIT DASHBOARD button.

46. Click on the tab for our first dashboard and open the PROPERTIES (see Figure 9.22).

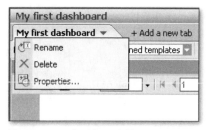

Figure 9.22 Dashboard Menu

47. The PROPERTIES dialog lets you select a style for your dashboard (see Figure 9.23).

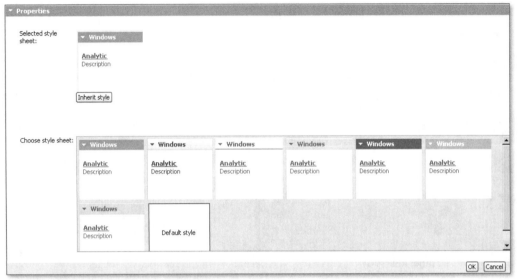

Figure 9.23   Dashboard Properties

48. Select a style and click OK.

49. Click the ADD A NEW TAB option to create a second page as part of our dashboard (see Figure 9.24).

Figure 9.24   Add a New Tab

50. Enter `Finance dashboard` as the TITLE and select the FAVORITES folder as the storage LOCATION.

51. Click OK.

52. Select the FINANCE DASHBOARD tab and select EDIT DASHBOARD.

53. Select the LAYOUT option DOCKING.

54. Click the ADD COLUMN and REMOVE COLUMN buttons to make sure your dashboard contains two columns.

55. Drag the Web Intelligence finance report from Chapter 4, Section 4.7, Customer Case Study — Financial Reporting with Web Intelligence, to the left columns.

56. Drag the Crystal Reports–based balance sheet from Chapter 3, Section 3.5, to the right column.

57. You will see that the content is only consuming half of each of the columns and that there is no menu option that allows you to configure the size of the content (see Figure 9.25).

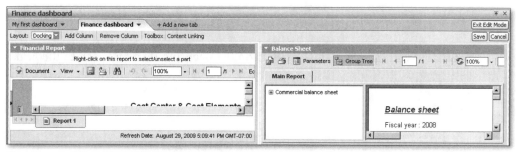

Figure 9.25 Finance Dashboard with Content

58. You can use the mouse pointer to resize the content to make sure it fills the column.

59. Resize the columns to cover the height of your screen.

60. Click SAVE.

61. Use the ADD A NEW TAB option to create a third tab in your dashboard.

62. Enter Sales dashboard as the TITLE and select the FAVORITES folder as the storage location.

Favorites vs. Public Folders

The reason you can only select the FAVORITES folder during the activities is because we're using the MY DASHBOARDS functionality. When you use the CORPORATE DASHBOARD functionality, you can store the dashboard in a public folder.

---

63. Click OK.

64. Select the SALES DASHBOARD.

65. Click EDIT DASHBOARD.

66. Select the LAYOUT FREEFORM option.

67. Activate the SNAP TO GRID option and set the GRID SIZE to SMALL (see Figure 9.26).

Figure 9.26 Freeform Design

68. Now you can place any elements on the page and they will snap to the grid.

69. Open the ANALYTIC TOOLBOX by clicking TOOLBOX in the toolbar.

70. Select the NEW ANALYTIC tab in the ANALYTIC TOOLBOX (see Figure 9.27).

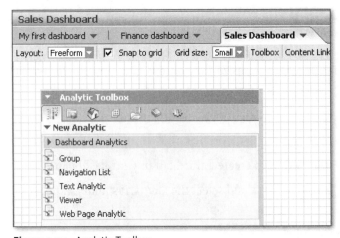

Figure 9.27 Analytic Toolbox

71. Drag and drop a NAVIGATION LIST to your new page.

72. Drag and drop a VIEWER next to the NAVIGATION LIST.

73. Navigate to the CORPORATE ANALYTICS tab in the ANALYTIC TOOLBOX.

74. Browse to the folder where we stored all of our reports so far.

75. Drag and drop all of the reports we created in the previous chapters to the NAVIGATION LIST.

76. Click the 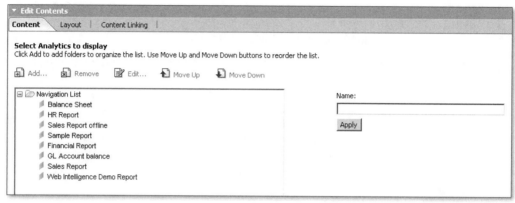 symbol in the heading of the NAVIGATION LIST to open up the edit modes (see Figure 9.28).

Figure 9.28   Edit Content — Navigation List

77. You can use the buttons above the NAVIGATION LIST to create a folder structure and to move the content objects up and down (see Figure 9.29).

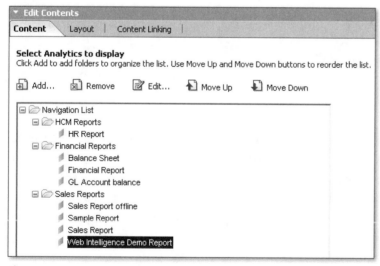

Figure 9.29   Navigation List with Folder Structure

78. Create a corresponding folder structure and assign the objects to the folders.

79. Click OK.

80. Resize your VIEWER analytic to leverage most of the page.

81. Click SAVE to save the changes to the page.

82. Click EXIT EDIT MODE.

83. Select any element from the NAVIGATION LIST.

84. Each selection in the NAVIGATION LIST will be shown in the VIEWER (see Figure 9.30).

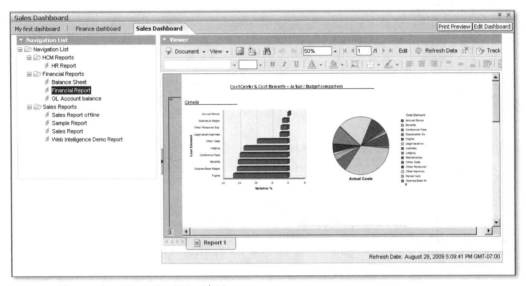

Figure 9.30 Navigation List with Viewer

Up to this point, you've learned how to create a dashboard page and how to leverage the existing content on your BusinessObjects system. Creating a Corporate Dashboard follows the same steps, except that a Corporate Dashboard is saved to a Public Folder in your BusinessObjects system and that instead of following the DASHBOARDS • MY DASHBOARDS menu path, you follow DASHBOARDS • CREATE CORPORATE DASHBOARD.

9.3.2 Creating Analytics

In this section, we'll look at how you can create new analytics based on the analytic templates in Dashboard Builder. In general, the analytics are based on a Universe, which, in the case of your SAP data sources, means that you can only build analytics on top of SAP NetWeaver Business Warehouse (BW) with either a relational universe leveraging Data Federator (see Chapter 4, Section 4.3.3, Relational Universes and SAP NetWeaver BW) or Online Analytical Processing (OLAP) universes (see Chapter 4, Section 4.3.2, OLAP Universes and SAP NetWeaver BW).

To create a new analytic, you have three options:

1. You can follow the NEW • ANALYTIC menu path in InfoView (see Figure 9.31).

Figure 9.31 Menu New • Analytic Menu Path in InfoView

2. In InfoView, you can follow the menu path OPEN • DASHBOARD AND ANALYTICS and select the option DASHBOARD BUILDER to create new analytics (see Figure 9.32).

3. You can use the ANALYTIC TOOLBOX when creating a dashboard in the NEW ANALYTIC tab (see Figure 9.33).

Figure 9.32 Dashboard Builder

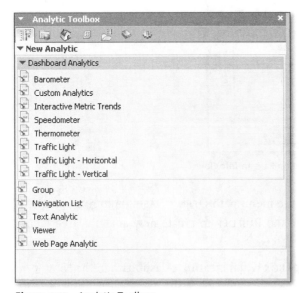

Figure 9.33 Analytic Toolbox

In our case, we'll use the NEW menu from InfoView to create new analytics and focus on the workflow.

1. In InfoView, follow the menu path: NEW • ANALYTIC (see Figure 9.34).

2. Select SPEEDOMETER (see Figure 9.35).

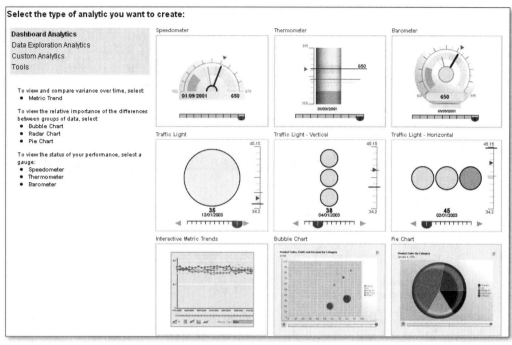

Figure 9.34 Selection of Analytic Type

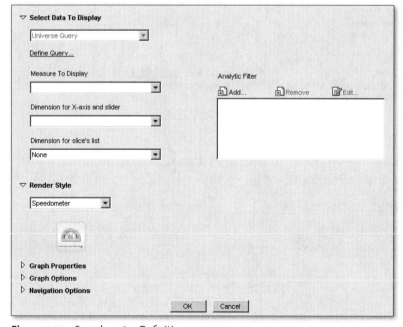

Figure 9.35 Speedometer Definition

3. Now you can define a query based on a Universe and define which measures you want to display.

4. Click DEFINE QUERY.

5. Select the Universe we created in Chapter 4, Section 4.6.

6. Add the CALENDAR MONTH characteristic and the ACTUAL SALES key figure to the RESULT OBJECTS (see Figure 9.36).

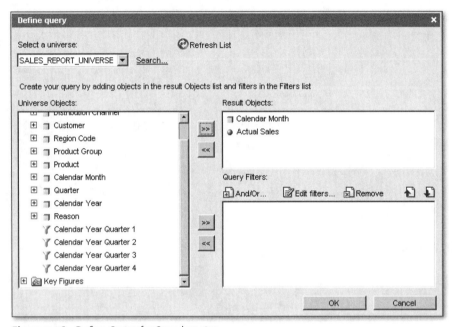

Figure 9.36 Define Query for Speedometer

7. Click OK.

8. Set ACTUAL SALES as MEASURE TO DISPLAY and set CALENDAR MONTH as DIMENSION FOR X-AXIS AND SLIDER (see Figure 9.37).

9. Open GRAPHIC PROPERTIES.

10. Define a range based on your data and set the color coding from red to yellow to green (see Figure 9.38).

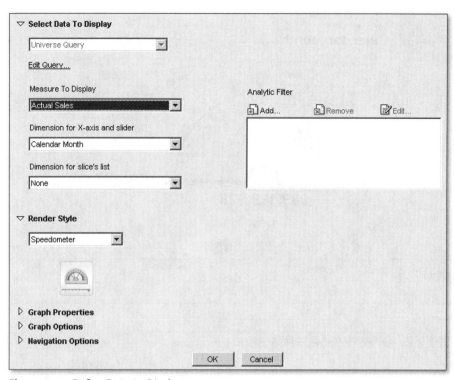

Figure 9.37 Define Data to Display

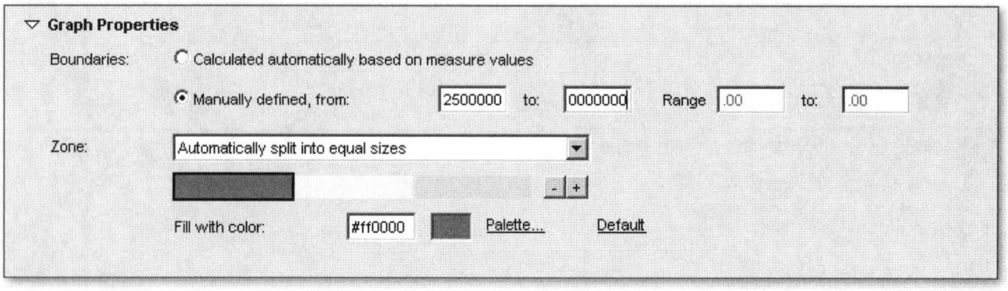

Figure 9.38 Graphic Properties

11. Click OK (see Figure 9.39).

12. Use the SAVE AS option to save the newly created SPEEDOMETER to InfoView (see Figure 9.40).

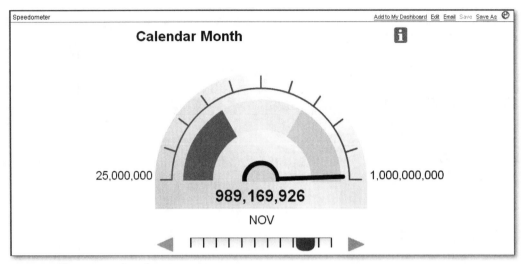

Figure 9.39 Speedometer

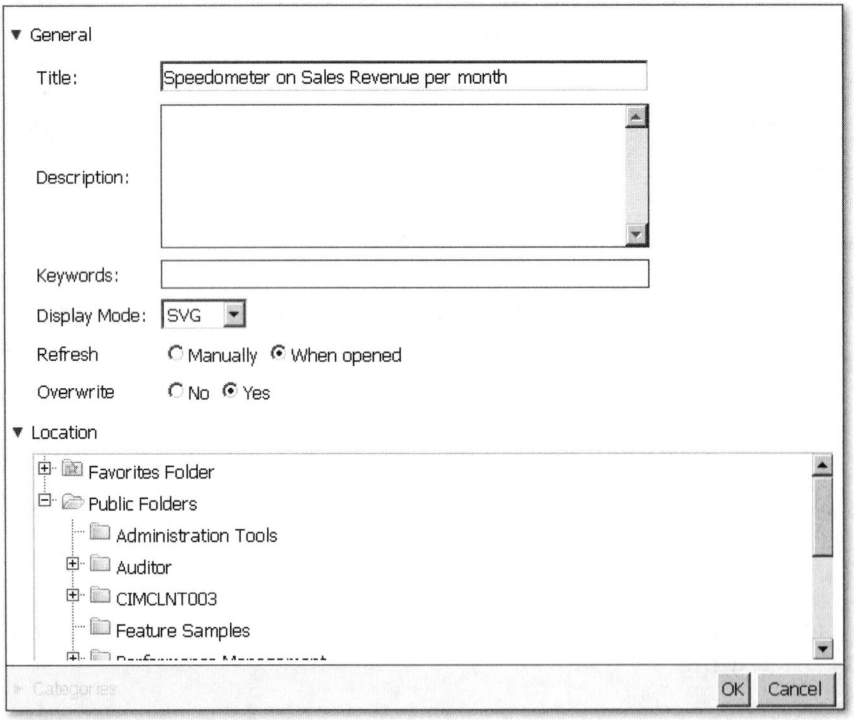

Figure 9.40 Save as Dialog

13. Enter a TITLE, set the REFRESH option to WHEN OPENED, and select a folder to save the analytic.

14. Click OK.

You have saved the analytic to the InfoView folder structure and you can also leverage it as part of any dashboard via the Analytic Toolbox.

15. Click DOCUMENT LIST in InfoView.

16. Follow the menu path NEW • ANALYTIC.

17. Select INTERACTIVE METRIC TRENDS.

18. Click DEFINE QUERY (see Figure 9.41).

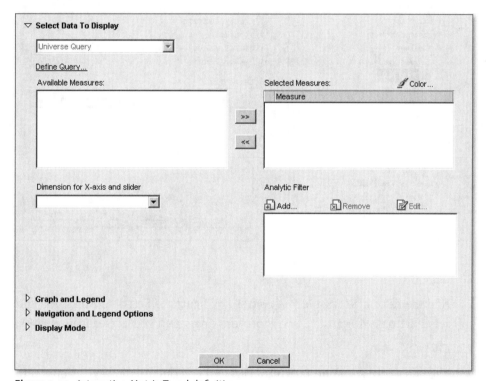

Figure 9.41 Interactive Metric Trend definition

19. Select the Universe we created in Chapter 4, Section 4.6, and add the following objects to RESULT OBJECTS (see Figure 9.42).

- ► CALENDAR MONTH
- ► CALENDAR YEAR
- ► PRODUCT GROUP
- ► ACTUAL SALES
- ► PLAN SALES

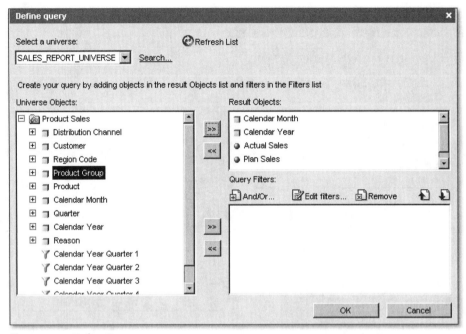

Figure 9.42 Define Query

20. Click OK.

21. Add the ACTUAL SALES and PLAN SALES key figures to SELECTED MEASURES and set CALENDAR MONTH as DIMENSION FOR X-AXIS AND SLIDER (see Figure 9.43).

22. Click OK.

23. The INTERACTIVE METRIC TREND appears and you can use the SAVE AS option to save the analytic to InfoView (see Figure 9.44).

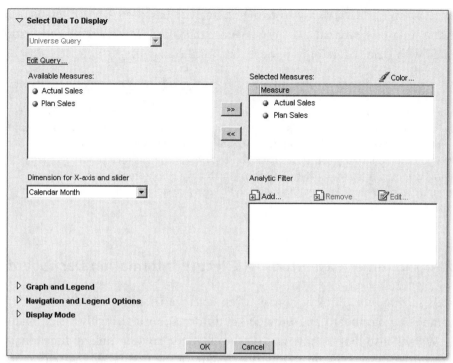

Figure 9.43 Select Data to Display

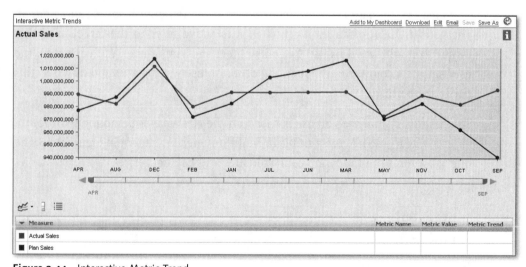

Figure 9.44 Interactive Metric Trend

As you can see, it's very easy to create an analytic based on a set of templates. With regard to the SAP data, you can leverage the OLAP Universes and Universes created with Data Federator to retrieve data for the analytics.

Analytics and SAP Variables/Prompting

When you create analytics based on Universes with prompts, the prompting dialog from the analytics doesn't provide a list of values, which makes it very difficult for your end users to leverage the analytic without knowing which values are possible. Because of this, you should leverage Universes based on top of SAP sources only when there are no prompts required for the analytic. If you need to have the prompt and a list of values, you may want to consider creating the analytic with Xcelsius and then include the Xcelsius objects in the dashboard.

9.4   Customer Case Study — Execute Information Dashboard

In this section, we'll look at how you can leverage Dashboard Builder to offer a compelling dashboard and provide key information in a highly visual manner. We will also look at how you can leverage the content linking functionality from Dashboard Builder to link the content of the dashboard to each other. The content linking functionality lets you link several content objects, such as Xcelsius, Crystal Reports, and Web Intelligence, and define a source and a target. The source analytic can then act as an interactive filter to the target analytics. In our example, we'll use an Xcelsius object showing a map and each time the user selects a country in the map the other objects will get filtered down to this particular country.

The first query that we will use is based on the NetWeaver demo model InfoProvider 0D_NW_M01 Actuals and Plan MultiProvider. As shown in Figure 9.45, the query contains the following characteristics and key figures:

- ▶ Country
- ▶ Net Sales
- ▶ Product Costs
- ▶ Open order value

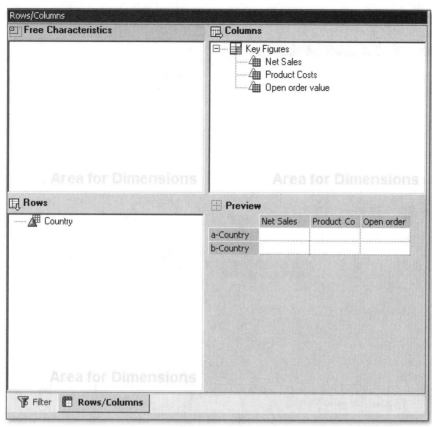

Figure 9.45 Query for Xcelsius Dashboard

We'll use this query to create our source analytic as an Xcelsius dashboard display-ing a map and showing the net sales revenue per country. In addition, we created a second query based on the same InfoProvider but with slightly different objects as shown in Figure 9.46.

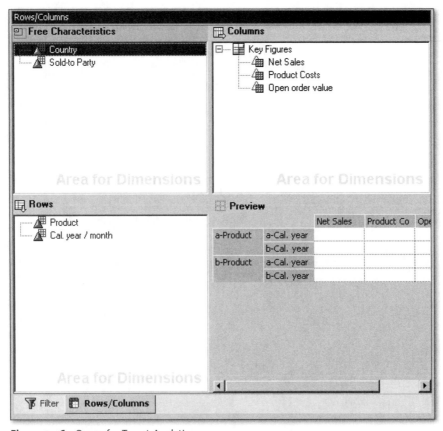

Figure 9.46 Query for Target Analytics

This query contains the following objects:

- ▶ PRODUCT
- ▶ CAL. YEAR/MONTH
- ▶ SOLD-TO PARTY
- ▶ COUNTRY
- ▶ NET SALES
- ▶ PRODUCT COSTS
- ▶ OPEN ORDER VALUE

In addition, the query includes a variable based on the COUNTRY characteristic for single values. We will use this query for three target analytics displaying information filtered for a single country based on the selection from our source analytic.

Because we want to host the Xcelsius object inside InfoView, we can't leverage the new SAP NetWeaver Business Intelligence (BI) connectivity, because such an Xcelsius file will not work properly when hosted in BusinessObjects Enterprise XI 3.1 Service Pack 02. Therefore, we will use a Live Office and Crystal Reports combination to bring the data to our Xcelsius dashboard.

SAP NetWeaver BI Connectivity for Xcelsius

The newly offered Xcelsius connectivity for SAP NetWeaver BW queries is available as of Release XI 3.1 Service Pack 02 does not work with BusinessObjects Enterprise XI 3.1. An Xcelsius object leveraging this connectivity can't be hosted in the BusinessObjects Enterprise system, but can be hosted in the BEx web runtime. This is on the roadmap for a future service pack so that an Xcelsius object using this connectivity can be hosted in BusinessObjects Enterprise.

---

1. Start Crystal Reports by following the menu path: START • PROGRAMS • CRYSTAL REPORTS • CRYSTAL REPORTS 2008.

2. Follow the menu path SAP • SETTINGS.

3. Make sure the USE MDX DRIVER WITH SUPPORT FOR MULTIPLE STRUCTURES option is activated.

4. Follow the menu path SAP • CREATE NEW REPORT FROM QUERY.

5. Authenticate yourself for your SAP NetWeaver BW system.

6. Select the BW query that we created as shown in Figure 9.45.

7. Add the following fields to the DETAILS section of your report:
   - Country (SAP NW Demo) Name
   - Country (SAP NW Demo) Key
   - Net Sales Value

8. Follow the VIEW • PRINT PREVIEW menu path. Your report should look similar to Figure 9.47

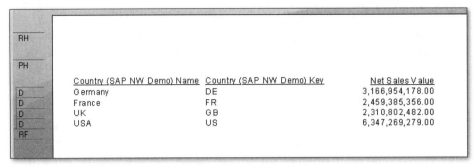

Figure 9.47 Crystal Reports Preview

9. Follow the SAP • SAVE REPORT menu path to save the report to your SAP NetWeaver BW system and then to publish the report to your BusinessObjects Enterprise system.

10. After you publish the report make sure you can view the report using your SAP Credentials and the SAP authentication mode in InfoView.

11. Close the Crystal Reports designer and start Microsoft Excel.

12. Select the LIVE OFFICE menu and the OPTIONS menu item. Here, you can navigate to the ENTERPRISE tab.

13. Here, you need to enter your system details. The Web Service URL follows the standard syntax:

    http://[APPSERVER]:[PORT]/dswsbobje/services/session

    In our example:

    http://vmwsap20:8080/dswsbobj/services/session

14. Make sure you set SAP as the AUTHENTICATION mode and you leave the username and password empty (see Figure 9.48).

15. Uncheck the USE SPECIFIED LOGON CRITERIA option.

16. Navigate to the VIEW tab and in the COLUMN HEADING area select to show the FIELD DESCRIPTION.

17. Click OK.

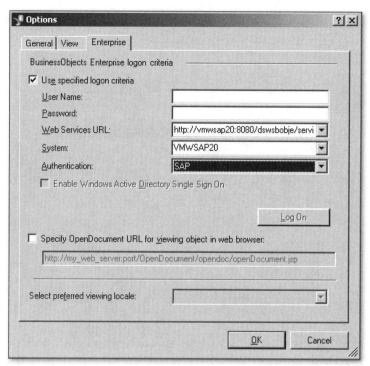

Figure 9.48 Live Office Options

18. Follow the LIVE OFFICE • INSERT • CRYSTAL REPORTS CONTENT menu path. Live Office will come up with a logon screen. However, Live Office does not have a SAP-specific logon screen with the System ID and the Client number; therefore you need to use the following syntax:

```
<SAP System ID>~<SAP Client number>/<SAP user name>
```

19. After you authenticate against the system, Live Office will present you with the repository of your BusinessObjects system. You can use the My Roles shortcut to navigate directly to the roles that contain content for your SAP credentials.

20. Select the Crystal Report object from the role folder where you published it. The report is shown to you in a preview as shown in Figure 9.49.

21. Click NEXT.

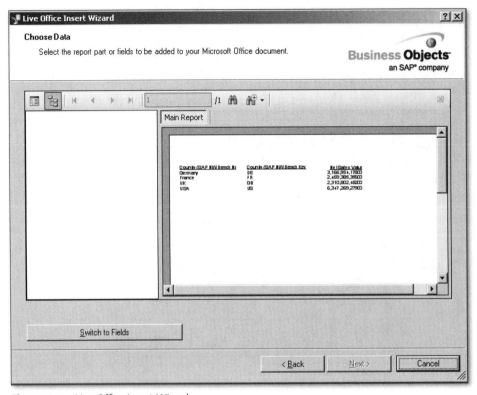

Figure 9.49   Live Office Insert Wizard

22. Select the SWITCH TO FIELDS option.

23. Add all three fields to the list of SELECTED FIELDS.

24. Click NEXT.

25. Click NEXT.

26. Click FINISH.

27. The data from the underlying source — in our example, a SAP NetWeaver BW query — is shown as live content in Microsoft Excel (see Figure 9.50).

28. Follow the LIVE OFFICE • PUBLISH TO BUSINESSOBJECTS ENTERPRISE • SAVE TO BUSINESSOBJECTS ENTERPRISE menu path to save our Live Office document to the BusinessObjects Enterprise system so that we can leverage it with Xcelsius.

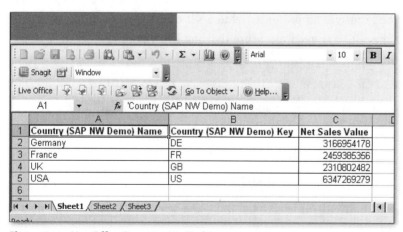

Figure 9.50 Live Office inside Microsoft Excel

29. Start the Xcelsius designer via the menu path START • PROGRAMS • XCELSIUS • XCELSIUS 2008.

30. In the Xcelsius designer, follow the menu path: DATA • IMPORT FROM ENTERPRISE.

31. Log on to your BusinessObjects Enterprise system.

32. Select the Live Office document we created in the previous steps (see Figure 9.51).

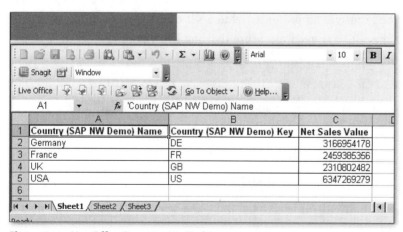

Figure 9.51 Live Office Document in Xcelsius

33. Follow the DATA • CONNECTIONS menu path.

34. CLICK THE ADD button.

35. Select LIVE OFFICE CONNECTIONS.

36. On the DEFINITION tab in SESSION URL, replace the <webserver> placeholder with the name of your application server.

37. Set the REFRESH ON LOAD option on the USAGE tab.

38. Click CLOSE.

39. Follow the menu path: FILE • DOCUMENT PROPERTIES.

40. Set the canvas size to 400 x 400.

41. Drag and drop a EUROPE BY CONTINENT map from the MAPS area in the COMPONENTS to your canvas.

42. Right-click on the map component and select PROPERTIES.

43. Click the ⬚ button next to DISPLAY DATA and select the data and country name from columns B and C. In this case, we are using the COUNTRY KEY value to ensure that the dashboard still works properly when refreshed with a different language.

44. Click the ⬚ button to ensure that you are matching the correct key to the correct region. You will be presented with a set of COUNTRIES and keys so you can edit the list. You need to ensure that the key values are assigned to the correct region.

45. Navigate to the ALERTS tab.

46. Set the ENABLE ALERTS option and select the BY VALUE option.

47. Activate the HIGH VALUES ARE GOOD option (see Figure 9.52).

48. Navigate to the GENERAL tab.

49. Set the INSERTION TYPE to the ROW option.

50. Click the ⬚ button next to SOURCE DATA and select the data and columns B and C.

51. Click the ⬚ button next to DESTINATION and select, in our example, cells A1 and B1 in the second spreadsheet of your Xcelsius file (see Figure 9.53).

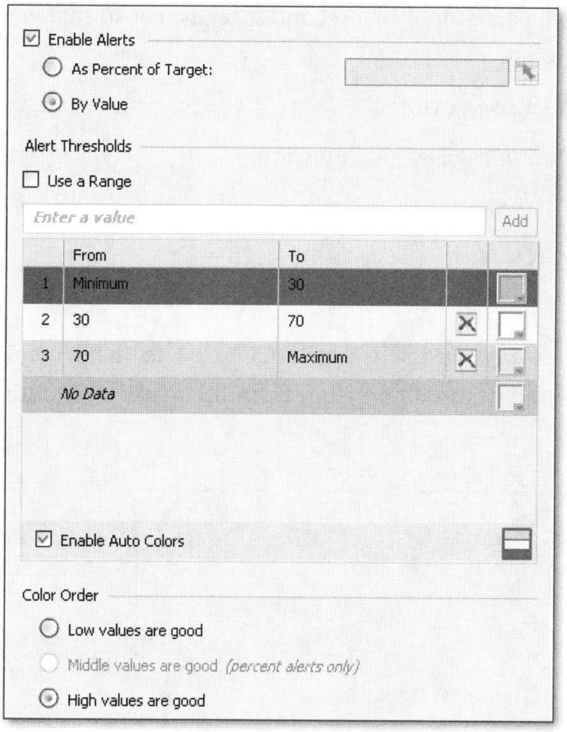

Figure 9.52 Alert Properties

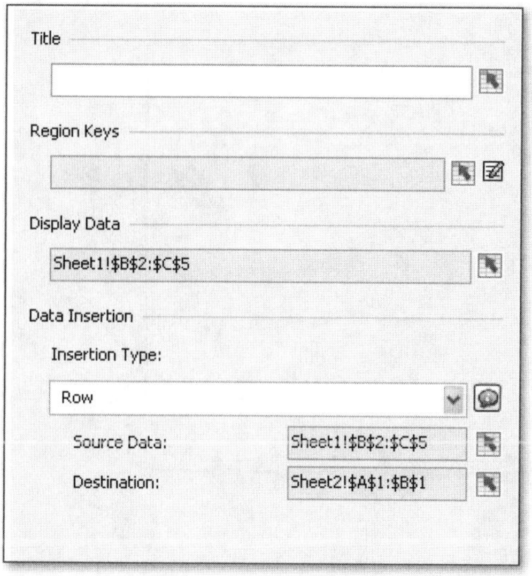

Figure 9.53 Map Properties in Xcelsius

52. The COUNTRY key and the value are stored in a second spreadsheet so that we can use it for our content linking.

53. Follow the menu path: DATA • CONNECTIONS.

54. Click the ADD button to add a PORTAL DATA connection.

55. Set the CONNECTION TYPE to PROVIDER.

56. Enter `Provider` as the RANGE NAME.

57. Set the RANGE TYPE to ROW.

58. Click the ▣ button next to RANGE and select cells A1 to B1 in the second spreadsheet, where we store the destination values from the map (see Figure 9.54).

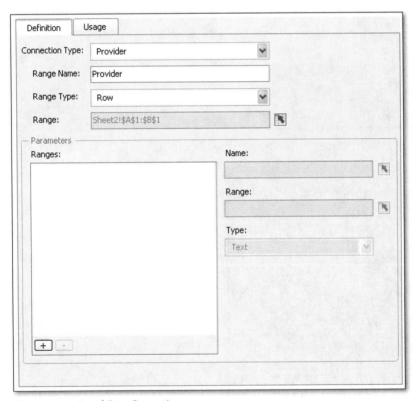

Figure 9.54 Portal Data Properties

59. Navigate to the Usage tab .

60. Click the ▣ button next to Trigger cell and select cell A1 in the second spreadsheet.

61. Set the When Value Changes option.

62. Click Close.

63. Follow the File • Export • BusinessObjects platform menu path to export your Xcelsius design to the BusinessObjects Enterprise system.

64. Follow the File • Save to Enterprise menu path to save the actual design of your dashboard to the BusinessObjects Enterprise system as well.

Now we will create a second Xcelsius object based on Live Office, which will act as the target analytic of our map and filter the data based on the selections in the map.

1. Start Crystal Reports via the menu path: Start • Programs • Crystal Reports • Crystal Reports 2008.

2. Follow the menu path SAP • Settings.

3. Make sure the Use MDX Driver with support for Multiple Structures option is activated.

4. Follow the menu path SAP • Create New Report from Query.

5. Authenticate yourself for your SAP NetWeaver BW system.

6. Select the second BW query that we created as shown in Figure 9.46.

7. Add the following fields to the Details section of your report:

   ▸ Product (SAP NW Demo) Name

   ▸ Net Sales Value

8. Follow the menu path Insert • Group.

9. Use the Product (SAP NW Demo) Name field as the field to group on (see Figure 9.55).

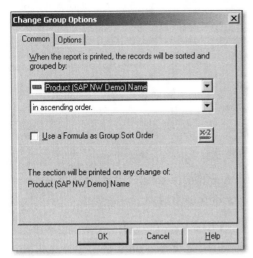

Figure 9.55 Crystal Reports – Insert Group

10. Click OK.

11. Right-click on the NET SALES VALUE field and follow the menu path INSERT •
    SUMMARY.

12. Select SUM and select GROUP#1 as the summary location.

13. Click OK.

14. Move the summary field from the GROUP FOOTER to the GROUP HEADER.

15. Follow the menu path REPORT • SECTION EXPERT.

16. Select DETAILS from the list.

17. Activate the SUPPRESS property.

18. Select GROUP FOOTER #1 from the list.

19. Activate the SUPPRESS property.

20. Click OK.

21. Follow the menu path VIEW • PRINT PREVIEW.

22. Use the SET TO NULL option for the parameter.

23. Click OK.

24. Your report should look similar to Figure 9.56.

Product (SAP NW Demo) Name	Net Sales Value
Compact Screen 17	223,888,592.00
Easy Hand III	125,524,170.00
Easy Hand V	124,634,936.00
Ergo Screen	187,479,924.00
Flat Future	187,148,331.00
Large Screen 21	217,679,089.00
Notebook Basic 15	289,972,006.00
Notebook Basic 17	280,038,762.00
Notebook Standard 15	299,789,447.00
Notebook Standard 17	286,167,447.00
PDA Professional	185,003,583.00
PDA Standard	196,216,406.00

Figure 9.56 Crystal Reports Preview

25. Follow the SAP • SAVE REPORT menu path to save the report to your SAP NetWeaver BW system and then send the report to your BusinessObjects Enterprise system.

26. After you publish the report, make sure you can view the report using your SAP credentials and the SAP authentication mode in InfoView.

27. Close the Crystal Reports designer and start Microsoft Excel.

28. Select the menu LIVE OFFICE and select the menu item OPTIONS. Here you can navigate to the tab ENTERPRISE.

29. Follow the menu path LIVE OFFICE • INSERT • CRYSTAL REPORTS CONTENT.

30. After you authenticate against the system, Live Office will present you with the repository of your BusinessObjects system. You can use the MY ROLES shortcut to navigate directly to the roles that contain content for your SAP credentials.

31. Select the Crystal Report object from the role folder where you published it.

32. Click NEXT.

33. Select the SWITCH TO FIELDS option.

34. Add the two fields from the group summary (see Figure 9.57).

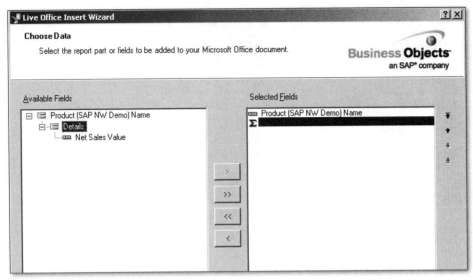

Figure 9.57 Live Office Insert Wizard.

35. Click NEXT.

36. Click NEXT.

37. Click FINISH.

38. The data from the underlying source — in our example, an SAP NetWeaver BW query — is shown as live content in Microsoft Excel.

39. Follow the menu path LIVE OFFICE • PROPERTIES FOR ALL OBJECTS.

40. Select the Crystal Reports object in the list.

41. Navigate to the PROMPTS tab .

42. Select the parameter in the list and click the PARAMETER VALUES button.

43. Select the CHOOSE EXCEL DATA RANGE option.

44. Click the ▦ button next to the CHOOSE EXCEL DATA RANGE option and select cell A1 in SHEET 2 of the spreadsheet. Remember, we selected cells A1 to B1 in SHEET 2 for the PORTAL DATA PROVIDER in the Xcelsius map. A1 is the key for the COUNTRY characteristic.

45. Click OK.

46. Click OK.

47. Follow the menu path LIVE OFFICE • PUBLISH TO BUSINESSOBJECTS ENTERPRISE • SAVE TO BUSINESSOBJECTS ENTERPRISE to save our Live Office document to the BusinessObjects Enterprise system so that we can leverage it with Xcelsius.

48. Start the Xcelsius designer via the menu path: START • PROGRAMS • XCELSIUS • XCELSIUS 2008.

49. In the Xcelsius designer, follow the menu path: DATA • IMPORT FROM ENTERPRISE.

50. Log on to your BusinessObjects Enterprise system.

51. Select the Live Office document we created in the previous steps.

52. Follow the menu path DATA • CONNECTIONS.

53. CLICK THE ADD button.

54. Select LIVE OFFICE CONNECTIONS.

55. On the DEFINITION tab in the SESSION URL, replace the <webserver> place-holder with the name of your application server.

56. Click the ▨ button next to TRIGGER CELL and select cell A1 in SHEET 2 of the spreadsheet.

57. Set the WHEN VALUE CHANGES option .

58. Use the ADD button to add a PORTAL DATA connection.

59. Set the CONNECTION TYPE to CONSUMER.

60. Enter Consumer as the RANGE NAME.

61. Set the RANGE TYPE to ROW.

62. Click the ▨ button next to RANGE and select cells A1 to B1 in the second sheet (see Figure 9.58)

63. CLICK CLOSE.

64. Drag and drop a column chart to the canvas.

65. Right-click the column chart and select PROPERTIES.

66. Enter Net Sales by Product as the TITLE and remove the SUBTITLE.

67. Select the BY SERIES option and use the "+" symbol to add a new series.

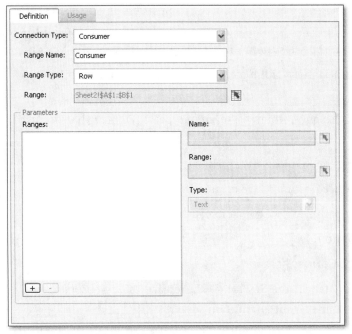

Figure 9.58 Portal Data — Consumer

68. Click the ▣ button next to VALUES (Y) and select cells B2 to B50 in our Live Office document.

69. Click the ▣ button next to CATEGORY LABELS (X) and select cells A2 to A50 in our Live Office document.

70. Navigate to the BEHAVIOR tab and set the IN SERIES and IN VALUES options.

71. Navigate to the APPEARANCE tab and select the TEXT tab.

72. Select HORIZONTAL (CATEGORY) AXIS LABELS.

73. Set the FONT size to 8.

74. Follow the menu path FILE • EXPORT • BUSINESSOBJECTS PLATFORM to export your Xcelsius design to the BusinessObjects Enterprise system.

75. Follow the menu path FILE • SAVE TO ENTERPRISE to save the actual design of your dashboard to the BusinessObjects Enterprise system as well.

76. Start InfoView.

77. Log on with your SAP credentials using SAP authentication.

78. Select DOCUMENT LIST.

79. Follow the menu path DASHBOARDS • MY DASHBOARDS.

80. Select the SALES DASHBOARD we created previously.

81. Click the EDIT DASHBOARD button.

82. Click the +ADD A NEW TAB button.

83. Enter `Navigation Example` as the TITLE.

84. Click OK.

85. Select the NAVIGATION EXAMPLE tab.

86. Click the EDIT DASHBOARD button.

87. Select the LAYOUT option TEMPLATE.

88. Select the 2 COLUMNS template.

89. Activate the SCALE WIDTH and SCALE HEIGHT options.

90. Click the TOOLBOX button in the Toolbar.

91. Navigate to the CORPORATE ANALYTICS tab in the ANALYTIC TOOLBOX.

92. Drag the Xcelsius object with the map to the left column.

93. Drag the Xcelsius object with the chart to the right column (see Figure 9.59).

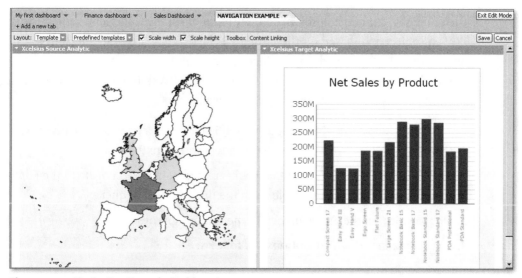

Figure 9.59 Navigation Example Dashboard

94. Click the CONTENT LINKING button in the toolbar.

95. Select the Xcelsius object with the map as SOURCE ANALYTICS and then activate the checkbox for the Xcelsius object with the column chart (see Figure 9.60).

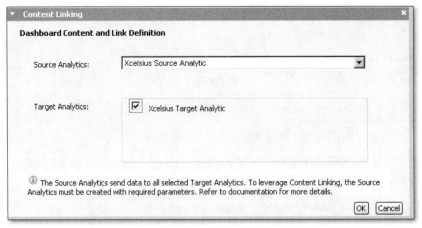

Figure 9.60   Content Linking

96. Click OK.

97. Click SAVE.

98. Click EXIT EDIT MODE.

Each time you click on a different country in the map, the value sent to the second Xcelsius object and, based on the design we created, is picked up and sent to the underlying Live Office and Crystal Reports documents to refresh the data. In addition to the Xcelsius column chart, we will now create Web Intelligence and Crystal Reports objects and link them to the Xcelsius object.

1. Follow the steps described in section 4.3.5 and create a new OLAP Universe on top of the SAP NetWeaver BW query shown in Figure 9.46.

2. In the Universe designer with the newly created universe, navigate to the Filter that was created for the variable from the underlying BW query.

3. Double-click on the FILTER object to open the properties.

4. The syntax in the WHERE option is as follows:

```
<OPTIONAL><FILTER KEY="[!V000001]"><CONDITION OPERATORCONDITION="Equa
l"><CONSTANT   TECH_NAME="@Prompt('VAR_COUNTRY','A','Country\LovVAR_
COUNTRYBase',mono,primary_key)"/></CONDITION></FILTER></OPTIONAL>
```

5. As you can see, the prompt name is VAR_COUNTRY, which is also the technical name of the variable in the BW query. We will need to leverage the technical name of the prompt later on.

6. Export the Universe to BusinessObjects Enterprise.

7. Start InfoView.

8. Log on with your SAP credentials using SAP authentication.

9. Select DOCUMENT LIST.

10. Follow the menu path: NEW • WEB INTELLIGENCE DOCUMENT.

11. Select the universe that we created previously.

12. Add L01 CAL. YEAR/MONTH and NET SALES to the RESULT OBJECTS (see Figure 9.61).

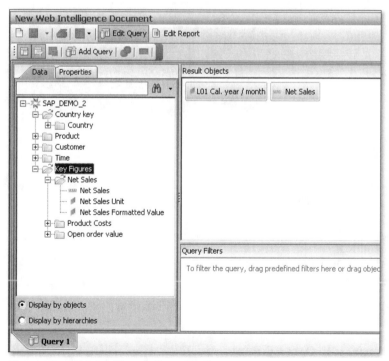

Figure 9.61 Web Intelligence Query Panel

13. Click EDIT REPORT.

14. Remove the table from the report.

15. Drag and drop a BAR CHART from the TEMPLATES tab to your report.

16. Use L01 CAL. YEAR/MONTH as a dimension and NET SALES as a measure for the chart.

17. Remove the REPORT TITLE and place the chart in the top-left corner of the report.

18. Click REFRESH DATA.

19. Leave the list of values for the parameter empty for now and click REFRESH DATA (see Figure 9.62).

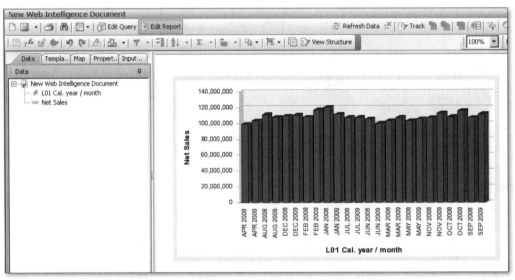

Figure 9.62 Web Intelligence Report

20. Save the Web Intelligence report to your BusinessObjects Enterprise system.

21. Start the Xcelsius designer via the menu path START • PROGRAMS • XCELSIUS • XCELSIUS 2008.

22. In the Xcelsius designer reopen the Xcelsius dashboard we created that contains the map.

23. Follow the menu path DATA • CONNECTIONS.

24. Use the ADD button and select the FS COMMAND option from the list.

25. Select the newly created connection.

26. Enter `queryparams` as the COMMAND.

27. Click the ⬛ button next to PARAMETERS and select cell A3 in our SHEET 2 of the embedded spreadsheet (see Figure 9.63).

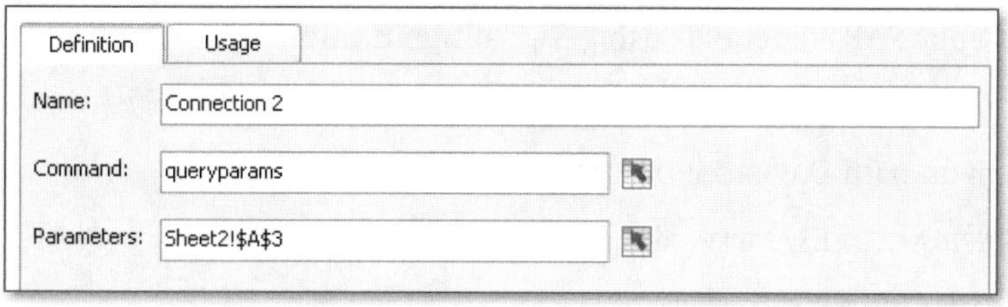

Definition	Usage		
Name:	Connection 2		
Command:	queryparams		⬛
Parameters:	Sheet2!$A$3		⬛

Figure 9.63 Connection Properties

28. Navigate to the USAGE tab.

29. Click the ⬛ button next to TRIGGER CELL and select cell A1 in SHEET 2 of the embedded spreadsheet. Remember, we store the map values in cells A1 and B1 in SHEET 2.

30. Select the WHEN VALUE CHANGES option.

31. Click CLOSE.

32. Enter the following formula into cell A3 in SHEET 2 of the embedded spreadsheet:

```
="&lsSVAR_COUNTRY="&Sheet2!A1
```

- ▶ The syntax `lsS` is part of the standard syntax of the web application Open Document.
- ▶ `VAR_COUNTRY` is the name of our parameter.
- ▶ Cell A1 stores the key value from the selected country.

Open Document

Open Document is a standard application with a set of standard parameters for calling content objects such as Web Intelligence, Crystal Reports, or Xcelsius from the BusinessObjects Enterprise system. You can find more details about the standard syntax at *http://help.sap.com* under the BusinessObjects category.

33. Follow the menu path FILE • EXPORT • BUSINESSOBJECTS PLATFORM to export your Xcelsius design to the BusinessObjects Enterprise system. In this case, overwrite the existing version.

34. Follow the menu path FILE • SAVE TO ENTERPRISE to save the actual design of your dashboard to the BusinessObjects Enterprise system as well.

35. Start InfoView.

36. Log on with your SAP credentials using SAP authentication.

37. Select DOCUMENT LIST.

38. Follow the menu path DASHBOARDS • MY DASHBOARDS.

39. Select the NAVIGATION EXAMPLE tab.

40. Click the EDIT DASHBOARD button.

41. Use the SPLIT HORIZONTALLY option in the heading toolbar of the Xcelsius object displaying the chart (see Figure 9.64).

Figure 9.64 Split Horizontally

42. Click the TOOLBOX button in the toolbar.

43. Navigate to the CORPORATE ANALYTICS tab in the ANALYTIC TOOLBOX.

44. Drag and drop the Web Intelligence report that we created to the empty space in the right column.

45. When the Web Intelligence report appears, right-click on the chart in the report and use the SELECT THIS REPORT PART menu item.

46. Click CONTENT LINKING in the toolbar.

47. Activate the checkbox next to the Web Intelligence report (see Figure 9.65).

48. Click OK.

49. Click SAVE.

50. Click EXIT EDIT MODE.

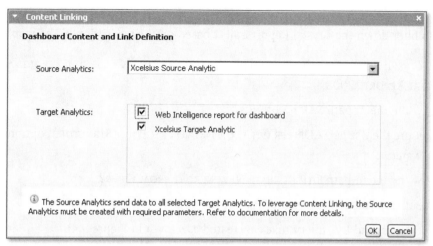

Figure 9.65 Content Linking

51. Now each time you select a different country in the map, not only is Xcelsius filtered but the Web Intelligence report as well (see Figure 9.66).

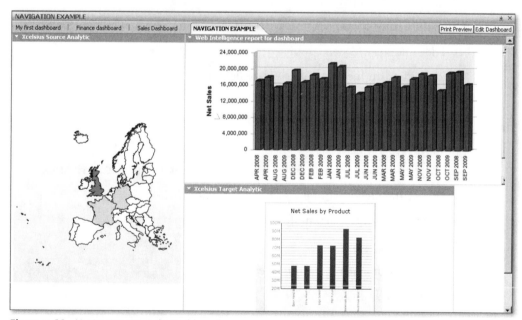

Figure 9.66 Navigation Example Dashboard

Finally, we'll create a Crystal Report object and leverage the same logic as previously to filter down the Crystal Report object based on the navigation in the map.

1. Start Crystal Reports via the menu path: START • PROGRAMS • CRYSTAL REPORTS • CRYSTAL REPORTS 2008.

2. Follow the menu path SAP • SETTINGS.

3. Make sure the USE MDX DRIVER WITH SUPPORT FOR MULTIPLE STRUCTURES option is activated.

4. Follow the menu path SAP • CREATE NEW REPORT FROM QUERY.

5. Authenticate yourself for your SAP NetWeaver BW system.

6. Select the second BW query that we created as shown in Figure 9.46.

7. Add the following fields to the DETAILS section of your report:

   ▸ SOLD-TO PARTY (SAP NW DEMO) NAME

   ▸ NET SALES VALUE

8. Follow the menu path INSERT • GROUP.

9. Use the SOLD-TO PARTY (SAP NW DEMO) NAME field as the field to group on.

10. Click OK.

11. Right-click on the NET SALES VALUE field and follow the menu path: INSERT • SUMMARY.

12. Select SUM and select GROUP#1 as the summary location.

13. Click OK.

14. Move the summary field from the GROUP FOOTER to the GROUP HEADER.

15. Follow the menu path REPORT • SECTION EXPERT.

16. Select the DETAILS section from the list.

17. Activate SUPPRESS.

18. Select GROUP FOOTER #1 from the list.

19. Activate SUPPRESS.

20. Click OK.

21. Follow the menu path INSERT • CHART and place the chart in the report header.

22. Follow the menu path VIEW • PRINT PREVIEW. Your report should look similar to Figure 9.67.

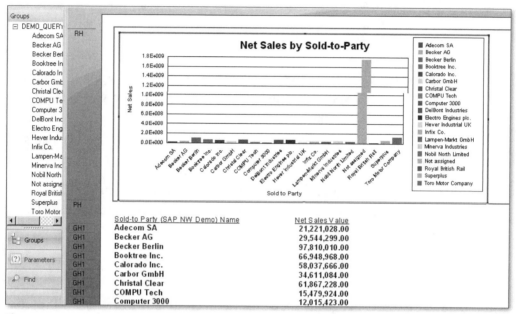

Figure 9.67 Crystal Reports Preview

23. Follow the menu path: REPORT • GROUP SORT EXPERT.

24. Select the TOP N option.

25. Set the value for N to 10.

26. Click OK.

27. Select VIEW • FIELD EXPLORER and open the list of Parameter fields. Take note of the parameter names, which in our example is the name of the SAP variable with [ ] brackets around the name (see Figure 9.68).

Figure 9.68 Field Explorer

28. Follow the menu path SAP • Save Report to save the report to your SAP NetWeaver BW system and then to publish the report to your BusinessObjects Enterprise system.

29. After you've published the report, make sure you can view it using your SAP credentials and the SAP authentication mode in InfoView.

The name of the prompt in Crystal Reports is different from that in Web Intelligence. Therefore, we need to add another Portal Data connectivity to our Xcelsius object.

1. Start the Xcelsius designer via the menu path Start • Programs • Xcelsius • Xcelsius 2008.

2. In the Xcelsius designer, reopen the Xcelsius dashboard we created that contains the map.

3. Concatenate the following formula into cell A3 in Sheet 2 of the embedded spreadsheet:

```
&"&lsS[VAR_COUNTRY]="&Sheet2!A1
```

4. Your complete formula should look similar to the following:

```
="&lsSVAR_COUNTRY="&Sheet2!A1&"&lsS[VAR_COUNTRY]="&Sheet2!A1
```

5. Use the menu path File • Export • BusinessObjects platform to export your Xcelsius design to the BusinessObjects Enterprise system. In this case, overwrite the existing version.

6. Follow the menu path File • Save to Enterprise to save the actual design of your dashboard to the BusinessObjects Enterprise system as well.

7. Start InfoView.

8. Log on with your SAP credentials using SAP authentication.

9. Select the item Document List.

10. Follow the menu path: Dashboards • My Dashboards.

11. Select the Navigation Example tab.

12. Click the Edit Dashboard button.

13. Use the Split Horizontally option in the heading toolbar of the Xcelsius object displaying the map.

14. Click the Toolbox button in the toolbar.

15. Navigate to the Corporate Analytics tab in the Analytic Toolbox.

16. Drag and drop the Crystal Reports report that we created to the empty space in the left column.

17. Click Content Linking in the toolbar.

18. Activate the checkbox next to the Crystal Reports object as well.

19. Click OK.

20. Click Save.

21. Click Exit Edit Mode.

Now each time you select a different country in the map, not only is the Xcelsius object filtered but the Web Intelligence and Crystal Reports objects are filtered as well.

9.5 Summary

In this chapter, we used Dashboard Builder in conjunction with Xcelsius, Web Intelligence, and Crystal Reports to provide our users with an interactive and compelling user experience by linking content together. You learned how to create your own dashboards, how to create new analytics based on SAP data sources, and how to link the content together based on common filter values.

In this chapter, we'll discuss the functionality of InfoView and its tools, including Search, Discussions, and Encyclopedia.

10   Using BusinessObjects InfoView

Now let's turn our attention to InfoView and how you can use it to perform common tasks such as viewing, editing, or scheduling a report.

10.1   InfoView — Introduction

InfoView is a web-based environment that lets you perform common tasks, such as viewing or scheduling a report, without having to deploy any software on your client computer. InfoView provides you with all of the end user functionality out of the box and provides your end users with access to the functionality in your BusinessObjects system.

In the following sections, we'll take a step-by-step look at the most common tasks using InfoView. In addition, we'll look at the InfoView features that are only available when you deploy the BusinessObjects Integration for SAP solutions.

10.2   InfoView — User Authentication

In this section, we'll look at user authentication for your BusinessObjects system using InfoView.

1. Launch InfoView via the URL *http://<Application Server>:<port>/InfoViewApp* (see Figure 10.1) or you can follow the menu path: START • PROGRAMS • BUSINESS-OBJECTS XI 3.1 • BUSINESSOBJECTS ENTERPRISE • BUSINESSOBJECTS ENTERPRISE JAVA INFOVIEW.

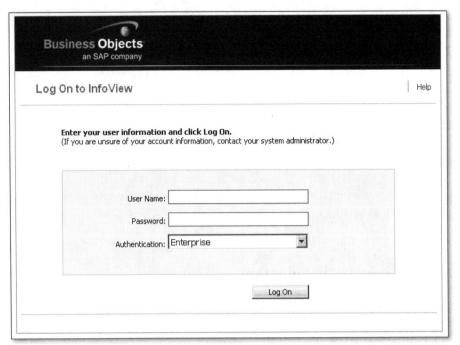

Figure 10.1   InfoView User Authentication

2. Select SAP as the AUTHENTICATION from the list (see Figure 10.2).

3. The logon dialog is being changed and we can now enter our SAP credentials, SAP System ID, and SAP client number; a prerequisite for SAP authentication to work is the deployment of the BusinessObjects Integration for SAP solutions and the successful configuration of the SAP authentication in the Central Management Console (CMC).

4. In cases where you see a logon screen for your BusinessObjects system that doesn't ask for an SAP system ID and an SAP client number, you can use the following syntax: <SAP System ID>~<SAP client number>/<SAP user ID>, for example CIM~800/DEMO.

If your BusinessObjects system landscape administrator has defined a default SAP system for SAP authentication, which can be configured in the Options tab in the SAP authentication of the CMC, and you would like to log on to the default system, you don't have to enter the SAP System ID and SAP client number because the BusinessObjects system will then try to verify your user ID for the default system. It is recommended to always enter the SAP System ID and SAP client number for authentication.

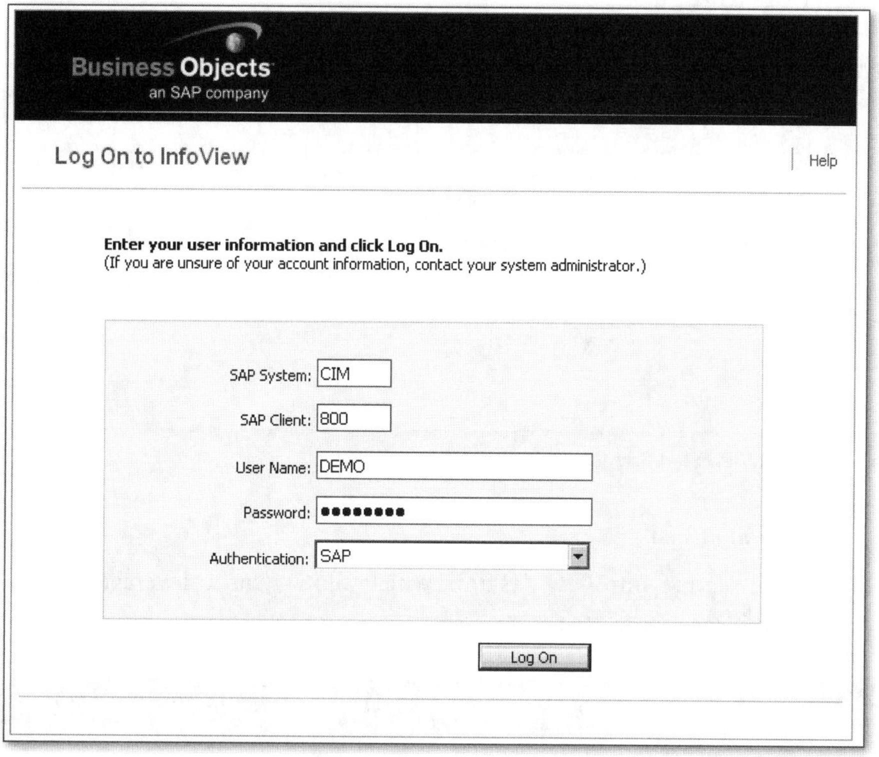

Figure 10.2 SAP Authentication for InfoView

5. Click LOGON to authenticate yourself for the BusinessObjects system.

Configuration via Web.xml

As shown in Figure 10.1, the InfoView logon screen shows the USER NAME, PASSWORD, and AUTHENTICATION. You can configure the options to be visible or not in the web. xml file. In case of a default installation on Windows with Tomcat used as application server, the file can be found at \Program Files\Business Objects\Tomcat55\webapps\InfoViewApp\WEB-INF.

10.3   InfoView — Web Desktop Overview

In this section, we'll look at some of the common tasks and menus in InfoView.

1. After you authenticate your BusinessObjects system, you will see the initial screen (see Figure 10.3).

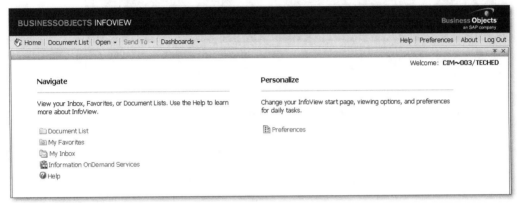

Figure 10.3   InfoView Start Screen

2. Click Document List.

3. Next, you'll see the InfoView desktop, which allows you to leverage the full functionality (see Figure 10.4).

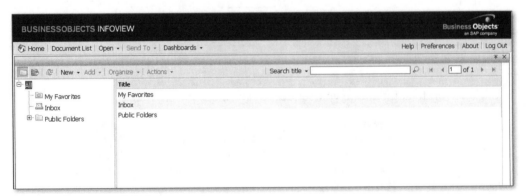

Figure 10.4   InfoView

In the toolbar, there are several menu items:

▶ With the symbols [□][📂] you can switch between a view by folder structure or a view by categories. Each report object is stored in a folder and can be assigned to a category.

▶ With the NEW menu (see Figure 10.5) you can create new content objects, such as a new Web Intelligence report. The list of content types depends on the license for your BusinessObjects system.

▶ The ADD menu lets you upload a local Crystal Report document or a local file, such as Microsoft Excel or Microsoft PowerPoint, or other file types (see Figure 10.6).

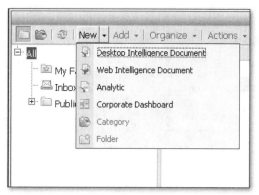

Figure 10.5 InfoView Menu — New

Figure 10.6 InfoView Menu — Add

▶ The Organize menu lets you cut, copy, and paste objects and create shortcuts for objects (see Figure 10.7).

▶ The Actions menu lets you perform actions like viewing a report. The list of actions you can perform depends on the actual object type (see Figure 10.8).

▶ The Open menu (see Figure 10.9) lets you open My InfoView (see Section 10.9, InfoView — My InfoView), Encyclopedia (see Section 10.11, InfoView — Using Encyclopedia), and Dashboards (see Chapter 9, Combining Content into Dashboards).

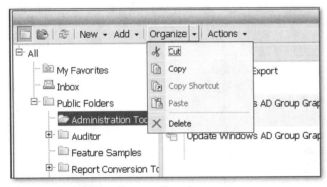

Figure 10.7 InfoView Menu — Organize

Figure 10.8 InfoView Menu — Actions

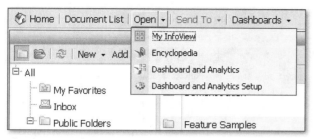

Figure 10.9 InfoView Menu — Open

10.4   InfoView — Folders and Categories

InfoView organizes objects by folders and categories. You can switch views between the folder structure and the categories using the buttons on the far left of the toolbar [ ]. When storing an object in your BusinessObjects system, only Web Intelligence offers you the option of assigning the report to a category. For Crystal Reports objects, this needs to be configured after the objects have been saved to your BusinessObjects system.

To assign a category to Crystal Reports objects, follow these steps:

1. Launch InfoView using the URL *http://<Application Server>:<port>/InfoViewApp* (see Figure 10.1) or as an alternative you can follow the menu path START • PROGRAMS • BUSINESSOBJECTS XI 3.1 • BUSINESSOBJECTS ENTERPRISE • BUSINESS-OBJECTS ENTERPRISE JAVA INFOVIEW.

2. Select SAP as AUTHENTICATION from the list.

3. Enter your credentials and click LOGON.

4. Navigate to the folder for the objects we created in the previous chapters.

5. Right-click on the Crystal Reports object and select CATEGORIES (or follow the ACTIONS • CATEGORIES menu path (see Figure 10.10).

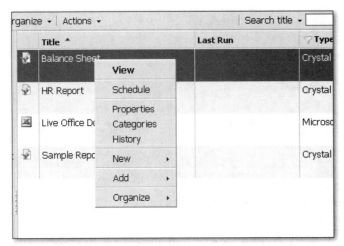

Figure 10.10 Assigning Categories

6. The list of available CATEGORIES is shown and you can select one (see Figure 10.11).

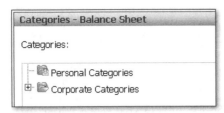

Figure 10.11 Categories

7. Select a CATEGORY and click OK.

If you want to create new folders or categories, follow these steps:

1. In InfoView, click the ⬜ 🖿 buttons in the toolbar to switch to a FOLDER view or a CATEGORY view.

2. Navigate to where you want to create a new folder or category.

3. Select the NEW menu and FOLDER to create a new folder or select CATEGORY to create a new category (see Figure 10.12).

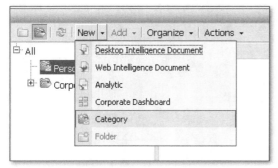

Figure 10.12 Creating a New Category

Folders, Categories, and SAP Roles

You can use the folders and categories to organize all of the content in your BusinessObjects system. Keep in mind that, if you use Crystal Reports with the publishing integration for SAP NetWeaver Business Warehouse (BW), you'll also be able to leverage the SAP role structure in the BusinessObjects system for organizing the content (see Section 10.8, InfoView — Integration for SAP Solutions).

10.5   InfoView — Setting User Preferences

In InfoView, each user can configure a set of preferences based on the credentials used for authentication. These preferences have an impact on how the system behaves in several areas. The preferences let you configure which viewers to use for Crystal Reports and Web Intelligence, how many objects to display by default in the list of objects, which language to use, and several other items.

1. In InfoView, click the Preferences button in the toolbar to open up the list of PREFERENCES the user is able to configure.

2. Open the GENERAL category in PREFERENCES (see Figure 10.13).

3. In the GENERAL category, you can (see Figure 10.13 and Figure 10.14):

   ▶ pick the START PAGE for InfoView.

   ▶ configure the initial view to be based on FOLDERS or CATEGORIES.

   ▶ set the NUMBER OF OBJECTS displayed per page.

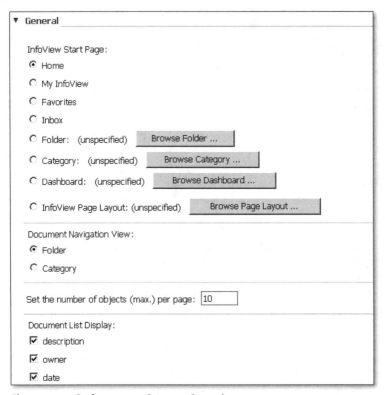

Figure 10.13 Preferences — Category General

- ▶ configure the information shown per object.

- ▶ configure how documents are viewed — in place or in a new window.

- ▶ set the product local, which requires the installation of language packs for BusinessObjects.

- ▶ configure the time zone.

- ▶ configure PREFERRED VIEWING LOCAL, which is important because Preferred Viewing Local is used to replace the SAP logon language when viewing a report, and therefore it can influence the data that is being shown in that one user can view the report in German and another in English, assuming the objects in the report have been translated in your SAP system or by using the Translation Manager from BusinessObjects.

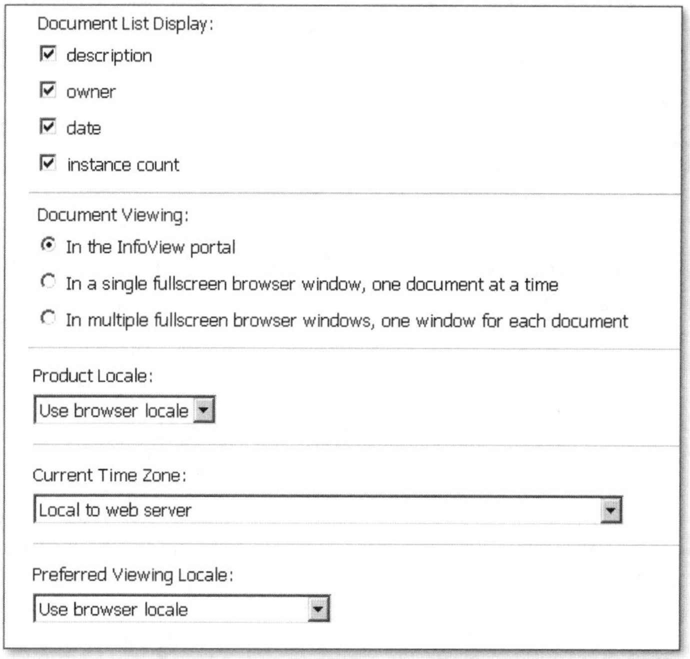

Document List Display:
- ☑ description
- ☑ owner
- ☑ date
- ☑ instance count

Document Viewing:
- ◉ In the InfoView portal
- ○ In a single fullscreen browser window, one document at a time
- ○ In multiple fullscreen browser windows, one window for each document

Product Locale:

| Use browser locale ▾ |

Current Time Zone:

| Local to web server ▾ |

Preferred Viewing Locale:

| Use browser locale ▾ |

Figure 10.14   Preferences — Category General

Preferred Viewing Local and SAP Logon Language

BusinessObjects Enterprise offers a large set of preferred viewing languages, including specific options like English (U.S.) and English (Canada). You can map the preferred viewing language to an SAP logon language code. As part of the BusinessObjects Integration for SAP solutions, you can leverage a file (default path for Windows environments: *\Program Files\Business Objects\Integration Kit for SAP 12.0\PVL Mapping*) named DefaultMapping.properties, where you can assign a SAP logon language to a preferred viewing language.

4. Close the GENERAL category and open the CHANGE PASSWORD category (see Figure 10.15).

5. This category lets you change the password to your account. Keep in mind that for users imported from your SAP system, the password is configured on the SAP system.

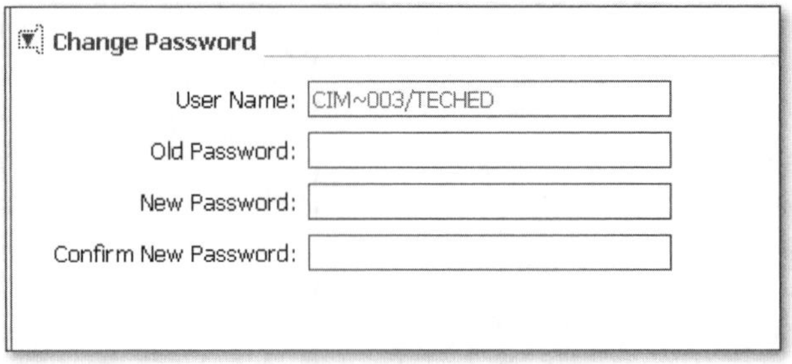

Figure 10.15 Preferences —Change Password Category

6. Open the WEB INTELLIGENCE category (see Figure 10.16).

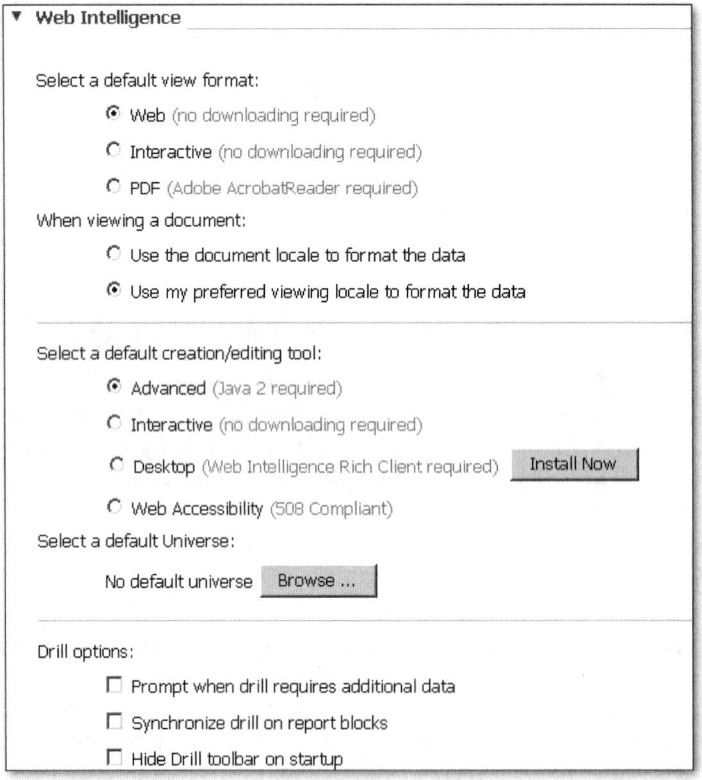

Figure 10.16 Preferences —Web Intelligence Category

7. In WEB INTELLIGENCE, you can influence the behavior of your Web Intelligence deployment.

8. VIEW FORMAT lets you specify if you would like to work with the WEB View format, INTERACTIVE, or view the content as a PDF (see Chapter 4, Section 4.5, Web Intelligence — Quick Basics, for details).

9. The option to select the locale lets you use your PREFERRED VIEWING LOCALE or the locale where the report was created.

10. DRILL OPTIONS lets you configure the behavior for drill operations in Web Intelligence.

   ▶ The PROMPT WHEN DRILL REQUIRES ADDITIONAL DATA option lets you configure a kind of warning message and prompt for you in case the drill operation results in a query for more data.

   ▶ The SYNCHRONIZE DRILL ON REPORT BLOCKS option lets you specify if all items in your report should be synchronized when you perform a drill operation.

11. With regard to the DESKTOP INTELLIGENCE category, you can decide which view format you would like to leverage for Desktop Intelligence (see Figure 10.17).

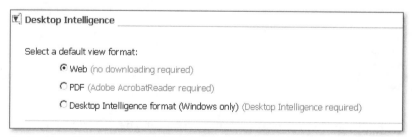

Figure 10.17 Preferences —Desktop Intelligence Category

Desktop Intelligence and SAP NetWeaver BW

Remember, Online Analytical Processing (OLAP) Universes are not supported in Desktop Intelligence.

12. In CRYSTAL REPORTS, you can set several options for using Crystal Reports (see Figure 10.18):

    ▸ You can decide which view format you prefer: DHTML, Active X, or Java.

    ▸ You can configure between a PDF-based printing and an Active X plug-in for printing.

    ▸ You can configure the resolution and the default measuring unit.

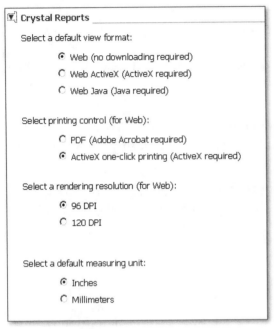

Figure 10.18 Preferences —Crystal Reports Category

13. The settings in the DASHBOARDS AND ANALYTICS category provide you with several settings to influence the view-time experience when using analytics created with the Dashboard Builder (see Figure 10.19).

14. In the VOYAGER category you can specify the default connection for creating a new Voyager workspace.

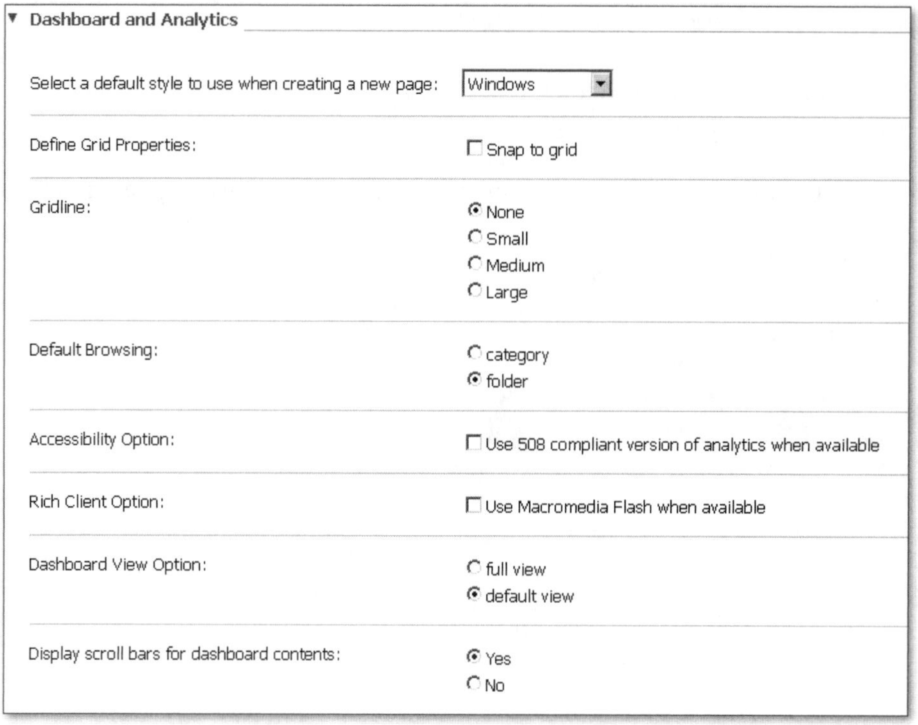

Figure 10.19 Preferences — Dashboard and Analytics

15. The SAP PREFERENCES category (see Figure 10.20) lets you specify if the parameter description in the SAP-specific prompting user interface (UI) in InfoView should be shown or not. This category is only available after you install the BusinessObjects Integration for SAP solution.

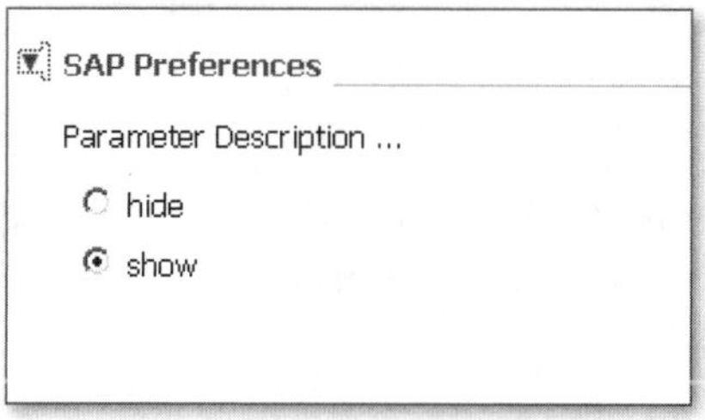

Figure 10.20 Preferences — SAP Preferences

10.6   InfoView — Using Objects

When using objects in InfoView, there are several actions you can take and several options for calling these actions.

1. In InfoView, navigate to the folder that contains the objects we've created so far.

2. Select one of the Crystal Reports objects.

3. Right-click on the Crystal Reports object (see Figure 10.21).

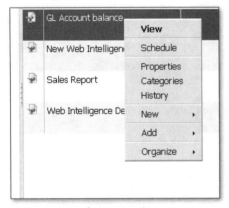

Figure 10.21   InfoView — Object Actions

4. Using the right-click menu, you can:

   ▶ VIEW and SCHEDULE the report.

   ▶ See the PROPERTIES of the report.

   ▶ Configure the CATEGORY assignment.

   ▶ See the HISTORY with a list of prescheduled reports (instances).

   ▶ Leverage the right-click menu options NEW, ADD, and ORGANIZE. These menus are identical to the NEW, ADD, and ORGANIZE menus in the toolbar.

5. Select the ORGANIZE menu (see Figure 10.22).

6. With the ORGANIZE menu you can create a copy from a report object or create a shortcut from an existing report. A shortcut provides you with a link to the original report, so you can leverage any changes to the original report. In cases

where you create a copy of the original report you are creating a physical copy, and changes to the original report are not incorporated into your own copy.

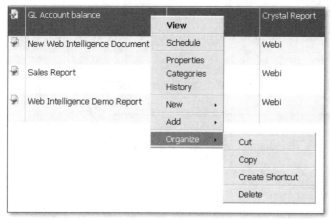

Figure 10.22 InfoView — Menu Organize

7. Right-click the report and select SCHEDULE.

8. The scheduling dialog lets you configure a process to execute the report as a batch process, and you can define criteria such as RECURRENCE, PARAMETERS, FILTERS, DATABASE LOGON, and others (see Figure 10.23).

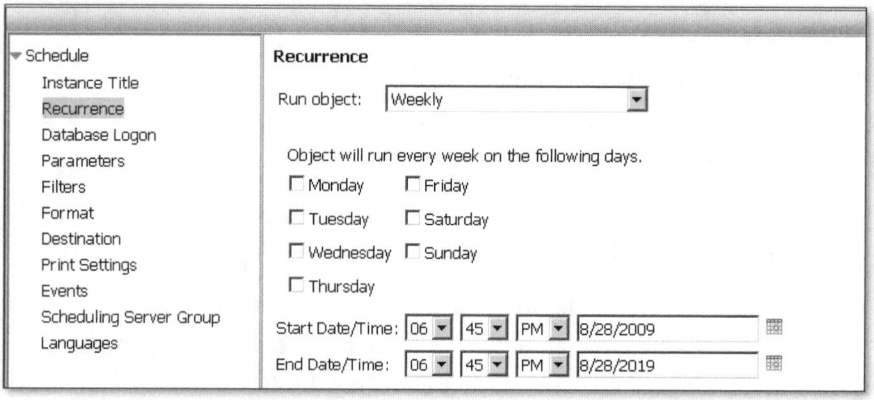

Figure 10.23 InfoView — Scheduling

9. After the scheduling process has finished, the report is available in the HISTORY.

10.7   InfoView — Search

In addition to all of the previously mentioned options that InfoView provides you, you can also search for objects. The search in InfoView lets you search for an object based on several criteria, such as the report title, report keywords, report owner, and several others.

1. In InfoView, navigate to the SEARCH dialog (see Figure 10.24).

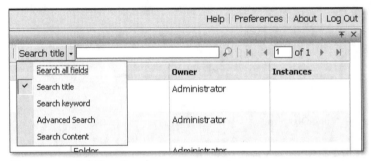

Figure 10.24   InfoView Search

2. You can select different options to become the default search options. By default, the search will only search for content objects in the folder that you select. In cases where you need to broaden the search, you can use the ADVANCED SEARCH option.

3. Select the ADVANCED SEARCH option (see Figure 10.25).

4. With the ADVANCED SEARCH option you can search based on several criteria and across folders and categories in a single step.

5. The most advanced search option is to search not by keywords or the title of the report, but a search based on the actual content of the report.

6. To enable this type of search, you first need to schedule the SEARCH INDEXING PROGRAM. In a default installation you will find the program in the SEARCH PROGRAM folder below the PUBLIC FOLDER (see Figure 10.26).

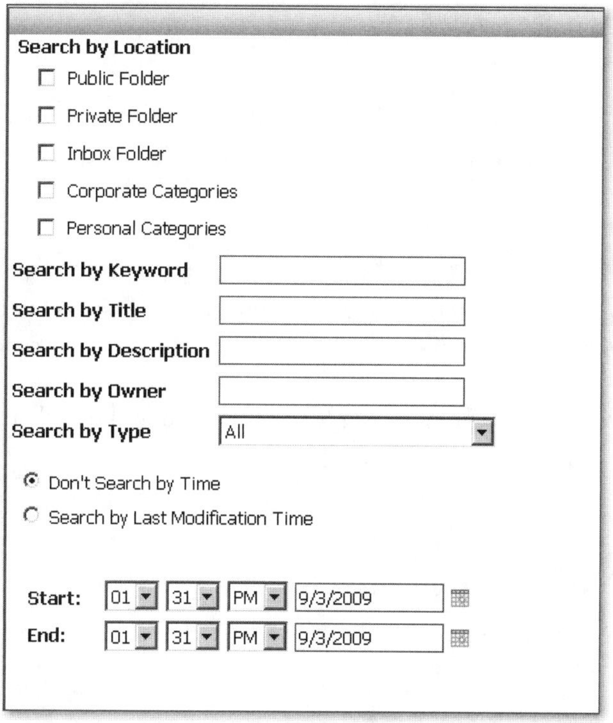

Figure 10.25 InfoView — Advanced Search

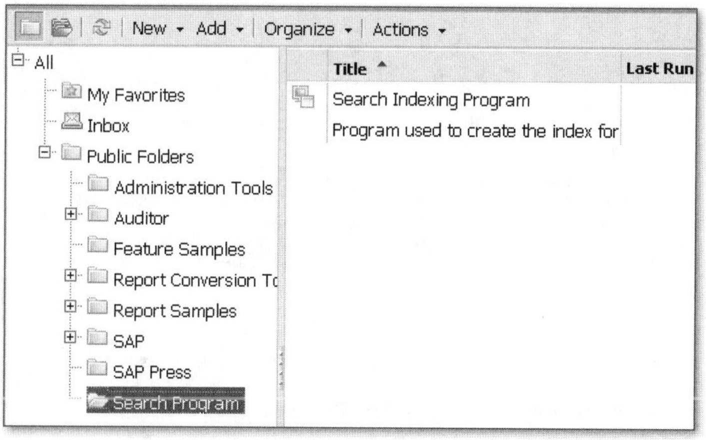

Figure 10.26 Search Indexing Program

7. Right-click on the Search Indexing Program.

8. Select the Schedule menu option.

9. Leave all of the parameters with their default values and press the Schedule button. In a real product environment, you would want to set up a recurring scheduling job for this program.

> **Note**
>
> This is a program that is being executed, so you need to make sure that the Program Job Server is started and enabled on your BusinessObjects system.

10. After the program has successfully finished, set the search type in the toolbar to the Search Content option (see Figure 10.27).

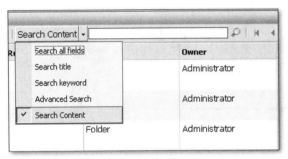

Figure 10.27 InfoView Search Options

11. Type USA as a search term and you will see a screen that looks similar to Figure 10.28.

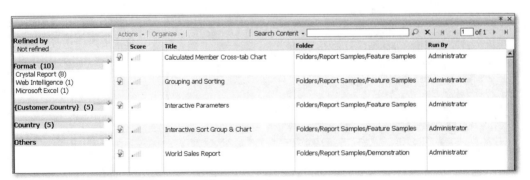

Figure 10.28 InfoView Content Search Result

Not only does the search show the reports by content type and country, it also makes suggestions for other reports (see Figure 10.29).

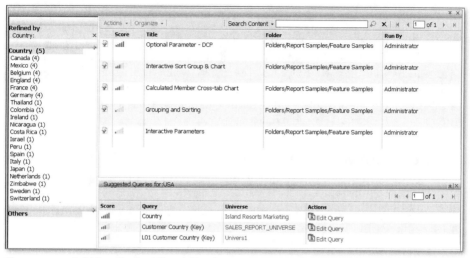

Figure 10.29 InfoView Content Search Results

10.8 InfoView — Integration for SAP Solutions

After you install and deploy the SAP BusinessObjects Integration for SAP solutions, you can leverage some specific features in InfoView.

The most notable feature is the MY GROUPS entry in the InfoView folder structure (see Figure 10.30).

Figure 10.30 InfoView — My Groups

The MY GROUPS entry acts as a shortcut to all of the role folders that have been used to publish Crystal Reports–based content to your BusinessObjects system that the user is allowed to see.

> **Crystal Reports Publishing and Other Content Types**
>
> If you use the publishing integration of Crystal Reports with SAP NetWeaver BW, you'll see that the roles from your SAP NetWeaver BW system will result in folders in the BusinessObjects system. You can also use these role folders to store other content types, such as Web Intelligence or Live Office documents, and that way leverage a well-known structure for the end user based on the roles.

The other specific functionality you will recognize is Crystal Reports–specific and related to the scheduling of Crystal Reports based content (see Figure 10.31).

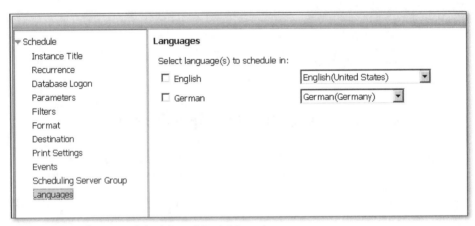

Figure 10.31 InfoView — Scheduling of Crystal Reports

When scheduling a Crystal Reports object that was published from SAP NetWeaver BW with the purpose to be translated, you can schedule the report in InfoView for several languages in a single step.

In addition to the scheduling, you will notice that when viewing Crystal Reports content based on SAP NetWeaver BW, there is a list of values for parameters, which is retrieved online from the underlying SAP NetWeaver BW system (see Figure 10.32). In addition to the list of values, the prompting dialog is also offering the functionality for personalizing variable values.

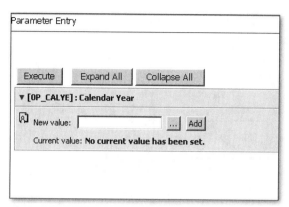

Figure 10.32 Crystal Reports Parameter

10.9 InfoView — My InfoView

The My InfoView functionality creates a small-scaled dashboard-style page in Info-View and each user can create their own page layout, which can be called via MY INFOVIEW.

1. In InfoView, follow the OPEN • MY INFOVIEW menu path (see Figure 10.33).

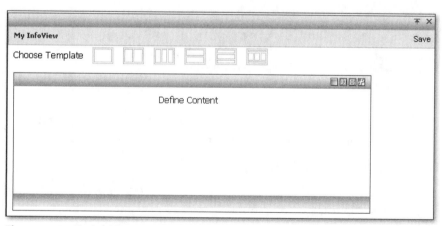

Figure 10.33 My InfoView

2. Next, select a TEMPLATE to define the layout of your page from the list of templates shown in the toolbar.

3. Select the second option with two panels in the page.

4. Click DEFINE CONTENT for the first panel (see Figure 10.34).

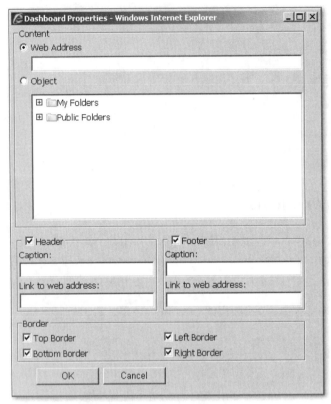

Figure 10.34 Define Content for My InfoView

5. Select the Finance report we created in Chapter 4, Section 4.7, Customer Case Study — Financial Reporting with Web Intelligence.

6. Click DEFINE CONTENT for the right panel.

7. Select the Sales report we created in Chapter 4, Section 4.6, Customer Case Study — Sales Reporting with Web Intelligence (see Figure 10.35).

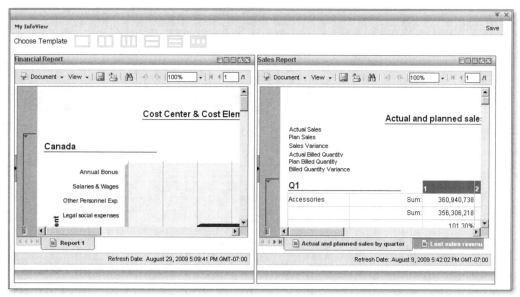

Figure 10.35 My InfoView

8. Click SAVE.

9. Now you can open MY INFOVIEW using the OPEN • MY INFOVIEW menu path and the content will be shown to you.

10. You can also use SAVE AS and save your defined dashboard to your folder structure in the BusinessObjects system so you can leverage more than one custom page layout.

10.10   InfoView — Using Discussions

DISCUSSIONS is an integrated panel in InfoView that lets you create notes and share information about a report in an easy-to-use way.

1. In InfoView, navigate to the reports that we created in our BusinessObjects system.

2. Select one of the report objects.

3. Now open the DISCUSSIONS panel, which is located at the bottom of InfoView (see Figure 10.36).

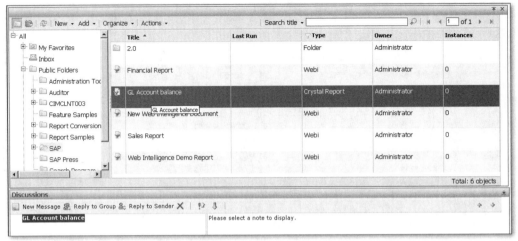

Figure 10.36 InfoView with Discussions Panel

4. You can use the NEW MESSAGE option to create a new message for the report and you can use the REPLY TO GROUP and REPLY TO SENDER options to create responses to entries from other users (see Figure 10.37).

Figure 10.37 Discussions

10.11 InfoView — Using Encyclopedia

Encyclopedia is a feature in InfoView that lets you and your users provide more information about the reporting and analytics content in your BusinessObjects system. You can provide background information to the reporting content and provide suggestions on reports that might be of interest or relevance as well.

1. In InfoView, navigate to the reports that we created in our BusinessObjects system.

2. Select one of the report objects.

3. Follow the OPEN • ENCYCLOPEDIA menu path (see Figure 10.38).

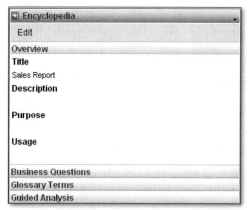

Figure 10.38 Encyclopedia

4. The ENCYCLOPEDIA panel has four main areas: OVERVIEW, BUSINESS QUESTIONS, GLOSSARY TERMS, AND GUIDED ANALYSIS.

5. For our example, let's select the sales report, which we created in Section 4.6.

6. Click EDIT and you can start entering information on the report (see Figure 10.39).

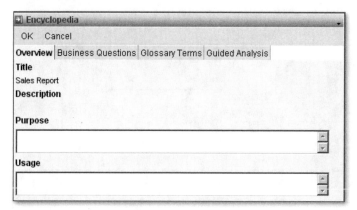

Figure 10.39 Editing Encyclopedia Information

7. Enter a PURPOSE and USAGE for the report.

8. Navigate to the Business Questions tab .

9. Enter a Business Question into the empty Business Questions field.

10. Click New.

11. Move the newly created Business Question from the Available list to the Selected list (see Figure 10.40).

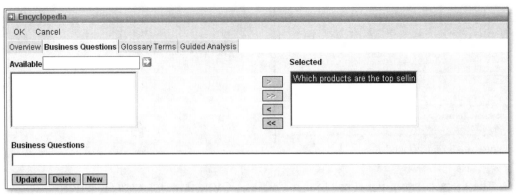

Figure 10.40 Encyclopedia — Business Questions

12. The Business Questions area lets you associate your report with a set of Business Questions that you can define. Each Business Question can be assigned to more than one report.

13. Navigate to the Glossary Terms tab (see Figure 10.41).

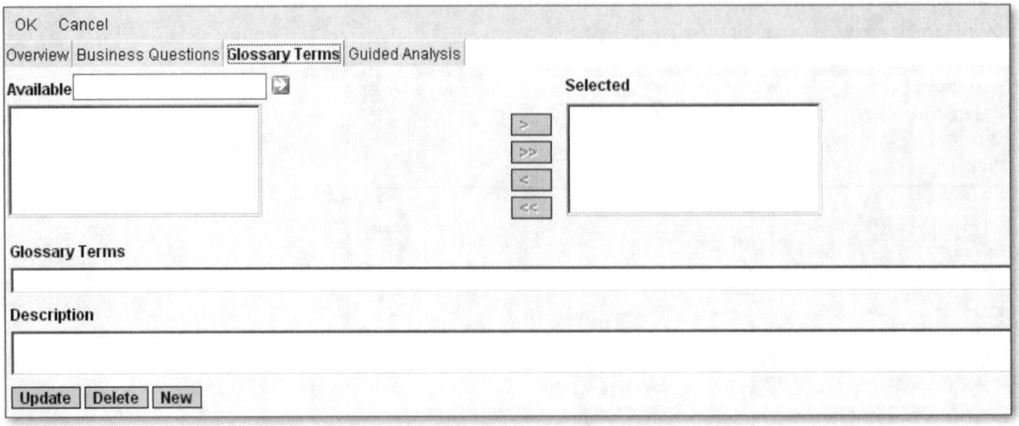

Figure 10.41 Glossary Terms

14. In the GLOSSARY TERMS tab you can define new terms and their definitions and associate them with the report. This is especially helpful for when you create calculations in your report and would like to share how you reached the numbers and how you calculated certain Key Performance Indicators (KPIs).

15. Navigate to the GUIDED ANALYSIS tab. The GUIDED ANALYSIS tab provides you with the opportunity to create a storyline for your report object and to share information with your users (see Figure 10.42).

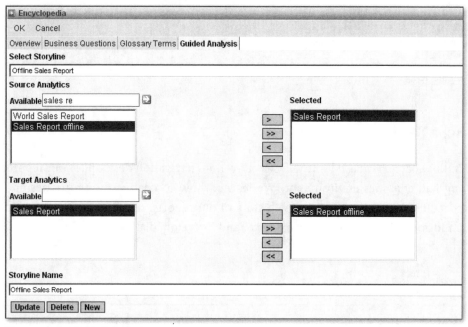

Figure 10.42 Guided Analysis

16. In our example, we used our Web Intelligence sales report as the SOURCE ANALYTICS and the Live Office offline report with Microsoft PowerPoint as the TARGET ANALYTICS to highlight that there is an offline option available.

17. In InfoView, this will look like Figure 10.43.

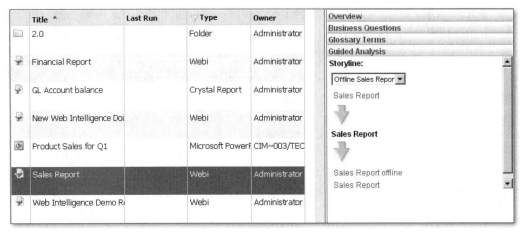

Figure 10.43 Sales Report with Guided Analysis

10.12 Summary

In this chapter, we used InfoView as our central navigation desktop for our reporting and analytics environment. We learned how to change the properties and schedule, and how to review the history of our reports. In addition, we provided an introduction to Discussions, Search, and Encyclopedia.

Understanding the Best Practices for the SAP BusinessObjects Business Intelligence (BI) tools, in conjunction with SAP NetWeaver, will help you leverage the tools and avoid common pitfalls.

11   Best Practices for SAP BusinessObjects BI Tools

In the following sections, we'll look at a set of Best Practices, tips and tricks, and known limitations for data connectivity, Business Warehouse (BW) query design, security, performance, and several other topics. These Best Practices will help you leverage the SAP BusinessObjects BI tools and avoid some common pitfalls. Please note that the information in this chapter is made based on SAP BusinessObjects XI Release Service Pack 2 and that the behavior of the tools might change in future releases.

11.1   Selecting the Right Tool

Before we go into the details of the best practice approach, we should point out that the most important part of your overall project approach is the proper selection of the tools. You should spend time learning a consumer's requirements, needs, and skill level. Based on that information, consider the right tool. Requirements gathering, and fully understanding them, are crucial to your project. Try to speak directly to the consumer as much as possible and let them describe their needs, day-to-day workflows, and how they plan to use the information. Understanding these things is crucial for the success of the project.

For example, if the financial controller describes to you the information he needs every day, you could easily provide him the information with Crystal Reports or Web Intelligence. However, if the financial controller also explains to you that he needs the information as part of his monthly planning, and that he always exports the data from the report to a Microsoft Excel spreadsheet, your solution could change to Live Office — offering the consumer a Microsoft Excel spreadsheet with live data via Live Office.

You can apply as much of the best practice approach as possible in the project, but if the initial step, gathering and understanding the requirements, and the second important step, mapping the tools to the requirements, are not done thoroughly, the project will likely fail because expectations will not be met.

Please keep this in mind when applying these Best Practices and feel free to refer back to Chapter 2, Reporting and Analysis — Customer Case Study, where we discussed customer requirements and how to map the tools to these requirements in more detail.

11.2 SAP NetWeaver BW Query Design

In this section, we will focus on the SAP NetWeaver BW query and how the properties and settings in the BW query influence behavior in the SAP BusinessObjects BI tools. In this section, you won't find BW query design recommendations for performance, because those are included in Section 11.5, Performance Considerations.

11.2.1 Relationship: BW Query and Report

In the past, most customers had a one-to-one relationship (or close to it) between a BW query and a report. In this case, a one-to-one relationship means that you are using a BW query for a single Business Explorer (BEx) Analyzer or BEx web report. These situations lead to lot of administrative overhead and, given the SAP BusinessObjects BI solution, you can now improve this situation.

The BI tools are able to explicitly select only elements from the BW query (see Section 11.5) and therefore there is no need for a one-to-one relationship between a BW query and a report created with the SAP BusinessObjects BI tools

On the other hand, this does not mean that you can now create a single BW query on top of each InfoProvider and leverage this single BW query for all of your reporting needs. The impact of such a BW query regarding performance has been improved, but you'll still see a difference in performance between such a large BW query and a more dedicated BW query. Therefore, it is recommended that you create BW queries that represent the common denominator. You should try to break down the requirements of your BW environment into groups of characteristics and key figures that represent a high commonality, but also represent a manageable number of BW queries. If you're not sure if the BW queries that you create are too large in terms of number of elements, you can easily use the tools to trace the runtime of your BW queries and then take the necessary steps to make the required changes.

11.2.2 Elements of an SAP NetWeaver BW Query

A BW query can contain elements in the following sections (see Figure 11.1):

- ▸ Rows
- ▸ Columns
- ▸ Free Characteristics
- ▸ Filter/Characteristic Restrictions
- ▸ Default Values (new in SAP NetWeaver BI 7.x)

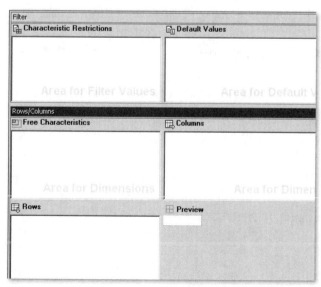

Figure 11.1 SAP NetWeaver BW Query Designer

When you use an SAP NetWeaver BW query in conjunction with the SAP Business-Objects BI tools, you can apply the following generic rules (unless we mentioned exceptions in the previous chapters):

▶ All elements in the ROWS and COLUMNS will be shown in the SAP BusinessObjects BI tools.

▶ All elements in FREE CHARACTERISTICS will be shown in the SAP BusinessObjects BI tools.

▶ Filters configured in the FILTER/CHARACTERISTIC RESTRICTIONS area using a fixed list of values get applied to the data retrieval but the actual filter values are not available to the report designer or the consumer (exception: Xcelsius).

▶ Filters configured in the FILTER/CHARACTERISTIC RESTRICTIONS area using variables will be available in the SAP BusinessObjects BI tools and the variables will result in prompts for the consumer.

▶ Elements specified in the DEFAULT VALUES area will not be leveraged by the SAP BusinessObjects BI tools. In such cases, the default values will be ignored (exception: Xcelsius and Pioneer). Please note, default values specified for variables are available and will be shown to the consumer.

▶ Custom structures defined in the BW query are available to the report designer and consumer, but a custom structure is represented by a single object in the SAP BusinessObjects tools and the report designer does not have each element as a separate element during the report design available. As a result, the report designer can't preselect a list of elements from the custom structure or apply conditional formatting or highlighting based on technical names or keys for elements in the custom structure.

▶ Conditions defined in the SAP NetWeaver BW query are not transferred to the SAP BusinessObjects BI tools (exception: Xcelsius and Pioneer).

▶ Exceptions defined in the SAP NetWeaver BW query are not transferred to the SAP BusinessObjects BI tools.

▶ BW queries need to be configured with the Allow external access property in the BW query designer, so that the SAP BusinessObjects tools can leverage them (exception: Xcelsius and Pioneer).

11.2.3   Using Variables in a BW Query

With regard to the use of variables in the SAP NetWeaver BW query, you should consider the following:

▸ Variables need to be configured with the Ready for input property to be considered by any SAP BusinessObjects BI tool as a prompt.

▸ The Selection option variable type, which provides the user with the functionality to select an operator and to decide between the option to include or to exclude the values, is fully supported by Voyager and Pioneer; the other SAP BusinessObjects BI tools try to map it as close as possible. For example, Crystal Reports and Web Intelligence will provide a range value prompt in such a case.

▸ Text variables in a BW query influence the description of the elements in the BW query, and therefore influence the metadata that is important to the SAP BusinessObjects BI tools. Proper support for text variables is only provided in Xcelsius and Pioneer. Other tools are technically capable of supporting text variables that don't ask for user input, but it will impact the meta data and lead to further complications.

▸ Exit and authorization variables are fully supported by the SAP BusinessObjects BI tools.

▸ The functionality of exit variables is a capability that the semantic layer on the SAP BusinessObjects product stack can't provide in the current release. Therefore, you should consider using exit variables in cases where you need to provide a fixed time range based on the system date to the consumer, such cases are much easier to implement using exit variables.

11.2.4   Display Relevant Settings

The SAP NetWeaver BW query offers several display-relevant settings in the BW query designer. In Figure 11.2, you can see the display settings for a characteristic, and in Figure 11.3 you can see the display settings for a key figure.

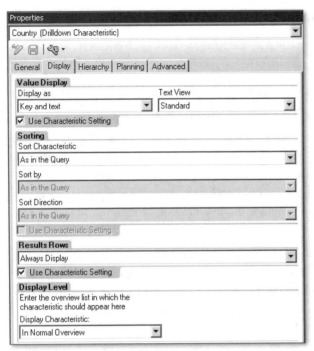

Figure 11.2 Display Settings for a Characteristic

Figure 11.3 Display Settings for a Key Figure

These settings are relevant to the display of the object and these settings are not leveraged by most of the SAP BusinessObjects tools in the current release (Business-Objects XI Release 3.1 Service Pack 2).

For characteristics, this means:

▶ Crystal Reports via the BW Multi-Dimensional eXpressions (MDX) driver and Web Intelligence via the Universe always offer the key and descriptions of a characteristic, regardless of the display setting.

▶ Xcelsius leverages the display setting for the key and description of a characteristic when using SAP NetWeaver BI connectivity.

▶ Sorting is done in the SAP BusinessObjects BI tools.

▶ The option to suppress result rows is only leveraged by Xcelsius and it is highly recommended to suppress the result rows so that it does not influence the overall dashboard design (see section 5.3).

For key figures, this means:

▶ Key figures will be shown to the SAP BusinessObjects BI tools, even though you might have configured to hide them in the BW query designer.

▶ The scaling factor, number of decimals, and sign for the key figure can be leveraged in the SAP BusinessObjects tools via the formatted value per key figure. The formatted value is a string value and cannot be used for calculations. When you use the numeric value (referred to as raw value in Xcelsius), these settings will not be leveraged and you will instead be presented with the plain numeric value.

11.3   Data Connectivity and Metadata Management

In this section, we'll look at some Best Practices for data connectivity and metadata management for Universes.

11.3.1   Data Connectivity

In general, it is recommended to leverage the BW query as the entry point for the SAP NetWeaver BW system for data connectivity; however, this doesn't mean that this recommendation will not change in the future. We will look at the roadmap for data connectivity and metadata management in more detail in Chapter 12.

As of XI Release 3.1, it is recommended to leverage the BW query as the data source because the query offers functionality that is not available in any of the BI client tools, such as creating exit variables or creating custom structures.

A direct connectivity for the InfoProvider level will result in the loss of metadata as shown in Table 3.2. The comparison shown in Table 3.2 is valid for all SAP BusinessObjects BI client tools that are based on the public Online Analytical Processing (OLAP) Business Application Programming Interfaces (BAPIs), which are Crystal Reports and Web Intelligence (and Live Office) as of Release XI 3.1 Service Pack 02. Please note that direct connectivity to the InfoProvider level will lead to a situation where you can't leverage authorization variables in the BW query anymore and the report designer will need to ensure that each consumer is only receiving the information that he is allowed to see. The reason for this behavior is that SAP NetWeaver BI authorizations are not acting automatically like a filter, which is why there is the functionality of authorization variables.

With regard to Crystal Reports, you will notice that you have a BW MDX driver and a BW query driver available. The BW query driver has data connectivity for SAP NetWeaver BW that was established in the Original Equipment Manufacturer (OEM) relationship between SAP and Crystal Decisions. This connectivity has not been enhanced for several releases and it is recommended to leverage the BW MDX driver successor connectivity.

11.3.2 Metadata Management

Metadata management in this case refers to leveraging the metadata from your SAP landscape in conjunction with the SAP BusinessObjects Universe.

In previous versions of the SAP BusinessObjects BI tools (prior to Service Pack 02) you might have experienced several issues and problems with updating a Universe after a BW query has been changed. In this area in particular, there have been several enhancements and it is highly recommended to apply at least FixPack 1.8 for XI release 3.1 or to apply Service Pack 02.

With these changes in place, you can fully leverage the updated functionality in the Universe designer and use this functionality in a complete product environment.

Please note, that there is still caching happening on the connection to the SAP NetWeaver BW system and therefore it is common practice to restart the Universe Designer before you trigger the update of the universe via the menu VIEW • REFRESH STRUCTURE.

Overall you should try to approach this topic — changes to the data elements and meta-data — with some strict rules in place as a change in the underlying structure can impact not only a set of universes, but also a large set of Web Intelligence, Crystal Reports, and Xcelsius objects.

11.4 User Security

In regards to data level security for the SAP BusinessObjects BI tools, leveraging SAP NetWeaver BW as a data source the recommendations are very simple. In such a scenario, the recommendation is to leverage the SAP NetWeaver BI authorizations simply because as of Release XI 3.1 there is no such capability available in the SAP BusinessObjects portfolio. You can define data level security in Universes on top of relational sources, but you cannot create data level security in OLAP Universes.

For data level security when connecting to the SAP ERP system, you can leverage the Security Definition Editor as part of the SAP BusinessObjects Integration for SAP solutions, which allows you to define row and column level security on top of the tables in your ERP system. For the connectivity for classic InfoSets in the ERP system, it is recommended to set up security in the ERP system as part of the InfoSet and to leverage security by using Single Sign-On (SSO) for the SAP BusinessObjects tools.

For cases where it is required to broadcast a report to a larger audience but still keep security intact, or if you would like to precalculate the report and create an offline version of the report and keep the security intact, it is recommended to leverage the functionality of the reports on the SAP BusinessObjects Enterprise backend. The SAP BusinessObjects Integration for SAP solutions lets you establish server-side trust with the SAP NetWeaver BW system (for example, based on the SAP Cryptographic Library) and that way you can set up a passwordless publication process that can create an instance of the report per user.

Integrating BusinessObjects XI 3.1 BI Tools with SAP NetWeaver

With regard to the installation and deployment of the BusinessObjects XI 3.1 Release in conjunction with your SAP landscape, you can find the complete details the author's first book, *Integrating BusinessObjects XI 3.1 BI Tools with SAP NetWeaver*, published by SAP Press.

11.5 Performance Considerations

The following is a list of recommendations regarding performance:

▶ Several significant performance enhancements have been made since the acquisition of BusinessObjects by SAP. These performance enhancements have been incorporated into the following releases:

  ▶ SAP NetWeaver BW 7.0 Enhancement Package 01 (7.01) SP03

  ▶ SAP BusinessObjects XI Releases 3.1 FixPack 1.3

  It is highly recommended that you move to these releases for your reporting and analysis landscape to leverage these performance improvements.

▶ All SAP NetWeaver BW performance topics are still valid and are relevant for integration with the SAP BusinessObjects BI tools. Topics such as setting up aggregates and creating database indexes are all still important for your performance.

▶ Use your BW statistics to identify the most used and the slowest-performing BW queries, and to identify the reasons for the performance results.

▶ Use Transaction ST03 to evaluate the need for aggregation of the BW queries that you're using for reporting. Pay particular attention to the overall time spent on the database and the ratio between the database-selected records and the transferred records. An indicator of missing aggregates would be a ratio higher than 10 for the records and 30% or higher database time compared to the overall time.

▸ With regard to setting up aggregates on the SAP NetWeaver BW side, you need to ensure that you match the aggregates to the data request from the reporting tool, which is different for each tool:

    ▸ In Crystal Reports, the request will only include elements used in the report itself — even though the BW query might include more elements.

    ▸ In Web Intelligence, the request is based on the elements that have been included into the Web Intelligence query panel and not on the actual report itself.

    ▸ In Xcelsius, using the new SAP NetWeaver BI connectivity, the data request is based on the definition in the DATA PREVIEW tab per connection in the Xcelsius designer.

▸ With regard to the BW query, you should enable the USE SELECTION OF STRUCTURE MEMBERS setting, which can be enabled in Transaction RSRT as part of the query properties (see Figure 11.4).

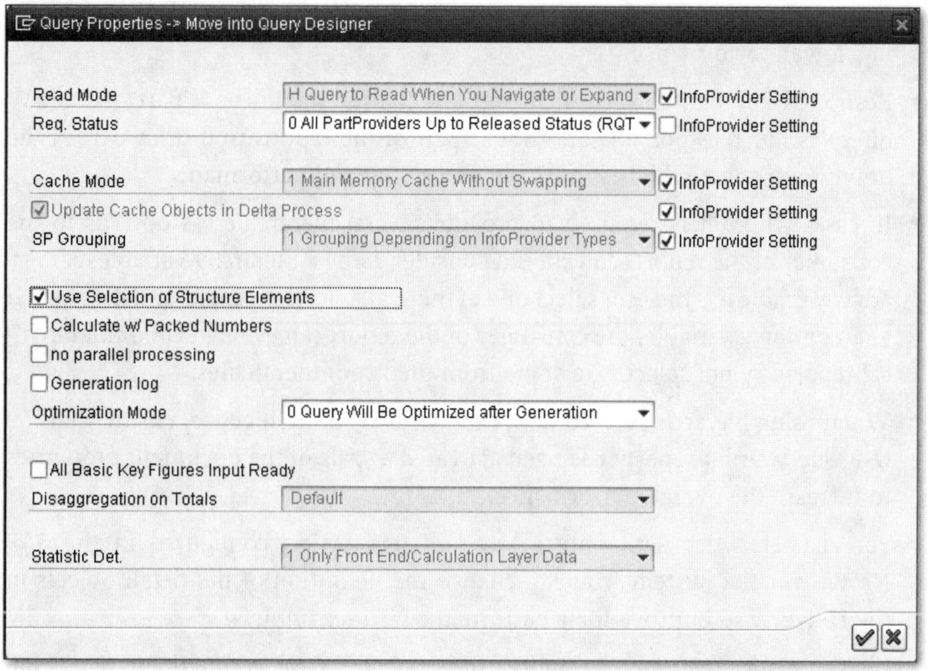

Figure 11.4 Query Properties

▶ When offering filtering of the data retrieval for the consumer, it is highly recommend to leverage as many variables as possible in the BW query to ensure an online retrieved list of values and a server-side filtering. Note that Crystal Reports can't pass manually created filters or parameters as a filter into the MDX statement and therefore it will result in a client-side filtering situation.

▶ In cases where variables offer a large set of values, you should consider using the Delegated Search property for the defined list of values in the Universe. By enabling the Delegated Search property the user will not retrieve a list of values automatically, but instead is forced to search for the values, which can be very helpful in cases with a very large list of values.

▶ When using Xcelsius with the new direct SAP NetWeaver BI connectivity, leverage the DATA PREVIEW in the Xcelsius designer as much as possible to define the data level that is required for the Xcelsius dashboard.

▶ When defining selections or filters in the BW query, make sure you use the option to include values instead of excluding values as much as possible, as the exclusion of values is not able to access the database indices, which will result in a lower performance.

▶ Restricted key figures and calculated key figures should be a part of the BW query as much as possible and not as part of the report itself or as part of the universe to ensure the best possible processing and performance.

▶ In cases where it is required to provide several hierarchies as options to the consumer of the report, you should consider using a hierarchy variable. A hierarchy variable lets the user select one of the available hierarchies, and if designed as an optional variable, the consumer of the report can even view nonhierarchical reports by not selecting a value from the list of hierarchies.

▶ When using hierarchies in combination with Web Intelligence, ensure that the Use Query Drill property has been activated as part of the document properties to increase the overall performance.

▶ For characteristics with only a key and description configured in the SAP NetWeaver BW system, you can change the definition of the detail objects in the Universe to improve their performance. For example:

Characteristic Customer (technical name: 0CUSTOM) resulted in two detail objects. The definition of the key objects would look like [0CUSTOM].[LEVEL01]. [[20CUSTOM]].[VALUE] and you can change the definition to [0CUSTOM].

[LEVEL01].[NAME]. Accordingly, you can change the definition for the description from [0CUSTOM].[LEVEL01].[[10CUSTOM]].[VALUE] to [0CUSTOM].[LEVEL01].[DESCRIPTION].

▶ It is especially important for objects that will be leveraged for List of values in Universes to have a key associated with them, otherwise the values sent to the SAP NetWeaver BW system might not be unique. Ensure that those objects have a key associated with them that follows a similar syntax: [<characteristic>].[TECH_NAME] or [<characteristic>].[LEVEL<xx>].[TECH_NAME], where you need to replace <characteristic> with the technical name of the InfoObject.

▶ In cases where you need detailed information in combination with highly aggregated data, you might want to consider the functionality to link from one report to another (for example, Xcelsius to Web Intelligence) and passing the context between these reports.

▶ You should also pay attention to the SAP system and the number of connections being leveraged at the same time. Based on the assumption that you are offering the reporting and analysis tools to a large audience, you need to ensure that the number of possible dialog users is configured appropriately.

With regard to the overall sizing of your SAP NetWeaver BW system or your SAP BusinessObjects Enterprise landscape, it is highly recommend to engage the field services organization from SAP and consider a sizing workshop where you can receive detailed information on the important factors for sizing your landscape. A complete sizing guideline would go far beyond the scope of this book. In addition, it is recommended to consider a staged approach and to use all available monitoring tools, like the BW statistics and auditing functionality on the SAP Business-Objects Enterprise system, to gain as much information as possible to ensure a properly sized landscape.

11.6   Known Limitations

In this section, we'll list all of the known limitations as of XI Release 3.1 Service Pack 02 per product. Please note, this list can change in the future and these limitations might get resolved in a future service pack or a future release of the product.

11.6.1 Crystal Reports

▶ The BW MDX driver is not capable of passing values from manually created filters or manually created parameters in Crystal Reports as actual WHERE clauses to the underlying SAP NetWeaver BW system, which means that those situations will result in client-side filtering. Therefore, it is recommended to leverage variables in the BW query for those situations.

▶ When creating a new report using the SAP toolbar, saving this report directly to the BusinessObjects Enterprise system results in a situation where SSO will fail because of missing information in the database connection. The report designer needs to either leverage the FILE • NEW menu path when creating the report and then use the FILE • SAVE AS menu path to store the report to BusinessObjects Enterprise, or use the SAP toolbar when creating the report and then use the SAP • SAVE REPORT menu path to save the report to BW and publish it to BusinessObjects Enterprise.

▶ When using the FILE • NEW menu path to create a new report using the BW MDX driver, any list of values for a parameter will be empty and needs to be uploaded with values manually. This is only in the Crystal Reports designer; the list of values will be retrieved online from the SAP NetWeaver BW system in InfoView after the report has been published to the BusinessObjects Enterprise system.

▶ When using the SAP toolbar to create a new report, the list of values for parameters can be limited to a fixed amount by using the registry value MaxPickList-Size in the registry branch HKEY_LOCAL_MACHINE\SOFTWARE\Business Objects\ Suite 12.0\SAP\BWQueryReportWrapper.

▶ An online list of values is only available for the BW MDX driver and not for any of the ERP connectivity for Crystal Reports.

▶ Crystal Reports is always asking for NON EMPTY in the MDX statement when retrieving data from the SAP NetWeaver BW system, which means that you cannot create a report based on the master data of a characteristic or on the master data design of a hierarchy.

▶ A hierarchy node variable is shown as a flat list in the Crystal Reports designer, but it is shown as a hierarchical tree in InfoView after the report has been published to BusinessObjects Enterprise.

▶ Crystal Reports does not support hierarchy version variables.

▶ A selection option variable is turned into a complex parameter Crystal Reports offering single, multiple, and range values as input options, but without the option to set an operator or choose between include and exclude.

▶ A custom structure is represented in Crystal Reports as a single field and each element of the structure is shown as a row in the data set. The report designer does not have access to the technical names of each structure element.

▶ Only a single key date variable is supported. In cases where the BW query contains more than one key date variable, Crystal Reports will only leverage one and ignore the others. It is recommended to use one key date variable as part of the global BW query properties.

▶ In cases of a hierarchy and hierarchy node variable combination, the list of available hierarchy nodes in the Crystal Reports designer is only retrieved for the first hierarchy. After the report has been published to the BusinessObjects Enterprise system, the list of available hierarchy nodes and leafs will be retrieved online after the hierarchy has been selected.

11.6.2 Web Intelligence and Universe Designer

▶ Web Intelligence always asks a NON EMPTY MDX statement when retrieving data from SAP NetWeaver BW, which means that you cannot create a report based on the master data of a characteristic or on the master data design of a hierarchy.

▶ A selection option variable created in the BW query will result in a range prompt in the Universe. As a result, the consumer of the report can't select an operator or choose to include or exclude the values.

▶ Default Values, defined as variables in the BW query, are shown to the consumer of the report. In cases where the variable is optional and the user is explicitly removing the default value from the prompt screen, the data is still filtered based on the defined default value in the BW query. It is recommended to remove the default value from the variable in the BW query in such situations to ensure a consistent user experience.

▶ A client-side Secure Network Communication (SNC) authentication is not available for the Universe designer.

▶ In cases where the underlying SAP BW query contains time-dependent hierarchies or a time-dependent hierarchy structure, the Universe designer will leverage the system date as the date to retrieve the valid metadata. As of this writing, there is no workaround available.

▶ In cases where you leverage a hierarchy and hierarchy node variable combination, the prompting dialog from Web Intelligence will offer you a list of all available hierarchies and nodes for the hierarchy node variable, instead of only offering the nodes from the selected hierarchy. An error message will be shown to the user when selecting a node from a hierarchy other than the one selected for the hierarchy variable.

▶ The key figure data type TIMS is not fully supported by Web Intelligence. In cases where you leverage the value of the key figure, you will notice a #DATA-TYPE error in the report. You can leverage the formatted value and you receive the formatted time value for the key figure as a string value.

▶ A custom structure is represented in Web Intelligence as a single field and each element of the structure is delivered as a row in the data set. The report designer does not have access to the technical names of each structure element.

▶ Web Intelligence and the Universe designer do not support hierarchy version variables.

11.6.3 Xcelsius

▶ Xcelsius offers data based on hierarchies when using the direct SAP NetWeaver BI connectivity, but as of Service Pack 02 there is no component displaying data in a hierarchical way as part of the Xcelsius designer. However, there are partner solutions offering such functionality.

▶ A custom structure is represented in Xcelsius as a single field and each element of the structure is delivered as a row in the data set. The report designer does not have access to the technical names of each structure element.

▶ An Xcelsius dashboard created with the new direct SAP NetWeaver BI connectivity will not work when hosted in an SAP BusinessObjects Enterprise environment.

11.6.4 SAP BusinessObjects Explorer

The following list is based on the Release XI 3.1 Service Pack 01 and the limitations are in relation to the SAP BusinessObjects Explorer solution in combination with SAP NetWeaver BW Accelerator (BWA).

> **SAP BusinessObjects Explorer Service Pack 01**
>
> Please note that SAP BusinessObjects Explorer Service Pack 01 is not supported with the combination of Service Pack 02 for SAP BusinessObjects Enterprise. Service Pack 02 for SAP BusinessObjects Explorer is expected to be released by the end of 2009.

▸ SAP BusinessObjects Explorer can only leverage a single language for all SAP NetWeaver BWA indexes.

▸ Display attributes are not supported.

▸ Key figures with exception aggregation are not supported.

▸ Restricted and calculated key figures are not supported.

▸ External hierarchies for InfoObjects are not available.

▸ Only a single BI authorization object can be assigned per user for the enhanced BWA index. Hierarchy node authorizations can't be leveraged.

▸ The current date is always used for time-dependent objects.

▸ BWA indexes are only based on InfoCubes, but there is a solution for creating BWA indexes based on MultiProvider (see SAP Notes 1332090 and 1332392 for further details).

11.6.5 Data Federator

The known limitations for Data Federator are shown in Table 4.3 and Table 4.4.

11.7 Report Design–Relevant Topics

In this section, we will look at some tips and tricks for report design. The topics are kept on a generic level and are applicable to most of the SAP BusinessObjects tools.

▶ None of the SAP BusinessObjects BI tools in Release XI 3.1 offers a multicurrency functionality as consumers might expect based on their experience with BEx Analyzer or BEx web reporting. In particular, the functionality to summarize totals based on a set of different currencies is not available, and therefore it is highly recommended to leverage a single currency in the underlying BW query. An alternative approach is to leverage a variable as part of the BW query, which provides the consumer with the option to select a target currency for the report or to have multiple version of a single key figure — one per needed currency — created in the BW query layer.

▶ The topic of hierarchies and hierarchical navigation in the report is often the reason for misunderstandings and user expectations not being met. In the previous chapters, you saw the capabilities of each tool and how each tool can leverage a hierarchy and the type of navigation that is possible in each of the BI tools. It is important to acknowledge the different options and to ensure that the consumer understands the different options for using a hierarchy and navigating a long a hierarchy to make sure you do select the right tool for the reports.

▶ Number formatting and date formatting are based on the preferred viewing locale for each user (unless mentioned otherwise in previous chapters). This preferred viewing locale is available as part of the user preferences in InfoView on a user by user basis. If you are using the formatted value for a key figure, which is available as a string value in the BI tools, the formatting is based on the settings in Transaction SU3 per user.

11.8 Tracing and Troubleshooting

The following represent a list of tools that you can leverage to trace and troubleshoot most parts of the integration between SAP NetWeaver and SAP BusinessObjects:

▶ You can use Transaction RSRT (Query Monitor) to execute a single BW query, change the properties of the BW query, and execute the BW query in a debug mode, including the retrieval of BW statistic values, SQL statements, and information on the use of aggregates.

- You can use the SAP NetWeaver BW trace tool RSTT to create a detailed trace for a dedicated user and to analyze this trace for the complete details on BW statistics and time spend on the BW backend.

- You can use Transaction MDXTEST to manually execute MDX statements without involving any SAP BusinessObjects BI tools to either ensure the MDX statement is correct and retrieves data, or to see the performance of the retrieved MDX statement.

- You can find details on how to enable tracing on the SAP BusinessObjects Enterprise system in SAP Note 1235111 (for Unix platforms) and SAP Note 1260004 (for Windows platforms).

Integrating BusinessObjects XI 3.1 BI Tools with SAP NetWeaver

With regard to the installation, deployment, and troubleshooting of the BusinessObjects XI 3.1 Release in conjunction with your SAP landscape, you can find the complete details in the author's first book, *Integrating BusinessObjects XI 3.1 BI Tools with SAP NetWeaver*, published by SAP Press.

11.9 Summary

In this chapter, you learned about Best Practices and steps you should consider to ensure the best possible solution, stability, and performance for your BI solution. We also reviewed the current limitations of the BI tools and some report design considerations. In the next chapter we'll look at the future of the BI roadmap.

After learning about the current integration of SAP BusinessObjects Business Intelligence (BI) tools with your SAP system, we will now take a glimpse into the future and look at some of the upcoming changes in the integration between SAP NetWeaver and the SAP BusinessObjects BI platform.

12 Product Integration Outlook

At the time of this writing (August 2009), the integration of SAP BusinessObjects and SAP was in full swing and all areas where working on a better and deeper technical integration. In the following sections, we will outline the most important areas for future enhancement and integration.

12.1 SAP BusinessObjects BI Client Tools

In this section, we'll look at future developments for SAP BusinessObjects BI client topics, such as Web Intelligence, Pioneer, and SAP BusinessObjects Explorer.

12.1.1 Pioneer

Probably the most anticipated development is the release of Pioneer, which is the first release of the new Online Analytical Processing (OLAP) client for SAP NetWeaver Business Warehouse (BW) and non-SAP OLAP clients, like Microsoft Analysis Services.

Pioneer, which is the codename for the project and the final product name might differ, is a combination of Voyager, Business Explorer (BEx) Web Analyzer, and BEx Analyzer (see Figure 12.1). The first release of Pioneer is scheduled for the first half of 2010.

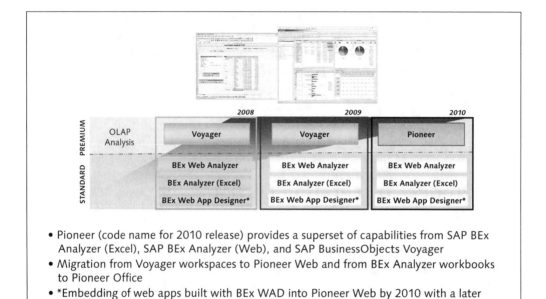

		2008	2009	2010
PREMIUM	OLAP Analysis	Voyager	Voyager	Pioneer
STANDARD		BEx Web Analyzer	BEx Web Analyzer	BEx Web Analyzer
		BEx Analyzer (Excel)	BEx Analyzer (Excel)	BEx Analyzer (Excel)
		BEx Web App Designer*	BEx Web App Designer*	BEx Web App Designer*

- Pioneer (code name for 2010 release) provides a superset of capabilities from SAP BEx Analyzer (Excel), SAP BEx Analyzer (Web), and SAP BusinessObjects Voyager
- Migration from Voyager workspaces to Pioneer Web and from BEx Analyzer workbooks to Pioneer Office
- *Embedding of web apps built with BEx WAD into Pioneer Web by 2010 with a later migration to the Pioneer Design SDK

Figure 12.1 SAP BusinessObjects Roadmap — Pioneer

Pioneer is set to be released in two versions: Pioneer Office and Pioneer Web. Pioneer Office will focus on SAP NetWeaver BW–specific functionality and add additional innovations on top of its capabilities. Pioneer Web will focus on new innovations and will serve as the vehicle to introduce new functionality to SAP customers. The plan is to provide 80% of the SAP NetWeaver BW– and Microsoft Analysis–specific features with Pioneer Web and to expand this number over time.

As shown in Figure 12.2, the focus of the first Pioneer release is to provide a stable Pioneer Office and Pioneer Web environment based on the SAP BusinessObjects Enterprise platform. The 2010 release will offer migration support for customers using Voyager. The next release after 2010 will focus on topics such as Design SDK, Lifecycle Management, support for Essbase, and support for the common semantic Layer. In addition the second release of Pioneer will provide migration for BEx Analyzer workbooks to Pioneer.

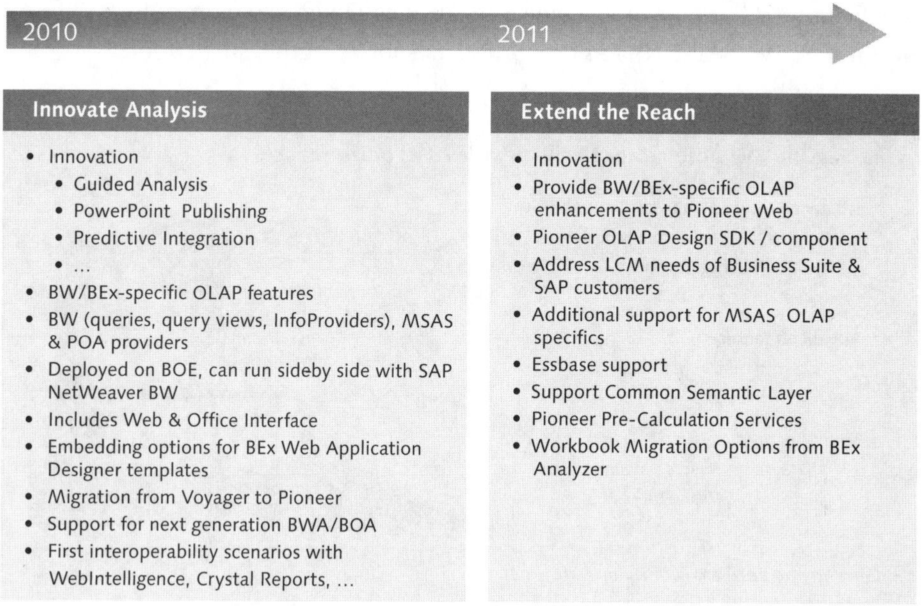

Figure 12.2 Preliminary Pioneer Release Schedule

12.1.2 SAP BusinessObjects Explorer and SAP NetWeaver BW Accelerator (BWA)

The combination of SAP BusinessObjects Explorer and SAP NetWeaver BWA provides high-performing access to very large data sets. Up to now, this data is based purely on SAP NetWeaver BW.

Figure 12.3 shows the direction of SAP NetWeaver BWA with plans to integrate it with SAP BusinessObjects Data Services, particularly SAP BusinessObjects Data Integrator. This integration will provide customers with the opportunity to not only use SAP NetWeaver BW data, but also leverage SAP ERP and non-SAP data as part of an indexed data set handled via SAP NetWeaver BWA.

These new capabilities — loading SAP and non-SAP data in BWA — lets customers index all of these different data sources, but more importantly, by using the SAP BusinessObjects Explorer and SAP NetWeaver BW Accelerator combination (see Figure 12.4), you can leverage SAP BusinessObjects Explorer on top of SAP NetWeaver BW, SAP ERP, and non-SAP data sources with a single tool.

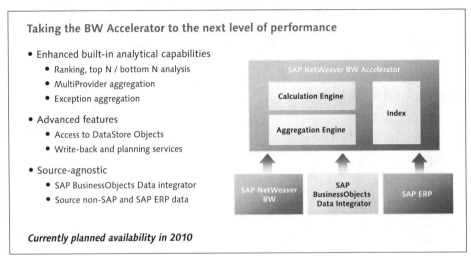

Figure 12.3 SAP NetWeaver BW Accelerator — Roadmap

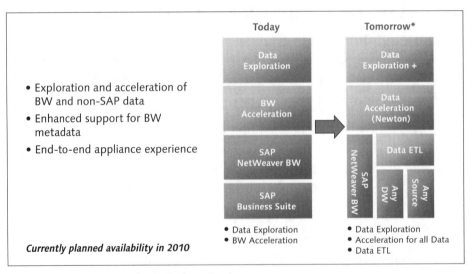

Figure 12.4 SAP BusinessObjects Explorer Roadmap

The COMMON SEMANTIC LAYER (see Figure 12.5) is one of the most important projects in the integration of SAP NetWeaver and SAP BusinessObjects BI tools. The COMMON SEMANTIC LAYER provides a single access point for all SAP BusinessObjects BI client tools for SAP NetWeaver BW and any other data sources. Currently, this will be released in 2010.

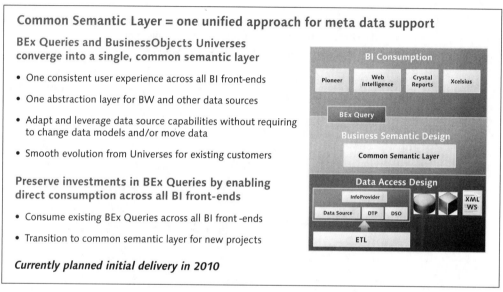

Figure 12.5 Common Semantic Layer

12.2 SAP BusinessObjects BI Client Tools Integrated into SAP Applications

The integration of the SAP BusinessObjects BI client tools into SAP applications is called Embedded Analytics and is meant to provide users of SAP applications the functionality to leverage BI tools and BI content as part of their overall workflow. The goal is to provide analytics in a way that the context of the application is leveraged by the client tools. There are three integrations for this planned in the first half of 2010.

The first part of Embedded Analytics will allow you to leverage the ABAP List Viewer (ALV) in conjunction with Crystal Reports (see Figure 12.6). This integration will give you the ability to leverage an existing ABAP report that uses the ALV and uses Crystal Reports to generate a layout-focused report using the data provided by the ALV.

- Enable SAP Business Suite customer to show SAP BusinessObjects tools immediately across the whole suite without dedicated investment for specific applications
- Enable the usage of Crystal Reports as layout option for Web Dynpro ALV and SAP GUI ALV layouts
- Enable the usage of Crystal Reports templates to provide coverage for all standard ALVs
- Integration of Crystal Reports layouts into the Lifecycle of the ALV

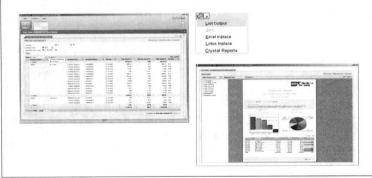

Figure 12.6 Embedded Analytics and ABAP List Viewer (ALV)

The second part (see Figure 12.7) of Embedded Analytics focuses on integrating the BI client tools into SAP NetWeaver BW and the Business Content delivery mechanism. You will be able to integrate Crystal Reports and Xcelsius into the typical lifecycle mechanism of SAP NetWeaver BW and the SAP applications will deliver content from Crystal Reports and Xcelsius using BI Business Content. In addition, the content will be integrated into the Report Launchpad and provide the functionality to leverage the given context of an SAP application as part of viewing the report.

The third part of Embedded Analytics (see Figure 12.8) focuses more on developer-oriented integration, where you can leverage Xcelsius-based dashboards with Web Dynpro and create custom applications with bidirectional communication between Xcelsius and Web Dynpro.

- Integration of SAP BusinessObjects tools into the SAP NetWeaver BW landscape
  - Data retrieval via existing BI queries
  - Integration into existing SAP NetWeaver BW Lifecycle Mgmt and repository
- Integration into the Report Launchpad and SAP Enterprise Portal content of the Business Suite application with context awareness for the Business Content

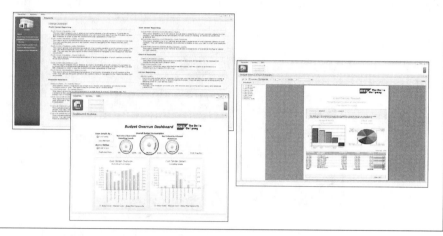

Figure 12.7 Embedded Analytics and SAP NetWeaver BW

- Enabling very tight application integration which includes analytical components like Xcelsius
- Enable bi-directional communication between the integration and the analytical component
- Include analytical components into the Lifecycle Mgmt and deployment of the application
- Support for Flash Islands in Web Dynpro ABAP and Java

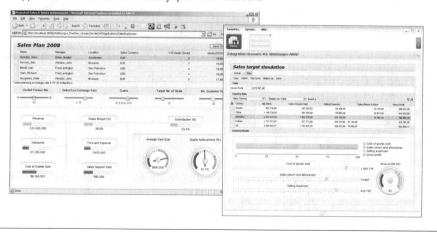

Figure 12.8 Embedded Analytics and Web Dynpro

12.3 Two Platforms — SAP BusinessObjects and SAP NetWeaver

In Figure 12.9, you can see an overview of the SAP NetWeaver and SAP Business-Objects combined landscape with a focus on reporting and data warehousing.

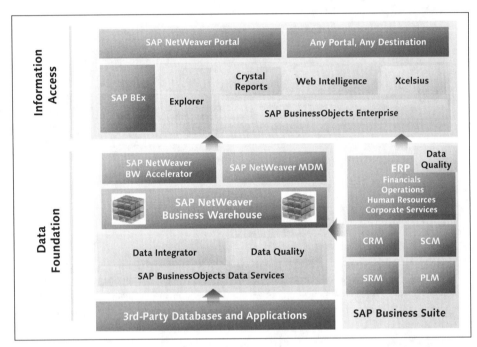

Figure 12.9 SAP NetWeaver and SAP BusinessObjects

There are two main areas where the SAP BusinessObjects portfolio will be integrated and where you can expect a lot more functionality in the future. The Enterprise Information Management (EIM) portfolio from SAP BusinessObjects will integrate with SAP NetWeaver BW for data loading, extraction, transformation, and data quality. Customers will be able to leverage SAP BusinessObjects Data Services to load any data into the SAP NetWeaver BW data warehouse or into the SAP NetWeaver BWA. The second area is Information Access, where the tools from SAP BusinessObjects will play an important role. Tools like Crystal Reports, Xcelsius, Web Intelligence, SAP BusinessObjects Explorer, and Pioneer will become the leading tools for BI and you can expect major investments in these tools to improve and extend the integration with SAP NetWeaver and SAP ERP.

> **Product Roadmap Disclaimer**
>
> The descriptions of future functionality are the author's interpretation of the publically available product integration roadmap. These items are subject to change at any time without any notice and the author is not providing any guarantee on these statements. A regularly updated product integration roadmap is available on the SAP Developer Network (*http://sdn.sap.com*).

12.4 Summary

In this chapter, you received a brief outlook into some areas of future integration between SAP BusinessObjects BI tools and SAP NetWeaver and SAP applications. With the existing solutions, you can already leverage the SAP BusinessObjects portfolio and deliver compelling and scalable BI solutions on top of your SAP landscape. By looking at only small portions of the product roadmap, you can easily see that there is a very interesting future for each of us on waiting to use SAP BusinessObjects BI tools in conjunction with SAP NetWeaver and SAP applications.

A   Installation and Configuration of the Data Federator Connectivity

In this section, we'll look at the installation steps for leveraging the Data Federator connectivity for SAP NetWeaver Business Warehouse (BW).

A.1   Required Software Components

For you to leverage the Data Federator connectivity for SAP NetWeaver BW, you will need the following components:

- ► SAP NetWeaver BW 7.0 Enhancement Package 01 (7.01) Service Pack 03 (or higher).
- ► SAP BusinessObjects Enterprise XI Release 3.1 FixPack 1.1 (or higher).
- ► Data Federator XI Release 3.1 Service Pack 01 (or higher).
- ► SAP frontend 7.x is required for the configuration steps.

In the following sections, we will assume that we have access to an SAP NetWeaver BW and SAP BusinessObjects Enterprise system with the correct release and patch level.

A.2   Installation of Data Federator

The following steps outline the Data Federator installation:

1. After downloading the installation software, start the installation routing for Data Federator (see Figure A.1).

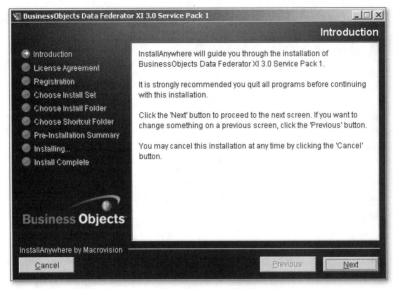

Figure A.1 Data Federator Installation — Introduction

2. Click NEXT.

3. Select the I ACCEPT THE TERMS OF THE LICENSE AGREEMENT option and click NEXT (see Figure A.2).

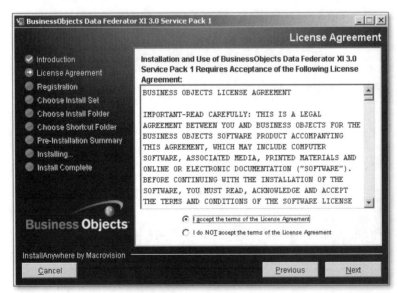

Figure A.2 Data Federator Installation — License Agreement

4. You need to provide a valid license key (see Figure A.3).

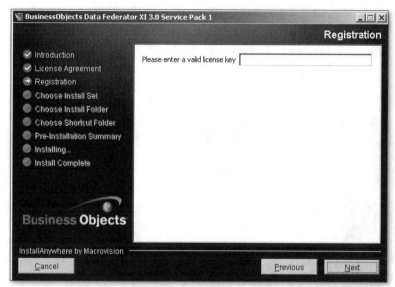

Figure A.3 Data Federator Installation — Registration

5. Click NEXT.

6. Select the CUSTOM option (see Figure A.4).

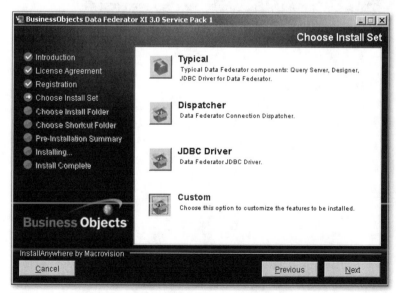

Figure A.4 Data Federator Installation — Installation Type

7. Select the following components (see Figure A.5):

- ▶ DATA FEDERATOR QUERY SERVER

- ▶ DATA FEDERATOR DESIGNER

- ▶ DATA FEDERATOR WINDOWS SERVICES

- ▶ DATA FEDERATOR JDBC DRIVER

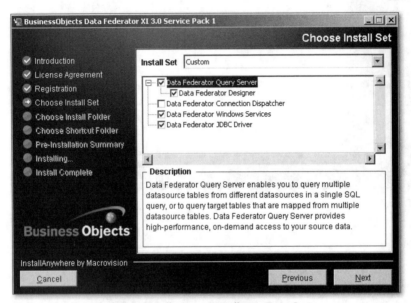

Figure A.5 Data Federator Installation — Installation Type Custom

8. Click NEXT.

9. Select the installation folder (see Figure A.6).

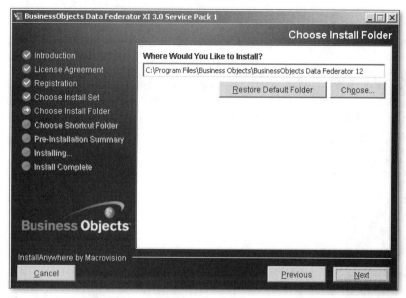

Figure A.6 Data Federator Installation — Installation Folder

10. Click NEXT.

11. Select the options to create the shortcut entries (see Figure A.7).

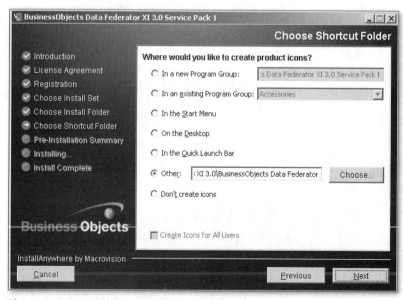

Figure A.7 Data Federator Installation — Shortcut Folder

12. Click NEXT.

13. A summary with all of the settings will be shown to you (see Figure A.8).

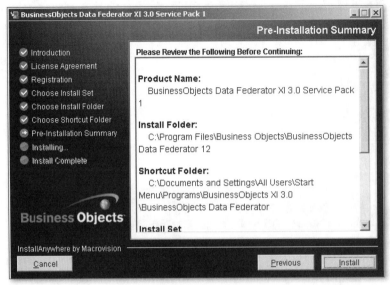

Figure A.8 Data Federator Installation — Summary

14. Click INSTALL.

15. After you successfully install the software, you should find the entries in the folder you configured during the installation process (see Figure A.9).

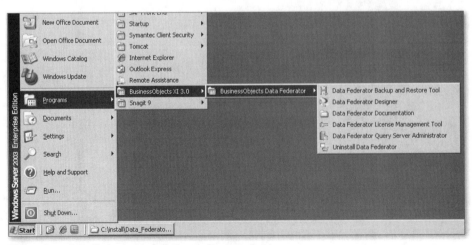

Figure A.9 Data Federator Installation — Program Entries

In the next couple of sections, we'll configure the Data Federator software and the SAP NetWeaver BW system so that we can create a relational universe on top of an InfoProvider and leverage the Universe with Web Intelligence.

A.3 Configuration Steps for SAP NetWeaver BW and Data Federator

In this section, we'll configure the SAP NetWeaver BW system and the Data Federator software so that you can create a new relational Universe based on an InfoProvider.

The following steps need to be configured:

▶ Callback Registration for Data Federator and SAP NetWeaver BW

▶ Configuration of the data access driver for Data Federator

▶ User configuration for Data Federator

Callback Registration for Data Federator

For Data Federator to retrieve data from the SAP NetWeaver BW system, you need to register a callback ID with the SAP NetWeaver BW system.

1. Log on to your SAP NetWeaver BW system.

2. Start Transaction SE37.

3. Enter RSDRI_DF_CONFIGURE as the FUNCTION MODULE (see Figure A.10).

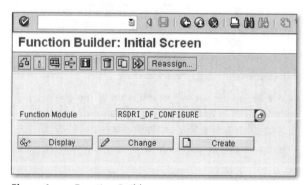

Figure A.10 Function Builder

4. Press F8 or follow the FUNCTION MODULE • TEST • SINGLE TEST menu path to execute the function (see Figure A.11).

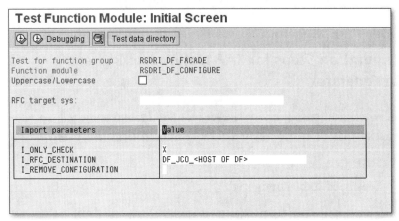

Figure A.11   Function Module RSDRI_DF_CONFIGURE

5. Use Table A.1 to enter the values for your system.

Import Parameter	Value
I_ONLY_CHECK	Use "X" as a value to verify an existing configuration and use an empty value to create a new configuration. In our example, use empty.
I_RFC_DESTINATION	Enter DF_JCO_<HOST OF DF> where you replaced <HOST OF DF> with the host name when you installed the Data Federator query server. You can also use DF_JCO_<HOST OF DF>_<SID> and replace <SID> with a unique system ID for cases where you have to differentiate between multiple connections with the same host name. In our example, use VMWSAP21.
I_REMOVE_CONFIGURATION	Use "X" as a value when you want to remove a configuration and use an empty value when you want to create a new configuration In our example, use empty.

Table A.1   Data Federator Configuration Values

6. Enter the configuration details (see Figure A.12) and execute the function by pressing ⌑F8⌑ or following the FUNCTION MODULE • EXECUTE menu path.

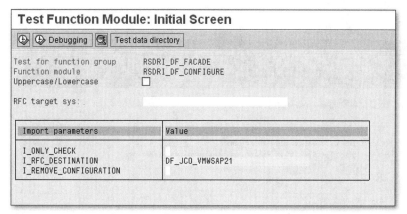

Figure A.12 Data Federator Configuration

7. You should receive a message similar to Figure A.13.

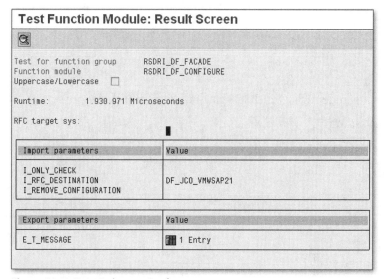

Figure A.13 Data Federator Configuration

After we configured the callback ID in the SAP NetWeaver BW system, we need to configure the ID in the Data Federator Administrator.

1. Follow the menu path: START • PROGRAMS • BUSINESSOBJECTS XI 3.0 • BUSI-NESSUBJECTS DATA FEDERATOR • DATA FEDERATOR QUERY SERVER ADMINISTRATOR (see Figure A.14).

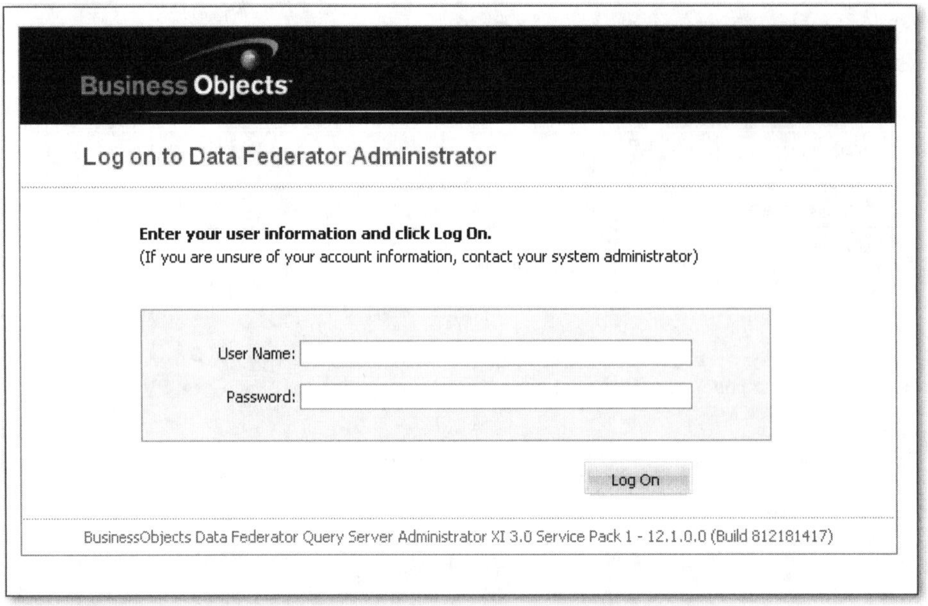

Figure A.14 Data Federator Administrator

2. Use the following credentials, which are part of a default installation:
   - User: sysadmin
   - Password: sysadmin
3. Click LOG ON.
4. Navigate to the ADMINISTRATION tab (see Figure A.15).

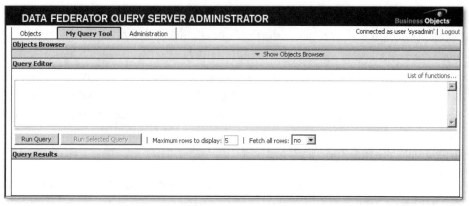

Figure A.15 Data Federator Server Administrator

5. Select CONNECTION SETTINGS from the list on the left side (see Figure A.16).

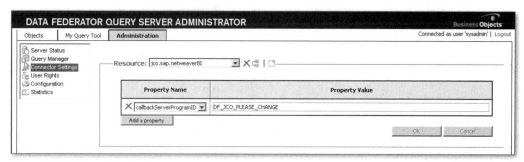

Figure A.16 Connection Settings

6. Make sure JCO.SAP.NETWEAVERBI is selected as a RESOURCE.

7. For CALLBACKSERVERPROGRAMID, enter the name you previously configured in Transaction SE37. In our example, use DF_JCO_VMWSAP21.

8. Click OK.

Now that we've configured the callback ID on the SAP NetWeaver BW and Data Federator system, let's configure the data access driver for Data Federator.

Data Access Driver for Data Federator

In this section, we'll continue with the deployment of Data Federator in conjunction with SAP NetWeaver BW and configure the data access driver. Data Federator offers connectivity to the Universes via Java Database Connectivity (JDBC) and therefore we need to update a configuration file to enable the newly added SAP NetWeaver BW connectivity. In addition, we need to configure a Strategy file for the Universe designer, so that the creation process of a Universe can leverage this Strategy file and offer you a wizard-style workflow.

1. Navigate to the following folder: *\Program Files\Business Objects\BusinessObjects Enterprise 12.0\win32_x86\dataAccess\connectionServer\jdbc*.

2. Open the *jdbc.sbo* file with an editor like Notepad.

3. Search for the phrase "Data Federator Server" in the file.

4. Add the following lines after the <JDBCDriver> tag:

```
<ClassPath>
<Path>C:\Program Files\Business Objects\BusinessObjects Data Federator
12\JdbcDriver\lib\thindriver.jar</Path>
</ClassPath>
```

5. The file should now look like the following:

```
<DataBase Active="Yes" Name="Data Federator Server">
<JDBCDriver>
<ClassPath>
<Path>C:\Program Files\Business Objects\BusinessObjects Data Federator
12\JdbcDriver\lib\thindriver.jar</Path>
</ClassPath>
<Parameter Name="JDBC Class">LeSelect.ThinDriver.ThinDriver</Parameter>
<Parameter Name="URL Format">jdbc:leselect://$DATASOURCE$;catalog=&quot;$DATABASE$&quot;</Parameter>
</JDBCDriver>
```

6. Save the changes to the file.

In addition, we now need to enable the Universe designer to leverage the Strategy for creating a Universe on top of SAP NetWeaver BW. A Strategy is a script that offers you classes, subclasses, dimensions, measures, and detail objects as part of the process when creating a new Universe.

1. Navigate to the source folder for your Data Federator installation files.

2. Find the subfolder named BOE-ADD-ONS.

3. In this subfolder, you will find a file named *datafederator.stg*.

4. Copy the *datafederator.stg* file to *\Program Files\Business Objects\BusinessObjects Enterprise 12.0\win32_x86\dataAccess\connectionServer\jdbc*.

5. Navigate to *\Program Files\Business Objects\BusinessObjects Enterprise 12.0\ win32_x86\dataAccess\connectionServer\jdbc*.

6. Open the *jdbc.sbo* file with an editor like Notepad.

7. Search for the phrase "Data Federator Server" in the file.

8. Add the following parameter to the file as part of the PARAMETERS:

```
<Parameter Name="Strategies File">datafederator</Parameter>
```

9. The file should now look like the following:

```
<DataBase Active="Yes" Name="Data Federator Server">
<JDBCDriver>
<ClassPath>
<Path>C:\Program Files\Business Objects\BusinessObjects Data Federa-
tor 12\JdbcDriver\lib\thindriver.jar</Path>
</ClassPath>
<Parameter   Name="JDBC   Class">LeSelect.ThinDriver.ThinDriver</
Parameter>
<Parameter Name="URL Format">jdbc:leselect://$DATASOURCE$;catalog=&q
uot;$DATABASE$&quot;</Parameter>
</JDBCDriver>
<Parameter Name="Strategies File">datafederator</Parameter>
<Parameter Name="Family">SAP BusinessObjects</Parameter>
<Parameter Name="Version">datafederator_jdbc.setup</Parameter>
```

10. Save the changes to the file.

11. Restart your Data Federator Services.

Next, we need to configure the Data Federator credentials to access the data.

Data Federator User Configuration

After you install Data Federator, you will have the user `sysadmin`, by default, as part of your deployment, but for actually leveraging Data Federator in your SAP landscape, you should create additional users so that you can differentiate them based on their role in the organization.

1. Follow the menu path: START • PROGRAMS • BUSINESSOBJECTS XI 3.0 • BUSINESSOBJECTS DATA FEDERATOR • DATA FEDERATOR QUERY SERVER ADMINISTRATOR.

2. Use the following credentials, which are part of a default installation:
   - User: sysadmin
   - Password: sysadmin

3. Click LOG ON.

4. Navigate to the ADMINISTRATION tab.

5. Select the USER ACCOUNTS tab (see Figure A.17).

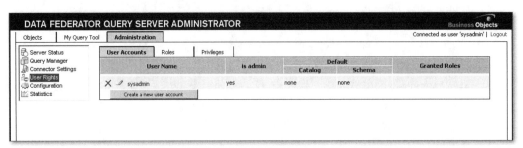

Figure A.17 Data Federator Query Server Administrator

6. Click CREATE A NEW USER ACCOUNT.

7. Enter `NW_DESIGNER` as the USER NAME, ensure the IS AN ADMINISTRATOR checkbox is clear, and grant the user the role DESIGNER (see Figure A.18).

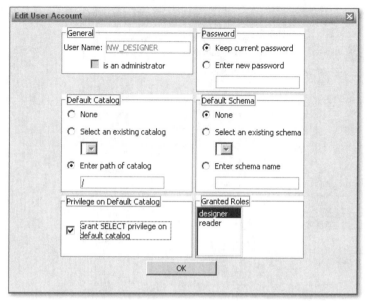

Figure A.18 Create User Account

8. In addition, select DEFAULT CATALOG, in our example we select the root and activate the GRANT SELECT PRIVILEGE ON DEFAULT CATALOG checkbox.

9. Click OK.

10. Click CREATE A NEW USER ACCOUNT.

11. Enter NW_VIEWER as the USER NAME, make sure the IS AN ADMINISTRATOR checkbox is clear, and grant the user the role READER (see Figure A.19).

Now you can use the NW_DESIGNER user to create Data Federator projects and we will use the NW_VIEWER user to retrieve data in Web Intelligence.

Data Federator user

In the example in this section, we are only configuring the Data Federator credentials with very basic security configurations. In a production environment, you want to make sure that security is not assigned on the Default Catalog "/" — unless the user is supposed to be an administrator for all catalogs.

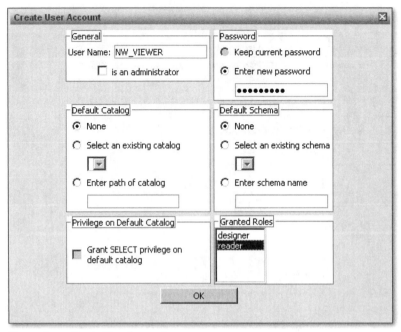

Figure A.19 Create User Account

A.4 User Handling between Data Federator and SAP NetWeaver BW

In Release XI 3.1 Service Pack 02, the connectivity from Data Federator for SAP NetWeaver BW can't leverage the SAP authentication from your SAP BusinessObjects Enterprise system with Single Sign-On (SSO), therefore, we will describe the user handling between the different systems in this section (see Figure A.20). Please note, the capability to leverage the SAP authentication with SSO is under consideration for a future service pack for Data Federator and you should consult the roadmap for further details.

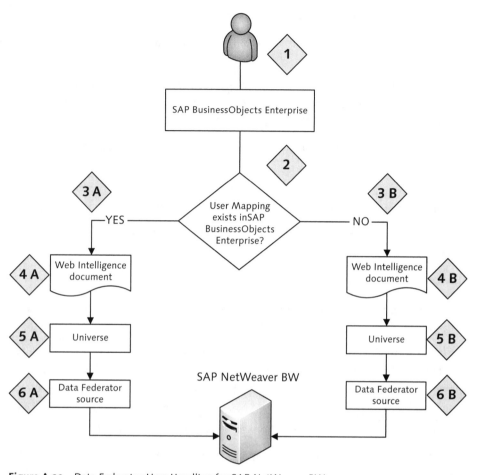

Figure A.20 Data Federator User Handling for SAP NetWeaver BW

The following steps outline Step 1 to Step 6 A:

▶ Step 1: The user is authenticating towards the SAP BusinessObjects Enterprise system with the credentials USER_A.

▶ Step 2: After logging on to SAP BusinessObjects Enterprise, the system verifies if the user has been configured with user mapping. In our steps USER_A has been configured with USER_B in the SAP BusinessObjects Enterprise credentials mapping.

633

- Step 3 A: The configured credentials USER_B are used for the next steps.

- Step 4 A: The user is creating or opening an existing Web Intelligence report based on the Universe.

- Step 5 A: The Universe has been configured with the authentication method USE BUSINESSOBJECTS CREDENTIALS MAPPING. In our example this means the Universe will leverage USER_B and pass USER_B to the Data Federator server.

  It is important to note at this point, that USER_B needs to exist as a Data Federator user.

- Step 6 A: Data Federator is using the credentials USER_B and uses USER_B to authenticate towards the SAP NetWeaver BW system.

  It is important to note, that USER_B needs to exist as user in the SAP NetWeaver BW system.

The following steps outline Step 1 to Step 6 B

- Step 1: The user is authenticating towards the SAP BusinessObjects Enterprise system with the username USER_A.

- Step 2: After logging on to SAP BusinessObjects Enterprise, the system verifies if the user has been configured with user mapping. In our steps USER_A has not been configured with USER_B in the SAP BusinessObjects Enterprise credentials mapping.

- Step 3 B: The credentials from USER_A are used for the following steps.

- Step 4 B: The user is creating or opening an existing Web Intelligence report based on the Universe.

- Step 5 B: The Universe has been configured to leverage the specified user in the connection of the Universe.

- Step 6 B: Data Federator is using the configured credentials from the Universe connection to connect to the SAP NetWeaver BW system.

  It is important to note, that the user from the Universe connection needs to exist as user in the SAP NetWeaver BW system.

Data Federator and data level security

Because a full SSO solution is not available for the current release (XI 3.1 Service Pack 02), you have two options to ensure data level security:

Option 1 is to leverage a single Data Federator user, which also needs to exist on the SAP NetWeaver BW system. You can then create the data level security for your SAP BusinessObjects Enterprise credentials in the Universe itself.

Option 2 is to leverage the BI Authorizations from your SAP NetWeaver BW system, which means that you need to maintain several Data Federator users and credentials mapping in your SAP BusinessObjects system.

Data Federator user credentials

As shown in the preceding steps, there are two main scenarios for connecting from Data Federator to the SAP NetWeaver BW system. Regardless of which route you choose, you need to realize that users leveraged in the different systems need to exist in each of the systems involved with the exact same username and the exact same password.

A.5 User Mapping for Data Federator Connectivity

The following outline shows the configuration steps to let a SAP BusinessObjects Enterprise user leverage the Data Federator connectivity in conjunction with SAP NetWeaver BW. For these steps, we will assume that your SAP BusinessObjects Enterprise system has been configured with the SAP authentication and that you created a Data Federator project on top of SAP NetWeaver BW already (see Chapter 4, Section 4.3.7, Creating Your First Relational Universe on Top of SAP NetWeaver BW).

1. Log on to the Central Management Console (CMC) of your SAP BusinessObjects Enterprise system.

2. Navigate to USERS AND GROUPS.

3. Select USER LIST.

4. Select the user that you will use to authenticate for the SAP BusinessObjects Enterprise system.

5. Right-click on the user and select PROPERTIES (see Figure A.21).

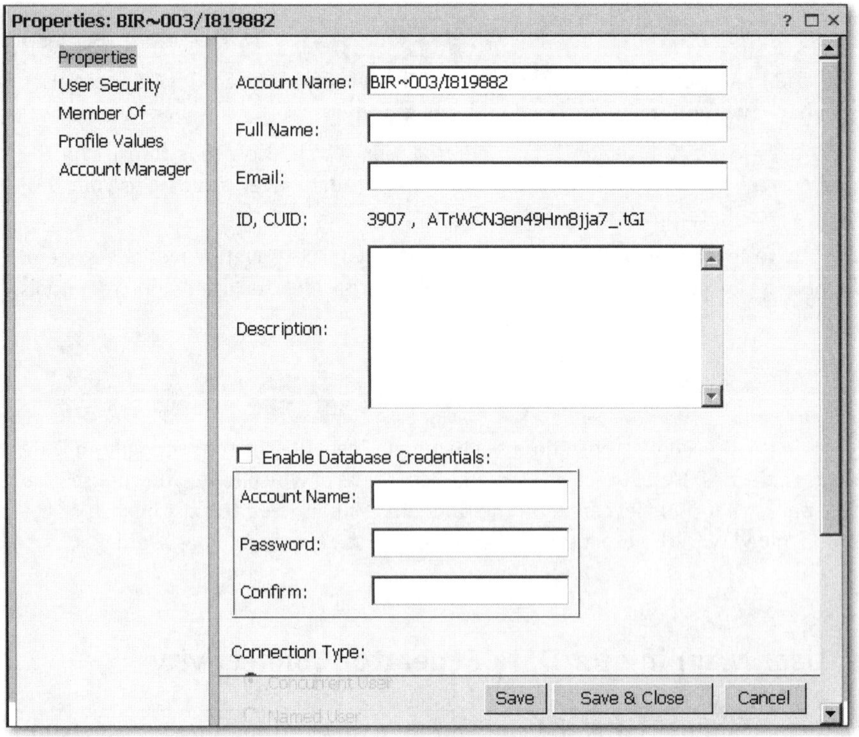

Figure A.21 User Properties

6. Activate the ENABLE DATABASE CREDENTIALS option.

7. Enter the Data Federator credentials that you would like to use into the ACCOUNT NAME, in our example, NW_VIEWER.

8. Enter the PASSWORD and confirm the password by repeating it in the CONFIRM box.

9. Click SAVE & CLOSE.

10. Close the CMC.

11. Start the Data Federator designer via the START • PROGRAMS • BUSINESSOB-JECTS XI 3.0 • BUSINESSOBJECTS DATA FEDERATOR • DATA FEDERATOR DESIGNER menu path.

12. Log on with credentials that have been configured as the Data Federator designer, in our example, NW_DESIGNER.

13. Open up the Data Federator project from the activity in Chapter 4, Section 4.3.7.

14. Navigate to the DATASOURCE of your project (see Figure A.22).

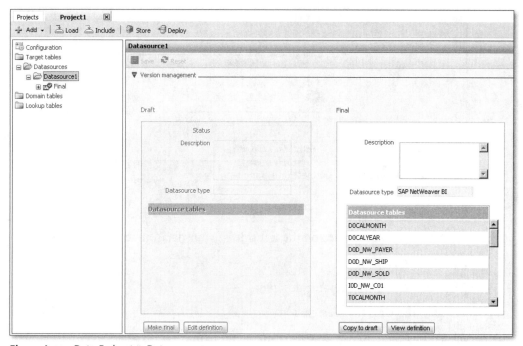

Figure A.22 Data Federator Datasource

15. Click COPY TO DRAFT so that you can change the definition.

16. Click EDIT DEFINITION.

17. Make sure you set the AUTHENTICATION MODE to USE DATA FEDERATOR LOGON (see Figure A.23).

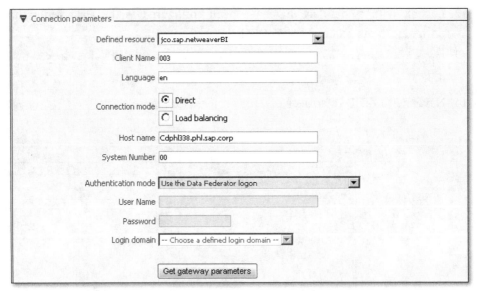

Figure A.23 Data Federator Connection Parameters

18. Click SAVE.

19. Navigate to the folder on the left side of your datasource (see Figure A.24).

20. Click MAKE FINAL.

21. Close the Data Federator designer.

22. Start the Universe designer.

23. Follow the TOOLS • CONNECTIONS menu path.

24. Select the connection you created on top of the Data Federator project.

25. Click EDIT.

26. Set the AUTHENTICATION MODE to USE BUSINESSOBJECTS CREDENTIALS MAPPING (see Figure A.25).

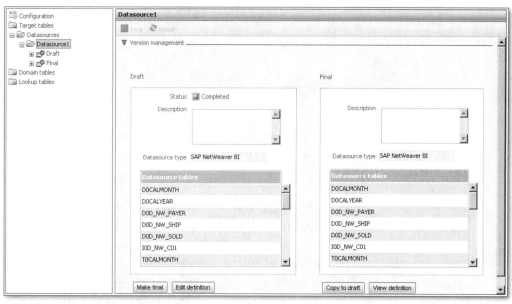

Figure A.24 Data Federator Datasource

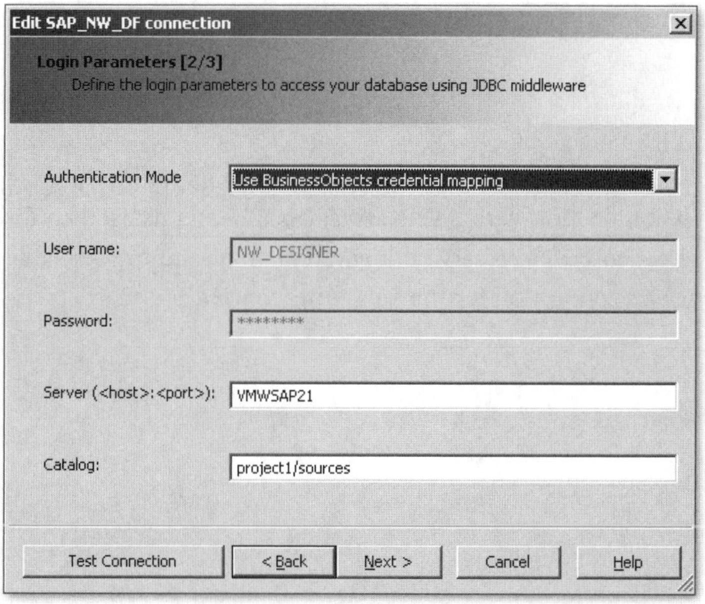

Figure A.25 Login Parameters

27. Click NEXT.

28. Click FINISH.

29. Click FINISH.

30. Close the Universe designer.

At this stage, we configured an SAP BusinessObjects Enterprise user based on the SAP authentication with mapped credentials. In addition, we configured the Data Federator datasource to leverage the Data Federator logon and configured the Universe connection to leverage the BusinessObjects credentials mapping.

We configured the user NW_VIEWER as the mapped credentials, and therefore user NW_VIEWER needs to exist in the Data Federator Administration and in the underlying SAP NetWeaver BW system. Please note, the user needs to exist in these systems with identical passwords. Based on the earlier configuration, you should be able to authenticate with the configured user for the SAP Business-Objects Enterprise system and view the Web Intelligence report based on the Data Federator datasource. Based on the credentials mapping, the connectivity for the SAP NetWeaver BW system will be established with the user NW_VIEWER.

A.6   Summary

In this chapter, you learned about the installation and configuration of the Data Federator software in conjunction with SAP NetWeaver BW as a datasource for your reporting. You learned the necessary configuration steps and the available options to ensure a secure connection for the data for each user.

B   The Author

 **Ingo Hilgefort** started with Crystal Decisions in Frankfurt, Germany, in 1999 as a Trainer and Consultant for Crystal Reports and Crystal Enterprise. In 2001, he became part of a small team working at SAPs headquarters in Walldorf for Crystal Decisions as a Program Manager. During this time, Ingo was working closely with the SAP BW development group and helped design and shape the first integration of Crystal Reports with SAP BW, which then became an OEM relationship between SAP and Crystal Decisions. With the acquisition of Crystal Decision by BusinessObjects, he moved into a Product Management role for the integration between the BusinessObjects product portfolio and SAP. In 2004, Ingo moved to Vancouver, which is one of the main development sites for BusinessObjects.

In addition to his experience in Product Management and Engineering, Ingo has been involved in architecting and delivering deployments of BusinessObjects software in combination with SAP software for a number of worldwide customers. He has also been recognized by the SDN and BusinessObjects communities as an SDN Mentor for BusinessObjects and SAP integration-related topics.

Recently, Ingo focused on Embedded Analytics, where he is working with members of the BusinessSuite to integrate the BusinessObjects portfolio into the business processes of SAP applications.

He is also the author of the book *Integrating BusinessObjects XI 3.1 BI Tools with SAP NetWeaver*, which is published by SAP PRESS and focuses on the installation, deployment, and configuration of the BusinessObjects software in the SAP landscape.

Index

F

G

H

Q

R

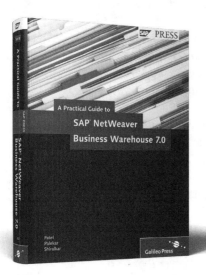

Understand the core functionality of
SAP NetWeaver BW 7.0

Learn from a step-by-step, practical,
sales scenario-based approach
developed from concept to reality

Explore BW reporting using both the
BEx and BusinessObjects suite of
tools

Bharat Patel, Amol Palekar, Shreekant Shiralkar

A Practical Guide to SAP NetWeaver Business Warehouse (BW) 7.0

This book is intended to provide a comprehensive and practical
understanding of SAP BW 7.0, utilizing a real-world, scenario-based
approach to detail the core, fundamental components, and features. This
book is intended as an up-to-date replacement for SAP BW Professional
(017). This new book provides a functional overview of SAP BW with
practical, real-world insight into how best to use the technology.
Coverage topics include data architecture, data modeling, master
data management, data transformation, business planning, and reporting
with both the BEx tools and BusinessObjects tools.

approx. 600 pp., 69,95 Euro / US$ 69.95
ISBN 978-1-59229-323-0, Jan 2010

>> www.sap-press.com